Americans and the Soviet Experiment, 1917–1933

AMERICANS AND THE SOVIET EXPERIMENT,

1917–1933 / *Peter G. Filene*

Harvard University Press, Cambridge, Massachusetts   1967

To My Parents

Acknowledgments

In the course of preparing this book, I received help and encouragement from many people, all of whom deserve more thanks than I can compress into a few paragraphs. First of all is Professor Frank Freidel, who guided my work from the beginning and who gave warm concern and constant support for which I shall always be grateful. Professor Ernest R. May subjected the completed manuscript to his keen criticism and suggested many valuable improvements. At two key moments, Professors Christopher Lasch and Lewis S. Feuer answered my requests with important advice. None of these persons, of course, is responsible for my errors or interpretations. Lastly, the Woodrow Wilson National Fellowship Foundation provided a different but equally important kind of contribution: a Dissertation Fellowship which enabled me to complete this book without interruption.

During my search through various manuscript collections, innumerable librarians and archivists provided me with their expert assistance. I wish to thank the staffs of the Library of Congress, the State Historical Society of Wisconsin, the New York Public Library, the Yale University Library, the University of Chicago Library, and the Widener and Houghton libraries of Harvard University. Of all these individuals, Frank G. Burke of the University of Chicago Library deserves specific mention because of his exceptionally kind assistance. I am grateful, too, for the generous permission

ACKNOWLEDGMENTS

granted me to quote from the various collections of private papers.

I have reserved for last my thanks to two persons who have played the most intimate role in my writing of this book. From beginning to end, William G. Rosenberg participated as a scholar of Russian history, an acute critic, and a friend. At the same time, I depended on my wife, Jeanette, for doing more than any wife should be asked to do. She was always there to listen, criticize, encourage, assist, or simply endure, always with understanding and patience.

P. G. F.

June 1966

Contents

Illustrations

Americans and the Soviet Experiment, 1917–1933

On Method and Matter

The traditional historian is committed to the burden of making order out of events which are arranged only temporally; that is, they are not arranged at all, but simply happen. Yet because events participate in the world of causality, they usually are amenable, within the limits of existing evidence, to narrative and explanation. The historian of ideas undertakes the more uncertain responsibility of ordering materials which, existing in human minds and memories, escape the objective causal world; ideas do not happen, but develop, alter, disappear, or spread. Yet because they represent attempts to communicate and to be understood, they too are amenable to the historian's retrospective search for order, though it will be a less precise, more interpretative order.

The historian of attitudes has none of these advantages. Attitudes not only occur within men's minds, but are intellectually inferior to ideas, often being little more than a complicated form of taste. "Dirt is the badge of Bolshevism" reports an elementary attitude, but nevertheless an attitude. As a result, the data for this third type of historian tend to be undeveloped, irrational, paradoxical. To adopt the succinct definition of Wilbur Schramm, a social psychologist: "By attitudes we mean inferred states of readiness to react in an evaluative way, in support of or against a given stimulus situation." [1]

Attitudes are predispositions to action, in other words, directly involving values. Since they are essentially dynamic

1

and abstract, the historian can fully visualize them only in process. He must analyze them in the dimensions of direction, intensity, and salience, if he wants to analyze their content.[2] Furthermore, unlike opinions, which are explicit statements about a situation, attitudes are the implicit mental reservoir from which opinions derive. The historian of attitudes engages in a delicate enterprise of probing or interpreting the verbal surface in order to reach the attitudes concealed beneath. In this book, therefore, I devote most of my attention to opinions, because they are the specific and substantive data in which attitudes find expression. Ultimately, however, this study attempts to go beyond the ephemeral, often atypical appearance to the underlying and motivating intellectual process. In effect, it attempts to discover not simply what was said, but what was *meant*.

This quality of inarticulateness implies another discouraging fact about attitudes: all but a fraction of them have irretrievably disappeared along with those who held them. This mortality is particularly characteristic of a period preceding the work of Gallup, Roper, and the other pollsters. The historian of American attitudes before 1933 must resign himself to dealing with printed matter (or the reminiscences of survivors) and therefore with the attitudes of those who are most powerful, or noisy, or educated, or fanatic, rather than most representative. He cannot forsake the archives in order to interview carefully selected samples of the public. Instead, he is confined to the mute, unmalleable materials bequeathed to him by a departed generation.

In modern America, of course, these materials are voluminous, since the mass media have provided more evidence than ever before in history. Yet the historian's dilemma thereby becomes only further complicated, for he then confronts the question not only of whether the media were reflecting or shaping popular attitudes, but also of whose attitudes they reflected or shaped.[3] Since contemporary social scientists of public opinion have failed to settle this twofold dilemma, I have carefully sought to evade rather than grapple with it. In reporting that most newspapers held a particular view of the Soviet regime at a given time, for example, I make no inference that their readers held the same view. Such an inference would be an unprovable guess — no more. This book, then, analyzes the opinions and attitudes only of those who made their views known. Only these persons or publications populate the categories like "Americans" or "business leaders" which appear throughout this study.[4]

For all the preceding reasons, the historian of attitudes must be extremely cautious and self-conscious. He must recognize that his generalizations will be partial and tentative, for his evidence will always be an excerpt from the total reality. In addition, his synthesis must respect, or at least attempt to convey, some of the irrational, half-formed, paradoxical character of his materials, even as it shapes them into an artifice. For this historian most of all, history hovers on the tense thread hung from art to reality.

The topic of this book, American attitudes toward Soviet Russia, involves all these general methodological questions. It also arouses several specific questions about purpose, scope, and presentation. The purpose of isolating this special theme in American thought during 1917–1933 is not simply to document a subject hitherto neglected or casually discussed by others. My more ambitious hope is that intensive analysis of this single intellectual theme will indirectly describe Americans' conceptions of democracy, of capitalism, and of themselves as a society and nation. For the Bolshevik Revolution and its aftermath implicated all these broader themes. The USSR was — to use a favorite metaphor of the period — an "experiment" that tested a political, economic, and ideological system antithetical to American values. In effect it was test-

3

ing the American way of life. The emphasis, then, is on American attitudes toward Soviet Russia, not toward Communism in general. The distinction is crucial.

The chronological scope of the book extends from the February Revolution in 1917 to American recognition of the Soviet regime in 1933. This period is too long to permit thorough reading of all the written data, particularly newspapers. The drawback is balanced, however, by the opportunity to view attitudes as they evolved during more than a decade and a half. By selecting a long time span I hoped to avoid mistaking opinions for attitudes, to discover the motive intellectual forces underlying the flux of transient polemic. Furthermore, the context of the First World War, the subsequent period of prosperity, and then the Depression formed critical epochs in American history which, because they deeply involved and challenged American attitudes, also exposed more clearly the nature of those attitudes. The end of 1933 seems a natural point of conclusion because diplomatic recognition transformed the intellectual framework, closing the question of the formal American relationship to Russia which the October Revolution had opened. The question persisted in modified form thereafter, of course, but it no longer permitted the fundamental doubt of whether the Soviet regime had a *right* to exist.

As for the substantive scope, I believe that full understanding of American attitudes toward the Soviet Union requires inclusion of everyone's attitudes. Because the reaction to the Soviet system ultimately involved basic American values, all attitudes — ridiculous or sophisticated — are important and instructive. So wide a scope incurs the danger of losing both the historian and the reader in a wilderness of detail. On the other hand, with all the data laid out, "the figure in the carpet" may emerge. In other words, a myriad of attitudes is presented in order to surmount it and contemplate

4

the meaning of the whole. That totality is what social scientists generally call "culture," the set of common habits and assumptions with which a society confronts its environment.[5] The concluding chapter looks back over a decade and a half of American attitudes toward Soviet Russia in order to assess whether they embodied not only obvious and constant disagreements, but also a common "culture" of thought.

Because of the heterogeneous nature of American society, my analysis is structured primarily by groups rather than by attitudes; that is, by speakers rather than by their ideas. This categorization is based on certain premises.

(1) The attitudes derived from the character and social role of the speaker. Business leaders, for example, had ideas about Russia different from those of literary writers or labor leaders.

(2) More true and therefore more important, the attitudes revealed something about the way business leaders, writers, and others functioned within the American scene during 1917–1933. I have tried to relate views of Russia to the larger context of American history during this period — to the total "culture." In so doing, I did not pursue a causal relationship, but simply used the attitudes toward Russia as a symptom of a more general set of attitudes.

(3) Both of these premises assume the basic claim that such groups did in fact exist and are identifiable. This claim is indisputable for business leaders, engineers, economists, writers, ministers, and labor leaders, each of whom considered themselves to be a group with special interests and aims in society. For others, such as journalists, educators, social workers, congressmen, and housewives, the use of a group classification is less informative. In the first place, individuals tend to overlap classifications. John Dewey, for example, was a philosopher, educator, and political organizer. Second, as Thomas Cochran has noted, there is "the danger of ambiguity

between the abstract or normative concept and the role actually played by an individual." [6] Norman Thomas began as a minister, but his important activity was as leader of the Socialist Party; that is, his ministerial role was an office more than a social role. Similarly, Raymond Robins was acting as an unofficial diplomat rather than a social worker while he was in Russia during 1917–1918. Third, the attitudes of Dewey, Thomas, and Robins reveal little about educators, ministers or social workers, but much about liberalism and radicalism. A new group enters here, one defined by attitudes rather than the other way around. It is more informative to discuss Hamilton Fish as a conservative than as a congressman, or Oswald Garrison Villard as a liberal than as an editor. And it is unavoidable that the attitudes of an editorial or a petition to Congress are discussed as such, since the writers were anonymous; no individual can be identified with the words.

This classification by attitudes is not circular, however, because conservatives, liberals, and radicals defined their attitudes by a general set of principles rather than by views on Soviet Russia alone. In this book, the term "conservatives" is used to include those who upheld individual freedom as unqualifiably higher in priority than general welfare by governmental action; "liberals" includes those who countenanced the use of governmental power to obtain general welfare but who also insisted on parliamentary process of government and the undeniable value of individual freedom; "radicals" includes those who accepted the methods of revolution and class dictatorship for obtaining social justice and welfare.

Thus, most of my analysis is structured in terms of the major functional groups in American society. In dealing with the attitudes of journalists, congressmen, and so on, however, I have retained the group classification only when appropriate. For individuals who overlapped categories, I have used

6

more natural arrangements, such as "liberals" and "patriots." For relatively anonymous speakers, I have simply dealt with the attitudes themselves. Throughout, I have minimized analysis of the Communists and of Administration officials other than Herbert Hoover. In the case of the Communists, their attitudes represented Moscow's views rather than their own; also, Theodore Draper, in *American Communism and Soviet Russia*, has thoroughly covered the matter. As for the attitudes of Administration officials, that subject more naturally falls within the discipline of diplomatic history, an area that is not of concern here.

Finally, a word about the importance of historical study of attitudes seems in order. Although subject in especially acute form to the limitations and liabilities of any historical endeavor, analysis of attitudes is also especially important to an American historian and to Americans. As the twentieth century reveals with increasing impact, this is a nation in which "the people" play a more central role than ever before. Popular education, popular taste, and popular emotion have become unavoidable considerations for American diplomats and politicians, as well as for psychologists and advertisers and, of course, historians.

The sympathetic symbol of the bear, flanked by Judas-Trotsky and the grim Kaiser and haunted by the vultures of Russia's chaos, indicates a favorite American view of the Brest-Litovsk Treaty in mid-1918.

"The Bear That Walks Like a"—Lamb!

—From The New York Herald.

I / Two Revolutions and One Betrayal

Here is a fit partner for a league of honour.
— Woodrow Wilson, War Message to Congress, April 2, 1917

On March 15, 1917, after a week of riots, strikes, and troop mutinies in St. Petersburg, Nicholas II, Tsar of the Russian Empire, abdicated his throne. The Russian Revolution had taken place. Its repercussions quickly reached around the world. In Washington, D.C., on March 22, Woodrow Wilson announced that the American government was the first to extend diplomatic recognition to the new regime. Probably he was unaware that, by a quirk of history, Russia had been one of the last governments to recognize the American republic, in 1809. Meanwhile, in Zurich and New York, Vladimir Lenin and Leon Trotsky were hastily preparing to return to their native land and participate in the drama of which they had dreamed so long. By November they were leading actors on the world's stage, having led a second Russian revolution which overthrew the Provisional Government in the name of the soviets. This time the American government was less precipitous in its welcome. Sixteen years passed before another Democratic President, Franklin D. Roosevelt, finally recognized the Soviet regime, thus ending the second period of silence in Russian-American diplomatic relations. Despite this official silence, however, Americans in newspapers, periodicals, and books were extremely vocal about

9

Soviet Russia, expressing attitudes which comprise an important part of the Russian-American relationship.

"[A]utocracy has received its death blow; democracy has triumphed. All of America rejoices to see the dawn of the new day for Russia." [1] The editor of the Boston Methodist weekly, *Zion's Herald*, certainly was presumptuous in speaking for his whole country, but he also was accurate. Editors, labor leaders, political statesmen, nineteen state legislatures or governors, as well as groups gathered in public meetings, issued enthusiastic statements hailing the February Revolution.[2] The events in St. Petersburg obviously had touched a great feeling of sympathy in Americans. On the day after American recognition of the new government, for example, the *Washington Star* editorialized: "A free people naturally wants all the other peoples of the world to be free. It is the American hope that Russia will hold its new freedom, develop it and through it work out a great national destiny." [3] Similarly, in a message sent to a mass celebration at the Manhattan Opera House, Theodore Roosevelt said: "I rejoice from my soul that Russia, the hereditary friend of this country, has ranged herself on the side of orderly liberty, of enlightened freedom, and for the full performance of duty by free nations throughout the world." [4] From this meeting developed the American National Committee for the Encouragement of the Democratic Government of Russia, including among its members such prestigious individuals as Charles Evans Hughes, Alton B. Parker, Jacob H. Schiff, Charles W. Eliot, John Grier Hibben, and George Haven Putnam.[5]

The unanimity of this lavish response to the Revolution can be partly explained in the context of American hostility toward tsarist Russia during the preceding generation. Two major groups had been particularly concerned about Russia.

On the one hand, immigrant Jews, arriving in increasing numbers since the 1880's, had publicized the repressions and pogroms of the Romanov empire from which they had fled. Americans responded with a sympathy which periodically swelled to outrage after notorious pogroms, such as the Kishinev slaughter in 1903. Probably this reaction was mixed with middle-class apprehension at the influx of poor, radical foreigners adding to the economic and social problems of Eastern cities. In 1911 these two viewpoints coincided in a massive protest against the tsarist policy of denying visas to Russian-American Jews who wanted to visit their homeland. So strong was popular feeling, not confined to Jews or to the northeastern United States alone, that Congress prepared to abrogate the 1832 commercial treaty between the two nations. When the House of Representatives passed a joint resolution to that effect and sent it to the Senate, President Taft personally intervened to avoid an overt international insult. Even he could succeed only in quietly arranging for the treaty's termination.[6]

The second group focusing hostility toward tsarism originated from George Kennan's reports about conditions in Siberian prisons. Sent to Russia by *The Century Magazine* in 1885, Kennan established a reputation as an authority by a series of indicting articles from 1888 to 1890 and then by a two-volume book, *Siberia and the Exile System* (1891). These writings not only were extremely influential in shaping American ideas about Russia, but they prompted the formation of the Society of the Friends of Russian Freedom in the 1890's as a vehicle for aiding Russian revolutionaries. Kennan, Samuel Clemens, and William Lloyd Garrison (son of the abolitionist) were among the founders. By 1917 the society, though less active, included such distinguished persons as Lyman Abbott, Jane Addams, Samuel Gompers, Norman Hapgood, Robert M. La Follette, Julius Rosenwald, Jacob Schiff, Cyrus L. Sulzberger, Ida Tarbell, Oswald Garrison Villard, and Stephen S. Wise.[7]

These two channels of hostility were complemented by a virtual cult of Russia, expressing itself in the popularity of Russian writings and ballet and developing a sentimental image of the oppressed, quasi-mystical peasantry seeking beauty and freedom. This was "Russia's Message," according to William English Walling in a book he wrote under this title in 1908 and then republished in 1917.[8]

It is not surprising that, with these precedents, Americans — and, above all, American Jews — joyfully welcomed the February Revolution.[9] Yet immediate events were more important in determining the nature of the response. At the end of January 1917, Germany had declared unlimited submarine warfare against the Allies, thereby increasing the probability that the United States would join Britain and France in the war. As the major power on the Eastern Front, Russia was a crucial military factor in the Allied cause. But President Wilson insisted on regarding the war from a moral as well as a military perspective; to make the world safe for democracy with the aid of the troops of tsarist autocracy would have been an uncomfortable paradox. The Revolution occurred at a providential moment, therefore, enabling Wilson to tell Congress and the world, in his war message of April 2, that the United States had "a fit partner for a league of honour." He did not stop here, however. With that genius for tuning American attitudes at a fervent and universalized pitch, the President reassured his countrymen that Russia had, by her revolution, adhered to all the premises of his war program. This was a battle between democracy and autocracy to achieve peace, not victory, and to sustain the rights of peoples, not the might of governments; in this battle, he asserted, Russia now was "a fit partner." Despite her tsarist

12

rule, he declared, Russia was "always in fact democratic at heart, in all the vital habits of her thought, in all the intimate relationships of her people that spoke their natural instinct, their habitual attitude towards life." [10]

Wilson's words endorsed rather than created what a majority of Americans had already concluded. As soon as the tsar had abdicated, newspaper editorials and national spokesmen had interpreted the event not only as a victory for democracy, but as an enormous benefit to the Allied war effort. Now the Russian people would be inspired to fight all the harder because they were fighting for themselves rather than a corrupt tsarist regime generally suspected of being pro-German.[11] Self-interest thus magnified the Revolution's meaning to Americans, but it also distorted that meaning into grossly unreal proportions. In the first place, a central cause of the St. Petersburg uprisings was the war itself, in which millions of Russian soldiers had died and from which the whole country had suffered enormous economic and social injury. The popular disgust with the war had been partly responsible for the Revolution; thereafter it continued to furnish the main platform of the Soviet, the council of workers' and soldiers' deputies which constituted a radical political force parallel to the Provisional Government and soon more powerful than it. When American spokesmen welcomed the new Russia as a reinvigorated belligerent, they engaged in a self-contradiction which, because they were unaware of it, distracted and eventually blurred their perception during 1917. They could not believe that the majority of Russians would heed the Bolshevik cries for peace; to American ears, those cries sounded like the "traitorous" and "pro-German" appeals of pacifists in the United States. But the more the Provisional Government sought to pursue the war effort, the stronger became the Soviet which, in American opinion, was the enemy of Russian democracy.[12]

By joining the ideas of war and democracy, Wilson created a further dilemma of contradiction and confusion in American attitudes toward Russia. In the same way that Americans assumed that victory had become as overwhelming a concern for Russians as for themselves, they also assumed that Russia, freed of the tsar, had become a democratic nation. George Kennan, still regarded as the authority on Russia, proclaimed "the complete triumph of democracy." [13] This sort of confidence exemplifies the tone of other commentators.[14] The editorial position of the *New York Times* was typical. In mid-March this conservative paper foresaw at best a constitutional monarchy under Paul Miliukov; a month later, following Wilson's war message and American entry into the war, it declared, "Democracy is the very soul of the Russian revolution, the sustaining principle of the new Government." [15] In retrospect, such emphatic optimism arouses rather than satisfies doubts. What justified the claim that Russia had been transformed, within a few weeks, from a despicable autocracy into an admirable democracy? True, the new regime had promised numerous reforms to be implemented by a future constituent assembly elected by universal suffrage. But these were only promises, after all, and Russian history was notable for promises given and then retracted by despotic rulers. Still more basic, what in fact did Americans mean by "democracy"? Prince Lvov and his colleagues were large landowners whereas the vast majority of the population were peasants with little or no education and much hostility to the landholding class. This situation hardly seemed ripe for parliamentary process and consensus.

Some commentators acknowledged doubts of this kind, but found satisfactory answers by pointing to various institutions operating in Russia since long before the Revolution. In their opinion, the zemstvos (boards of local citizens performing

14

various functions of local government), the dumas (elected representative bodies on the national, regional, and city level), the mirs (peasant bodies supervising agricultural and social affairs in their respective villages), and finally the numerous cooperative societies (effectively handling a large part of internal commerce) had created a tradition and a framework of elective, respresentative government. The Revolution, they said, was simply a coup ridding Russia of a vestigial despot at the head of a growing democracy.[16] More often, however, observers ignored Russian institutions in preference for the Russian "soul." Like President Wilson himself, they relied on an amorphous "instinct" for democracy inherent in the Russian masses. An editorial in *The Outlook,* for example, was confident that Russia would not forsake the path of democracy, because "there is something deep and fine about the spirit of Russia." [17]

This analysis was perilously close to an abstraction so vague as to mean nothing at all. The point is that the writer thought he was saying something of substance. Even ambiguous rhetoric is illuminating if part of a general tendency. And in the three years following the Revolution, Americans habitually inclined toward just such generalizations about the soul of the Russian people. Indeed, the relationship to the Wilsonian principles of a war fought for the self-determination of peoples is too close to be accidental. Just as Americans could not extricate the meaning of the Revolution from the success of the war they were fighting for democracy, so they could not perceive the political conditions of Russia except in reference to the Russian people at large. It was a simplified and naive view but, for that very reason, compelling and convenient. Thus Abraham Cahan, editor of the *Jewish Daily Forward,* could exclaim in March 1917: "We no longer distinguish between the Russian government and

15

the Russian people; both are one in soul and spirit: we now love both." [18]

Between individuals and maybe even between "peoples" a relationship of love is possible, but a relationship between governments involves interests, power, and policy. Americans sought to evade that unromantic fact when talking about Russia in 1917; like Theodore Roosevelt, they wanted to talk of "Russia, the hereditary friend of this country." [19] This habit not only introduced a crucial element of abstraction and naiveté in their attitude toward Russia, but it concealed a central self-deception. For in translating the complexities of the situation after the February Revolution into convenient terms, Americans also imposed *American* terms on that situation. In explaining the reasons and purposes of American participation in the war, Wilson assumed that Russia would conform to the same principles. As "a fit partner," Russia was, in effect, to be a Slavic version of the United States. Not surprisingly, then, Russian "democracy" was expected to be a replica of the American model.

An appropriate illustration of these ideas appears in a letter by the American ambassador in Moscow, former Governor David R. Francis of Missouri, which he wrote to his son in May 1917: "I have not lost faith," he said, "in Russia coming out of this ordeal as a republic and with a government which will be founded on correct principles." [20] The final phrase betrays his conviction of a standard of political right and wrong borrowed from his own American experience and applied indiscriminately to a country of totally different circumstances.

That individuals are "culture-bound" is neither a new nor an astonishing concept. But when the perception of a diplomatic representative is narrowed, it decisively limits his utility both to his own government and to the government with which he is dealing. When the basic impulse of a nation's

16

foreign policy seeks to apply or discover preconceived principles rather than to operate within the conditions as they are, it is in grave danger of misunderstanding and failure. Wilson's relationship with Russia suffered from precisely that misunderstanding and failure. He fought the war in order to convert other nations to his ideals, and he dealt with Russia on the same terms. In this role as missionary, he was repeating in intensive form a messianic theme familiar in American history.[21] This was ideological manifest destiny turned eastwards. As a result, Americans easily adopted both his rhetoric and his attitudes in evaluating Russia. It is to be expected that the editors of *The Missionary Review of the World* would regard the Revolution as an opportunity for evangelical harvests. But others, in a secular mode of thought, expressed the same missionary spirit. The *Pittsburg Leader*, for example, recalling the American colonies' struggle for freedom, paternally argued: "It is democracy's duty and obligation to see Russia through." And an editorial in *The Nation* declared that the United States, as the first large modern democracy, was "more qualified than any other nation to understand the aspirations of the Russian people." [22]

On the contrary, with hindsight it is clear that this claim to a privileged status not only was a function of misunderstanding the Russian Revolution, but bred further misunderstanding. Citing a supposed brotherhood in democracy, many Americans unwittingly adopted an arrogant or condescending attitude which, when contradicted by events or rebuffed by the Bolsheviks, was to become anger born of a sense of betrayal. *The Nation* eventually realized its initial errors, but most critics projected them onto the Bolsheviks or onto Russians in general, not onto themselves.

This tension between Russian facts and American assumptions began in May 1917, when Russia's military stability began to deteriorate so markedly that even confident American observers became apprehensive. The press began to speculate that Russian soldiers would take longer than expected to overcome the intoxication of sudden liberty. The *New York Evening Sun* predicted that the United States might have to grant extensive supplies to rehabilitate the Eastern Front. The *Milwaukee Free Press* went so far as to question whether Americans had the right to strengthen Russia for war if the masses wanted peace, to which *The Literary Digest* directed a stern rebuke: "Fortunately, these conscientious scruples against urging Russia not to betray her Allies are not shared by our press in general." [23] By August, the *Baltimore Sun* was pleading with Kerensky to restrain the democracy which had gone "mad with freedom." [24]

In an effort to halt the growing disruption in Russia, President Wilson decided to send a commission, headed by Elihu Root, to reassure the Provisional Government of American friendship and to inspire Russia back into the war. In addition to the conservative, elderly Root, the commission included other fairly conservative figures such as James Duncan, Charles R. Crane, and John R. Mott, along with one prowar socialist, Charles E. Russell.[25] The experience of the commission symbolized the dilemma of policy and attitude through which Americans struggled in 1917.

For about six weeks the commissioners traveled through Russia, giving speeches, arranging interviews, and collecting evidence for recommendations to the Administration. During this time none of them, except Russell and Crane, sufficiently escaped either their own prejudices or respectable Russian society to understand the facts of Russia's condition, much less the strength of the Bolsheviks.[26] They had come to reassure, strengthen, and convert, with little willingness or capacity to learn. Root hinted at a possible open-mindedness when, in a speech to the Council of Ministers in June, he acknowledged that Russia would develop institutions appropriate to her own needs and circumstances.[27] But that soon proved to be an exception. After returning home, he told various American audiences what they had long believed or wanted to believe: by reason of a spirit strong in kindness, idealism, and self-control, the Russian people "have again found themselves" and were successfully creating a free, democratic government which would effectively fight Germany.[28]

Actually, he was deliberately promoting an illusion. While in Russia he had privately telegraphed the President that "we have found here an infant class in the art of being free containing one hundred and seventy million people and they need to be supplied with kindergarten material; they are sincere, kindly, good people but confused and dazed." [29] But even this more candid report derived from a conservative prejudice rather than from a genuinely empirical investigation. For one thing, at this point Root had been in Russia for only two weeks. Moreover, in his final report to the Secretary of State he repeated the same optimistic message that he gave in public speeches.[30] Perhaps one can credit with greatest reliability a casual remark he made while walking through a Siberian village in June: "I am a firm believer in democracy, but I do not like filth." [31] Neither in predisposition nor in final evaluation was Root equipped to understand Russia. His disability was shared in 1917 by most Americans, whether in Siberian villages, in New York editorial offices, or in Washington.

The findings of the Root Commission easily reassured the doubting American public and thus made all the keener their bewildered frustration when the Russian political and military situation continued to disintegrate.[32] The disastrous conclusion to an attempted Russian offensive against the Germans, followed by the abortive Bolshevik uprising in mid-

July, had been ominous events for which the reorganization of the Provisional Government under Alexander Kerensky offered only small compensation. The *New York Times* urged patience and understanding on July 22, but two days later was suggesting a dictatorship by Kerensky. By the beginning of August, it was arguing that patience "with wrong-headed men, with mistaken men," can go just so far. "What is social reform, political reform, agrarian reform now," the editorial asked, "when all Russia should be saving her existence" by fighting the Germans? After General Lavr Kornilov attempted a coup in favor of conservative political policies and strong military action, the *New York Times* expressed its approval and harshly criticized Kerensky for dismissing the General.[33] The *New York Tribune*, the *Springfield Republican*, and the *St. Louis Post-Dispatch* were equally hopeful of a "strong man" like Kornilov to replace Kerensky's vacillations.[34] *Collier's*, a family magazine reaching a million subscribers, said that Russia must fight or forsake the success of her revolution.[35]

The tension between American values of democracy in Russia and victory against Germany was increasing to the detriment of the former. Just as, within the United States, victory had taken priority over free speech, so Americans were being forced into similar choices when discussing Russia. Most observers continued to praise the loyal, freedom-loving Russian people and to proclaim American faith, but a defensive tone now pervaded their entreaties.[36] Perhaps the stubborn adherence to first principles is most vividly illustrated by Wilson's decision to send Edgar Sisson to Russia late in October. Sisson's assignment was to set up an office of George Creel's Committee on Public Information, from which American propaganda would inspire Russia and demoralize Germany.[37] Here again the United States sought

20

to be a missionary to "the people." As the historian George Kennan (first cousin twice removed of the older Kennan) shrewdly notes, the Creel committee, operating independently of the State Department and trying to influence peoples, not governments, signified the change from dynastic to national diplomacy.[38] Sisson's mission was only another indication of the broader American perspective on Russia.

Although becoming anxious, Americans still clung to their original premises about the February Revolution. Moreover, in the Bolsheviks they found a way to avoid admitting that any error discolored those premises. The followers of Lenin and Trotsky served as the villains of the morality play which Americans had written for Russia. The fact that the Bolsheviks preached a form of revolutionary socialism was in itself sufficient sin for those Americans who, during the summer of 1917, were becoming used to damning and imprisoning domestic antiwar socialists, anarchists, and just plain radicals. The Bolsheviks' frankly avowed goal of withdrawing Russia from the war set most of the American public unhesitatingly against them. The indictment, filled with labels such as "escaped murderers" and "hysterical, criminal, and impatient socialist fanatics," grew in volume and venom through the autumn.[39] The charge that the Bolsheviks were German agents now began to gain prominence.[40]

When the Bolsheviks actually seized power, on November 7, newspaper and magazine writers, as if in shock, suddenly lapsed into a more sedate but grimly optimistic attitude. The impossible had happened but, because it was impossible, it would soon cease happening. George Kennan explained that the new regime would fail because it violated "certain fundamental economic laws." Others were equally sanguine prophets at first.[41] As the Bolsheviks remained, however, observers began to be afraid, angry, and aggressive. The confident expectations about Russia's future, derived from Wilsonian premises about peoples and democracy, had gone awry, whereupon Americans repeated them with greater vehemence. Reviving the familiar themes, they now injected belligerent undertones. Thus the *New York World* reminded its readers of their missionary responsibility: Russia "cannot be abandoned, neither to Germany nor to anarchy." [42] A few observers, however, slipped from shock into disgust with the old assumptions. *The Outlook,* for example, remarked: "It is hard to preserve faith in a people who allow such men as Lenine and Trotsky to get into power." [43]

Disillusionment was still exceptional. Despite the drastic events in Russia, most American writers did not doubt the validity of their premises, unlike the reaction in 1919 when the Allied "betrayal" at Versailles drove so many Americans to retreat from international application of their ideology. At the end of 1917, in any case, the war was still going on and they could not afford to ignore Russia. On the contrary, the Bolshevik success, combined with German victories in Europe, made the question of a revived Eastern Front all the more pressing. Americans *had* to have faith in the Russian people, despite the character of the Russian government. At the moment they saw no other alternative.

This self-imposed commitment to faith was temporarily successful. Indeed, it produced the curious effect, in many cases, of extending the delusive confidence in Kerensky's government to his Bolshevik successors as well, despite the latter's armistice with Germany on December 5. *The Public,* for example, which only three months before had vilified Lenin's party as "ideologists who flourish on decomposition and chaos," in January 1918 criticized the "peevishness" of American commentators on Russia. If Russia is demoralized, the editorial argued, the Soviet regime is a product, not a cause; and if Russia is exhausted, the armistice is irrelevant. It concluded that Lenin probably was using the armistice to play for time and advantage before renewing the war in the summer.[44] Many other publications were also anxious, around the turn of the year, to put the best possible light upon Russia's military future and, by reflection, upon the Bolsheviks as well.[45]

American optimism refused to dim, even if it required enormous distortion to survive. "Shall We Abandon Russia?" asked Senator William E. Borah in the title of his *New York Times* article of December 2. Numerous groups and individuals answered "No!" The Society of the Friends of Russian Freedom joined representatives of the American-Russian Chamber of Commerce in January to form the American League to Aid and Cooperate with Russia. Samuel N. Harper, a University of Chicago professor who served for a while on the league's executive committee, urged Americans to believe in the "fundamental ideas" of the Revolution and to ignore its excesses and the demagogues temporarily in control. John R. Mott, a member of the Root Commission and head of the International Section of the Young Men's Christian Association, told a New York City audience in January: "It is the duty of a Christian people to stand by any people groping toward larger light and larger liberty." [46]

Such pep talks were effective in the winter of 1918, despite the Brest-Litovsk Treaty by which Russia formally withdrew from the war. Businessmen and public meetings urged economic aid for Russia while religious leaders continued to plan confidently for evangelizing the peasant masses.[47] Typical was a statement which Lansing proposed to Wilson on January 10 but which, in the end, he never made public: "the Government of the United States is convinced that the spirit of democracy continues to dominate the entire Russian nation. With that spirit the United States feels a profound sympathy and believes in the ultimate effect of its cohesive power upon the Russian people as a whole." [48]

Two months after the second Russian revolution, Americans still thought in the terms of "instinct" and "people" with which Wilson had greeted the first revolution in March, and they clung to the same desperate optimism. This attitude was partly caused by continued anxiety about victory in the war. Partly, too, it resulted from an emotional inability to deal with more than one enemy. Hate propaganda had focused so exclusively on "the Hun" that Americans found it difficult to conceive of an equally despicable enemy, "the Red." Rather, the initial tendency was to pity Russia as the victim of brutal German ambition. [49]

But the optimists did not monopolize American discussion of Russia. Lansing himself, despite the cheery platitudes of the draft he had sent to Wilson, only a week earlier had privately told the President: "Lenine, Trotsky and their colleagues are so bitterly hostile to the present social order in all countries that I am convinced nothing could be said which would gain their favor or render them amenable to reason." [50] This darker vision was shared by a growing portion of the general public as the Bolsheviks divided landlords' estates, then nationalized the land as well as banks and factories, repudiated the national debt, and confiscated church property. Writers castigated the Bolsheviks as traitors to the Allies and their own nation. Skillfully solving the problem of dividing American hatred between two enemies, they joined them by the simple maneuver of making the Bolsheviks into "German agents." In the words of a *Collier's* reporter on the scene, the October Revolution was Germany's "masterpiece in Russia," designed by those willing German tools, Lenin, Trotsky, and the others. [51]

This campaign of defamation began in December, follow-

24

ing the Russian-German armistice, and reached a climax after the final ratification of the Brest-Litovsk Treaty in March.[52] Just as the optimists had allowed their confidence to extend from the Russian people to the Bolsheviks, so many critics included the Russian masses in their anti-Bolshevik hostility. The Slavic population, they said, was ignorant, superstitious, fickle, and anarchic. To expect that such "children" (a favorite epithet of these American critics) would create a democracy was absurd. As a writer in *The North American Review* confessed: "We have optimistically — and somewhat credulously — called Russia free, a republic, a democracy. Russia has not, for a single day, been either a republic, a democracy, or free." Along with other observers he argued that the only hope for freedom and democracy lay in the establishment of a dictatorship.[53]

Disillusionment weakened the entire structure of assumptions so carefully built in 1917. The loss of faith in Russian possibilities provoked William T. Ellis, returning from relief work in Russia, to write in terms that foreshadowed the xenophobic temper of the next decade. The United States, he argued, must exclude immigrants from Russia and elsewhere, for they are alien to American ideals: "Self-preservation is America's first and highest duty to world-wide democracy. If America means to the world what some of us have clearly perceived, then our most sacred obligation is to conserve the American type for the American mission." [54] Thus he inverted the confident missionary spirit into defensive patriotism. The new emphasis, though not yet typical, was significant in exposing the latent tendency in American attitudes toward Russia and the world. Congressman Clarence B. Miller of Minnesota represented an earlier stage of that tendency. In a speech to the House of Representatives on January 18, he declared that Russia would never re-enter the war. The Bolsheviks had murdered all the army officers and were "abandoned to all lusts of the flesh." "The plain truth is," he advised, "just forget Russia" and attend to fighting Germany on the Western Front.[55]

Americans still had too great an investment — military, economic, and ideological — in the fate of Russia simply to forget her. For a large group of American liberals, those whom Christopher Lasch calls "anti-imperialists," this was especially true.[56] Russia served them not simply as the "acid test of . . . good will," in Wilson's vivid phrase of January 1918, but as the test of liberalism itself.[57] Until the fall of 1917 they had shared the general view of Russia as an ally struggling to fulfill the role of a democracy and a belligerent. Like other observers, these liberals professed confidence in the Russian people's desire to defeat autocratic Germany, and they condemned the Bolsheviks for seeking to deflect the nation into peace and political extremism.[58] They did not welcome the October Revolution with enthusiasm, therefore, but neither did they adopt an attitude of blind outrage. Rather, they sought to understand what had happened, and to understand in a more analytic fashion than most other critics were able or willing to assume. Their fundamental advantage was an inclination to recognize that Russia was different from the United States, not merely a distant field in which to plant American values.

Lincoln Steffens lucidly discussed the subject in a letter of January 5, 1918: "As to Trotzky and the Bolsheviki, I am not surprised that you misunderstand them. Everybody does, so they are evidently not easy to 'get.' But I do think that in matters so remote and so difficult to comprehend, we might be slow to condemn and suspend our verdicts till we are measurably clear." Then he enlarged the idea in significant fashion: "It doesn't matter that we Americans misunderstand the Russians. . . . The point is that we are so cocksure of the rightness of our own false ideas that we are likely, now that we are getting into world politics, — we are pretty sure to misunderstand every people and every crisis that rises. Which means more wars; which means more boys for soldiers; which means more and more educated ignorance and illiterate misery. See?" [59]

This sort of open-mindedness did not always produce unerring insight. Like other observers of Russia, liberals often drew false conclusions from the evidence. In this same letter, Steffens emphatically denied that the Bolsheviks were seeking a separate peace, while *The New Republic,* a week earlier, had asserted that Lenin's government would be doomed if it violated the Constituent Assembly.[60] Furthermore, these liberals often reached their flexible attitudes by the same dubious reasoning that led others to rigid opposition. An editorial in *The New Republic,* for example, explained the October Revolution as a peculiar development resulting largely from the psychology of the Russian people whose "sources of moral action are religious and social rather than political." [61] This was another instance of the dangerous habit of diagnosing "the national mind."

Nevertheless, liberals such as Steffens and the editors of *The New Republic* had attained a perspective closer to insight than to cliché. One of the men who most fully personified this perspective and was most influential in educating others to it, during 1918 and 1919, was Raymond Robins. Although officially a member of the American Red Cross Mission to Russia (and by December its head), Robins extended his power and personality far beyond the limits of his office. As he wrote to his wife from Petrograd, on December 20, 1917, with his relish for a grandiose gesture against a heroic backdrop:

I shall have a tale to tell in my old land — a tale that is a tale! Each hour the situation grows more grave. Civil war is now added to the troubles of sick and suffering Russia. . . . Our diplomacy is past speaking about. Could it be better told than in this fact, I a Red Cross man am the only person in any authority that is permitted by our government to have direct intercourse with the de facto government that has complete control over three fourth [*sic*] of Russian territory and more than five sixths of the bayonetts of the Russian people.[62]

This unusual status derived from the fact that the United States had withheld recognition from the Bolshevik regime and prohibited the American ambassador from communicating with the new rulers in Russia. Moreover, Ambassador Francis himself was an elderly, quite conservative man whom diplomatic inexperience and a rumored love affair with a suspected German agent had made virtually ineffectual. Into this diplomatic vacuum stepped individuals from various organizations on the scene, including the Young Men's Christian Association, the Committee on Public Information, and the American Red Cross. Although highly unorthodox and certainly confusing, the situation at least permitted the officials in Washington to obtain information by indirect contact with Lenin's government. Of these ersatz ambassadors, Robins soon attained the greatest intimacy with the Bolsheviks. By February 1918, despite Wilson's personal grudge against him that came from his Progressive activities in the 1912 Presidential campaign, he earned Administration approval of his activities.[63]

Robins arrived in Russia during August 1917, possessing all the conventional American attitudes raised to an almost ecstatic pitch. He came as a robust missionary, anxious for the adventure of a revolution and dedicated to helping the Slavic nation fulfill its destiny of freedom and brotherhood. "To help this happen," he wrote to his wife from Petrograd on August 18, "is the greatest task in the world. Russia is a giant long asleep that has been wakened roughly and has not yet found complete consciousness." [64] Combining this ambition with an unshakeable belief in American democracy, a determination to revive Russia's participation in the war, and, finally, opposition to Bolshevik economic and political principles, Robins apparently diverged not at all from the common American view.[65] The difference became clear after the October Revolution. Unlike most of his compatriots, he understood that "Revolutions never go backward." [66] He was neither shocked nor bewildered, therefore, when the Bolsheviks seized control. Rather, he was prepared to work with them to attain his objective of restoring Russia's military role. His cooperative attitude did not mean that he had forsaken liberal and patriotic values. It only meant that he realized the permanence of Lenin's coup and made a pragmatic choice between impotently boycotting the new government and seeking to deal with it.[67]

Of course his decision presupposed that there was at least a potential coincidence between Bolshevik and American purposes. Even disregarding larger points of ideology, it is clear in retrospect that, on the immediate and crucial issue of a separate peace, Robins was wrong in his presupposition. His fervent self-confidence as well as his taste for heroism probably were responsible for deceiving him here. Historians have persuasively argued that, no matter what Robins or the United States might have done, the Bolsheviks were determined to withdraw from the war. After all, the cry of "peace" to a war-weary populace had been one of the major reasons for the success of the October Revolution.[68]

The point is, however, that Robins' whole personality and his friendly relationship with the Bolshevik leaders inclined him to the opposite view. More important, enough circumstances allowed him to make a strong case that the United States, not Soviet Russia, was responsible for the Brest-Litovsk Treaty. Just as Americans used the Bolsheviks as a means of exonerating themselves from the fallacies in their

29

reasoning about Russia, Robins maintained confidence in the Bolsheviks by blaming the Wilson Administration for his failure to deter Russia from a separate peace. According to Robins, on March 5, 1918, Trotsky confided to him that Lenin was apprehensive of German ambitions and would refuse to ratify the Brest-Litovsk Treaty if he could be assured of economic and military support from the Allies. Robins excitedly conveyed the proposal in a memorandum to Ambassador Francis for telegraphic transmission to the State Department. When the Fourth All-Russian Congress of Soviets met on March 16, he reluctantly told Lenin that he still had received no reply from Washington, whereupon the Bolshevik leader mounted the stage and led the delegates in ratifying the treaty. In Robins' opinion, the only possible inference was that the bitter anti-Bolshevism of his government was to blame for the separate peace.[69] In fact, however, he had exaggerated the meaning of the Russian proposal: Trotsky had only asked a hypothetical question and had never promised that the treaty would be rejected.[70] Nevertheless, Robins' version of the incident was what the American public learned when he testified before the Senate Judiciary Subcommittee in March 1919. And it was this same version, with all its implications, that he told privately to his friends when he returned home in May 1918.

On the eve of his departure, Robins wrote to Lenin: "It has been my eager desire for over five months to be of some use in interpreting this new democracy to the people of America and I shall hope to continue efforts in this behalf upon my return to my own land." [71] During the next few years, those efforts shaped the opinions of a vast circle of American liberals.

His influence had begun already during his first few months in Russia. William Boyce Thompson, a millionaire mining engineer who was Robins' predecessor as head of the Red

Cross Mission, quickly succumbed to his colleague's attitudes. Although he had given a million dollars out of his own pocket to strengthen the Provisional Government's war effort, he swiftly imitated Robins' adjustment to the Bolsheviks' *fait accompli*. In December he left for London and then the United States in order to persuade the Allied governments to adopt a pragmatic tolerance toward the Russian situation. Wilson refused to see him, but Thompson vigorously persisted in telling his countrymen of the "democracy" he had just visited.[72]

Another admirer of Robins was Arthur Bullard, serving in Russia first as unofficial representative of Wilson's adviser, Colonel Edward M. House, and then as director of the Moscow office of the Committee on Public Information. Historian George Kennan, not prone to hasty superlatives, asserts that "Bullard's was the best American mind observing on the spot the course of the Russian Revolution," and claims that his long and frequent letters to House were probably more important than the ambassador's reports in shaping American policy toward Russia.[73] In his letters after the October Revolution, Bullard emphatically echoed Robins: Bolshevism, although "wrong-headed," was the only real political power in Russia; to deny the fact would be "sheer blindness and dangerous stupidity," and to charge the Bolsheviks with being German agents "is at best an unproven guess"; the new government sincerely wanted to fight Germany and therefore Washington should "go the limit in cooperation with the present *de facto* government — short of formal recognition."[74] Others, such as Professors Edward A. Ross and Samuel N. Harper (although the latter was to become disenchanted with Robins' point of view), returned from Russia to preach the same gospel.[75]

President Wilson, who had his own gospel, ignored the suggestions of Robins and his circle, but many Wilsonian liberals did not. Their receptivity marked a significant development in American liberalism. Ever since the February Revolution, the question of Russia had never escaped the context of the World War. Most Americans, including a large group whom Christopher Lasch appropriately calls "war liberals," granted sympathy to Russia only as long as there was a possibility that she would restore the Eastern Front; the Brest-Litovsk Treaty definitively ended their tolerance. But for others, the "anti-imperialists," the choice was more complex. They had rallied behind the war effort because Wilson had promised a peace without victory and a world of democracy. The Bolsheviks, although ruthless to a degree disquieting to American liberals, nevertheless cried out with an appealing vigor for peace and democracy. Of course the Americans would have preferred peace only with a defeated Germany and democracy within a parliamentary structure. But they conceded that the conditions of Russia — exhaustion after three years of war and a population of illiterate peasants inexperienced in representative government — required more flexible standards. The question was how far toward flexibility they were willing to go. Would they yield so much that they would surrender their values altogether and become pure relativists or radicals?

During the interval between the October Revolution and the Brest-Litovsk Treaty, they never had to confront this ideological challenge. Instead, they fixed their attitude toward Russia at a degree of warm sympathy and focused attention neither on themselves nor on Russia, but on the Wilson Administration. If the Bolsheviks were negotiating with Germany for a separate peace, they argued, the responsibility lay with the American government, which refused to redefine its war aims. Wilson should declare the aims for which the United States was fighting, they insisted, and then Russia would be induced to return to battle for the moral cause.

When the President finally satisfied this demand, in the Fourteen Points speech of January 8, 1918, the liberals applauded but did not revise their attitude. Rather, two months later, they easily excused the Brest-Litovsk Treaty by claiming that the United States had acted too late. This was the state of mind which Robins met on his return in May. Naturally he had no trouble persuading his friends to believe his story about Trotsky's proposal and the Administration's silence on the eve of ratification. He merely confirmed their previous suspicions. The "betrayal" of which most Americans accused the Bolsheviks actually was, according to these liberals, an American betrayal.[76]

Not all of the Robins coterie survived the challenge of Brest-Litovsk. As ratification became imminent, Bullard, for one, began to adopt the idea that the Bolsheviks were German agents and to argue that American economic aid would only contribute to the "tragic farce" toward which the Soviet leaders were guiding Russia. For liberals like Bullard, the pull of victory was stronger than the pull of peace.[77] But a large segment of American liberals reacted differently. They thus enacted a rehearsal of the larger drama of 1919–1920 when they, along with others, finally freed from fear of Germany, would revive the charges of Allied betrayal at Versailles. Russia indeed was an "acid test," a test not simply of "good will" but of Wilsonian liberalism itself.

The question of a separate peace proved less troublesome to the "anti-imperialists" than the question of democracy in Soviet Russia. In the first months after the October Revolution, few Americans had a clear sense of what principles the Bolsheviks advocated, and they certainly could have acquired only further confusion and miseducation from American newspapers and magazines. (A minor masterpiece of misinformation was the report by a writer in the November 1917 issue of *The North American Review,* that the real

Lenin had died two years ago in Switzerland and that the present imposter was in fact a man named Zederblum.[78]) Sympathetic liberals shared this general ignorance even though they rejected the popular prejudices. As a result, they often resorted to invocation of the same faith in Russian democracy which they, along with so many others, had trumpeted during 1917. A typical comment appeared in a *New Republic* editorial of November 17, 1917: "In word, thought and deed Americans should . . . be loyal to the Russian revolution." [79] This vague exhortation, along with the failure to recognize that there now were *two* Russian revolutions, implies the liberals' uncertainty about the meaning of events in Russia.

Throughout the winter and spring of 1917–18, vagueness only advanced to vacillation. Editorials in *The Nation* of March 1918, for instance, emotionally declared: "The healthy fruits of the Russian Revolution must be saved" from German imperialism, for the sake of both "the great Slav people" and "the ideal of a community of free nations." With an earnestness transcending a concern for metaphorical consistency, *The Nation* went on to deplore "the Bolshevik tide" which had temporarily submerged those Russians loyal to the Revolution. Developments in Russia, it admitted, had been a disappointment to liberals. Yet it drew back from any suggestion that the Revolution had failed. Rather, it insisted that the condition of the Russian people was decidedly better than before the February Revolution. By June this liberal periodical, still conceding that the Bolshevik ideas might be erroneous, urged the Administration to consider diplomatic recognition of the Soviet regime, which had proved to be stable, popular, and congruent with the democratic impulses of the Russian masses.[80] *The New Republic* went through similar contortions. In a single editorial of April 6, for example, it said that the Bolshevik social and economic programs were "wholly unsound" and bound to be "calamitous" if applied, yet praised the Revolution as a milestone in the history of liberty; in a desperate effort at coherence, the editors went on to explain that the Bolsheviks were necessary to Russia's survival during her present crisis, after which the "Russian democracy" would overthrow them. The only really lucid analysis came near the end of the editorial: "We sympathize with them [the Bolsheviks] for the moment because of the enemies they have made." [81]

This intellectual tangle, always beginning and ending in sympathy for the Soviet regime, accurately represented the position of a growing number of liberals during the half year after the Bolshevik coup. They did not have the advantage of radicals like John Reed, Bessie Beatty, Louise Bryant, and the editors of *The Liberator*, who believed in the Revolution with single-minded devotion. As Reed wrote to Robins in January 1918: "I am working for international democracy *from below*, the only way I believe it can come," while Robins was involved in waging a war under a ragged banner of war aims which were "still a little Alsace-Lorrainish, if I may put it so." [82] Like Louise Bryant, Reed's wife, these radicals used the faces of the Russian people as a mirror in which they saw "a vision of world democracy." Along with pacifists and anarchists, these radicals rejoiced at the separate peace as a liberation from an imperialist war and as an incentive to Germany's proletarian revolution. They did not need to reassure themselves by an elaborate discussion of war aims and Administration actions. They possessed the certainty that the liberals had had early in 1917 and now were losing. They had given up faith in the United States and turned to Russia as the land of promise. [83]

The "anti-imperialist" liberals professed their faith in Russia but had not yet, in the spring of 1918, given up on their own country. This uneasy suspension between the

Wilsonian and Leninist ideologies accounted for the emotional squirming and intellectual confusion they exhibited. But under the impetus of events they began to slide eastward. To liberals, Allied hypocrisy about war aims contrasted sharply with the Bolsheviks' publication of the secret treaties and their sincere, though naive, search for a just peace at Brest-Litovsk. The Bolsheviks were not Western-style liberals, but they preached a form of democracy appropriate to backward Russia. And ultimately, as *The New Republic* explained, the anti-imperialists loved Russia for her enemies. Those enemies were increasing during the first half of 1918. Within Russia the Whites were organizing for counterrevolution. Britain, France, and Japan were clearly preparing to support them. Meanwhile, the American public was beginning to call more and more stridently for intervention in Russia. In response to these forces, the liberals began to back into the pro-Soviet camp, their progress being in effect a reluctant retreat from their old loyalties. As Samuel Harper complained to Walter Lippmann, in a letter written on January 18, 1918: "We have allowed the Bolsheviki to steal our moral thunder." [84]

An incident in March vividly underscored his insight. President Wilson, still preaching his familiar message of universal democracy, sent a statement to the All-Russian Congress of Soviets just before the Brest-Litovsk Treaty was to be ratified. (This was not a reply to Trotsky's proposal to defer ratification in return for American aid.) "The whole heart of the people of the United States," Wilson wrote, "is with the people of Russia in the attempt to free themselves forever from autocratic government and become the masters of their own life." But, he regretfully added, the United States could offer no economic aid to them. [85]

In reply, the Congress thanked "the toiling and exploited classes of the United States of North America" and expressed "its warm sympathy and its firm confidence that the happy

36

time is not far distant when the toiling masses of all bourgeois countries will throw off the yoke of capitalism and will establish a socialist order of society, which alone is capable of assuring a firm and just peace as well as the cultural and material well being of all the toilers." [86] Suddenly Americans were hearing their own gospel, in Bolshevik translation, returning to them like an ironic and ominous echo. Two missionaries were now competing for the souls of the peoples of the world.

With military intervention and then the Red Scare, feeling toward the Soviets intensified. In place of the pathetic Russian bear, the fierce bearded Bolshevik presses a bloody hand against "civilization."

ON THE THRESHOLD!

—Gale in the Los Angeles *Times*.

II / Intervention and Withdrawal

We want to show them that treaties are sacred and debts and religion. They've all become atheists, and I'm for blockading them and starving them and killing them till they return to their senses and become decent Christians again.
— from William C. Bullitt's novel, *It's Not Done* (1926), p. 274

During the first half of 1918, Americans became less and less able to sustain a posture of watchful waiting toward Soviet Russia. The nationalizing and confiscatory decrees of the Bolshevik regime, as well as the separate peace, quickly discouraged those optimists who, in the first months after the October Revolution, had stubbornly claimed that Russia would obey American expectations. The combined pressure of Soviet actions and the German menace stifled their vague assurances, leaving an empty and broadening middle ground between the bitterly hostile critics, on one side, and the reluctantly pro-Soviet liberals on the other side. As in 1917, the war effort was the primary factor in American considerations: while the liberals were driven to defend Russia by disillusionment with Allied war aims, the expanding camp of conservatives argued that Russia would be saved for democracy only if she were first saved for the Eastern Front.

As salvation by faith or by the inspiration of George Creel's Committee on Public Information proved impotent, Americans began to look for other solutions. Secretary of State Lansing pointed to the answer as early as December 1917. He recommended to President Wilson that the United

States should support General Kaledin, hetman of the Don Cossacks and soon to be one of the many Whites organizing counterrevolutionary armies within Russia: "It seems to me that nothing is to be gained by inaction, that it is simply playing into the Bolsheviki's hands, and that the situation may be saved by a few words of encouragement, and the saving of Russia means the saving of this country of hundreds of thousands of men and billions of dollars. I do not see how we could be any worse off if we took this course because we have absolutely nothing to hope from continued Bolshevik domination." [1]

Betrayed by events and the work of Bolshevik "devils," the American preachers prepared to take up arms. With their country waging war in Europe in order to make a democratic peace, they now included Russia under the same framework of national purpose and policy. All the attitudes of 1917 had prepared for this decision. Few Americans doubted the premise that the Russian people were democratic at heart and anxious to defeat the German autocrats. The ones to blame for the Revolution's deterioration into a proletarian dictatorship and a separate peace, they said, were those "German agents," Lenin and Trotsky, the first of whom had come to Russia in 1917 in a train provided by the German General Staff and the second of whom was really Bronstein, a Jew. The Bolsheviks, many Americans comfortably concluded, were not really Russians at all.

But in seeking a label for the Soviet rulers, the critics disagreed. Many simply contented themselves with the term "socialists" as sufficient condemnation. [2] Others preferred to call them "anarchists" whose application of utopian doctrines had produced the inevitable consequences of economic chaos, social disorder, and general immorality. In the vivid language of Senator Lawrence Sherman of Illinois, the Soviet government "is a compound of slaughter, confiscation, anarchy, and

40

universal disorder. It is the paradise of I.W.W.'s and the superlative heaven of anarchists and direct-action socialists." [3] At the same time, a large number of opponents charged the Bolsheviks with being dictators. *The Saturday Evening Post*, for example, told its two million subscribers that, whereas Germany practiced despotism by an elite, Lenin's government was a "despotism by all the lowest." [4] This uncertainty about definition occasionally produced strange amalgams such as "anarchistic autocrats" or "socialistic anarchists." [5] Precision was unnecessary, however. As the *New York Times* explained, "anarchy and despotism are the two ends of the same stick." Indeed, the same newspaper declared that precision was a trifling consideration when it is "not alone the rescue of Russia that is involved, it is the safety of civilization." [6]

However they were defined, the Bolsheviks were an evil which the Wilson Administration diplomatically boycotted and which the majority of American observers vehemently opposed. Given the opportunity, they argued, the Russian people would overthrow these intruders and reassert the fundamental impulses of the Revolution. With the German Empire strengthened by the annexations at Brest-Litovsk, that opportunity had to be provided quickly. Thus, American idealism neatly coincided with and sanctioned a policy of armed intervention which might otherwise have carried a suspicious aura of counterrevolutionary imperialism.

The international situation was changing in unison with American attitudes. While the Bolsheviks were demonstrating their radical intentions and the Whites were beginning their counterrevolution, Japan, Britain, and France were preparing for action of their own. Japan made the first move in April 1918, by sending troops to Vladivostok on the eastern coast of Siberia, for the ostensible purpose of guarding munition stores there. The editorial response by American

41

newspapers was "overwhelmingly" in approval, according to *Current Opinion*'s survey. There were exceptions, of course: the *Chicago Herald* and *Chicago Evening Post* wanted Japanese guarantees of nonannexation and eventual withdrawal; the *New York Evening Post* and the *Springfield Republican* condemned the action as immoral and impractical; the Hearst press passionately cried out against the "yellow peril." Some important anti-Soviet individuals, meanwhile, warned that the Russian people would regard armed intervention as invasion and would defend themselves, with German arms if need be. But these various dissents were submerged by a bellicose deluge from Florida to Massachusetts to California, an endorsement especially significant in view of continual American suspicions of Japanese ambitions since 1904. In the words of the *San Francisco Chronicle*: "Either the Japanese must be permitted to occupy as much of Siberia as they want or the Germans will take all they can get." Meanwhile, the *New York Times* scoffed at suspicions of Japan's motives for intervening.[7]

This sort of enthusiasm was still quite different from advocating intervention by American troops. The *New York Times*, for example, endorsed the Japanese action but expressly stated that American participation was not necessary. That was on March 3, however, two weeks before the formal Soviet withdrawal from the war. During late March and April, the demand for American intervention became clamorous, based on the familiar dual rationale. On the one hand, and in appropriate parable, *The Congregationalist and Advance* cited missionary responsibility for Russia: "On the Jericho road of history," it editorialized, "she has fallen in with the robber. May America be the Good Samaritan to lift her wounded out of the dirt, to pay her hospital expenses, if need be, and to restore her to sane and civilized society."[8] By intervening to put Russia on her democratic feet, Kennan and other respected figures assured Americans, the United States would have the support of the vast majority of Russians.[9] In any case — and here the second rationale enters in — even if American troops met popular resistance, the fate of the United States and the whole world depended on defeating Germany and therefore partly on rescuing Russia from the German-serving Bolsheviks. Senator James Reed of Missouri presented the case with startling succinctness shortly after the American decision to intervene: if Russia rises up against the entering troops, he told the Senate, then that will only prove that "Russia is already Germanized." [10] During May and June 1918, the advocates of American intervention gained still further in numbers and vehemence.[11]

The Wilson Administration was exposed simultaneously to this growing public clamor and to pressure on a diplomatic level. From January through April 1918, it was obliged to make six formal rejections to Allied proposals for concerted entry into Siberia. But Britain, France, and Japan, with motives as much anti-Bolshevik as anti-German, continued to urge intervention as a way of re-establishing the Eastern Front, despite Wilson's objections on moral, political, and military grounds.[12] Many of the President's own diplomatic advisers in the Far East and Russia joined the interventionist side.[13] The most noteworthy defection was that by Ambassador Francis, who reversed his earlier position at the end of April.[14] The double pressure began to take effect in Washington. Already by April, Wilson showed an unprecedented interest in Siberia, while in May the Secretary of State told the British ambassador that northern Russia, being closer to the German front, was more suitable than Siberia as a site for intervention.[15]

Two developments within Russia converted this timid tendency into conclusive action. First, reports that the Bolsheviks were arming German and Austrian prisoners of war, although firmly denied by British and American observers sent to verify the facts, alarmed the government and the nation at large.[16] Second, and ultimately decisive, on May 18 the Czechoslovak Legion staged an uprising against Soviet forces in Siberia. These Czech soldiers, including members of Czech colonies in Russia and deserters to the Russian side, had fought against the Central Powers until the Brest-Litovsk peace; then they had arranged with the Soviet and Allied governments to travel to the Western Front via Vladivostok and a global journey. Although they had promised to disarm in order to calm the Soviet fear of counterrevolutionary action, the Czechs resisted the Soviet troops who demanded their weapons. The clash became widespread war against Soviet authority, the legion being joined by the White forces and being supported by France and Britain. By May 29 a Czech contingent had seized Vladivostok and was asking for Allied cooperation in helping its compatriots in the Russian interior.

News of the Czech appeal arrived in Washington on July 2; it climaxed the growing realization of Wilson and his advisers that they had been providentially given a solution to their dilemma over intervention. In a so-called aide-mémoire sent to the Allied ambassadors on July 17, Wilson announced his decision to intervene in order "to help the Czecho-Slovaks consolidate their forces and get into successful cooperation with their Slavic kinsmen and to steady any efforts at self-government or self-defense in which the Russians themselves may be willing to accept assistance" and, third, to guard military stores on the Siberian and northern coasts of Russia. Yet the statement also defined military intervention as "merely a method of making use of Russia, not a method of serving her," and it earnestly disclaimed any intention of interfering in internal Russian affairs.[17]

On August 3, the American public officially learned that

its government was intervening in Russia to guard military stores and to defend the Czechs against German and Austrian prisoners of war (the prisoners were not mentioned in the aide-mémoire).[18] In their enthusiastic response, commentators did not question the reasons or purposes of the decision. Already stirred by the heroic, beleaguered Czechs and of course still loyal to the vision of a democratic Russia, most Americans eagerly endorsed intervention as satisfying both commitments. The *New York Tribune* declared that the arrival of American and Allied troops was the means to a "true realization of the hopes of the revolution." [19] If any criticism was made in the popular press, it was that the United States was sending too few troops; Senator Reed boldly called for an army of 500,000 Americans in Russia.[20]

This enthusiasm overlooked certain difficulties in the official justification of intervention. For one thing, the statement of August 3 spoke of the Czechs moving westward, *away* from the coast, whereas the ostensible goal was to help the Czechs reach the eastern Siberian ports. Second, contrary to the general American belief, only a few thousand prisoners, mostly Austrians, were armed, and they presented little danger. Finally, even if no one knew or admitted that the Czechs were fighting the Soviet forces, how could the United States avoid interference with internal Russian affairs either when its troops defended the Czechs or when they aided "the Russians themselves" to form a democratic government? Both the Administration and the public ignored these ambiguities in the summer of 1918. Instead, they declared that intervention was purely to aid the Czechs' safe passage through German forces and to foster Russian democracy. A later generation of historians, provoked by the obvious inconsistencies, has argued that American intervention was a secret check on Japanese imperialism or a frankly anti-Bolshevik drive. Whatever the real motive, in popular understanding it became another expression, in military terms, of the delusive American faith in the Russian people's democratic desires, complemented by the determination to ignore the Bolsheviks as transient, German-supported pretenders to Russian power. In the late summer and fall of 1918, few Americans perceived intervention as in fact a war against the Bolsheviks rather than Germany.[21]

This context of direct involvement in Russia and of reinforced commitment to false assumptions encouraged Americans to develop an anti-Bolshevik mythology of huge proportions during the second half of 1918 and early 1919. The Bolsheviks became convenient monsters to be dressed with one's favorite prejudices or fears. The claim that the Soviets had ordered Russian women to be "nationalized" became the most notorious myth. In October 1918, the *New York Times* printed a British press wireless report that, in certain Russian provinces, every eighteen-year-old girl was required to register at a government "bureau of free love" and was then given a husband without her consent or, vice versa, could choose a man without his consent. In January 1919, Senator Sherman of Illinois quoted the same report in a Senate speech.[22] Despite the arguments by Robins and others that the decree was the work of an anarchist, not Bolshevik, group, the licentious rumor did not die. On the contrary, Senator Hiram Johnson of California wrote to Robins in April 1919 about "the extraordinary publicity" which the smaller western papers were giving to the nationalization of women; he himself — a loyal member of the Robins coterie — apparently was uncertain about the truth of the matter.[23] As late as 1922, the myth still was being repeated.[24]

In addition to sexual sensationalism, anti-Semitism provided fertile ground for anti-Bolshevik attitudes. Samuel N. Harper, for example, expressed fears of "the Jewish gang in Washington" which, he said, was maneuvering for a more tolerant policy toward Soviet Russia.[25] A Methodist Episcopal minister, returning to the United States after a decade of work in Petrograd, ascribed the Bolshevik activities to Jewish agitators from New York.[26] In response, American Jewish leaders, who had welcomed the February Revolution with such ardor, took pains to disown the Soviet leaders. Louis Marshall, president of the American Jewish Committee, declared: "Everything that real Bolshevism stands for is to the Jew detestable." At the same time, Jewish spokesmen rebuked those Jews such as Rabbi Judah Magnes who urged a liberal policy toward Lenin's regime.[27]

The most important myth was the charge that the Bolsheviks were German agents. This idea became more and more common during the months after the October Revolution until, with the publication of the famous Sisson documents in October 1918, the American government officially endorsed it. Edgar Sisson, while serving in Russia as the representative of the Committee on Public Information, had deviously acquired documents which appeared to him to prove a Bolshevik-German conspiracy. In September, the Creel committee released them to the press (without State Department approval) and then, a month later, published them in a pamphlet which included the opinions of Professors Harper and J. Franklin Jameson that the documents were authentic.[28] "Lenine and Trotzky German Agents: Secret Documents Unearthed in Petrograd Prove that Bolshevist Leaders Are Paid Traitors." This headline in *Current History* was typical of the excited credulity with which the public received Sisson's revelations. The devastating analysis by the *New York Evening Post* reached only a small company of skeptics.[29]

In fact, the *Evening Post* was right; the charge of "German agents" was, like the nationalization of women, an alarmist fabrication, and the Sisson documents were forgeries.[30] Harper himself, though convinced that the Bolsheviks had accepted German money and were serving German ends, confided to a colleague, in November 1918, that he did "not like the way he [Sisson] uses the term German agent." But Harper did not state his reservations publicly nor did he ever doubt that the documents were genuine.[31] Even more to the point, President Wilson himself had authorized Creel's release of the documents. Throughout 1917 and 1918 the dedication to defeating Germany had distracted and distorted American attitudes toward Russia; the Sisson documents were only a particularly lurid scene in the tragedy of errors.

"As to Lenin, and Trotzky, and the Bolsheviks, the President has been poisoned. All Washington has." In a letter written on October 31, 1918, Lincoln Steffens generously made the President a victim, not a co-conspirator, of the interventionist atmosphere.[32] But the events of 1918 had been a more embittering experience for other liberals of Wilsonian loyalties. To many of them, intervention seemed a stab in Russia's back, with American as well as Allied hands guiding the knife.

In March 1918, for example, Harold Stearns still was confident enough to write in *The Dial*: "Others may abandon Russia, but he [Wilson] will not." [33] But William C. Bullitt, serving as adviser to both the State Department and the President and therefore more familiar with the Administration's thinking, was more alarmed. In a memorandum to Acting Secretary of State Frank Polk on March 2, he wrote that the United States could preserve its moral position only by frankly opposing Japanese entry into Siberia. The rudiments of democracy existed in Russia, he declared, but equally certain was the fact of Bolshevik control. In his opinion, Wilson had the alternatives of joining the Allies in support of reactionary Whites or of standing by the Soviet regime and Russian democracy against intervention. Bullitt concluded with passion: "We cannot stand aside and maintain our moral integrity. We cannot wash our hands of this matter. Unless we oppose, we assent. Pontius Pilate washed his hands. The world has never forgiven him." [34] By late June he wrote to Colonel House that he was "sick at heart" because of the tragic prospect of Siberian intervention.[35]

Sickness at heart spread throughout the ranks of "anti-imperialist" liberals during the spring and early summer of 1918. Nevertheless, consistent with their posture of reluctant retreat from Wilsonian policies, they refused to lose hope that the Administration would produce a constructive and sympathetic policy toward Soviet Russia. It was on this basis of lingering loyalty that *The Nation* and *The New Republic* warned that Russia would and must save herself. Military intervention, they insisted, would only provoke civil war between the Russian people and the Bolshevik regime, on one side, and the White armies backed by Allied troops on the other. The only moral and practical intervention would be an economic mission dispensing aid. When Wilson promised that the United States would "stand by" Russia, in his Red Cross speech on May 18, these liberals significantly interpreted him to mean that he was endorsing their own position. In other words, although they criticized the President, it was a loyal criticism based on continuing faith that he and they shared the same ideals. Meanwhile, they had never been so firm in support of the war effort, believing that only Germany's defeat would erase Russia's subjection to Germany at Brest-Litovsk.[36]

In claiming Wilson's position as their own, these liberals in fact had unwittingly made themselves prisoners of his terms. The American decision to intervene dragged them and their protests in its wake. With consternation they sought to make the best of a bad situation by an awkward straddling of fences. *The New Republic*, for example, first defended Wilson as having been forced to choose this path — so injurious to Soviet-American understanding — as a lesser evil than Allied intervention unaccompanied by American restraints and as the only way of reviving Russia's role in the war. But the same editorial went far beyond Wilson's purposes by stating: "Possibly the Soviet regime is declining to its fall, and that in spite of apparent aggression we may be able to effect an understanding with a democratic counter-revolution." Three weeks later it again sought to stand on both sides of the dilemma. The Allies ought to defend the Czechs against the armed prisoners of war, the editorial stated; but it went on to repeat, without contradiction, both the official Soviet denial that the Czechs were in danger and the Soviet demand that the Allies state the real motive for aiding the Czechs.[37]

The Nation evaded the situation with more candor. The editors recalled their consistent opposition to armed intervention but now urged, in view of the *fait accompli*, that intervention be done well so that stability and an elective, representative government could be introduced into Russia.[38] This pragmatic stand implied, however, that the Bolsheviks were providing neither law nor order nor a democratic regime, and thus it could also imply the counterrevolutionary program which *The New Republic* had momentarily suggested.

Public and diplomatic pressures had driven Wilson to compromise his opposition to intervention; now his action was eroding the shaky structure of liberal attitudes toward Russia. Liberals could not long sustain this loyalty to the President's policy except at the cost of intellectual dishonesty or of finally surrendering any pretension of sympathy with Soviet Russia. Bullitt indicated his choice to House in September 1918. Although still praising Wilson's "wisdom and noble intentions," he bluntly charged that "we are fighting Great Russia" and driving her into a military alliance with Germany.[39] By October, as the end of the European war became imminent and thus removed that central factor in the American evaluation of Russia, *The New Republic* began to demand a substitution of economic for military intervention. Like Bullitt, however, it retained trust in the President. Early in November an editorial declared that continued military action in Russia would undermine Wilson's drive to apply his principles of justice after the war.[40] When the war ended and the Allied troops remained in Russia, the liberal outcry against intervention became increasingly forceful and bitter. *The New Republic* conceded, at the close of the year, that intervention "was a mistake from first to last."[41]

By this time, however, the dissenting liberals were neither so exceptional nor so courageous. Once Germany's defeat had erased the main rationale for intervention, a growing number of Americans, sharing none of the liberals' Soviet leanings, began to demand a withdrawal of troops from Siberia and northern Russia. As early as October 1918, Samuel Harper noticed a growing dissidence outside of the usual liberal circles and privately warned that, unless the government stressed economic assistance more than military action, there would be a "break" in American feeling toward Russia.[42] This proved to be a perceptive prediction. From all levels of American society, during the winter of 1917–18, people protested the continued intervention.

On November 27, Secretary of War Newton D. Baker wrote to the President that the presence of American troops in Siberia not only distracted Russians from reaching political solutions, but served as a cloak disguising Japanese entrenchment and annexations. "I do not know that I rightly understand Bolshevikism," he confessed. "So much of it as I do understand I don't like, but I have a feeling that if the Russians do like it, they are entitled to have it." [43] Newspapers and magazines claimed that intervention had only strengthened the Soviet regime by antagonizing the Russian people; if Bolshevik principles were so reprehensible and destructive, many writers argued, then the United States would do best by leaving the Bolsheviks to commit their own suicide, intervening only with aid to relieve the suffering masses.[44] During a month of nationwide lecturing for Russia and against intervention, Louise Bryant excitedly wrote to her husband, John Reed, about the warm reception from her audiences.[45] The Acting Secretary of State had the same feeling. "Public sentiment is extremely restive on the whole subject of Russia," he exclaimed in January 1919.[46] Michigan residents were more than restive; they were bitter that their sons were still suffering and fighting in northern Russia while American troops were coming home from Europe. Their letters, telegrams, and resolutions, demanding withdrawal of the interventionary forces, crowded the desks of their congressmen.[47]

The halls of Congress resounded with sympathetic echoes. In the House of Representatives, Speaker Champ Clark of Missouri drew vigorous applause when, on January 22, he called for the immediate return of American troops from Russia and all of Europe. Only a few weeks earlier, Representative Ernest Lundeen of Minnesota had introduced a resolution to the same effect.[48] In the Senate meanwhile, the prestigious Progressive leaders, Senators Johnson, La Follette, and Borah, began a concerted attack on Wilson's Russian policy. Borrowing ammunition from Raymond Robins, they delivered a series of speeches vehemently opposing the undeclared war against the Bolsheviks and castigating American dealings with Russia, in Johnson's words, as "an exhibition of the crassest stupidity" that contributed to "the awful tragedy there." All three emphatically denied any sympathy for Bolshevik doctrines or practices; on the contrary, their indignation derived from profoundly American loyalties. They wanted to let the Russian people practice self-determination, even if that meant continued Soviet rule, so that the American people could return both its armies and its attention to its own shores.

In 1917, Borah had supported American entry into war because it was "an American war to be carried on, prolonged, or ended according to American interests and to be adjusted upon American principles." A year later, he had supported intervention in Russia. By 1919 he and his Progressive colleagues felt that American responsibilities overseas were done. Senator Johnson spoke for them when he said: "I am opposed to American boys policing Europe and quelling riots in every new nation's back yard," thus tacitly including such back yards as Siberia and northern Russia. "It is time for an American policy," he continued. "Bring home American soldiers. Rescue our own democracy. Restore its free expression. Get American business into its normal channels. Let American life, social and economic, be American again." On February 7, the California senator's resolution urging withdrawal of American troops from Russia was defeated, 37 to 32, on a partisan split; intervention had become a Democratic issue now, not a national necessity. But apparently even the Democrats were not sure why American troops still were in Russia, for on June 27 the Senate unanimously approved a Johnson resolution asking for an explanation by the Administration.[49]

Within a few months, Borah, La Follette, and Johnson — the "irreconcilables" — levied the same sorts of arguments against the treaty which Wilson brought back from Versailles. Once again the World War — in this case its conclusion — was the lens through which Americans looked at Russia. And once again a group of Americans defended Soviet

Russia not because of ideological commitment, but because of hostility to American motives and actions. During the coming decade, these isolationists were to remain in the seemingly anomalous position of advocating tolerance and diplomatic recognition for the Bolshevik regime.

The issue of continued American intervention was only the most controversial and immediate aspect of the larger problem of Soviet Russia. It never defined attitudes toward that larger problem because it functioned in such various ways. Many anti-Bolsheviks objected to intervention as a futile venture into Russia's civil war, while many liberals, willing to give the Bolsheviks a chance, at first favored intervention as an anti-German move. When the Armistice removed the war as a preoccupation for liberals, they conceivably might have been able to construct a disinterested perspective on Russia, consonant with the open-mindedness they demanded of others. But the context of prolonged intervention, the Versailles Treaty, and the Red Scare prevented the "anti-imperialists" from achieving such a perspective. They continued, instead, to use Russia as a counterargument, as a weapon in the ideological battle they were waging at home. Their portrait was always policy.

After the end of the war, anti-imperialist liberals began to urge, with unprecedented vigor, the substitution of economic assistance for military intervention. They argued that only this constructive and cooperative relationship to the Soviet rulers would remedy the economic and political disorder within Russia. By this proposal they assumed, of course, that the Bolsheviks would be willing to cooperate. Even more rashly, they asserted that the introduction of American aid and techniques would cause an evolution of the Russian social and economic system toward capitalist principles.[50] As a corollary to this economic proposition, they insisted that the

Soviet dictatorship of the proletariat would inevitably develop in a democratic direction because of the underlying political structure of the mir. This village organization for local self-government had been cited in 1917 by those who were trying to prove the democratic character of the February Revolution.[51] Liberals now revived the idea, arguing that the soviets were simply modern expressions of the historical mirs. Some liberals also emphasized the presence of cooperative societies as stabilizing and democratizing forces. Finally, some were content to assert, with a dogmatic confidence rivaling that of Ambassador Francis himself, that the mere presence of time and the responsibilities of leadership would necessarily liberalize the Soviet regime.[52]

Lincoln Colcord, a correspondent for the *Philadelphia Public Ledger* until August 1918, was a particularly ardent victim of these misinterpretations. On December 14, 1918, an editorial in *The Dial* had declared that in Russia "we are confronted with an economic revolution instead of a merely political revolution." Writing in the same journal two weeks later, Colcord desperately tried to hurdle the implications of this insight. In "a certain divine sense," he wrote, "the proletariat of Russia is striving to accomplish for his world much the same ideals which our forefathers laid down for theirs." From this basis he continued: "In fact, has not the thought arrested liberals everywhere that in the Soviet system we see a foreshadowing of the next step forward in the machinery of democratic government, bringing our present machinery, a heritage from a past era, abreast of the new industrialized world?" Within this sublimely culture-bound perception he vehemently denied a place to the Bolsheviks' "transitory class dogma," which the "logic of life and history" would destroy. Bolshevism, he exclaimed, was a plan for "a free and outright representative democracy." [53]

The extravagance of these claims suggests a need and will

to believe. Certainly there was no inherent justification for liberals to embrace Soviet Russia with such warmth. In contrast to radicals like Reed, Louise Bryant, Max Eastman, and the left-wing American socialists, who admired the ruthless policies of Moscow without moralistic qualms, liberals were uncomfortable with the theory and practice of class revolution.[54] "Between ends and means there is an infallible contamination," *The New Republic* proclaimed in protest against the Soviet Terror. In the same editorial, however, it condemned the equally murderous Allied blockade preventing medical supplies and machine parts from reaching Soviet Russia.[55] Neither side was uncontaminated, but the thrust of events made liberals unable to stand aloof from the plague of both houses. Throughout 1917 and 1918 they had remained loyal to Wilson, pardoning his lapses with increasing distress. By March 1919, Colcord told Colonel House that "American liberals do not trust him [Wilson] any longer." Colcord attributed the break to disgust with the continued intervention and blockade:

> The word is getting around that the Administration is keeping the truth from the people in order to cover up a mistake in Russian policy.
> And the strange fact remains that everything the President stands for, every tenet and principle of his new world, and the whole success of his liberal campaign, are bound up, as they have been from the first, in that very solution of the Russian situation which he cannot bring himself to make.[56]

In their disillusionment, the liberals began to see the Soviet regime more as victim than malefactor. Just as they had previously excused the Bolsheviks' separate peace by accusing the Allies of failure to define their war aims, now they evaluated Soviet Russia through the filter of intervention and blockade. But in 1918 they had still had faith in Wilson's idealism. With that faith finally betrayed, they turned to the only hope left to them: the democratic dawn in the Soviet East.

This realignment of the liberals' devotion might not have been so severe if Wilson had not continued to damn himself in their eyes during 1919. While in Paris he tried to dissolve the Russian impasse by new actions. In January 1919, he persuaded the Allies to invite all the "governments" of Russia — both White and Red — to meet with the Allies at Prinkipo, the island near Constantinople, and arrange for peace and stability in Russia. The proposal apparently had in mind some division of the Russian nation among the contending factions; it certainly was nothing close to recognition of the Soviets. Nevertheless, the Bolsheviks agreed to attend the conference, although refusing the Allied request that they set a date for a truce in the civil war. That refusal allowed the Whites to decline the whole invitation. American liberals had experienced an initial surge of hope that the Prinkipo proposal signified a Soviet-American entente, but the dismal denouement reconfirmed their disenchantment with Wilson.

The Administration — in this case, House and Lansing — did not give up hope, however, and sent William C. Bullitt, Lincoln Steffens, and Captain Walter W. Pettit to Moscow to negotiate the basis for another conference. By mid-March, Bullitt was wiring his superiors in Paris not only that the Bolsheviks had accepted the conditions of the new invitation, but that the Revolution had created an orderly and constructive situation in Russia. Again the conference never took place, this time because conservative forces within the American party at the peace conference sabotaged any policy except an anti-Bolshevik one.[57] Once again the fine words and intentions toward Russia had ended in nothing. Wilson's hold on liberal loyalties was vanishing.

The President's crucial crime, in the liberals' opinion, was the peace treaty of Versailles. Even *The New Republic,* whose editors had been so influential in the shaping of the Fourteen Points, now turned away in anger. It condemned the treaty as a vindictive and imperialistic creation, a "shameless" pretense of peace which subjected liberalism "to a decisive test" of its principles.[58] Meanwhile, Bullitt was writing his own text of disillusionment. In a letter of resignation on May 17, 1919, he explaind to Wilson that the treaty betrayed the principles of justice and permanent peace which once had induced Bullitt and so many others to follow the President. As for Russia, that problem "has not even been understood." The letter ended in quiet anger: "I am sorry that you did not fight our fight to the finish and that you had so little faith in the millions of men, like myself, in every nation who had faith in you." [59] During the next decade, Bullitt retired to the Riviera to write a novel and married John Reed's widow, Louise Bryant. His next public appearance in the Soviet-American drama was in 1933 — as the first American ambassador to the Soviet Union.

Perhaps the last word on American liberal attitudes during this period is most appropriately left to Lincoln Steffens, the self-appointed student of revolutions and the mentor of the liberals. After returning from Moscow to Paris, he experienced strong reactions to the work of the Versailles negotiators. "So they have failed," he wrote to Allen Suggett in April. "They have the appearance of success, but, — they have failed. And it does not matter. The problem will be solved. Other, newer men, with a fresher culture, — the men I have seen lately, — they will have their turn now. And they are on the job." [60]

American intervention in Russia did finally end. The last troops withdrew from northern Russia in June 1919 and from Siberia in April 1920, while the Allied blockade was lifted in January 1920. In the interim, however, the attitudes of a large number of Americans froze into bitter, often bizarre, hostility toward "Bolshevism." The fervor aroused by the war against Germany, of which the joyful welcome for the February Revolution had been a part, now became distorted into hysteria. It was as if the emotions of the war crusade, not yet satisfied, frantically sought new objects. But the mission to save Russia from the Bolsheviks lacked the noble and confident spirit possessed by the mission to save the world for democracy. Instead, vindictiveness and xenophobia, the underside of the missionary spirit, predominated; the conservatives and reactionaries took command.

During 1919, opponents of Bolshevism portrayed their enemy in paranoiac proportions. As one observer wrote: "Bolshevism means chaos, wholesale murder, the complete destruction of civilization." [61] Such bombast colored most anti-Bolshevik diatribes. According to one headline in *Current History*, the issue was "Bolshevism Against Civilization." [62] These anti-Bolsheviks saw in Russia only economic collapse, social chaos, and political anarchy, with the Bolshevik "criminals" waging a reign of terror surpassing anything by Robespierre.[63] The constant distortion is most vividly conveyed, perhaps, by the fact that the *New York Times,* during the two years after the October Revolution, ninety-one times predicted that the Bolsheviks were near the end of their rope or had reached it, four times reported that Lenin and Trotsky were planning flight and three times that they had already fled, five times claimed that the Soviet regime was "tottering," twice announced that Lenin planned to retire, three times reported his imprisonment, and once reported his death.[64]

From this perspective, these opponents of the Soviets naturally regarded intervention as the only way of rescuing Russia — now from the "Reds" rather than the "Huns." The

Communist revolutions in Hungary and Germany, during the winter of 1918–19, underscored their sense of urgency: the Allies had to overthrow the Bolsheviks before the Bolsheviks overran Europe.[65] But advocates of intervention still dressed their purposes in a Wilsonian costume of democratic self-determination. They staunchly defended the various White leaders as liberals, Admiral Kolchak in Siberia winning particularly large admiration. State Department officials in Siberia were as guilty of this misleading characterization as writers in the United States, whose views could be excused by their dependence on biased press reports. As late as November 1919, Secretary of State Lansing was still considering diplomatic recognition of Kolchak.[66] At the same time, the interventionists persisted in believing that, as Senator William A. Smith of Michigan asserted, "the Russian people, God bless them," were anxious to overthrow the Bolsheviks and to fulfill "a noble destiny." [67] Arguing that the vast majority of the Russian population opposed the Soviet regime, they repeated the familiar faith in the democratic virtues and aspirations of "the people." [68] And of course that "democracy" would be constituted, as Lawrence F. Abbott of *The Outlook* said, along "the principles of constitutional administration, recognized by the common conscience and the common practice of mankind." [69] Doubtless he meant American mankind.

But a new, skeptical theme began to intrude into the ritualistic optimism. According to some anti-Bolsheviks, the Russian masses were unfit for the burden of self-government, having been disabled by illiteracy and centuries of autocracy. These skeptics argued that the sensible solution was to make Russia a trusteeship under the League of Nations and thus to supervise her gradual entry into "civilization." [70] These views were expressed by only a few in the anti-Bolshevik camp, but they signify the spirit behind the postwar crusade to save

Russia. The original trust that the Russian people would follow the path to democracy, guided by American encouragement, had given way to a fierce determination to impose law and order on anarchic Russia, with freedom as an afterthought or eventuality.

A growing number of Americans in 1919, however, were restive under the onerous responsibility of saving Russia. Military intervention without an anti-German motive now appeared to them a costly maneuver, likely to produce only further complications and frustrations if, in fact, the Bolsheviks fell. William Allen White, so often a barometer of American opinion, expressed his forebodings to the secretary of Cyrus McCormick in October 1919: "There is no question but that Russia is in for a long bloody time, no matter what happens. And the blood letting will come, no matter who wins. It is in the Russian people." Visualizing this prospect, he felt that the best policy would be "an economic cordon" around the Bolsheviks, denying food to the government while neutral agents distributed food to all classes. From then on, he concluded bitterly, "let the thing fry in its own grease so far as interior Russia is concerned. The whole trouble with Russia is Russia." [71]

This retreat to irresponsibility in no sense signified or produced a tolerance of the Soviet regime. Rather, it was part of a retreat to fight "Bolshevism" at home. Already in December 1918, Hiram Johnson prefaced a Senate speech on Russia with a denial that he was a Bolshevik; this disclaimer was necessary, he explained, because of the prevailing national temper, which bullied or terrorized even the mildest, most hesitant dissent.[72] During the following months, that temper blossomed into full hysteria and earned the title, the Red Scare. After the Armistice, organized labor engaged in a flurry of strikes to obtain a share in the inflationary prosperity. But the public viewed these developments in a conspiratorial context much broader than a merely economic one. The Seattle general strike in February, the series of bombs sent to public officials in April, the Boston police strike in September — these and other events incited a volatile fear of Bolshevik revolution. In response, numerous state legislatures passed syndicalist and sedition laws to prohibit membership in organizations advocating violent overthrow of the government, while mobs destroyed socialist offices and beat up or lynched IWW members. As a grand climax to the Scare, Attorney General A. Mitchell Palmer launched his famous Red raids, arresting for deportation 450 supposed Communist aliens in twelve cities on November 7, 1919, and then seizing 4,000 more suspects in thirty-three cities on January 2. On December 21, 1919, 249 persons were actually deported on the "Soviet Ark," the *Buford,* including the well-known anarchists Emma Goldman and Alexander Berkman.[73]

This climax also proved to be a finale; early in 1920 the hysteria suddenly subsided after the public learned how few genuine Communists had been taken in the raids and after the New York state legislature went so far as to seek the expulsion of six elected socialist members. But the damage had been thoroughly done: American attitudes toward radical dissent and especially toward Soviet Russia were molded into deep suspicion or even hatred. For almost two years the nation had concentrated on victory in the war, developing an incipient nativism into fierce attacks on Germans at home as well as in Germany. The Bolsheviks' seizure of power and their separate peace added to American nativism a strong antiradical motivation. Both emotional strains were rationalized on nationalistic grounds, a patriotism which Wilson directed out at the world but which also took the domestic guise of "100 per cent Americanism." When the war ended, the emotional fervor persisted, now twisted into rabid and xenophobic directions. To state the case in oversimplified terms, the Red Scare was Wilsonianism turned inside out, confident messianism become paranoiac, intolerant Americanism seeking to purify the nation of alien and disturbing elements.

It is not surprising that Soviet Russia became a scapegoat, for the Bolsheviks were, in popular opinion, German agents who preached world revolution. On the one hand, *The Saturday Evening Post* could decry the "Russo-German movement that is now trying to dominate America," and, on the other hand, the *Chicago Tribune* could warn that "it is only a middling step from Petrograd to Seattle." [74] At the same time, the Senate subcommittee investigating German propaganda decided to extend its scope to include Bolshevik propaganda as well.[75] Hysteria nourished itself on an indiscriminate diet of conspirators. The catharsis of the Red Scare relieved the violence of nativist and antiradical emotions, but it did not erase them. In part, they simply settled into an apolitical complacency. Yet Soviet Russia continued to attract American attention because — rather than simply a nation emerging from a revolution — it was a nation *and* a revolution, the combination always challenging American values. Even if the American government refused to recognize Lenin's regime and the majority of the American people opposed it, they could not ignore it.[76]

Most Americans had discarded the Red Scare perspective by early 1920. Civilization's door no longer is wide open; the Russian, though still bearded, is simply a plaintive old man, vulnerable to intoxicating theories.

HE WANTS HER TO TAKE HIM BACK.

—Orr in the Chicago *Tribune*.

III / Popular Responses during the NEP

Bolshevism is the negation of civilization.
— Elbert Francis Baldwin, "Russia at Genoa,"
Outlook, CXXXI (June 21, 1922), 335

According to President Warren G. Harding, the Republican victory in the election of 1920 marked a "return to normalcy." In respect to Soviet-American relations, however, he and his two successors maintained the "abnormalcy" of nonrecognition. Wilson's Secretary of State, Bainbridge Colby, reaffirmed this diplomatic legacy on August 10, 1920. In Wilsonian language, Colby declared: "From the beginning of the Russian Revolution, in March, 1917, to the present moment, the Government and the people of the United States have followed its development with friendly solicitude and with profound sympathy for the efforts of the Russian people to reconstruct their national life upon the broad basis of popular self-government." He promised that the United States would not encroach upon the political or territorial integrity of Russia. But because the Soviet regime "is based upon the negation of every principle of honor and good faith" and violates the standards of international law by revolutionary propaganda against other countries, Colby said that his government would still refrain from official relations with Soviet Russia.[1] Although by July 1920 the United States had lifted the blockade and permitted private trade with Russia, the wall separating the two governments was as high as ever.

This renewed commitment to nonrecognition was appropriate to the general American mood developing at the beginning of the 1920's. The crusades for victory in Germany and Russia were over, leaving a parochial desire to ignore any responsibility for the world and to claim the rewards of combat — security, prosperity, and fun. Popular attention to foreign affairs declined markedly during the decade. One analysis of forty morning newspapers in 1927, for example, found that the average percentage of space devoted to foreign events ranged from less than 9 per cent to less than 2.5 per cent, with the newspapers of inland cities being especially negligent in their foreign coverage.[2] As for Soviet Russia, a survey of the *Readers' Guide to Periodical Literature* shows the following trend in the number of articles about Russian economic conditions.[3]

	1915–1918	*1919–1921*	*1922–1924*	*1925–1928*
Articles per 1000	.53	1.40	1.26	.51
Absolute number of articles	41.0	86.0	77.0	44.0

At the same time, the average number of books written annually by Americans about Soviet Russia fell from twelve, during 1918–1920, to less than five during 1921–1926.[4]

But this impulse to provincial irresponsibility was constantly diverted, over the decade, by the events in Soviet Russia. Most Americans agreed with their government's decision to shun the Bolshevik regime on the grounds of "honor and good faith," but they refused to shun it passively. Instead, they tended to praise themselves and to attack the Soviets with great vigor. Whether from righteous zeal or from fear, they refused merely to disdain Soviet policies and principles. The Red Scare persisted in subdued form.

During a speech to the Senate on April 28, 1920, Henry L. Myers of Montana synthesized the fundamental attitudes of his anti-Bolshevik countrymen in one angry paragraph. After quoting the decree for nationalizing women, which the Bolsheviks had supposedly passed, he exclaimed: "They have utterly destroyed marriage, the home, the fireside, the family, the corner stones of all civilization, all society. They have undertaken to destroy what God created and ordained. They defy alike the will of God, the precepts of Christianity, the decrees of civilization, the customs of society. It is hard to realize that such things exist and are tolerated by the civilized world." [5] Once again the Communists (as the Bolsheviks called themselves after 1917) were being defined as enemies of "civilization," a habit retained from the war years and continuing into the twenties.[6] But invariably — and significantly — the speakers did not bother to define the term "civilization"; instead, they used it as a verbal basket into which they threw all things good, just as they meant "Bolshevism" to include all evils. Even a trained philosopher like Nicholas Murray Butler, the president of Columbia University, variously spoke of civilization in a cultural, moral, or geographical sense or as restricted to Christianity or as synonymous with capitalism. But he was consistent in the claim that the Soviets were trying to remove "the traces of what we call civilization." [7]

Despite this ambiguity, Senator Myers and other anti-Communists made clear what values they had in mind: a monogamous family, belief in God, adherence to a democratic system of government as exhibited most splendidly in the United States, respect for individual freedom and private property, and a faith in human progress.[8] The Communist regime, dominated by atheists who were dedicated to the overthrow of capitalist governments by violent revolution and to the establishment of a proletarian dictatorship, obviously contradicted these values. Myths such as the nationalization of women only served as sensational confirmation of the obvious. Occasionally, too, American opponents of the Soviets would invoke racism, calling for extermination of the Asiatic menace to Western or Anglo-Saxon civilizations.[9] Whichever theme was cited, anti-Communist arguments usually combined defensive outrage with arrogant righteousness. Although the vehemence varied from critic to critic, the premises were the same. When William Allen White pleaded for a more flexible policy toward the Soviets, he reasoned that "the way to get the poison out of their blushing blood is to let civilization penetrate the country and let the people see what dubs and muckers they are by contrast with substantial American business men." [10]

During the prosperous twenties, these overconfident values survived with undiminished strength. Indeed, the achievement of material success, which was one part of the American creed, sanctioned all the other parts.[11] Social psychologists have discovered that people both seek and accept information congenial to their prior attitudes, are less open to counterargument if their attitudes are strongly fixed, and ultimately change their views not in rational surrender to contradictory evidence, but in response to the birth of a wholly new situation.[12] These generalizations describe and explain the predominant American reaction to Soviet Russia between the end of the war and the onset of the Great Depression. Judgments most often were prejudices, arrangements of facts into categories constructed on the basis of strong beliefs. A hostile stereotype of the Communists had been formed during the emotional intensity of wartime; the patriotic "boosterism" and unprecedented prosperity of the postwar decade did nothing to discourage the bias. Those who complained of distorted information about Soviet Russia falsely assumed that Americans would revise their views if given the facts.[13] On the contrary, the distortion was in itself an attitude — the attitude that contrary facts could not be true.

Secretary of State Colby's statement in August 1920 repeated the American policy of nonrecognition, but it also signaled the abandonment of any active attempts to overthrow the Soviet regime. By April the last American troops had left Russian soil, and within a few months private trade with Russia was resumed. Thus the Administration returned to its original posture of watchful waiting, a position winning the approval of the general public. After the abortive intervention, most commentators preferred less aggressive hostility. Throughout 1920, books, articles, and editorials portrayed the misery and chaos perpetrated upon the hapless Russian people by the vicious Soviet system. As Bruce Barton wrote in *The American Magazine,* rule by the underdog "has been proved a nightmare." For the next thirteen years, such was the last word on Russia by this family magazine, which was read in one out of every five homes in "Middletown" and by one and a half million subscribers across the nation.[14]

Most American writers agreed that the United States should have no dealings with a government of such brutal principles.[15] The most sensible course of action was simply patient attendance upon the Communists' defeat at the hands of the Russian people or by their own incompetence. The *Baltimore Sun* advised, early in 1920: "The less we meddle, the sooner Russia will throw her pirates overboard." Although such optimism became increasingly strained, some people stubbornly continued to give voice to it.[16] As for economic relations with the Soviets, a controversial issue once the blockade ended and the European countries began to resume commerce with Russia, the prevailing sentiment favored a boycott for standard reasons. The *Grand Rapids*

News epitomized the moral argument by declaring that the United States cannot "sell its honor for a ton of Russian gold." Others offered the practical argument that the internal disruption of Russia precluded any hope of steady or profitable commerce.[17]

The tangle of dogma and ignorance about Soviet Russia at the beginning of the twenties is most dramatically illustrated perhaps by a rough outline of a Senate debate on January 22, 1921. William H. King (Dem., Utah) began by declaring his opposition to diplomatic or commercial relations with Lenin's government. In reply, Joseph I. France (Rep., Maryland) noted that Great Britain was engaging in Soviet trade and suggested that perhaps the Bolshevik bogey was a British device for scaring Americans away from a lucrative market. Interjecting at this point, George Moses (Rep., New Hampshire) warned that Soviet-American commerce would lead to the entry of Communist anarchists and revolutionaries into the United States, whereupon France slyly implied that his colleague believed Britain to be more stable than his own country. Moses hotly denied this imputed unpatriotism, but still insisted on the need for restrictive immigration laws to defend against importers of revolution. This opened a vigorous controversy over the tactics employed by the Justice Department during the recent Red Scare. In short, the so-called debate spun a web of prejudices, indiscriminately joining the themes of Russia and Communism and immigration.[18]

Simultaneous with this prevailing vituperation against the Soviet regime, however, was a smaller, much more subdued dissent by those who continued to profess hope for a free and flourishing Russia. This minority did not base their expectations on the Bolsheviks' leadership, nor did many of them invoke Wilsonian faith in the Russian people's instinctive democracy.[19] Rather, they shared the capitalist premise of the anti-Bolshevik majority, but supplemented it with a

70

belief that capitalism would succeed where intervention had failed. An editorial in the February 1920 issue of *The Review of Reviews,* for example, began with an apparent echo of 1918: "It is to be hoped, and it may be reasonably expected, that the Russian people will by degrees transform this Soviet tyranny until Russia becomes a free country with democratic institutions." But then it added a new sort of reasoning: "With outside pressure removed, and with opportunities restored for selling Russian wheat, flax, and other products and buying manufactured goods, Russia may become a sane country within a few years." [20] This was Wilson's messianism updated into the New Era; in the 1920's the dollar would convert those who had been impervious to words and armies. On the face of it, this optimism had no more empirical justification than had the optimism of 1917–1919, and during 1920 it won only a few proponents. *The World's Work,* for instance, skeptically wondered whether the laws of economics would transform the Communist regime before the Communists inflamed the world with revolution.[21]

Early in 1921, however, the situation altered radically. Almost as if the wish were father to the facts, the facts were born. On March 17, 1921, Lenin announced, at the Tenth Party Congress, the New Economic Policy (NEP). Calling a halt to the rigid economic programs of War Communism, the Soviet premier proposed a much larger degree of internal private trade and enterprise in order to rescue Russia from the disaster toward which she had been heading under the impetus of industrial underproduction, food shortages (because of peasant resistance to government crop requisitions), inflation, and lack of capital. This new economic system was termed "state capitalism," a preparation for socialism.[22]

The repercussions from this shockingly sudden shift in the course of the Revolution were felt almost as quickly in the United States as within Russia itself. As usual, however,

Americans saw what they wanted to see. On August 3, an editorial in the *Chicago Tribune* strenuously insisted that the Communists had made a virtual "vacuum" of their huge nation by relying on "book theory" and ignoring individual incentive, "the mainspring of human effort." But two days before, Senator France had spoken in very different terms from within the vacuum itself. "Russia is reverting to capitalism inevitably, by the play of relentless natural forces," he told the *New York Times* correspondent in Riga after a four-week tour through Soviet Russia.[23] Both views missed the point. In actuality, Lenin was following a path midway between these two poles, permitting private trade in order to revive his stagnant economy but retaining crucial industries and foreign trade under state control. The NEP was still socialism, despite temporary and calculated qualifications.

During the years following the innovation of the NEP, numerous American commentators excitedly exaggerated these qualifications into the catastrophe they had so often predicted since November 1917. They announced that Communism had surrendered to capitalism and that Russia offered a huge field in which American investment could reap fabulous profits. Even Walter Duranty, the cautious correspondent on the scene for the *New York Times,* reported the end of Communism in the fall of 1921.[24] Many observers described the political future with equal exhilaration. *The World's Work,* abandoning its previous hesitation in November 1921 foresaw the possibility of a representative government emerging in Russia — under non-Bolshevik rulers. By February 1922, the periodical had discarded all restraints: "The time appears to be ripe to resume relations with Russia," the editors declared. Lenin "has an astonishingly open mind for a fanatic," they explained, and so he may learn the necessity for production by capitalistic methods.[25] As fast as capitalism was supposedly converting the Communists in

Russia, the NEP was dissolving the intransigency of their American critics. The American faith in a "new Russia," so vital in 1917, began to revive, nourished now on capitalist more than on democratic premises.

Not all anti-Bolshevik Americans yielded so ebulliently to their fondest hopes. Many found strong reasons, either in the strength of their own prejudices or in evidence from Soviet Russia, for remaining skeptical. On the level of popular journalism, stories of oppression and chaos continued to appear; this was the grim picture, for example, which more than two million readers of *The Saturday Evening Post* were given throughout 1922.[26] Meanwhile, among those individuals intimately concerned with pre-Soviet Russia, the NEP only agitated a set of fixed responses. In August 1921, Elihu Root wrote sardonically to Princess Julia Cantacuzène, granddaughter of Ulysses S. Grant and wife of a Russian noble émigré: "It is interesting to see a lot of chuckle heads talking about the change in Lenin and Trotsky; how they abandoned the dictatorship of the proletariat and are going to give the bourgeoisie and capital a chance to restore Russia." [27] In his opinion, the Soviet leaders could not revise their policies because, by definition — Root's definition — they were capable of pursuing only a Communist path; according to Root's reading of economic laws and human nature, that path would soon lead to the extinction of "the Bolshevik terror." A decade later he was still offering the same assurances to the princess and others.[28] George Kennan also remained adamant, until his death in 1924, that Communist rule had produced nothing but economic disorder.[29] Samuel Harper at first was equally skeptical of the NEP, but — perhaps because he was a generation younger than Root and Kennan or perhaps because he carefully studied Soviet documents for his courses at the University of Chicago — by November 1922 he conceded that "things are wakening up in Russia, particularly economically,

DESPITE the Soviet Government." A year later he went so far as to say that "a new life is emerging, which will make for a better and greater Russia." [30]

Harper's evolution toward tolerance indicates how powerful an effect the NEP could exert on those whose antagonism had appeared unshakable. For Americans directly on the scene, liberated from the filter of news media, the effect was even stronger and more startling. A group of congressmen, visiting Russia in the summer of 1923, inadvertently served as test cases for a historical experiment in the formation of attitudes. On the one hand, Representative James A. Frear (Wisconsin), Senators Burton K. Wheeler (Montana), Smith W. Brookhart (Iowa), and Robert M. La Follette (Wisconsin), in keeping with their Progressivist advocacy of social and economic legislation, found order, happiness, and constructive governmental policies in Russia. Although disturbed by the lack of freedom, they urged American trade as well as recognition. On the other hand, Representative Fred A. Britten, a Republican from Illinois, returned to tell of economic hardship and relentless terror, with dissenters being "shot behind the ear." His Republican colleague in the House, Carroll L. Beedy of Maine, also lamented Russia's "sad fate," yet he had seen enough evidence of economic revival to make him favor Soviet-American trade relations. Most fascinating was the reaction of William H. King, Democratic Senator from Utah. Four years earlier he had told the Senate: "Any man who supports Bolshevism is an enemy to civilization" and the American form of government; in 1921 he still vehemently opposed trade and recognition. After returning from Russia in 1923, he informed the Senate that he had discovered the Communists to be firmly in power and, under the aegis of the NEP, rehabilitating the stricken nation with striking success. Indeed, King was so impressed that he recommended resumption of economic relations with the Soviet Union. [31]

Thus, whether visiting Russia itself or reacting from across the ocean, Americans expressed varied and often surprising attitudes toward the NEP. Explanation as to why some saw the birth of a new, capitalist Russia while others saw only continued paralysis or strangulation by the Communists would require mass biography or even mass psychoanalysis. Prediction of these responses would have been impossible. One generalization emerges from the heterogeneity, however. The renewed optimism toward Soviet Russia, shared by a growing number of commentators during 1921–1923, focused on the NEP and was a form of prejudice rather than open-mindedness. It reflected the assumption that Soviet leaders were succeeding because they had surrendered to capitalism, to American methods and values. Ultimately, the skeptics and the optimists stood on different ends of a basic anti-Communist attitude.

The NEP produced such varied American reactions because it was ambiguous and complicated. It was a policy of compromise, a "strategic retreat" to an economy that blended capitalist and socialist components into a dynamic system. Even if observers from the United States understood the NEP, they usually had to simplify the facts for their audience; and if, more often, they only vaguely understood it, they necessarily snatched at simplifications. Whatever the reason, they could find ample evidence to tempt them toward the most convenient sort of simplicity, which is exaggeration.

In 1921 another major event occurred in Soviet Russia, one more comprehensible and more interesting to Americans. This was the great famine. Three main factors were responsible for the hunger of millions of Russians: devastation of land and agricultural machinery by the European and civil wars since 1914; the peasants' refusal to plant crops, because of Soviet requisitions, or to sell crops when there were no manufactured goods to be purchased; and, finally, drought. The famine entered into Soviet-American relations on July 13, 1921, when Maxim Gorky appealed to the West for bread and medicine to combat the suffering of his countrymen.

The question of famine relief for Soviet Russia was not new to Americans. In the spring of 1919, Herbert Hoover, then the chairman of the American Relief Administration (ARA), which had supervised massive distribution of supplies to starving Europeans from the Baltic to the Caspian seas, had suggested to President Wilson the creation of a second Belgian Relief Commission for Russia. In a long memorandum he defended the proposal as a more effective and humane method than military intervention for stabilizing the political tumult within Russia. But he demanded that the Bolsheviks cease all revolutionary and military activities before any relief be given; moreover, he stressed that his plea would entail no relationship with or recognition of "the Bolshevik murderers." [32] With the consent of the Allied representatives at the Paris peace conference, a proposal to this effect was sent to the Soviet leaders. Their reply, combining a readiness to negotiate and an angry refusal to lay down arms, incited the already hostile French to stifle any further negotiations.[33]

During the next two years, American interest in relief for Russia continued in various forms. Hoover himself tried to interest Wilson in the idea of forming a commission which would set up an economic dictatorship over Russia and, by healing the economic disruption, lay the basis for eventual self-government.[34] Other Americans, both advocates and adversaries of the Communists, worked along more feasible lines, creating organizations for sending food and supplies to starving Russians.[35] Popular opinion strongly favored relief as both a humanitarian and an anti-Soviet policy.[36]

In July 1921, **Americans were prepared, organizationally and emotionally, to take up Gorky's appeal.** Once again it was Hoover, by this time Secretary of Commerce as well as head of the ARA, who became the leader in negotiating arrangements for relief. On July 23, he offered aid on several conditions: that the Soviets release all American prisoners in Russia; that the ARA workers in Russia be guaranteed non-interference by Soviet officials; that they be permitted to organize local committees without Soviet control; and that they have free transportation, fuel, and buildings for their relief work. The Soviets quickly accepted these terms and, on August 20, signed a formal agreement with ARA representatives at Riga.[37]

Immediately Hoover set in motion a vast machinery of fundraising in the United States, trans-Atlantic transportation, and distribution of supplies within Russia. He assigned Colonel William N. Haskell (chief of the ARA Mission in Rumania and then Armenia and the Caucasus) to direct the entire operation. At the same time he met with representatives from numerous organizations — including the American Friends Service Committee (AFSC), the Federal Council of Churches, the Jewish Joint Distribution Committee, the Knights of Columbus, the National Catholic Welfare Council, the Mennonite Central Committee, and the International Committee of the Young Men's Christian Association (YMCA) — to coordinate their relief efforts under the aegis of the ARA. Such coordination was necessary because some of the groups, especially the AFSC, already were deeply engaged in helping needy Russians or, in the case of the YMCA, helping Russian émigrés. Hoover had no difficulty in persuading these groups to work under his experienced leadership, although the AFSC retained a more autonomous form of cooperation. By December, the ARA was feeding more than

568,000 Russians in 191 towns and villages throughout the famine area.[38]

Thus in mid-1921 there developed the apparent paradox of American relief to a nation led by men whom most Americans vilified as enemies of civilization; moreover, Herbert Hoover, spokesman for individualism and capitalism, was directing the relief mission. Yet analysis dissolves the paradoxical appearance into comprehensible reality. There is no doubt that Hoover was, from the beginning, a bitter enemy of the Soviet regime.[39] By attempting to overcome the Russian famine he was not surrendering this animosity, but simply practicing it in a form more devious than frank counterrevolution. As he had explained to President Wilson in 1919, Bolshevism feeds on hunger, disease, and discontent; without those conditions it would lose its appeal. What he said about the European Children's Relief in 1921 also held true for Russian relief: American charity "had planted the American flag in the hearts of all those little ones and it is a greater protection to the United States than any battleship." [40] This preoccupation with identifying relief as American explains his demand that the ARA be independent of Soviet control and that all American relief groups be subordinate to the ARA.[41] For Wilson, words served as the vanguard of democracy in Russia; for Hoover, food was the vanguard. Writing to Secretary of State Charles Evans Hughes in December 1921, Hoover declared: "The relief measures will build a situation which, combined with other factors, will enable the Americans to undertake the leadership in the reconstruction of Russia when the proper moment arrives." By "other factors" he meant the introduction of American investment and technology. In Hoover's opinion, then, the ARA would succeed where Allied armies had failed in rescuing Russia from the Soviets.[42]

The popular American response to the Russian famine was

immediate and impassioned. According to most newspapers, magazines, and individuals, the only issue was human suffering and the only response was immediate and total generosity. Once again, as they had done after the February Revolution, Americans adopted emotional, not political, reasoning and looked to the people, not the government, of Russia. The *Washington Herald* went so far as to rebuke Hoover for interjecting the political question of American prisoners. In the words of its editorial: "The American conscience, the American sense of right and humanity, rebels" against such a condition for relief. "It is the heart of America that goes out to the starving of Russia to save the children, who are guilty of nothing, not even of their parentage, surely not of an imposed government." The daily press from coast to coast echoed this sentiment.[43] Religious journals unanimously favored relief, some of them with the hope that it might also bring spiritual sustenance to the Russian masses.[44] Even Senator King, not yet converted by the NEP from bitter antagonism to the Soviets, proposed an appropriation of $5 million for the noble work of the ARA in Russia.[45]

This surge of humanitarianism did not erase the prevailing American hostility toward the Soviet regime: it merely put it temporarily aside. In fact, some observers combined sympathy for the starving with triumphant assertions that the famine marked the failure of Communist policies. According to the *Seattle Times,* for example, the famine derived from "the saturnine blunder fastened upon Russia by those two arch-plotters, Lenine and Trotzky." [46] But a small minority of Americans could not subscribe even to this backhanded benevolence. Elihu Root opposed the ARA mission because he was sure that the supplies would really go to the Moscow regime, not to the starving people.[47] Others argued that relief would be futile until Russia was liberated from Soviet tyranny.[48] Amid the popular emotional response to

79

WE ARE NOT RESPONSIBLE FOR HATS AND COATS.
—Thomas, in the Detroit *News*

The context of famine relief confirmed the amiable image of the Russian peasant whose Bolshevism was not a menace, only a condition of dishevelment.

the famine, however, these opponents of relief could sustain their position only with difficulty. The rigidly anti-Communist *Chicago Tribune*, for example, on July 29 insisted that, until Lenin called a constituent assembly and discarded ideas of world revolution, "these starving millions must continue to die." Four days later it warmly advocated aid to "the Russian people" despite their despicable government.[49]

Toward the end of 1921, this commitment to altruism was tested when Hoover asked Congress to provide $20 million, out of unspent profits by the United States Grain Corporation, for expansion of the Russian relief mission. The House of Representatives, the stage for bellicose anti-Bolshevism during the preceding five years, greeted the request with notably restrained debate. Only one congressman, Democrat John Box of Texas, objected that aid would bolster or sanction the Soviets. All other opponents cited the need for fiscal caution, the questionable constitutionality of using the Grain Corporation profits, or the advantages of private over governmental charity. After only a few hours of discussion, the bill passed by a large margin of 181 to 71. It was a highly partisan vote, Republicans forming most of the majority with Democrats predominating in the minority. As in the case of Hiram Johnson's resolution against intervention (1919), the vote focused on political parties, not on the Bolsheviks.[50] The Senate responded to Hoover's bill with similar amiability. The debate paralleled the one in the House. Again only one dissenter referred to the Soviet regime: Senator Borah argued that, if the United States could feed the Russian populace, it could also recognize the Russian government. Meanwhile, so conservative a Republican as Reed Smoot of Utah was urging his colleagues to support the appropriation, even though it might be unconstitutional, because it would save millions of lives. The Senate swiftly passed the bill, dispensing with a roll-call vote.[51]

The remarks by Representative W. Bourke Cockran of New York reveal to what extent American attitudes toward famine relief directly continued those originating in 1917. In his opinion, support of the ARA "is a duty it [the United States] owes to civilization, and what it owes to civilization it owes chiefly and above all to itself, the flower and center of civilization." [52] From 1921 to 1924, Americans answered the moral call. At home, government and people contributed almost $50 million in funds and goods, while in Russia hundreds of ARA workers struggled against natural and political forces to save lives.[53] Toward the end of the massive effort, Colonel Haskell, head of the relief operation, evaluated its success in a report to Hoover on August 28, 1923. "To the mind of the Russian common people," he wrote, "the American Relief Administration was a miracle of God which came to them in their darkest hour, under the Stars and Stripes. It turned the corner for civilization in Russia." Even more, it had left Communism "dead and abandoned" while proving to the Russian masses the superiority of the American system.[54]

Once again Americans had assumed the role of missionaries to "the people," bringing bread in one hand and a political creed in the other. The only innovation since the Wilsonian era was an increased optimism, provoked by the NEP, that not only the people but the Soviet leaders themselves would be Americanized.

This growing confidence in the future of Soviet Russia was severely set back when, on March 31, 1923, the Soviet government executed Monsignor Buchkavich, Vicar-General of the Roman Catholic Church in Russia, for alleged counterrevolutionary activity. Because of its violent and antireligious character, the deed instantly inflamed all the anti-Communist hysteria which had marked American attitudes before 1920. During the relative lull since the Red Scare, of course, neither the Soviet leaders nor their American critics had altered their basic principles. From the moment they came to power, the Communists had pursued a policy of weakening the Russian Orthodox Church, which had been so willing an ally of tsarism. Their major decrees of 1917–1919 separated church and state, nationalized church lands and buildings, reserved legality only to civil marriages and divorces, forbade organized religious instruction of persons under eighteen years of age, and sought to encourage an atheistic propaganda drive. By 1920, with the church and popular religious feeling still surprisingly strong, the Soviets temporarily called a truce. In 1921 they renewed the campaign because the actions of the émigré clergy aroused Communist suspicions that the church sought to exploit the famine as a goad to counterrevolution. The government therefore ordered secular control of all relief work and demanded church treasures not used in the services. When Patriarch Tikhon condemned the demand and when the donations proved pitifully small, the Communists arrested him and fifty-three other church leaders as plotters of treason. More important than the subsequent punishments was the organization, with Soviet encouragement, of the so-called Living Church, a faction of liberal clerics who cooperated with Communist policies.[55]

This official program of atheism, so alien to American values, inevitably formed a pervasive theme in American diatribes on Soviet Russia, usually being linked to the issue of Soviet persecution in general. Estimates of the number of victims officially executed by the secret-police organization, the Cheka, ranged from 9,000 to 1,766,118. This latter total, supposedly taken from official figures and dutifully reported by *Current History* and the *Baltimore Sun,* led one skeptical reader to calculate that the Cheka must have killed fifty persons an hour without intermission during more than four years.[56] Undaunted by arithmetic, many publications continued to print the charge, perpetuating a general image of barbarism which sympathizers with the Soviet Union could not erase.[57] The news of Monsignor Buchkavich's execution in March 1923 synthesized atheism and terror into a climactic event; immediately all the emotional subcurrents came to the surface with a burst of fury. Against this bloody deed the abstraction of the NEP became invisible and forgotten. This event, said the *New York Evening Journal* in a typical reaction, marks "the execution of priest and the suicide of a government by the same bullets." *Time* magazine bluntly accused the Soviets of despotism exceeding that of the tsars.[58]

Spokesmen for American Catholics reacted to the execution of the priest with horror and malediction. To them it was a savage climax to a history of what *America*, in 1922, had called "an orgy of blood and terrorism." The Reverend Edmund A. Walsh, Regent of the School of Foreign Service at Georgetown University, used the execution to intensify his propaganda campaign against the Soviets and to enlarge his reputation as one of the outstanding opponents of the Soviet Union throughout the interwar period. His work as director general of the Papal Relief Mission to Russia during 1922 had not appeased his hatred of the Communist regime. On the contrary, he repeated the estimate of 1.8 million executions, including 28 archbishops and 1,400 priests, and explained that human life was "always cheap in the East" where "Asiatic callousness and Byzantine haughtiness" characterized the ruling classes. Even the liberal Catholic journal, *The Commonweal*, saw hope only in a revived religious feeling arising some day from "the fires of Red anarchy and atheism." [59]

Protestants displayed a much more ambivalent attitude, however. During the first three years of the decade, some denominational journals and ministers had expressed the usual sort of antipathy, but a striking number insisted on tolerance toward Soviet Russia.[60] Methodist, Quaker, and interdenominational visitors to Russia admired the social

RECOGNIZED AT LAST
As being outside the Pale of Civilization!

The Soviet persecution of religion in the spring of 1923 revived the horrible specter of Bolshevism, intensified by the conjunction of civilization and Christianity.

and religious conditions. They were convinced that the government did not seek to kill religion, but to liberate it from state control and from the corruption of the Orthodox Church. In their opinion, Communist policies strengthened religion by providing the inherently faithful population with a purer object of devotion. One Quaker relief worker even described the Soviet social ideals as ones which "every Christian shares," and advised Americans to let future experience decide whether atheism or Christianity would more successfully attain those ideals.[61] *The Christian Century*, which one historian calls "Protestantism's most influential periodical," and *The Congregationalist* were equally dedicated to the sanguine view that Russian religion and Soviet virtues would continue to grow.[62]

The execution of Buchkavich had only a muffled impact as set against this precedent of Protestant sympathy. Some spokesmen angrily discarded their tolerance. *The Congregationalist*, for example, indignantly defined the deed as a declaration of war upon religion and therefore the beginning of the end of the Soviet government. But others, including John Haynes Holmes, *The Christian Century*, and the Boston Methodist weekly, *Zion's Herald*, were willing to believe that the priest had indeed been guilty of counterrevolutionary activity, scoffed at exaggerated claims of bloody terror, and stressed that free exercise of religion was permitted throughout Russia.[63] Religious as well as political motivations played a part in this reaction, of course. Buchkavich was a Catholic priest, after all, and his fate consequently had less effect on American Protestants. Moreover, the Soviet decrees against the Orthodox Church had opened unprecedented opportunities for sectarians to expand their religious activities. One writer in the Catholic journal *America* flatly accused the Baptists and other evangelical denominations of hypocritically tolerating Soviet atheism because of the advantage they received under it.[64]

The strength of either motive is difficult to measure. Certainly, though, the attitudes of leading Protestants remained exceptionally benign throughout the twenties. *The United Presbyterian* may have hailed Lenin's death with lurid exultation: "The great beast has gone down into the pit! Glory be to God!" [65] The Methodist Board of Foreign Missions may have sternly rebuked a Chicago bishop and the editor of *Zion's Herald* for impulsively promising, while in Russia, that the American Methodist Church would raise $50,000 for the Russian Church.[66] But the skeptics had to compete with the strong dissent of those who invested great hope in Soviet Russia and urged American tolerance or even, on the part of *The Christian Century*, diplomatic recognition.[67]

Among the three dominant religious groups in the United States, the Jews had the most intimate concern with Soviet Russia because of the large Jewish population there. Their initial hostility to the Communists had somewhat diminished during the early twenties because of the Soviet attempts to suppress the anti-Semitism so extensive and unchecked under tsarism.[68] It was clear, nevertheless, that the proletarian dictatorship sought to infringe on the autonomy of Jewish communities and discriminated against Jews for their petty-bourgeois status if not for their religion.[69] Because of these new disadvantages suffered by their brethren, American Jews harshly criticized the Soviets for religious persecution throughout the decade.[70] But at the same time, some Jewish leaders were actively cooperating with the Soviet government on a colonization project designed to transplant Russian Jews from the urban ghettos to rural areas where they could build cooperative farms. The American agency for this work was the American Jewish Joint Agricultural Corporation (Agro-Joint), a subdivision of the Jewish Joint Distribution Committee (JDC) that had been aiding Russian Jews since 1914. Formed in mid-1924 with an initial subsidy of $400,000 by the JDC, Agro-Joint proceeded to spend more than $7 million and to settle more than 50,000 Jews in the Crimea and the Ukraine during the next four years. In 1928 this organization was forced to disband because of the Zionists' objections that it was jeopardizing the more important goal of settling Jews in Palestine. Under a new name and with the generous backing of Felix Warburg, Louis Marshall, Julius Rosenwald, and others, the colonization work continued as successfully as before.[71] Ironically, however, American Jews who visited the new settlements could not agree on whether religious faith was fading or growing under the circumstances of a rural environment and an atheistic government.[72] Clearly the only valid generalization is that American Jews had mixed feelings about the effects of Soviet rule and were trying to make the best of an imperfect situation.

During the short period of 1921–1923, American emotions about Soviet Russia had been pulled violently in various directions: first toward pity by the famine, then toward outrage by the execution of Buchkavich, and constantly toward optimism by the NEP. Amid the jostling, a loose coalition of liberals tried to push the Administration toward diplomatic recognition of Lenin's regime. The chief contingents in this campaign were peace groups coordinated under the National Council for Prevention of War, joined by the National Women's Trade Union League, the National League of Women Voters, and similar organizations.[73] But the generals of the campaign, those who determined strategy, were Raymond Robins, Alexander Gumberg, and Senator William E. Borah. Once again, but now in the United States rather than in Russia, Robins sought to occupy a pivotal role in Soviet-American relations. Gumberg was his chief aide, just as he had been his interpreter and secretary in Russia, invaluable because of his vast network of correspondents and his familiarity with the latest events in his native Russia. Although both of his brothers had returned home, one to hold a high party office, Gumberg himself preferred, as he explained to a friend in 1923, "to remain a free lance, a sympathetic bystander and well wisher." [74] To this little private army, Borah added a crucial political weapon, especially when he inherited Henry Cabot Lodge's chairmanship of the Senate Foreign Relations Committee late in 1924. On December 9, 1922, Robins commended Gumberg to the senator as a valuable ally.[75] The triumvirate was formed and ready for its years of patient, futile fighting. The intricacies and vicissitudes of their battle, intensified by the (virtually Bolshevik) conspiratorial flair of Robins and Gumberg, do not in themselves constitute a part of America's attitudes toward Russia. They do serve as a sounding board for these attitudes.

In one sense the issue was perfectly clear. Since November 1917, the American government had refused to recognize the Soviet regime, claiming that it did not deserve membership in the family of nations until it paid the debts incurred by the Provisional Government, compensated American holders of property that had been nationalized, and stopped disseminating revolutionary propaganda through the Third International. This was the policy initiated by Wilson, amplified by Colby, Hughes, and Coolidge, and noisily echoed by the American Legion, the National Civic Federation, the American Federation of Labor, and other patriotic groups.[76] In another sense, however, the issue was quite obscure because, until 1912, American diplomatic recognition had been granted to all governments that demonstrably controlled their nation; Wilson had changed this tradition by requiring that a new government prove the legitimacy and morality of its power.[77] The new policy soon proved to be a quicksand of confusion. On the one hand, the American government denied that it was passing judgment on Soviet internal policies, yet on the other hand the obvious implications of nonrecognition were that the Soviets would be legitimate only after renouncing their basic tenets. Not surprisingly, popular opinion regarded nonrecognition as "America's moral boycott," to use a phrase of the *New York Evening Post,* thus maintaining in full force the righteous 1917 attitude toward Russia.[78]

The advocates of recognition also occupied the quicksand. Although Robins caustically remarked that Hughes "would like to have all the Bolsheviks join the Baptist Church," he and his allies fought on Hughes' ground. They argued that the Soviet leaders had created domestic order, would recognize Kerensky's debts and compensate propertyowners, did not spread revolutionary propaganda, and tolerated the church even if they did not join it.[79] This was a dangerous mode of argument. Just as "anti-imperialist" liberals had inadvertently imprisoned themselves within Wilson's terms during the prelude to military intervention, now they repeated their mistake. For in fact Soviet Russia was a revolutionary class dictatorship. American sympathizers either had to disguise this identity by desperate halftruths or firmly state that recognition was a diplomatic formality, not a stamp of approval. By choosing the first alternative, they put themselves inevitably on the defensive.

During 1922, for example, Robins and Gumberg became increasingly optimistic about the chances for recognition because of the tolerance produced by the NEP and the famine. "This is the Hour to Strike," Robins exulted.[80] By January 1923, Gumberg was proposing that Borah revive his tabled Senate resolution in favor of recognition and call a hearing before the Foreign Relations Committee as the introduction to a pressure campaign.[81] Even Samuel N. Harper was apprehensive of eventual success by the proponents of recognition.[82] The Buchkavich execution caused all these hopes to collapse. As Gumberg complained to Robins in April: "Believe me, those fellows still seem to be sitting up nights trying to think up some scheme which will get them in dutch with the world." [83]

This setback only made the recognitionists struggle more vigorously. By June 1923, Robins believed that he had almost converted President Harding, but the latter's untimely death ended this possibility.[84] Undaunted, Robins arranged two meetings with President Coolidge, in November and in early December, which aroused him to unprecedented optimism.[85] Indeed, although the President's message to Congress on December 6 repeated the main reasons for nonrecognition, he then cited evidence encouraging him to see hope for an imminent change in American policy. The Soviet Union, interpreting this as an overture, replied on December 16 with an offer to negotiate, only to receive Hughes' brusque response that "there would seem to be at this time no reason for negotiations." [86] A vast majority of newspapers, from every section and of all political loyalties, warmly applauded what the *Providence News* called a "moral document." [87]

Borah tenaciously continued the fight, first on the Senate floor in a bitter debate with Lodge, then in hearings before a subcommittee of the Foreign Relations Committee.[88] But the campaign could never free itself from its inherent liabilities. For one thing, Borah himself was remarkably ignorant on the subject of Russia, as he demonstrated not only in his private appeals to Robins and others for information, but during the hearings themselves.[89] In addition and more important, the whole strategy contained the fatal flaw of challenging the opposition on its own terms. It was all too easy for Lodge to dominate the Senate debate and for State Department officials to dominate the hearings by a deluge of documents demonstrating Communist propaganda in the United States.[90] Borah protested that this propaganda had little effect on the American people and would have even less effect after recognition; but in context the protest was a tacit surrender. After three days of testimony, the hearings were temporarily suspended on January 23, 1924, because the scandals in Harding's Cabinet interjected a more compelling issue for the

91

subcommittee members' attention.[91] Borah never resumed the exercise in futility.

Because the Administration was allowed to set the ground rules of the recognition debate, it always had an enormous advantage. When Representative Carroll L. Beedy of Maine, for example, drew applause from the House by promising never "to urge my people through recognition to put the stamp of American approval upon this godless government of Russia," he effectively precluded any dissent except the reply that Soviet atheism was not at issue.[92] By their failure to take up the amoral argument for recognition, Robins and his allies provoke the suspicion that perhaps at heart they too wanted to recognize only a liberal and democratic Soviet regime.

In the first session of every Congress throughout the next decade, Senator Borah dutifully filed a resolution for recognizing the Soviet Union; Robins and Gumberg sporadically sought to revive their own efforts; and patriotic societies as well as most of the press righteously opposed any sanction of sin.[93] In short, the issue lapsed into an impasse from which it did not escape until the Depression. Meanwhile, the general subject of Soviet Russia was losing the frenzied attention focused on it during the years of famine, the beginning of the NEP, and the religious persecutions. With the death of Lenin on January 21, 1924, the epic of heroes seemed suddenly to dwindle into a tawdry tale of mediocre men quarreling over power. Lenin's eminence in American eyes is indicated by the epithets the press laid upon his grave: "undoubtedly an evil man" (*Washington Star*) and "the most sinister and mysterious figure born of the war" (*New York Herald*) were mild in comparison to "the great destroyer," "a demon in a laboratory" (*Chicago Tribune*) and the *New York Post*'s prediction that "Nikolai Lenin will be remembered as Attila, Alaric, and Tamerlane are remembered." [94]

His successors, except for Trotsky, seemed relatively pale and anonymous. Even Stalin resembled an American political boss more than an exotic revolutionary.[95]

Also contributing to the decline in Russia's dramatic appeal after 1923 was the supposed ruin of the October Revolution. The *New York Times* headlined its obituary: "Lenin lived to see his theories fail." [96] This renewed confidence that the NEP marked the irrevocable submission to capitalism became an increasingly prevalent motif during the next five years.[97] Only a few recognized that, on the contrary, the decrees by the Twelfth Party Congress in 1924 instituted a definite reversal of the trend toward quasi-capitalism. During the four years after Lenin's death, private trade actually diminished from two fifths to one sixth of the total trade within the USSR.[98] Most American writers preferred, like the *Chicago Tribune* on the tenth anniversary of the Bolshevik Revolution, to condemn the Communists for their principles while sardonically noting the Soviet failure to uphold them.[99]

Without Lenin's charisma and amid the persistent assurance of capitalist victory, Americans were fairly inattentive to the power struggle between Trotsky and Stalin. Although the press discussed the intraparty conflict with surprising accuracy and depth, the subject was too intricate and apparently irrelevant to their national interests for American commentators to become emotionally involved. By American standards, it hardly seemed to matter whether one or the other side won. Trotsky's call for more democracy within the Communist Party persuaded only sympathizers like William Henry Chamberlin, the *Christian Science Monitor*'s correspondent in Moscow, to argue that the Trotskyite opposition foreshadowed an irresistibly democratizing trend in Russia.[100] Most Americans were skeptical of what a Communist meant by "democracy"; if they expressed any optimism, it was that the factionalism would destroy the Communist Party and permit a two-party system to emerge from the ruins.[101]

In any case, the rest of Trotsky's program made the dictatorial Stalin seem decidedly preferable. On the basic issues of agricultural policy and world revolution, Trotsky advocated a radically antipeasant and anticapitalist program, while Stalin urged moderation in both areas. Popular American opinion naturally tended to favor Stalin, the lesser evil, in the years preceding Trotsky's expulsion from the party in December 1927 and from Russia in January 1929. In the judgment of the *Arizona Republic,* the Trotskyites were "visionaries and malcontents," whereas Stalin was putting the USSR onto "a business basis." [102] Although a ruthless dictator, nevertheless he was restraining the Third International, thus appeasing the American paranoia about Communist propaganda. During 1926, the *New York Times* complacently noted the "virtual abandonment of the dreams of world revolution," while *The Independent* urged Soviet-American negotiations for resuming diplomatic ties.[103] Recognition still was distasteful for most Americans, however, according to the editorial comment in 1927 concerning the British rupture of relations with the Soviet Union on the grounds of revolutionary propaganda.[104] A few years of Stalin's moderation could not wholly displace a decade of mistrust, but they did dilute it. During the winter of 1927–28, for example, Soviet proposals for complete disarmament won a mixed reaction in the United States. Although most of the press derided what the *Cincinnati Enquirer* termed "a rather silly gesture," a few newspapers were willing to treat the plans on their merits, not on their authorship.[105] A small but distinct dent in American hostility had been made. Even *The Saturday Evening Post* conceded, after Trotsky's dismissal from the party, that "Russia seems to have made a turn from the left," though the magazine still wanted the proof of deeds.[106]

Like his foreign policy, Stalin's agricultural policy seemed reassuring to most Americans. In fact, it was the occasion for a revival of all the populist delusions of 1917–1919. Developments within Russia since the Revolution provided stronger evidence than ever before that the peasants would ultimately determine the history of their nation. Primarily because of peasant resistance to the industrial and urban bias of War Communism, Lenin had instituted the NEP. Since 1921, private ownership and cultivation of land had constantly grown, while the growing divergence between the prices of agricultural and manufactured goods (the so-called scissors crisis) had widened the split within the Communist leadership. Against the opposition's proposal to combine heavy industrialization with relentless collectivization of agriculture, Stalin turned the thrust of party control in favor of continuing the NEP.[107]

Walter Duranty, the influential Moscow correspondent for the *New York Times*, expressed the conclusion of most American observers when he wrote, early in 1926, that the peasant problem was the major reason for Russia's evolution toward capitalist methods. According to another journalist, an "economic counter-revolution" was taking place in the countryside.[108] Muzhik recalcitrance had political as well as economic implications to Americans. Loyal to the prevailing democratic-capitalist syndrome of values, some commentators on Soviet affairs predicted that the peasant individualism would force the USSR toward representative government, although they disagreed on whether the change would involve the downfall or the transformation of the Communist regime. In either case, the democratic agents were "the people," the hero of the Wilsonian myth, who had been schooled in the mirs, the zemstvos, and the cooperative societies.[109] The sentimental and dogmatic nature of the argument suggests that Americans were projecting onto Russia their nostalgia for a simpler, rural way of life, which had been steadily vanishing from the

United States. Such an interpretation certainly seems warranted by a *Saturday Evening Post* writer's prophecy, in 1925, of the "real democracy" to appear in Russia: "Perhaps a Slav Washington or Lincoln, now brooding in some village hut over the wrongs of his nation, may lead the way to emancipation. Whatever the agency and whenever the hour, there can be no doubt of the outcome." [110]

During the second half of the 1920's, the number of American visitors to the Soviet Union began to increase, foreshadowing the tourist hordes in 1929 and the early thirties. In 1928 and 1929, they accounted for seventeen of the twenty-one books written by Americans about Russia. They went primarily because of curiosity, but — as was constantly the case with American attitudes toward Soviet Russia — they regarded their destination as more than just a place on the map. The USSR was, to use their favorite metaphor, "a vast laboratory" in which an "experiment" was being conducted.[111] Two months after the Bolshevik Revolution, President Wilson had described Russia as "the acid test of . . . good will." Now both he and Lenin were dead, but the metaphor and attitude survived. In the Soviet Union two contrasting systems of government, history, thought, and morality were being tested.

Most of the American visitors failed to live up to the scientific point of view that their imagery invoked. Often their observations were no more than vivid versions of the prejudices they had brought with them. The gulf between evidence and conclusion sometimes was ludicrously wide. Bronson Winthrop Griscom, for example, was interviewed in his Park Avenue apartment after a trip to the USSR during the summer of 1929. Griscom complained of the lax service he received throughout Russia, even when he wanted merely a cup of tea. "I believe . . . that gradually the country will swing back to the capitalist system," he declared. "Certainly it can never go on under the present policy." At the other

96

extreme, a group of college students, after only ten days of observation, praised the Russian workers' success in their "gigantic attempt to revive the life of the nation on a basis of justice and humanity." [112] A year earlier, however, Representative Fred A. Britten of Illinois returned with bitter reports of terror and poverty imposed by a government of dreamers who rode in automobiles and lived in palaces.[113] He did not specify whether these palaces included the Kremlin.

Probably personal experience was more distracting than helpful in evaluating the Communist experiment. Baedeker's guide of 1914 had advised travelers in Russia to take sheets, towels, pillows, "a small india-rubber bath, and some insect powder," and warned that hotels in provincial towns "satisfy as a rule only the most moderate demands, and they often leave much to be desired in point of cleanliness." [114] After world war, revolution, civil war, and blockade, Russia could hardly have improved in these respects, while visitors accustomed to American living standards could hardly have failed to be shocked. Many quickly decided that "dirt is the badge of Bolshevism." [115]

But others either noted without political comment the pervasive drabness, the inadequate housing, and the lines of housewives waiting to buy the small supplies of goods, or they stressed the material progress made since the Revolution.[116] Even Samuel Harper, having muted his outspoken antagonism to the Communist regime (perhaps because this was a prerequisite to obtaining a Soviet visa), made only neutral comments after a three-month visit in 1926.[117] These people sought to penetrate appearances to the reality beneath. They found a dynamic situation which demanded more than a cliché of approval or disapproval. On the one hand, the limitations on personal freedom, accentuated by the omnipresent government propaganda and, at least in American apprehensions, the secret police, depressed even the most pro-Soviet visitors. Dorothy Thompson described Russia as "a mental prison" for any intellectual.[118] On the other hand, she and others saw the prison as a frontier, a new society reminiscent of the American West in its geographical expanse and contagiously vital in its tempo. "Russia is young!" exclaimed Anne O'Hare McCormick, a *New York Times* reporter.[119] This mood of adolescent fervor and expectancy, particularly in Moscow and among young Communists, persuaded these Americans that the future would eradicate the evils of the present. They quickly were awed by the determination of the ruling proletariat to create a radically new world. The prevailing temper seemed almost religiously ascetic in its dedication to Communist goals, contrary to the debauchery featured in anti-Bolshevik diatribes after the Revolution. Indeed, these American observers occasionally expressed regret that romance or sheer fun had so little part in the Soviet idealism, and they noted signs that the Russian people, especially the women, were resisting the austerity.[120] Thus their opinions circled back to dismay at the dogmatic dictatorship of the Soviets.

Whether they broke the circle at a point of sympathy or of hostility, or left it intact in its ambivalence, depended on their respective temperaments. Anna Louise Strong and Albert Rhys Williams always were ardent defenders of the USSR, while Dorothy Thompson, Anne O'Hare McCormick, Maurice Hindus, and Samuel Harper remained neutral. But the neutrality was not disinterest; it was the sum of diverse and keen emotions in balance.

During the 1920's, Soviet-American relations were freed from the context of world war and Allied intervention which had charged them with such intensity until then. Except for famine relief, the two nations engaged in no extensive relations. On the contrary, the American government shunned the Soviet regime as an outlaw. In response to this diplomatic calm, as well as to an absorbing prosperity at home and the economic normalization under the NEP in Russia, Americans paid less attention to Soviet developments. At least the number of books and articles on Russia was substantially less than the output during 1918–1920. If measured in emotional quality, however, American concern had not subsided. Complacent predictions of Soviet submission to capitalism and representative government, following the introduction of the NEP and the defeat of Trotsky, may have created a surface of serenity. But the original excitement still ran beneath, boiling up when Buchkavich was executed, when Robins and Borah pressed for recognition, and when Britain broke off relations with the USSR. Why did so many Americans react with such animation? Were they afraid of Communist revolution? Were they feeling the frustrations of unsuccessful missionaries of democracy? Were they merely borrowing a convenient but vestigial rhetoric? These questions are best deferred to the concluding chapter, following a survey of popular responses after the Wall Street crash. In a broader perspective, the fickle shifts of opinion can be blended into the more constant underlying attitudes.

One new mode of attitude toward Russia definitely appeared during this decade. Those visitors to the Soviet "laboratory" implied, by their metaphor, a drastic shift in emotional relationship. For them, Russia was neither a people in whose hearts Americans were to plant the American flag, nor was it a den of debauchery and chaos. Their relationship was not one of missionary involvement or of outraged boycott, but one of curiosity — extremely unclinical curiosity. Whatever their final evaluation, even if it was ostensible neutrality, they could not regard the Soviet experiment without passion. For these Americans believed that, in the laboratory, their own way of life was being indirectly tested. Just as nonrecognition was, in terms of attitudes, the most intense form of recognition, so the role of interested scientist was a more flexible but no less emotional form of concern.

The New Economic Policy signified to most Americans — especially to American business leaders — that Russia (after "having consumed all the golden eggs") was trying desperately and pitifully to repair the damage wreaked by Communist economic theories.

—*Dallas News.*

IV / Business Leaders and the NEP

In the long run facts will control.

> — Henry Ford, "Why I Am Helping Russian Industry,"
> *Nation's Business*, XVIII (June 1930), 22

The decade of the twenties was the Jazz Age, the age of nativism, the Republican reign — but above all it was the New Era in which prosperity soared to the breathless altitudes traced by graphs of stock-market averages. In these years the American businessman ruled with ebullient confidence; his values guided politics, defined success, even permeated religion. Henry Ford was known, at home and almost everywhere in the world, as the typical American, the spokesman for efficiency, innovation, prosperity. The prestigious status of the businessman is inversely confirmed by the enormous stir over Sinclair Lewis' caricature of him in *Main Street* and *Babbitt*. These apparently were regarded not simply as novels, but as lèse-majesté by citizens of the New Era.

"With the steam engine it was possible to found a civilization on prosperity. The 100 per cent American is saturated with the idea of prosperity and equality." [1] Such was the declaration which William Feather, a publishing executive, issued in the United States Chamber of Commerce's magazine, *The Nation's Business*, under the title, "A Fourth of July Speech — *New Style*," a century and a half after Jefferson's original statement. And indeed the style was new. Modernization apparently required that "life, liberty, and

101

the pursuit of happiness" be translated into economic terms. Philosophical abstraction did not satisfy the temperament of this spokesman for business. Similarly, when Ben W. Hooper, a Harding appointee to the Railway Labor Board, discussed individualism before the delegates to the 1923 convention of the National Association of Manufacturers (NAM), he talked of "this dynamo of individualism" driving "the machinery of society." [2] The industrial metaphor epitomizes the functional emphasis by which businessmen directed their thinking.

Yet the change of style should not conceal the fact that American economic spokesmen in the 1920's continued to operate from a set of ideas which Jefferson would have found quite familiar. Primary among these tenets was individualism, expressed positively in private enterprise and negatively in freedom from governmental interference. Human nature precluded any system other than laissez-faire, it was argued. Governmental intervention in economic affairs would only create disruption and inefficiency. In addition, human nature was heterogeneous, so that some people inevitably were more successful or powerful than others. Equal opportunity was just, but equality of any other sort was unnatural.[3]

Businessmen preached these themes incessantly and confidently, pointing to the prosperity of the New Era as proof. But they also reminded the American public that, even if the prosperity was unprecedented, the themes were part of the national heritage to which all citizens owed loyalty. Feather's reference to "the 100 per cent American" was a conventional bit of chauvinism born from a complex of Wilsonian rhetoric, wartime suppression of dissent, isolationism, and the anti-immigration movement. Business leaders believed that they represented not simply success, but American success created with American economic ingenuity and American moral principles. Thus the president of the NAM boasted to its 1922 convention: "There is not now nor has there ever been a country in which it was so easy as in this one for a little business to grow into a big one or for a little person to become as great as his mental and spiritual boundaries will permit. Ours is a land of undreamed of opportunity such as none but a Christian civilization and the genius of democratic institutions could create." [4] In a fashion typical of business leaders' pronouncements in this decade, economic pride easily expanded into extravagant patriotism, while "civilization" replaced "country." References to "civilization" were, in fact, so frequent during these years that the verbal habit forms a significant indication that businessmen identified wealth with the entire American culture and way of life. They defined by the dollar sign. The rhetoric became as monumental as the profits.[5]

Given these premises, it is hardly surprising to learn that American business leaders strenuously opposed the Soviet regime. For the Communist hostility to private property, enterprise and profit challenged the foundation of American civilization. The theory of class conflict frankly accused the bourgeoisie of preaching individual opportunity as a hypocritical disguise for the tyranny by the wealthy over the working classes. Bolshevik autocracy flagrantly ignored democratic principles, while official atheism clashed head-on with the beliefs of "Christian civilization." And finally, because the Bolsheviks withdrew Russia from the war, promising international revolution instead, American business leaders added treason and anarchism to the list of crimes with which they indicted the authors of the October Revolution.

Conceivably, opposition to the Bolshevik regime could have taken the form of quiet, confident anticipation of its inevitable failure, a verbal nonrecognition complementing the diplomatic nonrecognition by the United States government. But American capitalists refused to ignore this rude challenge to their premises. Journals and spokesmen of financial, commercial, and engineering groups felt impelled to demonstrate the fallacies and failures of Lenin's rule. *The Engineering and Mining Journal,* for example, supplemented its customary technical material with editorials of a very different order. "Nature's laws are immutable; and he that opposes them will be crushed," it announced in 1921. Communism is only "an ideal dream" which the Bolsheviks are applying with "ferocious and fanatical stupidity" in "ignorance of the laws of evolution, of human nature, of past and present events and their lessons." [6] Herbert Spencer himself could hardly have done better.

But to American businessmen, who tested ideas by application to reality, theoretical dispute was less conclusive than the argument of hard fact. And the fact was that, in dramatic contrast to the apparently limitless prosperity of the United States, Russia presented "the biggest business failure of history." [7] No matter how insistently the Communists quoted *Das Kapital,* the inescapable counterargument was that Russia was in chaos. As a consultant in industrial economics said, after talking personally with Lenin, the Soviet leader was "an impractical idealist" who might have been a shrewd engineer of revolution but who could not run a nation.[8]

With relentless and contemptuous detail, the various trade magazines documented the breakdown of the Russian economy. The deplorable example of the railroad system was analyzed by *Railway Age, Railway Review,* and *The Annalist.*[9] *The Iron Age* described the ruined condition of the metal industry while *Mining and Metallurgy* did the same for the mines.[10] Numerous observers noted the inefficiency of factory management and production under the inexperienced personnel who had replaced tsarist officials.[11] In reporting the failure of Soviet farm policy, *The Commercial and Financial Chronicle* remarked: "The expected has come to pass." [12] And *The Nation's Business,* which displayed an

104

especially hostile attitude (for a while in 1923 it headlined a series of news items as "Notes from Deluded Russia"), gleefully declared that, based on 1913 levels, the price index in May 1923 had reached 544,546,854.[13] The almost unanimous view of business spokesmen was that Bolshevik rule had proved a catastrophe. In Secretary of State Hughes' famous phrase, repeated by Secretary of Commerce Hoover, Russia was an "economic vacuum." [14]

Thus, all the moral objections which business leaders raised against the Soviet regime in the early 1920's were ultimately subsidiary to the practical and, in their opinion, crucial objection that the Communist economic system clearly did not work. Julius H. Barnes, president of the Chamber of Commerce, was incredulous that a nation, "living just above the verge of utter barbarism, attempts to instruct orderly America, busy with its expanded economic life and social opportunities, typified by its eighteen million automobiles and its towering skyscrapers." [15] Until the Soviet Union had an equal number of automobiles and skyscrapers, in other words, it had no legitimate or persuasive claim to superiority over American capitalism. Living amid the rosy optimism of the New Era, business spokesmen overlooked the danger in this basically economic definition of American success and Soviet failure. For what if the USSR should begin to approximate American material standards or, on the other hand, what if the boom of the twenties should bust? How would one criticize the Soviet system if the skyscrapers housed empty offices and if unpurchased automobiles crowded showrooms while Russia was achieving a five-year plan in four years? Before 1930, Barnes and his colleagues were oblivious to any of these possibilities and therefore confidently criticized Communism's economic ineptitude.

Moreover, the inextricable corollary to this line of attack was that improvement could *never* take place under Communist rule. The economic breakdown which the Bolsheviks blamed on the war and Allied intervention was, according to American business leaders, irreparable by socialist or communist practices. Herbert Hoover developed this point at length in an official statement immediately after taking office as President Harding's Secretary of Commerce. The economic rehabilitation of Russia, he explained, was impossible so long as the Bolsheviks remained in power, for their economic system necessarily stifled revival of production.[16] During the next few years he never wavered from the conviction that Soviet leaders would have to jettison their economic doctrines and adopt those of capitalism if they wanted to survive.[17] This conclusion both reflected the thinking of most business leaders in the early twenties and, the more often it was repeated, reinforced that thinking.

Contrary impulses did exist, of course. For one thing, speculative itch was aroused by the realization that "There is not in the whole world so enormous, so eager, and so empty a market as Russia."[18] Moreover, the 1920–1921 depression at home temporarily increased the need for new purchasers. But investment and trade also rely in large measure on confidence. Few commercial or financial figures could muster such confidence when the Secretary of Commerce himself, whose personal career and fortune attested to his economic wisdom, warned that profit in the economic vacuum of Russia was impossible or always in jeopardy of confiscation by the anticapitalist regime. Just as the government refused recognition until the Soviet leaders first honored debts and property rights, so did individuals refuse to commit their capital until the Soviet Union returned to some sort of normalcy. Practical difficulties, in any case, impeded a contrary policy. For despite its lifting of the embargo on Soviet-American trade, on July 7, 1920, the government refused to accept gold from Soviet Russia, on the grounds that it was confiscated from the tsarist treasury. Unable to pay, the Soviets were unable to buy. Moreover, without stability in political relations, long-term credits were not granted by Americans to the Soviet government, again hampering American sales.[19] In the face of theoretical, emotional, and practical obstacles, most business leaders agreed with the editors of *Electrical World* who graphically stated in 1922: "At present the situation looks to us more like poker than investment."[20]

The fate of those few adventurous capitalists who dared to deal with Soviet Russia seemed to confirm the validity of Hoover's advice. Indeed, the activities of one Washington D. Vanderlip developed into a virtual *opéra bouffe.* Vanderlip, a California mining engineer, visited Russia in 1920 as representative of an association of ten leading financiers in the far west. By October he obtained from Lenin a sixty-year lease of a huge area in Kamchatka in northeastern Siberia, with exclusive rights to develop coal, oil, and fisheries. The Bolshevik leaders, he said, quickly agreed that he be allowed to operate the $3 billion concession "in American fashion." In harmony with the rhetoric of other business leaders, Vanderlip proclaimed the creation of "an almost unbroken band of republicanism around the globe from the Atlantic to the Atlantic." Thus profit had higher sanctions. What he did not know was that Japan controlled most of the area and that Lenin's goal was not to develop Siberia, but to disrupt Japanese-American relations and to create a demand for recognition within American business circles. What Lenin did not know, however, was that he had confused Washington Vanderlip with Frank A. Vanderlip, an influential financier and former president of the New York National City Bank. By mid-1921, the whole comedy of errors had collapsed ludicrously.[21]

Nevertheless, Vanderlip's fumbling performance had derived from a keen speculative vision of the vast wealth latent in Russia's natural resources. More substantial American interests pursued similar goals with greater caution. The Standard Oil Company of New Jersey, for example, had purchased a joint interest in the old Nobel holdings in Soviet oil (although the Bolsheviks had nationalized the property). In December 1920, shortly after Vanderlip's contract, A. C. Bedford, head of Standard, rejected a Soviet offer of a fifty-year concession for development of a large segment of oil reserves; instead he demanded the return of his confiscated property. When Russia turned to the Royal Dutch Shell Company, the British rival of Standard, Bedford turned to Secretary of State Hughes for protection. The result was that the Genoa Conference of April–May 1922, which originally was called to consider Soviet debts and confiscations and which the United States did not officially attend, became the battleground for American and British oil interests. The conference broke up over other issues, but State Department pressure produced a truce between Standard and Royal Dutch in July: each declared the sanctity of private property and promised not to negotiate independently with the Soviets. In effect, Bedford had emerged victorious over Royal Dutch while maintaining his moral and economic boycott of Communist policies.[22] The victory was brief. Less than a year later, the lure of oil had induced Royal Dutch to make a deal with the Soviet Union and had tempted another of Standard's competitors, Harry F. Sinclair, to begin negotiations for a concession to all of the Caucasus petroleum resources. Sinclair signed a contract in 1923, only to have the Teapot Dome scandal divert his attention from the Soviet oilfields.[23]

The fitful quality of these dealings by Vanderlip, Bedford, and Sinclair indicates the tensions in the American business attitude toward Soviet Russia during the early 1920's: the possibility of vast profit in the disrupted market and undeveloped lands strained against capitalist prejudices and the deep suspicion of the radical Bolsheviks. It is difficult to hypothesize which way the conflict would have resolved itself, if at all, had the situation remained constant. But already in 1921 the situation had been drastically altered, with the result that — as Americans began gradually to recognize the change — the old terms of the Soviet-American economic dialogue gave way to new ones. For on March 17, Lenin announced what was to be labeled a "strategic retreat" from Communist principles: the New Economic Policy.[24] Numerous American capitalists reacted to this sudden change with exultation, tending to overlook the "strategic" and to interpret "retreat" as defeat. They believed that the utopian, fanatical Bolsheviks were yielding to the natural law which ordained capitalism. In short, they grossly misinterpreted the terms of the NEP. Hoover himself was prompted to mention, in a letter to Secretary of State Hughes on December 6, 1921, "the striking parallel of national economy of Russia and the United States." [25] Surely the enormous impact of the NEP could not be more vividly illustrated than in this comment by the Secretary of Commerce.

Yet Lenin's innovation dissolved the existing tension within the minds of American business leaders only to replace it with a subtler one. For the NEP could be interpreted as an erasure of the despicable communist principles which had ruined Russia and prohibited American business with her, or it could be seen as the portent of the final fall of the Soviet regime. In the first case, Americans would be justified and sensible in initiating investments and commerce. In the second case, they would simply sit back a while longer until, ready for profiteering, they could enter onto a stage cleared of Lenin and his wild ideas. Camps of assertive and noisy spokesmen developed around both interpretations.

In the same letter to Hughes quoted above, for example, Hoover followed his analogy of the Soviet and American economic systems with the hope that the Administration would maintain its aloofness toward trade with Russia. Eventually, he said, conditions will create a situation "which, combined with other factors, will enable the Americans to undertake the leadership in the reconstruction of Russia when the proper moment arrives." [26] Although its ambiguities are perhaps insurmountable, this statement obviously advocates no rush of American investors into Soviet Russia; one can even construe the mysterious references to "other factors" and "the proper moment" as a deliberately oblique anticipation of Bolshevik overthrow with American intervention. Whatever Hoover's exact meaning, the practical effect of such thinking, shared fully by Hughes, was to reinforce the policy established by the Wilson Administration. As the *New York Times* correspondent reported from Washington in April 1921, informed government circles expected the end of the Soviet regime in the foreseeable future.[27] Two years later, *The Iron Age* was still expressing expectation of equal confidence: "The Bolshevik Government is already close to the end of its rope." [28] For proponents of this view, the NEP was the signal for no change of American behavior, except perhaps to increase the arrogance of their habitual hostility.

The majority of business leaders reacted in a very different way, however. To them the announcement of the NEP seemed to open the door to Soviet economic sanity and to American profits in the huge Slavic market. The astonishing degree to which opinion changed is best revealed in the juxtaposition of two editorials by the prestigious *Commercial and Financial Chronicle*. In November 1920, the *Chronicle* issued a relentless denunciation:

whatever the antecedent causes that enfeebled the Empire, whatever the revolution failed to do in its short life, has not been corrected by Bolshevism. The descent, on the contrary, has been accelerated. And therefore the Commune itself is a colossal failure. . . .

It was born in blood and fire, it has lived by murder and pillage. And it seeks through the Internationale to subjugate other peoples and Governments to its own theoretical enterprise. More interfering than interfered with, it can point to no single influence for good that has irradiated the world . . . the bare, stark fact is that history does not record in its long and bloody annals another example of tyranny comparable to this theft of property, subversion of order, and systematic suppression of the individual — ending in hopeless famine and helpless suffering.[29]

Three months later the NEP began. Twelve months later the *Chronicle* declared: "The Bolsheviki Government already recognizes its great financial and industrial mistakes, and is trying to correct them." "Existing difficulties," the article continued, "though at present discouraging, are sure in time to be overcome in one way or another by individual enterprise, without waiting for steps to be taken by Governments, greatly desirable as these must be." Such was the tempering influence of the NEP on the apparently unyielding hostility of a leading business organ. By 1925, in fact, the *Chronicle* was willing to foresee Russia as the leading economic force in Europe.[30]

Other trade journals became equally sanguine as they reported or prophesied Soviet economic recovery under the NEP. *Electrical World,* for instance, enthusiastically reported on Lenin's plans for electrification of Russia, describing his "visions" without the derogatory sense which Americans had so often applied to Bolshevik aims.[31] Because the terms of the NEP were closer to those familiar to American capitalists, the latter in turn were more willing to study the Soviet situation rather than immediately to despise or dismiss it as the hell for Communist sinners.[32] By 1927 a writer in *The*

Annalist was convinced that the spirit of American capitalism had replaced that of the *Communist Manifesto*.[33]

The product of this new tolerance was extensive consideration of the ways in which American business could tap the latent profits of the Soviet Union. Before the 1917 Revolution, American investments in Russia had comprised more than 5 per cent of total foreign investments, most of them by ten large corporations including International Harvester, Singer Manufacturing Company, and the New York National City Bank. Trade, almost constantly in American favor, had consisted mainly of exports of raw cotton, machinery, motor vehicles, and metals, and imports of furs, manganese ore, caviar, flax, and other items.[34] Although always a small part of the American commercial pattern, the Russian market nonetheless could furnish a significant addition to American economic outlets, particularly during the depression of 1920–1921. At least business leaders argued in this way with increasing assurance after 1921. "That great possibilities exist for this country with regard to trade with Russia in the near future cannot be doubted," exclaimed a writer in *The Magazine of Wall Street* in 1922. For those who may have continued to doubt, *The Magazine* a year later assigned a staff member to present a special report on Soviet economic development. At a luncheon of the American Manufacturers' Export Association in New York, a recent visitor to Moscow and Petrograd described the same bright possibilities. *Railway Age* urged big business to "take the plunge" and invest in the Soviet future, for "Russia is now a country to be worked as a colony." [35] And so it went, an accumulating message of inspiration to American businessmen to enter the Bolshevik marketplace.[36]

As a further prod to investment and commerce, the advocates of Soviet trade pointed to the quickening interest among European competitors. American hesitation, they warned, meant greater European profits in, perhaps even domination of, the Soviet economic field. In January of 1922, the Latvian correspondent for *American Machinist* told readers that, unless they wished to allow Russia to be overrun by others, they had better begin to exploit Soviet economic possibilities immediately.[37] At the same time, William C. Redfield, Wilson's Secretary of Commerce, and S. R. Bertron, president of a Wall Street banking firm, were writing to the State Department in the name of the American-Russian Chamber of Commerce, a group of rather conservative commercial and financial men interested in trade with Russia. In their letter, Redfield and Bertron anxiously cited the formation by France, Britain, and Germany of an international corporation for creating Russian commerce. They appealed to the government to provide equal opportunity for American traders before this country was entirely excluded from the Soviet scene.[38]

As in the Vanderlip incident, the Soviet regime sought to make use of this capitalist flirtation for its own political interests. With an eye to possible American aid in constructing a strong barrier against Japanese expansion, the Kremlin in 1921 began to mute the noisy revolutionary propaganda of the American section of the International.[39] More directly relevant to American business circles, the Soviet leaders regained the hope for recognition which Secretary Colby had so bluntly shattered in August 1920. By encouraging Soviet-American trade, and by undertaking a determined effort to attract foreign concessionaires, they expected simultaneously to encourage growing business pressure on Washington for an end to the diplomatic impasse. This strategy correctly reasoned that nonrecognition hampered the security of commercial intercourse; but the reasoning had a double edge, for the very fact of insecurity hampered the growth of extensive trade in the first place. Thus, like the baffling question of

113

chicken versus egg, the necessary priority of recognition or of trade was unclear.[40]

Much more clear, much more dependable, was the capitalist reflex of profit seeking. By 1922, the NEP and the threat of European commercial advantage had aroused the interest and ambition of large numbers of American businessmen. But this concern still had to be synthesized into the form of actual commerce and investment. The most active and influential director of such efforts was Alexander Gumberg, whose futile activities to obtain Soviet diplomatic recognition, with the aid of Senator Borah and Raymond Robins, have already been described. He proved much more successful in the complementary campaign to strengthen Soviet-American economic relations.

Gumberg found an early and important ally in Reeve Schley, vice-president of the Chase National Bank in New York. Schley already was indirectly involved in the Russian question because his former law partner, Thomas D. Thacher, had been a member of the Robins group that went to Russia in 1917. But he became actively engaged only in 1923 when a Russian Textile Syndicate representative named Nogin, seeking a million dollars to clothe the people of his devastated homeland, was referred to the Chase official as someone who was open-minded toward the USSR. Schley was not only open-minded but constructive. He suggested that Nogin would more effectively obtain credits if he set up a corporation in the United States. The result was the Amtorg Trading Corporation, incorporated under the laws of New York in May 1924 and serving as the agency of the Soviet export and import bureaus.[41] Because it was an official Soviet organization and because Russia had no embassy in this country during the next nine years, Amtorg naturally (though tacitly) added political and propaganda activities to its formal commercial duties.

In the same search for textile credits, Gumberg also came to Schley in 1923. Negotiations between the two produced in December a $2 million loan by the Chase National Bank and, thereby, another corporation, the All-Russian Textile Syndicate. From 1924 to 1930, the Syndicate not only arranged cotton sales but actually handled one third of all Soviet-American trade.[42]

A few years later, Schley became involved with a third institution for encouraging trade with the Soviet Union, this one of American origin. The American-Russian Chamber of Commerce, consisting in 1920 of 125 firms (including Standard Oil of New Jersey, the Chase National Bank, Vacuum Oil Company, and others) and many prestigious economic leaders, had come into existence in 1916 in order to foster trade with Russia. After the February Revolution, it supported Kerensky and continued to do so even after he fell from power. Its activity declined sharply, however, when Bakhmeteff, the vestigial ambassador in the United States of the nonexistent Provisional Government, retired and left in June 1922. Bitterly anti-Bolshevik, the Chamber declared that it saw no commercial future for Russia until the Red regime was overthrown. As the Bolsheviks held on more and more firmly and as American businessmen began to subordinate political to economic considerations, the Chamber became increasingly anomalous. Finally, in June 1926, a major reorganization took place: Allen Wardwell, a member of John W. Davis' law firm and a former participant in Russian relief work, became vice-president, while Reeve Schley became president. Schley promised that the Chamber would refrain from political questions and would focus its attention solely on developing trade with the USSR.[43]

The All-Russian Textile Syndicate, the new American-Russian Chamber of Commerce, and, above all, Amtorg represented striking achievements for Gumberg and his allies

115

in their campaign for Soviet-American economic relations. These institutions served both as a dramatic indicator of the change in business attitudes around the middle of the decade and as an encouragement of further change. Investment in the Soviet Union no longer was like playing poker; increasingly it represented common sense, particularly as growing numbers of companies did business there and thus set precedents for more timid colleagues. The Allied American Corporation, for example, acting as the agent for thirty well-known American firms (Ford Motor Company, United States Rubber Company, and American Tool Works among them), signed a trade contract with the Russian Foreign Trade Monopoly in July 1923, providing for a yearly turnover of not less than $2.4 million and guaranteeing freedom from Soviet interference. Most of the exports to the United States were to be furs, flax, and other raw materials, while the imports were to comprise machinery, tools, and similar items for Soviet agriculture and industry. Within six months, the corporation had already exceeded its quota of turnover and seemed destined to quadruple it in the next six months. Meanwhile, an American fur company had purchased a million dollars of Russian furs which it sold at huge profits.[44] Yet these were trifling deals compared with the contract secured in 1925 by Lena Goldfields, a British mining corporation using American capital to finance half of the venture. Its thirty-year concession gave a million and a half acres of Siberian and Ural land, rich in gold, silver, copper, and lead, to be developed by the company. Estimates of the value of future production went as high as $150 million.[45]

Only two months later, however, even this colossal transaction seemed less breathtaking. For on June 12, 1925, W. Averell Harriman, son of one of the great robber barons, announced that he had obtained the sole right to exploit the Chiaturi manganese deposits in Georgia for twenty years.

116

The magnitude of Harriman's concession is clear only when one learns that the Chiaturi district contained the largest known supply of manganese ore, a mineral vital to the production of steel, that in 1913 it had furnished one half of the world's output, and that Harriman's 10,000 acres were judged to have an amount worth one billion dollars and sufficient to supply the world for the next half century.[46] If Harriman dealt on this scale with the Soviet rulers, surely lesser businessmen need no longer hold back. *The Engineering and Mining Journal*, which four years earlier had advised that "American mining men should not stake a penny on Bolshevist promises of concessions," now declared rashly: "The mere fact of this concession shows that the Soviets have sacrificed their fundamental principles for cash." [47]

Both Lena Goldfields and Harriman soon were to engage in acrimonious dispute with Soviet authorities, so that eventually their contracts were canceled.[48] At the moment, however, all gloomy portents were swept away by an enthusiastic tide of trade and investment. In 1924 the value of American imports from Russia increased sevenfold over the preceding year, while exports quadrupled to exceed the 1913 level. In 1925, imports almost redoubled, while exports increased 50 per cent. As usual, the balance was heavily in American favor. The United States was, in fact, providing almost one third of the Soviet Union's foreign trade.[49] As for investments, the United States by 1927 was second only to Germany in the number of concessions it was operating in the USSR.[50] The next year, so prestigious a corporation as General Electric entered this new field of profit, further sanctioning the respectability of Soviet Russia.[51]

The Standard Oil Company itself, which at the time of the Genoa conference had stood hand in hand with Secretary of State Hughes in defense of American hostility to the Bolshevik regime, now was embarrassed by a blatant defection from within its own ranks. For the Vacuum Oil Company, a subsidiary, and Standard Oil of New York (Socony) in 1926 began to purchase large quantities of Soviet petroleum. When the Standard Oil Company of New Jersey accused them of betraying American principles, the president of Vacuum, noting that the United States sold cotton and other products to Russia, asked: "Is it more unrighteous to buy from Russia than to sell to it?" He preferred "common sense" to stubborn idealism.[52] The incident made its peculiar effect, however, because on the day after Vacuum and Socony signed their contracts the press published evidence that Ivy Lee, Standard's public-relations man and "the best known and most expensive of publicity men," now favored recognition of Russia.[53]

Lee's conversion, no matter how much it derived from agile accommodation to shifting trade winds rather than from ideological conviction, was a symptom of the new attitude which had developed among American business leaders since the NEP. Russia now qualified as the newest member of the dynamic boom being created in the United States. Colonel Hugh L. Cooper, engineer for the Muscle Shoals dam and then for the immense Dneiperstroy hydroelectric project, told American delegates to the 1927 congress of the International Chamber of Commerce that responsible industrial leadership would bring Russia to a "new era," leadership which "can be found only in the United States." [54] The very novelty and size of the Soviet economy excited the American sense of the adventurous and the grandiose. The editor of *The New York Journal of Commerce*, traveling through the Soviet Union in 1926, described the nation as "a great capitalistic experiment — perhaps the greatest of modern times." [55] However uncomfortable the Soviet Communists may have felt under the bourgeois barrage of praise, they could at least take satisfaction in having successfully reached over the

American heads of state to the heads of corporations. And undeniably they needed the trade, investment, and technical assistance which the United States, more than any other nation, was able to provide.

The Soviet-American economic entente was, then, the product of compromise. Brutal distress compelled the Bolshevik authorities to replace War Communism with the NEP. In response, most American business leaders, confident that Russia was evolving toward capitalist "normalcy," were willing to overlook the continuance of Soviet rule and to resume economic interchange. By 1924, the marriage of Communist necessity and capitalist ambition was being widely celebrated. A large part of the business community, of course, as well as the government, continued to object. Within the Soviet leadership, too, great debates already were developing over the NEP, concluding in the First Five-Year Plan's return to purer communism.[56] As for American business leaders' ideological framework, that had not changed at all. In fact, their commitment to laissez-faire became more tenacious, if anything, as they thought they saw Russia's drift toward capitalism. Many believed, moreover, that their contact with the Soviet Union would accelerate the inevitable drift.[57]

Retrospect reveals, however, that the two sides shared certain fundamental attitudes — one is tempted to call them instincts — which neither of them clearly perceived or was willing to admit. More than economic circumstances was at work to subdue the supposedly unappeasable clash of ideologies. This fact emerges most dramatically from analysis of the relationship between the USSR and the archetypal American of the New Era, Henry Ford. That the two would relate at all seems, at first, preposterous. Ford's practice of mass production by means of the assembly line, his hostility to labor unions, his personal fortune, and, in general, his role as American capitalist par excellence — all this should have made him anathema to the Communists. Similarly, Ford, who had no use for "professional reformers" in any case or country, certainly should have had little tolerance for a system which preached economic equality, class conflict, and international revolution. And in fact he caustically remarked, in 1926, that "The professional reformers wrecked Russia." Earlier he argued: "Nature has vetoed the whole Soviet Republic," for the Communist rulers denied "the right to the fruits of labour." [58]

Nevertheless, on May 31, 1929, the Ford Motor Company signed a contract with Amtorg, the representative of the Supreme Economic Council of the USSR. Ford agreed to furnish detailed plant layouts and working projects for construction and equipment of a factory able to produce 100,000 units a year, including Model A cars, Model AA trucks, and heavier vehicles. In return, the Soviet Union would buy, via Amtorg, 72,000 Ford units on a four-year schedule and would use only Ford-made parts for repairs. In addition, Ford agreed to give full rights to make and use Ford machinery, to allow use of all Ford inventions or technical advances, whether patented or not, and to provide detailed drawings of all departments of a complete factory, including specifications and schedules of machinery and operation sheets. Finally, Russian engineers would have access to Ford's American plants so that they could acquire practical training, while the company would send its own engineers and foremen to the Soviet Union to help in the planning and operation of the new works.[59]

Hard business calculation by both sides, of course, provided the leading impetus to this vast transaction. This was no propaganda stunt. In any event, the two parties had already engaged in extensive business, though not on so elaborate a scale. From 1920 through 1927, the USSR purchased more than 24,000 Fordson tractors for agricultural production. At the end of that period, the Soviet authorities asked Ford to send a delegation to supervise the servicing of the tractors. They hoped to persuade Ford also to build a plant there, but the returning delegates convinced him that the dangers of nationalization and political interference precluded such a venture.[60] Three years later, Ford changed his mind.

At a time when all of Ford's activities and opinions were news, the 1929 contract was big news indeed. Yet many people were perplexed that Ford would help a regime which four Presidents and four Secretaries of State had castigated as a menace to American democracy and survival. In *The Nation's Business*, the journal of the United States Chamber of Commerce, Ford offered this explanation: "Russia is beginning to build. It makes little difference what theory is back of the real work, for in the long run facts will control. I believe it is our duty to help any people who want to go to work and become self-supporting. I have long been convinced that we shall never be able to build a balanced economic order in the world until every people has become as self-supporting as possible." [61] In succinct form he was repeating what many American business leaders had been arguing since the early days of the NEP: Communist theories necesarily shattered when applied to economic reality. He also was voicing the impulsive American generosity which had prompted famine-relief work and which now took the form of technical aid to a nation progressing toward recovery.[62]

Yet these were only the most explicit and familiar of an intricate complex of motives, most of which Ford did not articulate. In his mind, as well as the minds of numerous other New Era business leaders interested in Russia, these motives operated tacitly but nonetheless forcefully. Their agitation was responsible for the otherwise inexplicable, or at least peculiar, intensity of enthusiasm about Soviet invest-

121

ment and trade despite disapproval by the American government, despite alien Bolshevik theories, and despite the obvious shakiness of the USSR's economic present and future. Only the postulation of some incentive other than a strictly economic one will explain, for example, why so many businessmen interpreted the NEP as more than a "strategic retreat" and why they used it as the justification for a virtual gold rush into the Soviet Union and, finally, why they tended to use superlatives of praise in vivid contrast to their earlier superlatives of scorn. Their reaction was excessive; it went beyond what the facts permitted or required of an impartial observer, indicating the operation of emotional forces. In the comments by the numerous American engineers who went to work in Russia after 1929 on projects of the Five-Year Plan, these emotional forces are more clearly articulated and can be documented. For businessmen like Ford, who dealt with Russia at a distance, the evidence remains generally implicit and must be inferred. In either case, a phenomenon which might conveniently be dismissed as paradoxical is actually an acute reflection of human complexity.

Certainly Ford was not reluctant to express his views on the American scene. In numerous books, many of which unembarrassedly plagiarized their predecessors, he stressed the precepts that he felt were essential to a proper way of life. Individualism served as a virtual leitmotiv. To it he added, as harmonious complement, strenuous warnings about the ineptitude and injuriousness of governmental control of industry.[63] But if these two principles had been the only components of his industrial "philosophy," his admiration of and investment in the progress of socialist, dictatorial Russia would have made him guilty of gross inconsistency or grosser hypocrisy.

In fact, other attitudes were at work, overruling these initial objections. First of all, Ford recognized that the

122

Soviet leaders were basically practical. "So my advice to young men," Ford said in 1929, "is to be ready to revise any system, scrap any methods, abandon any theory if the success of the job requires it." As the October Revolution and the NEP had proved to him, the Bolsheviks adhered to the same belief. If a situation was not soluble by action in line with their theories, they could put their theories aside and improvise.[64] Indeed, Ford carried pragmatism to a point at which, in a crude way, it resembled the historicism of the Marxian system. "The universe is set in a certain direction," he declared, "and when you go along with it, that is 'goodness.' If you don't, you are getting an admonitory kind of experience." He added: "Rightness in mechanics, rightness in morals, are basically the same thing." [65] In an unsystematic fashion, he was approaching a deterministic, amoral theory not too foreign to the Marxian mode of thought.

Above all, however, Ford admired power, particularly the power of the machine. And to observers of the Soviet attempt to reconstruct a country spread over one sixth of the globe, the most striking fact was the monumental scale of the programs, especially the Five-Year Plan. The coincidence between Ford's and Soviet thinking becomes remarkable when one considers the following statement:

The way to liberty, the way to equality of opportunity, the way from empty phrases to actualities, lies through power; the machine is only an incident.

The function of the machine is to liberate man from brute burdens, and release his energies to the building of his intellectual and spiritual powers for conquests in the fields of thought and higher action.[66]

Although these words could easily have come from a Soviet poster or pamphlet in 1930, they were written by Ford in 1926. The spirit in which Lenin and Stalin sought to give a (Fordson) tractor to every peasant was the same as that in which Ford designed an automobile for the average American budget. Departing from different premises — Ford from democratic and individualistic ones, Lenin and Stalin from authoritarian ones — they converged in a common awe for the power and meaning of the machine.

The convergence is more than hypothetical. In the 1920's Ford became a hero in Russia. As one American writer declared in 1930: "If Lenin is Russia's God today, Ford is its St. Peter." [67] The symbol of American capitalism joined the symbol of Communism in a curious, thrilling hierarchy, a mixed metaphor born from the affinities just outlined. To Soviet leaders, Ford also was a great revolutionary because of the industrial techniques which he developed and they appropriated. To the Russian people, particularly the peasants, "Ford" was a familiar and revered name. Maurice Hindus describes a wedding in a village of the Volga region, the bride and groom sitting in a cart drawn by a Fordson tractor and the procession interrupted by a speech celebrating the progress due to Fordson. Ford's writings were used as handbooks for industrial managers. *Pravda* carefully traced the progress of "Fordization" in Russian factories. And in the 1936 edition of the *Bolshaya sovetskaya entsiklopediya,* Ford earned his own article, although applause of his economic achievements was by then mixed with criticism of his political views.[68] No wonder that Stalin sent representatives to Dearborn when he wanted to industrialize his nation.

Nevertheless, these various parallels — pragmatism, respect for the machine, enthusiasm for its social consequences — did not eradicate the fundamental fact that Ford's nation was capitalist and Stalin's was socialist and that neither could ultimately tolerate the other's system. Stalin accepted Western aid only to accelerate Russia into self-sufficiency. With that accomplished, with socialism's having been created in one country, he planned to spread socialism throughout the world. Thus, in 1934 he terminated the five-year-old contract with Ford, since the USSR could now make its own automobiles and tractors.[69] Ford's nationalism, though nonmilitaristic, had a significantly analogous tone of imperialism. As he declared: "The essential principles of Americanism are the goal toward which all civilization is striving." Then he added: "The United States was created as a nursery in which these principles could be brought to full growth, that all the nations of the earth might see, and seeing know, the practical nature of liberty in all things. The mission of the United States is to give a demonstration to the world of the reality and endurance of certain principles." [70]

This exalted view of the American role typifies the enormous self-esteem which American business leaders enjoyed in this decade. They regarded themselves, in the words of the president of the NAM, as the elite "in the vanguard of the procession of progress," agents for "civilization."[71] Under the incentive of such extravagant notions, they confronted Russia as Lenin himself, the leader of his own vanguard, confronted her in 1917: as missionaries entering a benighted land.[72] Soviet requests for buyers, investors, and engineers only confirmed many businessmen's belief that, just as the NEP had signaled the irreversible decline of communism, so now Soviet borrowing of American aid and Soviet imitation of "Amerikansky tempo" indicated the conversion of Russia to capitalism.[73] As it became clear, in the late 1920's, that the USSR was progressing, as Soviet leaders spoke in terms of "unprecedented" advances in the same way that New Era boosters boasted of their own "unprecedented" prosperity, that belief became still stronger. For progress on a noncapitalist basis was inconceivable to these capitalists. As a result, they demanded normalization of commercial and political relations with the Soviet Union.[74]

Not all business leaders were so credulous, so rash. The Chamber of Commerce, for example, still pledged loyalty to Hoover's 1921 dictum that trade relations with the Soviet

WE'RE BOUND TO RECOGNIZE THAT!

—Fitzpatrick in the St. Louis *Post-Dispatch*.

According to many Americans in 1929, Russia has gained a good suit and lost its beard, seeming impressive both in stature and luggage.

Union were a political rather than an economic question.[75] But that stand was less and less attractive as the decade passed. Other business spokesmen, such as Ivy Lee, reversed the priority and then went even further. Instead of developing an economic case for the resumption of trade relations, Lee asked: "And is it not possible that Western civilization is called upon in the case of Russia to make the greatest experiment in faith in human nature in all history?" [76] Lee, like many others, had faith, had a confidence nurtured by the New Era boom and elitist ideas. Communist propaganda was, from this perspective, merely verbal posturing and quite irrelevant.[77] Even Soviet confiscation of property was deemed incidental.[78] The reality in Russia was the machine, the "Amerikansky tempo," the growth of "civilization" from the preachings and practices of capitalist missionaries. Soon Ford would be God, and Lenin only St. Peter.

Ironically, then, the final affinity between American business leaders and the Soviets — a missionary fervor — placed the two nations in a relentless rivalry. Each nation considered itself the laboratory for a great experiment in faith. American capitalism was in competition with Communism for men's souls and the world's future. Each preached liberty and happiness for the common man, but each interpreted liberty and happiness in its own way. When William Feather, in his statement quoted at the beginning of the chapter, declared that "the 100 per cent American is satisfied with the idea of prosperity and equality," he was inadvertently speaking for the 100 per cent Communist as well.[79] But that confidence did not at all preclude the national rivalry; it created it. Each ism believed itself assigned by a higher necessity to be the sole servant of history and the sole leader of the world. Two manifest destinies collided.

It was originally asserted that many of the motives for business leaders' enthusiasm about the Soviet Union were not articulated or fully recognized. After the elucidation of the many affinities between Soviet and American attitudes during the late 1920's — respect for the machine and its power, a promise of liberty, equality, and prosperity by means of man's mastery of the machine, and, finally, a sense of supramaterial purpose and inevitability in the success of their economic programs — this peculiar relationship should be clear. At the same time, it may also have become apparent that Americans were not speaking with one voice or even disagreeing rationally. After the Revolution, sympathizers with its ideals urged recognition and trade relations as a means of benefiting the United States. They were met, instead, by a deluge of evidence proving that Russia was an "economic vacuum." Relinquishing this shaky ground, they then argued that the very prostration of Russia warranted American investment and extension of credits. Their opponents in turn shifted position and retorted that, as Hoover put it, the trade question "is far more a political question than an economic one so long as Russia is in control of the Bolsheviki." [80]

The innovation of the NEP in 1921 allowed the pro-Soviet camp to claim that the Bolsheviks had reformed the political and economic policies which Hoover found objectionable. This was a gross exaggeration but, for the various economic and emotional reasons discussed earlier, it persuaded many businessmen to deal with the Soviet Union. It did not at all weaken the equally exaggerated stance of the government and its supporters who, during the decade, increasingly stressed Soviet propaganda as the reason for their hostility. Both sides engaged in expedient distortions and the business leaders, who conceivably might have been expected to treat the question as an objective one of dollars and cents, acted from their own brand of distorting motives: namely, a set of emotional affinities with Soviet rhetoric and methods. When critics pointed out to them the blatantly anticapitalist

128

content of Soviet propaganda, these business leaders talked about civilization and thus evaded the problem. In short, no one really answered anyone else or treated objectively the question of trade with Russia. The question always provoked moral and emotional reactions which distorted perception and permitted only prejudices disguised by arguments of expediency. Contrary to Ford's assertion, facts did *not* control.

And in the long run, at the end of the 1920's, a wholly new set of facts took over. A year after the Five-Year Plan began, the stock-market crash exploded the New Era and, with it, the assumptions of its creators. Businessmen suddenly, painfully, had to reappraise their ideas and the world at large. In the process they also had to revise their views of the Soviet Union.

When Lenin died, the Communist *Daily Worker* portrayed with almost religious fervor its conviction—and the conviction of most American leftists — that the light of Lenin's revolution, the "Soviet star of hope," would continue to illuminate and inspire the world.

V / Dissident Responses during the NEP

For an old bitch gone in the teeth,
For a botched civilization.
                    — Ezra Pound, "Hugh Selwyn Mauberley" (1920)

In the spring of 1919, Harold Stearns began an intellectual journey away from old loyalties. Like other liberals, the *Dial* editor was dismayed by American misunderstanding of Soviet Russia, "the greatest economic experiment and social adventure in the history of the world." [1] But he also was angered by the "extraordinarily facile collapse" of the liberals themselves in the face of wartime shibboleths and emotionalism. Liberalism was not a program, he contended, but an attitude of candor, open-mindedness, and detachment.[2] By November, in a book entitled *Liberalism in America,* he synthesized the themes of Russia and the World War into a more refined explanation of the liberal failure. He argued that liberals had made themselves impotent and irrelevant because they continued to take political positions — and, in fact, positions at all points of the political spectrum — whereas the Communist Revolution demanded an economic mode of thought. By failing to recognize the crucial change produced by events in Russia, Stearns charged, liberals had become anomalous at the very time when the United States was most in need of liberalism's critical and creative virtues. He demanded that they fulfill their responsibility to the nation.[3]

Soon he was traveling from this implicitly hopeful demand to trenchant despair. In a series of essays, collectively pub-

131

lished in 1921 as *America and the Young Intellectuals,* Stearns gradually assumed the perspective of an outsider observing American materialism and conformity with biting, often bitter, disgust. At the same time, he no longer relied on liberalism to repair the situation, but instead put his stress on art.[4] This accelerating pessimism reached a smashing climax in his preface, dated July 4, 1921, to a group of essays written by thirty leading intellectuals and edited by Stearns under the title, *Civilization in the United States: An Inquiry by Thirty Americans.* Actually, it was an indictment more than an inquiry. Stearns epitomizes the tone in his prefatory remarks: "The most moving and pathetic fact in the social life of America to-day is emotional and aesthetic starvation, of which the mania for petty regulation, the driving, regimentating, and drilling, the secret society and its grotesque regalia, the firm grasp on the unessentials of material organization of our pleasures and gaieties are all eloquent stigmata." No longer did he suggest a remedy in liberalism or even in art. Now he advised: "we must change our hearts."[5] He himself chose a more immediate course of action by leaving for Paris, thus adding geographical emphasis to his intellectual journey. He was not to return for eleven years.

Stearns joined a band of artist-refugees whom Gertrude Stein labeled "the lost generation." Before the war they had waged a rebellion against the ruling genteel culture; now they found that their success was being celebrated in the popular arena and perverted into unaesthetic terms. From their point of view, the Roaring Twenties had simplified their artistic dissidence into carefree, mindless fun and had submerged their intellectual experimentalism beneath conformity, complacency, commercialism, and parochial patriotism. Rather than be ruled by "the clamped dominion of Puritan and Machine," as Waldo Frank described it, they extended their rebellion to exile. According to Glenway Wescott in 1924, "all writers are spiritual expatriates. Their position in this commonwealth is that of a band of revolutionaries or a cult of immoralists." With a few exceptions like Van Wyck Brooks, they denied any responsibility or possibility of reforming their country. The war years had demonstrated to them that political liberalism became a chauvinistic bulldozer, flattening ideas into clichés and destroying any dissent. They regarded both American culture and politics as machines against which human personality was helpless. As Matthew Josephson exclaimed in 1928: "Man in the mass is beastly; but masses of men subject only to the undirected machine are monstrous." Rather than be devoured by the gears, like Charlie Chaplin in *Modern Times,* these artists withdrew to the private world of sensibility.[6]

As dissenters from American capitalism, they conceivably might have been ardent supporters of Soviet Russia. It was the October Revolution, after all, which formed the initial basis for Stearns's critique of his fellow liberals. However, these artists were not revolutionaries, as Wescott contended, but rebels or bohemians. They resisted subjection to any political creed, whether conservative or radical. Like Stearns, they went to Paris rather than Moscow. Indeed, after Lenin instituted the NEP they saw little difference between Russia and the United States. Even Floyd Dell, on the staff of the pro-Soviet *Liberator,* admitted in 1922 that the poetry of Russia's revolutionary dawn had yielded to the period of prose, characterized by industrialization and hard work.[7] Along with Joseph Freeman and other radical writers, Dell lamented the lack of interest in Russia among American intellectuals, but he saw no solution to the problem. He himself was uncertain whether life under "Lenin's seven hundred million electric bulbs" would be preferable to capitalism. By 1923 *The Liberator* had succumbed to the heavy political prose of Communist dogmas, and a year later it entirely lost its old identity by becoming *The Worker's Monthly*. It had not survived the tension of revolution versus art.[8]

Most artists had none of Dell's ambivalence. In the words of one writer in 1928, Russia would evolve into "a sort of fat, complaisant, second-rate United States," eager for Americanization.

The country will become industrialized, radioized, movieized, and standardized, the huge population of illiterate peasants will be taught how to read advertisements, newspapers, and bibles, the country will develop a huge belly, and the Russian populace will placidly settle down to the preoccupation of money grubbing.[9]

American liberals surveyed the national scene with a dismay as strong as that of the artists. "What a God damned world this is!" William Allen White wrote to a friend at the end of 1920. "If anyone had told me ten years ago that our country would be what it is today, and that the world would be what it is today, I should have questioned his reason." [10] Other liberals had the same feeling. Lincoln Colcord, who had been so involved with political events during the war years, went home to Maine and, like his former fellow journalist, William Bullitt, devoted himself to literary fiction. In 1922, Colcord confessed to Colonel House: "I have no faith or hope left in politics. What disgusts me most is that politicians are such stupid politicians." [11]

But vehemence, disgust, and flight did not settle the matter. They merely were symptoms of the great inescapable question: could liberalism survive in the New Era and, if it could, in what form? Herbert Croly, editor of *The New Republic*, offered one answer in the fall of 1920. Liberalism had undergone an "eclipse," he wrote, because it assumed the existence of a classless society and therefore relied on political and educational techniques, when in fact the growing class cleavage in the United States demanded a partnership of liberals and labor to achieve industrial and social democracy.

He told his readers that he was going to vote for the Farmer–Labor presidential candidate. Four years later he supported Robert M. La Follette's Progressive campaign for the presidency, but his views were turning in new directions. Croly now defined liberalism as an affair of the human soul as much as of economic institutions. By 1927 he was arguing that, because democratic institutions were creating only greedy and complacent people, liberals must improve themselves by spiritual introspection before trying to improve the world.[12]

In effect, Croly admitted defeat. For if liberals turned their backs on popular democracy, then the paths toward the elitist cynicism of H. L. Mencken and toward the aesthetic aloofness of the expatriates were as open as Croly's road toward quasi-religion — and all three choices left aspirations of social reform far behind. There was another alternative, however, one which Roger N. Baldwin and others adopted. Writing in 1926, the director of the American Civil Liberties Union declared the death of political liberalism and the imprisonment of democracy by capitalism. "There is no 'Public'; the 'People' as a political party are unorganizable. Only economic classes can be organized. The only power that works is class power." [13] This was a fourth path, the path of radicalism, and at the end of it lay Soviet Russia. Throughout the twenties, those liberals who refused to escape from their dilemma by cynicism, aestheticism, or religion looked to the revolutionary dawn in the East and examined their dilemma in its light.

Ever since 1917, liberals had been intensely concerned with Soviet Russia, first as a potential belligerent on the Eastern Front, then as a challenger to Allied war aims, and finally as the victim of intervention. Invariably, Russia had been considered as part of a complex of world events and had been used as a convenient sounding board for liberal criticism of the Administration. During the 1920's, the question of Russia still was not totally free of the question of American diplomatic policy, but nonrecognition did not distract much of the liberals' energy. It was, after all, a passive policy, as compared with intervention, without overwhelming practical consequences either for Russia or for the West. The fact that it hampered Soviet-American trade produced annoyance but not passion among liberals. On the whole, the government's diplomatic and commercial boycott seemed so patently absurd to liberals that, if it had not symbolized the larger issue of American attitudes toward Soviet principles, they might have deemed it unworthy of discussion. By 1929, *The Nation* was calling nonrecognition "a sort of sermon in a vacuum," a gesture without effect on Soviet policies or Soviet-American trade and contradicted by the policies of major European countries. Within five years, the editors predicted, the whole controversy would seem ridiculous.[14]

But even if they occasionally adopted a supercilious tone, liberal spokesmen were never casual about Soviet Russia. After the years of war, intervention, and the Red Scare, so devastating to their expectations, they felt that they had only the October Revolution as a legacy of hope. When the United States lapsed into a "normalcy" which smothered dissent, Soviet Russia alone stood between the liberals and despair. They were ready to protect it, therefore, against any renewed American challenge. Given this emotional investment, it is not surprising that Herbert Hoover aroused the liberals to defensive fury by his American Relief Administration mission to Russia during the 1921–1923 famine. Hoover's well-known animosity to Bolshevism would have made him suspect in any case; his insistence on the release of all Americans in Soviet prisons as a prerequisite to American relief made him despicable to left-wing spokesmen.[15] And a series of incidents in 1921 soon made him, in the opinion of some liberals, a covert counterrevolutionary.

Already in January, at a meeting in Philadelphia of the

Medical Relief for Soviet Russia, Rabbi Judah Magnes had described attempts by the State Department, the ARA, and the Red Cross to restrict the relief work of the American Friends Service Committee in Russia, while they themselves abstained from any relief efforts. Magnes clearly implied that they had no tenable reason except political motives for this behavior.[16] These imputed sins of omission were provocative, but they paled in contrast to the sin of commission which T. C. C. Gregory, a former ARA director in Hungary, revealed in the June issue of *The World's Work*. With frank pride he explained how he had used the resources of his office to aid the overthrow of the Communist leader, Bela Kun, in 1919. *The Freeman* did not hesitate, therefore, to describe famine relief in Russia as the "latest intervention move." [17]

Having this evidence for their darkest suspicions, liberals decided to channel their relief through the AFSC rather than Hoover's ARA. By October of 1921, the Russian Famine Fund was formed for this purpose, with Allen Wardwell as national chairman and Robert M. Lovett as executive chairman.[18] But Hoover's insistence on centralizing all relief under his own agency only converted this potential solution into further friction. In the fall of 1921, he instructed the State Department to issue no passports to Quaker relief workers without ARA permission. Only after vehement complaints by the AFSC against this infringement of their autonomy did he cancel the order in January 1922.[19] At the same time, however, he initiated a publicity campaign against several relief groups which, he charged, gave their funds to the Soviet government for distribution according to political lines and without identifying the American origin of the funds. *The Nation* issued an angry censure: "With thousands starving to death, such national pride comes strangely close to murderous interference with the task of succor." [20]

The Russian relief effort ended with as much liberal bitterness as it had begun with. "Mr. Hoover Stabs Russia," the title of a *Nation* editorial accused in March 1923. The occasion was the ARA director's announcement that, according to reports from his chief representative in Russia, William N. Haskell, the famine needs had been met. On the contrary, *The Nation* argued, the full text of Haskell's cables called for reconstruction work to follow relief if the effects of the famine were to be really eradicated. *The Nation* concluded that Hoover had deliberately misquoted the cables in order to rationalize his termination of aid to Russia. *The Survey*, which had already been critical of ARA's reluctance to fight the famine with full vigor, vehemently echoed the charges of its sister journal.[21] Nevertheless, by June the ARA mission did end, and Hoover's announcement of its success effectively undermined the fundraising by groups like the AFSC.[22]

Thus the Russian relief effort, which temporarily displaced the general public's anti-Soviet feeling by warm sympathy for the suffering Russian masses, provoked among liberal and radical groups an accentuated sensitivity to that anti-Soviet feeling. Their accusations were occasionally so bitter and so unreasonable that they must be interpreted as the product of anxious defensiveness toward Soviet Russia. Even when the American government and people were acting with more apparent benevolence than at any time since the October Revolution, liberals suspected their motives. The suspicion contrasts vividly with their exhilaration in 1917: they no longer trusted the people, they were bewildered aliens in their own country.

Even if the liberals turned to Soviet Russia as an ideological refuge from the United States of the twenties, the fact is that they were refugees rather than converts. They refused to accept Soviet principles and practices simply because they were Soviet. Instead, they evaluated by their own standards.

138

In the apt phrase of Trotsky, they would be "fellow travelers," but no more.

The Nation celebrated the sixth anniversary of the Bolshevik Revolution with lusty acclamation: "In a world that is sick with the diseases that breed from capitalist-imperialism, the virility of Russia may hold out the best hope for civilization." [23] The metaphor blithely simplified a complex situation. In 1923 the crippling injuries of famine and economic dislocation were still quite apparent; hunger, disease, and poverty still pressed with appalling weight on the Russian populace. But the NEP had checked their growth and was beginning to exert a rejuvenating influence. This was the side which *The Nation* stressed and for which it could find enough evidence to convince those who were predisposed to hope for Soviet success. At the same time, those with hostile predisposition could find plentiful evidence for their dour observations and dire predictions. It was a question of what one wanted to see.

During the next five years, sympathizers presented statistics and reports which gave ample proof that the Soviet Union was moving swiftly toward economic stability.[24] As Lincoln Steffens discovered during a Soviet journey in 1923: "Moscow is booming. Russia is beginning to live bravely and smile." He based his enthusiasm on the "good news" that the Communists were "on their course, proceeding as they began and they intend to see it through ruthlessly." [25] The liberals' exultation, on the other hand, derived from very different premises, ones which would have disquieted the Soviet leaders. For they attributed Soviet success to the fact that, contrary to Steffens, the Communist leadership had taken the *new* course of the quasi-capitalist NEP. Indeed, their comments occasionally converged with those made by American antagonists to the Soviet regime. The editors of *The Freeman*, for example, who considered themselves to be radicals and friends of the Revolution, were relieved by Lenin's adoption of the NEP. As believers in the single-tax program of Henry George, they saw in socialist and communist doctrines only a "fantastic impracticability." [26] Similarly, *The New Republic* reported in 1927 that "it is rather what the Russian people have done for Communism which has enabled it to survive than what Communism has done for the Russian people." In May 1928, it regretted indications that Stalin might be abandoning pragmatic economic policy for the doctrinaire Communist approach advocated by Trotsky. Perhaps the lessons of the past decade had not been understood in Moscow, the editors speculated sadly.[27]

What, then, distinguished American liberals from those who denounced the Soviet Union without qualification? What redeeming virtues did they find to prevent their exceptions from becoming the rule? John Dewey offered the answer in his account of a visit to the USSR during 1928: "Perhaps the most significant thing in Russia, after all, is not the effort at economic transformation, but the will to use an economic change as the means of developing a popular cultivation, especially an esthetic one, such as the world has never known." [28] American liberals admired the October Revolution primarily for its cultural rather than its economic achievements. For visiting social workers, educators, and social scientists, who constituted such a large proportion of American tourists to the USSR during the twenties, Russia presented a living test of their ideas. It was for them a social laboratory." In the words of George S. Counts, one of Dewey's colleagues at Columbia Teachers' College: "No one can dwell long in Moscow without realizing that he is living in *the other half of the world*. The consequence is, I think, a gain in perspective which can be secured in no other way." [29] An advertisement in *The Nation* by the travel department of the

Amalgamated Bank of New York appealed directly to these motives and these people:

GO TO SOVIET RUSSIA

Intellectuals, social workers, professional men and women are welcomed most cordially in Soviet Russia. . . . where the world's most gigantic social experiment is being made — amidst a galaxy of picturesque nationalities, wondrous scenery, splendid architecture and exotic civilizations.[30]

After a generation of Progressive agitation for social justice, these liberals naturally were impressed with the numerous laws protecting and benefiting Russian workers. The free medical care, the paid vacations, the attention to improved factory conditions — these were among many aspects envied by American visitors in the land of the proletariat.[31] In 1927, for example, a group of women who took the title of the American Investigation Committee on Russian Women returned with praise for the unique freedom and status enjoyed by their sex in the Soviet Union. By contrast, they declared, the United States was decidedly retrograde in its treatment of women.[32] Numerous other American observers, particularly women, enthusiastically outlined the extensive Soviet program of free medical care for mothers, the ingenious system of nurseries for children of working women, and the legalization of abortion and the encouragement of birth control, which relieved women of unwanted children. Most controversial were the liberal divorce laws permitting either husband or wife to end the marriage without complex litigation or explanation, but which also required the husband to support his wife for six months or a year thereafter, if necessary.[33] "Russia since the revolution has been an experimental laboratory in sex relationship," one writer announced after a three-month visit in 1926. He and others concluded that the results were admirable: the government's healthy attitude

141

toward sex encouraged love, strengthened the family, diminished prostitution, and almost precluded pornography.[34] A few also remarked, however, that the new freedom had incited desperate conflict between traditional parents and the defiant revolutionary youth.[35] But as an official of the Young Men's Christian Association emphasized, the Communist generation rebelled in favor of social idealism, not jazz, automobiles, and petting parties.[36]

Soviet Russia was indeed "the other half of the world" where the laboring class had been elevated to social supremacy. The shabbily dressed crowds of workers in museums, theaters, and the new Parks of Culture and Leisure produced vivid impressions on American visitors. W. E. B. DuBois, the Negro social scientist, returned in 1926 with "astonishment and wonder at the revelation of Russia." Five years earlier he had taken a wait-and-see attitude toward the Revolution. But direct experience with a society of proletarian privilege overwhelmed this caution: "If what I have seen with my eyes and heard with my ears in Russia is Bolshevism," he wrote, "I am a Bolshevik." [37] The Soviet cultural program stirred American liberals to exult over the artistic awakening among the masses and to excuse the heavy-handed propaganda of movies and drama as an inevitable but transient product of the Revolution.[38] According to John Dos Passos, those American critics who disparaged Soviet theatrical productions were distracted by fear of the secret police, by the strange and uncomfortable conditions, and by ignorance of the language. "These gentlemen are completely wrong," he said. "It ought to be obvious to anybody that while the American theater is dying, the Russian theatre is at the beginning of a period of enormous growth." [39] Even more boldly, a highschool principal declared that the Soviets were preparing for "the very first culture to be truly human." [40]

Walter Duranty was obviously in a minority when he

pointed out that Russians preferred Charlie Chaplin, Buster Keaton, Jackie Coogan, and especially Douglas Fairbanks to the arid, didactic art of their own country.[41] Significantly, none of the visiting American liberals mentioned this fact. Their silence suggests a determination to find a new breed of men in Russia, one which appreciated the "truly human" culture of idealism rather than the all-too-human culture of Douglas Fairbanks and *The Saturday Evening Post*. After "the people" had failed them at home, they turned to "the people" of the USSR to rescue their hopes.

Because a society seeks to implant its fundamental values in its children, the reaction by Americans to Soviet education illuminates their general attitudes. The Communist Revolution signaled the beginning of a massive attack upon the illiteracy which kept three quarters of the total population, and even more of the peasantry, in mental darkness. In addition to enlarging the school system and bringing peasants and especially workers into it, the Communists sought to introduce a new curriculum which would integrate the classroom into the outer world. Classical subjects, rote learning, and authoritarian discipline were replaced by the Complex Method. With the teacher as guide rather than master, students would focus on practical problems of industrialization and agricultural cultivation, while forming student governments and Communist political organizations to implement their ideas. The turbulence of civil war almost totally prevented the Soviets from putting these aims into effect until the early 1920's. Even then, as many Americans noted, deplorable material conditions in the schools enormously hampered the application of the new educational philosophy.[42]

Actually, that philosophy was newer for Russians than for visiting Americans. As Soviet education officials readily admitted, the Complex Method was simply an imported and communized version of American progressive education. In

143

fact, between 1917 and 1927 at least five of John Dewey's books were translated into Russian.[43] It is hardly surprising, therefore, that Dewey, Counts, and other advocates of progressive education praised the work of Soviet schools. Yet their ardor went beyond mere authorial pride. Lucy L. W. Wilson, a Philadelphia highschool principal, exclaimed: "For the first time in modern history, a new school has risen out of the *ethos* of the people. For the first time in history, a people has a new cultural ideal on which to build." In her opinion, the new education system had implications stretching far beyond classroom boundaries: "The last hundred years have been ours; the next century may be Russia's." [44] Dewey restrained himself from such global inferences but, after his 1928 visit to the USSR, he concluded that educational reform would succeed only in a society based on cooperative rather than competitive principles. Although the Soviet leaders borrowed their educational ideas from the United States, he said, the noteworthy fact is that they were incorporating them more organically into their school system than American educators had ever been able to do.[45] Counts also came away inspired with the lofty social vision that "we should be endeavoring to make the school function in the building of a new civilization." [46]

Amid their enthusiasm, however, these American educators recognized that the Soviet school system was as much a political as an educational organ. They might exclaim over the harmony achieved between society and classroom, but that harmony also entailed total control by the Communist Party and its doctrines. During an address in 1916, Dewey crystallized one premise of his pragmatic philosophy into a succinct axiom: "the ultimate fate is the fatality of ignorance, and the ultimate wickedness is lack of faith in the possibilities of intelligence applied inventively and constructively." [47] A decade later he was confronting the Communist philosophy which subjected intelligence to a dogmatic view of history and man, which imposed the fate of infallibility on its subjects, condemning all dissent as ignorance or treason. Could Dewey and his disciples praise Soviet schools without violating their own ideals?

Lucy Wilson simply noted the intolerance of Soviet leadership and ignored the larger problem.[48] Counts went a step farther by explaining that *some* directing value system was necessary if educational anarchy was to be avoided, and he preferred the harsh social idealism of the USSR to the laissez-faire cynicism of the United States.[49] But Dewey adopted the most radical solution to the dilemma. Though recognizing that the Soviets identified education with propaganda, he insisted that Communist indoctrination would be displaced by intellectual independence and a cooperative mentality. "It seems impossible," he declared, "that an education intellectually free will not militate against a servile acceptance of dogma as dogma." [50] On its face, the assumption that Soviet education was intellectually free flagrantly contradicted his admission that it was propaganda. But Dewey had a broader perspective by which, presumably, he hoped to escape this impasse. In his opinion, the real Russian Revolution had not occurred in the government or economy, but in the hearts and minds of the people, whose energy and consciousness had been liberated. That psychological awakening was a type of education which, he believed, would survive any dogma of Marxian curriculum.[51]

This solution requires a synthesis of comments scattered throughout Dewey's report on Russia, a synthesis which he himself did not make and which, ultimately, is more confusing than convincing. Perhaps it is simpler to agree with the terse dictum of the *Bolshaya sovetskaya entsiklopediya*, in its quite friendly article on the American philosopher in 1931, that "Dewey looks upon education as a true bourgeois-liberal." [52] But Dewey and his fellow liberals denied any such definitive divorce between themselves and the Communists. The characteristic of their attitudes toward Soviet Russia was precisely the strained, often confused insistence on approving her Revolution — or as much of it as possible. Inevitably, the crucial test of their sympathy became the question of freedom. They could easily praise social legislation, culture, and education, but behind these appearances loomed the troubling fact of the class dictatorship which had created them. In confronting that fact, American sympathizers engaged in a startling variety of intellectual maneuvers.

Lincoln Steffens adopted one of the most articulate and confident positions. As he explained to a friend in 1926, the Russian Revolution "seemed to me to require a complete change of my mind, just, for example, as Einstein's relativity does. Nothing I used to think could stand in the face of that Russian experience." After 1917 he discarded liberalism and spent the rest of his life contemplating the significance of Soviet Russia. He set out to be the scientist of social change, explaining rather than judging events, surrendering the concepts of right and wrong which, he said, deterred liberals from understanding developments in Russia and elsewhere. Russia was "the future" and therefore one could not ignore or despise it without also isolating oneself from events of the world. He himself hoped to discover laws of revolution.[53]

Steffens' determined relativism led to strange conclusions. In a letter of July 1926, for example, he described the Soviet leaders as righteous fanatics who demanded total commitment and excused no mistakes. Life under the Soviets, Steffens said, was like service in an army at war — without kindness or tolerance. "But they are heroes too. I am for them to the last drop, I am a patriot for Russia; the Future is there; Russia will win out and it will save the world. That is my belief. But I don't want to live there." The younger generation could endure or even love the regime, "but for me who am ruined by the easy life of the old culture Russia is impossible. My service to it has to be outside here." [54] In other words, historical inevitability took precedence over personal feelings. His relativism was so firm that he felt bound to support Communism, however much he disliked it, because the laws of history indicated that his dislike derived from outdated values. Steffens was acting from more than an abstract conviction, however. As one historian has noted, he was "intrigued by the idea of change for the sake of change" and committed to "the pragmatic rule-of-the-result." [55] Because Soviet Russia satisfied these conditions, Steffens attached his relativist loyalties to Communist dogma.

Few other American sympathizers could imitate this delicate intellectual posture, so close to the brink of paradox. But, as Steffens was keenly aware, neither could they find comfortable safety in the liberal certainties of 1917–1919. Those certainties no longer applied to the world and therefore endangered any vestigial advocates. The experience of Emma Goldman in Soviet Russia poignantly proved that fact. In a pamphlet of 1918 she had expressed her ardent conviction that the October Revolution was "a miracle," that Lenin and Trotsky "have their ears close to the heart-beat of the Russian people," and that they "represent the most fundamental, far-reaching and all-embracing principles of human freedom and of economic well-being." [56] In December 1919, she and her fellow anarchist, Alexander Berkman, were deported to Russia by the Justice Department, only to discover that the miracle was, at first hand, a "phantom." It was as if she had suddenly come close to an Impressionist painting. The coherent brightness and bliss dissolved, under close scrutiny, into a "grotesque" reality of red tape, food rations, militarization of labor, and Communist tyranny. The Bolsheviks, she decided, had destroyed the Revolution.[57]

Her chronicle of disillusionment delighted antagonists of Soviet Russia and dismayed sympathizers, but it really told more about her preconceptions than about Russia. Certainly the Soviet leaders never pretended that they were fashioning a revolution to fit anarchist ideals, and they certainly would have scoffed at her expectation of finding a "great spiritual awakening." [58] They believed in Marxism, not miracles. Emma Goldman's defection was as irrelevant to the truth of the Soviet Union as was the unswerving loyalty of Isadora Duncan, who announced, shortly after her arrival in 1921, that she had looked "with clairvoyant eyes" beneath material things into Russia's "great collective soul" and had seen "the greatest miracle that has happened to humanity for two thousand years." [59]

As Floyd Dell remarked, the Revolution had moved from poetry to prose. Now the liberals had to re-examine their original criteria of evaluation if they were to escape the phantoms and fantasies of Goldman and Duncan. In 1920 it still might have been adequate to argue, as one correspondent wrote in *The Nation*: "Russia has no time for habeas corpus, free speech and such-like refinements which our own government found superfluous in time of war." [60] But as the decade continued and the Soviet dictatorship did not relent, such excuses no longer sufficed. In 1925, for example, Paxton Hibben frankly declared that judging the USSR by the standards of Western democracy was equivalent to criticizing a giraffe for not living in the water. The Communists conceived of government as an economic, not political, function, Hibben explained, and he admired them within that framework.[61] Another sympathizer, Jerome Davis, developed this point by telling readers of *Current History* that Russian workers, enjoying economic freedom, did not care that the government stifled opponents who would take these freedoms away.[62] Meanwhile, Oswald Garrison Villard, editor of *The Nation*, was annoyed by the newspapers' furor over his public criticisms of dictatorships everywhere, whether in Italy, Spain, or Russia. Contrary to the *New York Times* and other newspaper reports, he wrote to a friend, he was not "abandoning" the Soviet Union because he had never supported it. "I have only demanded fair play and straight news about it and expressed the hope that we should eventually get from it some residue of value in human government." [63]

Firm but qualified support became increasingly common among liberals during the twenties.[64] Roger Baldwin articulated this perspective with striking clarity in his book, *Liberty under the Soviets*. After a two-month Soviet journey in 1927, the director of the American Civil Liberties Union declared: "The fairest test by which to judge the Soviet experiment in relation to 'liberty' is not by Western standards of political or civil liberties, but by the effects of the dictatorship's controls and repression on its own avowed object of creating a 'free and classless society,' with the state abolished." [65] This was a thoughtful and consistent relativism, but it could not altogether appease the qualms of many American liberals. Baldwin himself noted that the Soviet leadership often was unnecessarily cruel and could safely permit more freedom.[66] Others, lacking his socialist beliefs, had much less patience. The execution of Monsignor Buchkavich in 1923, for example, provoked *The New Republic* to didactic anger at this "sinister piece of news." If the priest was indeed executed for having given religious instruction to persons under eighteen years of age, the editors said, "the outlook for the construction in the near future of anything like moral and social order in Russia is black indeed." [67] *The Nation* was in the embarrassing position of having predicted, only days before the incident, that the Soviet experiment would become more humane in its practices. Now it protested the execution but also criticized the American press for its silence on the plight of American political prisoners and on the British punishments of Sir Roger Casement and 172 Hindus.[68]

The clash between Trotsky and Stalin disquieted the liberals even more profoundly. After Trotsky's removal from several offices in 1925, *The Nation* voiced a guarded criticism: "The excommunication of Trotzky will convince many that a substantial core of truth lies behind the obviously exaggerated stories of indecent political persecution in the Soviet Republic. Russia, with her history of centuries of despotism, is not likely to adopt the Western forms of democracy at once if at all, but the form of dictatorship is bound to be modified." [69] The final comment was a bit of dogmatic optimism which context undercut as a nonsequitur and which Stalin's later actions converted into irony. Others struck out more bluntly. The socialist weekly, *The New Leader*, exclaimed that the Revolution was devouring its own children, while *The New Republic* denounced Stalin's dictatorial behavior as the path toward disastrous internal war of terror against terror.[70] The repercussions of the Trotsky affair spread everywhere, including the American Communist camp. Max Eastman, editor of the ill-fated *Liberator*, in 1926 published the secret "testament" in which Lenin urged the replacement of Stalin as General Secretary. According to Eastman, the destiny of the whole revolution was at stake in the Stalin-Trotsky struggle, and he warned: "A Dictatorship of the Secretariat is being substituted for the Dictatorship of the Proletariat." [71]

When *The Nation* celebrated the tenth anniversary of the Revolution, its editorial reflected the turbulence within Russia and within the minds of American sympathizers. On the one hand it hailed the USSR as "a land of hope" where the battle for literacy, health, and economic freedom was achieving impressive success. In vivid contrast to this rejuvenation, the West was wearied and disillusioned "after the emotional debauch of a war which almost drove democracy out of our

world." On the other hand, the editors recognized and condemned "the brutalities of the Red dictatorship. We have a
horror of all religious fanatics, of all men who feel so sure
of themselves that murder and lying become acceptable means,
however beautiful the goal or god to which they make their
sacrifices." Nonetheless, *The Nation* still felt a duty to defend
the Soviets, even if it required the unenviable tactic of justify-
ing one evil by a worse one. "But all things are relative; and
we live in a world which has just poured out the blood of ten
million boys, and our Western countries were ready to let
more thousands go to death if they could crush the workers'
republic of Russia." By the end of the editorial, this contrast
became positive and almost fervent: "The scars of the Czarist
centuries still lie deep, and the regime which brought so
much hope and freedom still fails of its broadest destiny;
but in this muddy age its ten years shine." [72]

The convolutions of *The Nation*'s argument embody the
predicament of American liberals as they evaluated Soviet
Russia in the twenties. Enthusiasm for Soviet social reform
competed with uneasiness at Soviet dictatorship, forcing
sympathizers to struggle laboriously before they could reach
an ultimate optimism. Yet they insisted on undertaking the
struggle and strained for even a qualified enthusiasm, until
the historian finally wonders: why all this exertion? Why,
in the first place, did they devote so much emotional and intellectual energy to the Soviet Union? And, given that they did,
why did they invariably seek to minimize or justify the distasteful aspects of the USSR? *The Nation* indicated one sort
of answer by its reference to the war and intervention.
Despite the passing years, the shock of these events still
affected liberals' thinking and still drove them, in mind and
often in body, toward Russia. A further answer was provided
in 1928 by a liberal who returned from the USSR with a
rhetorical question: "And is not a certain gorgeousness

created in the atmosphere beyond our Valley of Disillusion by the spectacle of vigorous, apparently intelligent, desperately sincere men devoting their utmost energy to the attainment and establishment of any ideal, old or new?" [73] In other words, he would admire *any* ideal, regardless of its content, simply out of the need to escape the American wasteland of mindless prosperity.

Yet the New Era's energetic pursuit of general happiness also represented an ideal. Moreover, it seemed extraordinarily like the Communist goal, even if it upheld capitalist method. To most liberals, however, the resemblances were merely verbal while the differences were profound. Instead of "trivial excitements" and "increasing cheapness," Soviet Russia was pervaded by "burning zeal," "religious ardor," "youth, enthusiasm and faith in what they are doing," and a "thirst for culture." In the words of John Dewey: "Freed from the load of subjection to the past, it seems charged with the ardor of creating a new world." [74] He and others acclaimed that ardor and believed in Soviet promises of a new world not because they were Communists, but because they were liberals whose world had suddenly become decadent. If the USSR was freed of its past, it also freed them of their own, which included the debacle of the Wilsonian crusade. The Communists allowed them to be reassured that their original ideals could still be fulfilled, even if by strangers' hands.

Moreover, as Dewey also remarked, they felt "a certain envy" for the Russian intellectuals who had "a unified religious social faith [which] brings with it such simplification and integration of life." Intellectuals in other countries could be only critical, he added, but in Russia they "have a task that is total and constructive. They are organic members of an organic going movement." [75] Thus Dewey generalized his admiration for Soviet schools to the whole Soviet experiment, using the same organic terminology. In so doing he also resolved, at least verbally, the troubling question of freedom: to function, even at the cost of the right to dissent, was preferable to impotent criticism. This was another instance of choosing the lesser evil, of course, but liberals could always justify the tactic by reviving their old premise that the USSR would eventually evolve toward political freedom. Oswald Garrison Villard, who visited the Soviet Union in 1929, even claimed that it might be the freest of all countries because "it has been spared the curse of Anglo-Saxon hypocrisy." [76]

Ardor and functionalism satisfied the liberals' need to hope and could even defer their demand for freedom, but they left unanswered the basic question of aims. On the one hand, as Heywood Broun sardonically noted, the Communists' ascetic and intolerant principles strikingly resembled the puritanism which American intellectuals had so vehemently condemned since before the war.[77] If those principles also characterized the future Soviet utopia, would the American liberals find it any more palatable than puritan American culture? To Joseph Wood Krutch the answer was clear. He shared the intellectuals' disgust with American culture but found equal fault in Soviet materialism, which, he said, evaded the fundamental problem of man's spiritual relation to the natural world.[78]

On the other hand, the Soviet Union's avid imitation and borrowing of American capitalist techniques, including a reverence for "Fordization," provoked the question of how Soviet success would differ from the New Era version. Indeed, the adoption of the NEP seemed to justify the claims by American business leaders that the USSR would evolve along American lines. What guaranteed that the present Soviet ardor and idealism, amid general poverty, would not dissipate into complacency and "trivial excitements" when the Communists attained their goal of general welfare?

The pro-Soviet liberals ignored these two treacherous problems, which could lead only to aesthetic aloofness, doctrinaire Communism, or confusion, none of which they found desirable. This intellectual evasion reveals the degree to which they still were Progressives. Lincoln Steffens had decided that liberalism was dead and turned to its successor, the Soviet program. But others disputed his diagnosis. In their opinion, liberalism had survived the wounds of war and the near-suffocation of the Red Scare and normalcy. They still were loyal liberals, though chastened and cautious, and they turned to the Soviet Union to find, not a new faith, but an outlet for their old one. Thus, they admired social legislation, progressive education, a quasi-capitalist economy, and, most of all, ardent idealism. At the same time, just as they had justified strong powers for the American government during wartime, they minimized the repressive dictatorship as a necessary transition to a future when prosperity would permit the leisure of dissent. But this confidence in the Soviet future collided with liberals' disgust at the way in which Americans had used belligerency and then prosperity to stifle dissent. Significantly, the liberals no longer spoke to or about "the people." Now, like Dewey, they envied their Russian counterparts who had organic membership in a movement practicing "democratic centralism." They would accept Progressive government without Progressive freedom. In this respect, liberalism was, if not dying, at least transformed drastically.

When the stock-market crash signaled the end of the New Era late in 1929, it also renewed the possibility for liberals to fulfill their ideals in their own country. Once again America called out for reform. But at the beginning of what some historians would later regard as the second Progressive era, the Progressive creed had become more complicated and ambiguous. It could either reassert the prewar faith or adopt the new faith preached by the new missionaries in the Soviet Union.

Despite the NEP and the famine relief, the Soviet regime still impressed most Americans as a treacherous evangel of bloody revolution. But, contrary to the sentiments of leftists, they were confident that workers would reject the Communist creed.

THE MISSIONARY

—Knott in the Dallas *News*.

VI / Labor and Proletarian Russia

Labor understands its mission in Russia.
— Sidney Hillman, address to the fifth biennial convention
of the Amalgamated Clothing Workers, May 1922

In a letter written in April 1920, Samuel Gompers, president of the American Federation of Labor, described the success of his union in these terms: "There is no labor movement in the world that has achieved for the workers the results that have been gained by the American Federation of Labor. There is no organization that has wasted less time in the pursuit of fantastic and untried theories." [1] Gompers had a right to this pride. During his almost uninterrupted leadership since 1886, the AF of L had increased its membership to more than four million, twice the total of 1914.[2] At the same time, labor as a whole had achieved impressively higher wage levels and, even more important, recognition in the Clayton Act of their right to organize. Gompers' personal prestige had risen correspondingly, so that it was a matter of course for President Wilson to appoint him in 1916 as labor's representative on the Council of National Defense. It was such evidence which provoked Gompers to make his complacent survey of the labor scene.

Yet his reference to "fantastic and untried theories" injected a shrill undertone into his complacency, implying a threat by invisible proponents of such theories. In his writings and speeches of the postwar years, Gompers permitted

157

no doubt as to whom he had in mind: the Russian Bolsheviks and their American supporters. Although he himself had become interested in unionism during the 1870's under the impetus of an adherence to socialism, he had quickly deferred theory for the practical problems of constructing a union. By the turn of the century, after enduring the attacks of Daniel De Leon's Socialist Labor Party and of the syndicalist International Workers of the World, he had become implacably hostile to both socialism and socialists. Instead of governmental ownership of industry, he preached "voluntarism," a doctrine which taught labor that progress would derive from self-help and self-rule.[3] As a leading supporter of the National Civic Federation, an organization founded in 1900 with the aim of reconciling unions and management, he scorned the tenets of class conflict as unworkable in the United States.[4]

The war years both intensified and, apparently, validated his hostility to socialism. On the one hand, as Gompers joined Wilson in the war effort, arguing that labor would protect its ideals and achievements only by constructive participation, the AF of L thrived. On the other hand, by contrast, the American socialist movement split into quarreling fragments as some socialists vainly preached pacifist internationalism to the bellicose American people while other socialists supported the war.[5]

At this very time of triumph over his domestic enemies, however, Gompers had to confront the new and more serious challengers establishing themselves in Russia. The Bolsheviks were, in his opinion, "pirates" who had "declared war upon the established order about which the fabric of civilized life had been woven." [6] Throughout the remaining seven years of his life after the October Revolution, Gompers incessantly and vitriolically assailed the Bolshevik regime. In 1921, with the aid of the socialist William E. Walling, he combined some of his indictments with a collection of the Communists' own statements, publishing the result under the suggestive title of *Out of Their Own Mouths*.[7] In the same year, the AF of L withdrew from the International Federation of Trade Unions, which he had helped to reorganize at Amsterdam in 1919, after the IFTU called on member unions to act against the blockade of Russia, to refuse to handle the arms and munitions bound for Poland in her war with Russia, and, finally, to participate in a general strike as a step toward socialism. Such purposes, said Gompers, were "wholly foreign" to those for which the IFTU was formed.[8] Meanwhile, he did not spare "the so-called liberals of America" who, by supporting the Communist regime and aims, had "fallen victim to a mania for mysticism," were scorning the American labor movement by rushing "with abnormal appetite into the social and moral violence of Moscow," were "guilty of betraying democracy in the most portentous situation of our time." [9]

Thus Gompers, the most powerful American labor leader, aided American employers in a defense of the capitalist system. After having joined the war against the armies of the Central Powers, he joined the war against the propaganda of Communist Russia, becoming a fervent patron of the Red Scare and, inescapably, an apologist for capitalism. Without embarrassment he declared that the AF of L "stands squarely and unequivocally for the defense and maintenance of the existing order." [10] For that order, although still open to innumerable improvements, possessed the fundamental virtues of democracy, liberalism, and the autonomy of the labor movement.[11] The bloodshed and oppression in Russia proved, he declared, that the Communists had no use for such virtues. They sought power, not justice, and achieved it at the expense of all classes, the working class included. Only sentimentalists were deceived by the unilateral theory which, imputing all evils to capitalism, sought to blur moral issues and responsibilities. Gompers saw no place in the American system for such theory.[12]

Gompers' conservatism is not surprising, in view of the fact that, by the end of World War I, he and his union were prospering. The Communist attack on American capitalism necessarily threatened the AF of L which had succeeded within the capitalistic framework and therefore had a vested interest in it. Even when that success began to dissipate during the twenties, when membership declined by one half, the union's official adherence to voluntarism and anti-Communism did not weaken.[13]

This intransigency was a reflection of the "bourgeois" views of most American workers. It was rigidified, however, by the autocratic control maintained by Gompers, loyally backed by an executive council of equally conservative views. The political structure of the AF of L permitted the larger unions to dominate the annual conventions and thereby the council, thus giving extraordinarily long tenure and oligarchic power to a small group of men.[14] William Green, succeeding Gompers in 1924, continued the firmly anti-Communist policy with no modification whatsoever, except an increased stress on the menace of Communism in America.[15] As a result, whenever the radicals at the conventions proposed a resolution tolerant of the Bolshevik regime, an enormous majority dutifully defeated it. By 1927, the radicals no longer pursued their Sisyphean task.[16]

Yet even if the conservative membership and oligarchic leadership were primarily responsible for the failure of dissidents to get their views accepted, in large part the failure was due to the minority's tactical and intellectual shortcomings. The actual strength of this group is impossible to determine. But scattered bits of evidence indicate that many workers did not share Gompers' views on Russia. One of Senator William Borah's constituents, for example, wrote to him in March 1918 that he "and all of my fellow workers" in Twin Falls, Idaho, were concerned that the Allies were in league with the Central Powers "to crush the workingmen's Government of Russia or to simply drive the workers of the same in the ranks of the Central Powers and thus prolong the war to the detriment of the workers of all Nations." [17] In January 1921, representatives of various labor organizations, claiming to speak for more than two million workers, testified before the Senate Foreign Relations Committee in favor of resuming trade with Soviet Russia.[18] From California to Florida to Wisconsin, AF of L groups in the early twenties passed resolutions or, in at least two cases, petitioned the Senate in favor of resumption of trade with Russia, diplomatic recognition of Lenin's regime, or both.[19] One delegate at the 1920 convention of the International Association of Machinists, after a majority had approved a resolution demanding recognition and affirming the interdependence of the working classes of all nations, even referred to Woodrow Wilson as "that thing in the White House" because of the President's role in the Russian military intervention.[20]

These protests were symptomatic but too sporadic to exert any effect on labor's top spokesmen. Those who took their dissents to the floor of the AF of L conventions were equally ineffectual. In the first place, despite outspoken support by several delegations and perhaps tacit support by others, the radicals failed to organize their forces effectively, if they organized at all.[21] Added to tactical insufficiency was intellectual clumsiness. In 1922, Timothy Healy, of the Brotherhood of Stationary Firemen and Oilers, and Max Hayes, of the Typographical Union, dissented from the hostile report on Russia written by the committee on which they served. Yet Healy was able to meet the majority's lengthy documentation of Soviet crimes with nothing better than evasion. "We are not dreamers or fanatics," he declared. "All my life I have been a believer in the principle that all people should establish governments according to their own ideals and they should not be dictated to by other peoples . . . and they should have the good will at least of the American Federation of Labor to back them up in their aspirations." [22] Yet one of the strongest and most undeniable points in the anti-Bolshevik attack was that the Russian people, being denied the right to vote or form opposition parties, were being "dictated to" by their own leaders.

Hayes chose a different but even more disastrous line of argument. "I sometimes believe that it really does not amount to much what action we take," for American capitalists would, he predicted, soon realize the richness of the Russian market and force Washington to provide official sanction and security for such trade. "That would mean," Hayes concluded, "that these tens of thousands of American workers would return to their jobs, where they are now [in the postwar depression] compelled to tramp the streets." Matthew Woll, a vice-president of the AF of L, a delegate from the International Photoengravers' Union, and one of Gompers' most faithful supporters, quickly caught Hayes in an embarrassing polemical squeeze. The minority report, he pointed out, urged recognition and trade relations "for a purely selfish motive, a motive of securing employment for American workers, and that alone." Having tacitly suggested the altruistic motives of the majority's stand, Woll went on to discredit Hayes's argument altogether. In advocating exploitation of Russia's natural resources by American capitalists, he said, the minority sought the accomplishment of the very thing which they condemned at home. "We who have been denouncing capitalism are now becoming the champions, the guardians, of capitalism," he remarked sarcastically.[23]

It is hardly surprising, then, that Gompers consistently held the upper hand; not only was the majority of his union's members conservative, but both his political machinery and his intellectual strategy were superior to those of the dissenters. His position was in many ways an easier one to uphold, of course, for he could rely on an emotional anti-Bolshevik bias throughout the nation and could cite facts which appealed to that bias. Counterargument, if it was to be at all effective, had to appeal to the more abstract concept that recognition and trade should be granted to any stable government, no matter how heinous or "un-American." In the aftermath of the Red Scare, such a stance was scorned as naive or as a disguise for Communist leanings. With proponents as awkward as Healy and Hayes, it collapsed utterly.

Gompers dominated his own union, but he could not extend his sovereignty to labor groups outside of the AF of L. And it was an independent union, the Amalgamated Clothing Workers of America, which posed the most forceful challenge to Gompers' views on Russia. Certainly the situation was ripe for such action. The needle trades were organized in the late nineteenth century under the tutelage of young Jewish socialist intellectuals from Russia. In the words of Joseph Schlossberg, the general secretary of the Amalgamated from its beginnings until 1940 and a radical socialist throughout his life: "The fight against the sweatshop was their fight against capitalism and for socialism." [24] At the outbreak of the world war, about one half of the union's workers were East European Jews.[25]

This intellectual heritage alone set the Amalgamated at odds with Gompers' tendency toward pragmatic, nonpolitical unionism. Yet the alienation assumed much more specific terms: at the 1914 convention of the United Garment Workers, the New York and Chicago delegations seceded from the AF of L union, protesting against the autocratic rule of Tom Rickert, its president and a friend of Gompers', and

against the AF of L's refusal to countenance industrial unionism. Following the rupture of relations, the rebels chose
Sidney Hillman to lead them into a new union organized by
industry rather than craft. In December 1914, the Amalgamated was formally born, and Hillman served as its president
until his death thirty-two years later. As a Russian Jew and
socialist who had fled from arrest by the tsarist police, he
was a natural choice for these men of similar background.[26]

The quarrel over the Bolshevik Revolution was, then, only
a segment of a much larger dispute about basic aims and
strategy of American unionism. Yet it was a segment synthe-
sizing these larger issues because, as had been noted before
and will be noted throughout this study, the issue of Soviet
Russia invariably aroused American observers to a pitch of
passion which exposed their basic values. Certainly this was
the case with Gompers who devoted a disproportionate
amount of energy, in the last years of his life, to the Bolshevik question. Correspondingly, Hillman and his followers
used that question as a focus for their general disagreement
with AF of L policies. In 1921, for example, an editorial in
The Advance, the Amalgamated's weekly newspaper, caustically commented: "Gompers has already solved all problems
of American labor, and being unable to live in idleness he has
turned his generous attention to the problems of Russian
labor." [27]

Russia served the Amalgamated as more than a weapon
of polemic, however. For many of the workers, it was a homeland where they had relatives, friends, and memories. The
February Revolution concerned them intimately, because it
seemed to complete their own revolutionary attempts or hopes.
The Bolshevik coup may at first have seemed as unfortunate
to Jews in the United States as it seemed to Jews in Russia;
but the Jewish massacres by General Denikin's White armies
soon made the Bolsheviks seem decidedly preferable.[28]

For President Hillman, Russia was the destination of three visits during the first half of the 1920's. Considering his revolutionary activities in tsarist Russia, Hillman's desire to see his homeland under Bolshevik rule is understandable. But in the fifteen years since his emigration, his ideas had changed. As a labor leader in America, he found that reformist unionism was far more relevant and effective in strengthening the position of workers than was the doctrine of socialism. Already he had acquired extraordinary success and respect because he bargained shrewdly but fairly with management, preferring negotiation to strikes, progress to class war.[29] Like Gompers, he had no use for theorists, for those whom he called dreamers, because he believed that "actual life is made by practical men, [although] inspired at times by the writings of the dreamers." [30] The leaders of the AF of L and the Amalgamated shared a pragmatic outlook, although they would not have admitted to sharing anything.

Hillman approached the Red experiment, therefore, in a spirit of curiosity mingled with apprehension. As he reported to the Amalgamated workers of New York, in a speech made on his return in November 1921, he had put three (very pragmatic) questions to himself: was the Soviet government stable, were the Soviet leaders capable and efficient, and were their policies workable? Soon after entering Russia, he answered each of these questions affirmatively. "There is no hope for America without Europe," he said, "and there is no hope for Europe without Russia. Sobered by the realization that the future of Europe is involved in what happens to Russia, and absolutely unbiassed, I came to the conclusion . . . that Soviet Russia is the most stable government in Europe today." As for the soundness of the Soviet policies, he continued, the best proof was that they were getting results, they were working.[31]

165

These confident conclusions by Hillman are highly dubious. After all, the "stable" Soviet government had just radically shifted from War Communism to the New Economic Policy because of terrific economic and social dislocations. Moreover, Lenin had introduced the NEP precisely because only *bad* results were forthcoming. The outstanding consequence of Soviet grain requisitions had been food shortages deriving from peasant resistance and magnified by drought into a famine of such dimensions that, in July, Russia had had to appeal to the United States for help. The gap between evidence and conclusion is insurmountable. In fact, it is so wide that it prompts the suspicion that perhaps Hillman went to Russia with answers as well as questions.

Obviously, Hillman's talent as an economic and political observer was limited. But his primary concern in Russia was less for such matters than for the intangible fact of human feeling. As he exclaimed in May 1922, after a second visit to Russia:

It is in Russia that labor appreciates that work is not something that one has to undergo as a punishment, but that work is something to be proud of. It helps build the world, because the world is built by work and not by the fellows who quibble in the legal profession, or otherwise. Labor understands its mission in Russia, and its mission in life is to build. There labor has learned to accept an iron discipline, because it realizes that no army can be successful in the struggle against life and against the other enemies unless it is disciplined.[32]

Hillman had gone to Soviet Russia with practical criteria for judging its success; yet he had returned with a vision of a promised land for labor. He believed that communism was alien to the demands of human nature and he sought in America to achieve freedom for his workers; yet he praised the "iron discipline" under which their Russian brothers lived.[33] How are these contradictions to be explained? To disparage them simply as muddled thinking is to ignore their implication of important facts about Hillman and about Bolshevik Russia. On the one hand, Hillman's exclamation about a mission for labor, a destiny to "build the world," reveals how strongly his earlier socialist impulses had survived. As president of the Amalgamated, working within the constraints of a developed capitalist society, he may have imitated Gompers' reliance on hardheaded reformism. But in the Soviet Union those constraints were absent, and the true difference between the two men reappeared. For Gompers saw nothing but the distress and oppression of the Russian present, while Hillman looked at the spirit beneath the conditions and saw there a future full of possibility. However much he dismissed the dreamers of the world, he was one of them in contemplating the Soviet Union.[34]

His own temperament was not solely responsible for these attitudes, however. The Bolsheviks engaged in the same apparent contradictions. Admittedly their revolution had created dictatorship and deprivation. Yet they justified these facts, negatively, by the necessity of overcoming natural and political enemies (as Hillman also had said) and, positively, by the eventual future of freedom and happiness for the proletariat. This argument of unavoidable means to ideal ends persuaded those like Hillman whose instincts made them susceptible to the Marxian dream of a "kingdom of freedom." Undoubtedly he was uncomfortable in tolerating any autocracy, even a temporary one, for he was always a liberal and a democrat. But the replacement of rigid, harsh Communism by the NEP deceived him, as it deceived so many others, into believing that the Soviet leaders preferred the most benevolent means toward their goals, that they would not be diverted by "this or the other 'ism,'" in Hillman's words, from the construction of a new social order.[35] Thus, both the idealistic and pragmatic aspects of his thinking could find satisfaction in the Russian phenomenon. Hillman could easily have uttered Lincoln Steffens' exclamation that "I have seen the future and it works," but the labor leader would have used "works" in its physical sense.

It was, in fact, this interest in Russia's industrial development which induced Hillman to arrange with the Soviets a startling and bold transaction. In his address to the Amalgamated's fifth biennial convention, in May of 1922, he announced that during his recent trip to Russia he and Soviet officials had agreed to launch a million-dollar cooperative enterprise by which American and Russian workers would jointly administer and operate all Soviet clothing and textile factories under a concession from the Soviet government. The Russian-American Industrial Corporation, as it came to be called, was to be capitalized by $10 shares sold to American workers and others interested in Russia's economic revival, while the Soviets would supply the factories, equipment, and raw materials. To do business with the Bolsheviks was in itself daring at this time; for a labor union to be one of the agents was unprecedented. According to *The Advance*, the delegates responded to their president's announcement with "the most glowing burst of working class spirit," cheering, applauding, pounding ashtrays, and, finally, deluging Hillman with flowers.[36]

This enthusiasm, combined with relentless fundraising efforts by Amalgamated officials, secured enough contributions to pay the first installment of $250,000 in January 1923.[37] By that time, however, complications had begun to disrupt the ambitious scheme. The public first learned of them in December from William O. Thompson, longtime counsel for the Amalgamated and former president of the American Cotton Oil Company. He, along with Professor Earl Dean Howard of Northwestern University, a famous labor-management arbitrator and friend of Hillman's, had accompanied the union president to Russia to supervise technical aspects of the textile concession. On his arrival back in the United States, Thompson told the press that he had advised against acceptance of the Soviet offer. Contrary to their expectations, he explained, the Americans found that they were to put up only money, not factories; that control over the funds as well as the production was to be in Soviet hands; and that no assurances about raw materials, tax rates, or investment security were to be given. For all these reasons, Thompson took a gloomy view of the entire proposition.[38]

Hillman promptly replied in detail to each of these points. But the crucial source of his disagreement with Thompson was over nontechnical matters. As he declared: "We are not offering stock in the Russian-American Industrial Corporation to those whose principal interest is in obtaining the largest possible security in an investment for purely money-making purposes. We are offering it to those who are interested in Russian industrial reconstruction and wish to help." [39] In other words, to him this was a venture in social rehabilitation, not in speculative capitalization. As he said a few days later in a speech at Carnegie Hall, Russia was seeking to answer the question whether labor must be "condemned to wage slavery forever." [40]

Hillman's attitude toward Russia shaped that of his union as a whole. At every one of its conventions during the decade, the Amalgamated approved a resolution calling for diplomatic recognition of the Bolshevik regime.[41] Meanwhile, the editorial columns of *The Advance* persistently pledged faith in the Communist experiment.[42] For these secessionists from the AF of L, the phenomenon of Russia embodied as much virtue as it embodied sin for Gompers and Green.

The International Ladies' Garment Workers' Union fluctuated between these two polar views, but managed thereby to establish a more valid attitude toward Soviet Russia than did either of the others. This median position paralleled its role in the world of American unionism. Like the Amalgamated Clothing Workers, the ILGWU had been formed by Russian Jews of socialist beliefs and preserved that heritage (especially under the presidency of Benjamin Schlesinger, 1903–1904, 1914–1923) as it acquired impressive strength and success in the second decade of the century. Unlike the Amalgamated, however, the ILGWU succeeded within the framework of the AF of L, becoming, by 1919, the fourth largest union in the federation.[43] When the debate over the Bolshevik Revolution began, therefore, the leaders of the garment workers sought a point of view satisfactory to both their ideological and institutional loyalties. The result was an unsatisfactory and restless ambivalence.

The columns of *Justice*, the official union newspaper, serve as a convenient index to the intellectual dilemma. On the one hand, the editor, S. Yanofsky, urged his readers to remember that the AF of L had the same lofty goals as they, however different its methods of attaining those goals.[44] In this way, apparently, he hoped to pacify anger at the anti-Bolshevik resolution adopted by the recent AF of L convention. A year later, after passage of another hostile resolution, *Justice* was still determined to find reasons for hope. The convention's stand was on the defensive now, according to one editorial, and had become apologetic rather than defiant in criticizing Lenin's regime. In any case, the editorial concluded in its own apologetic tone, many delegates had voiced strong dissent.[45]

When *Justice* was not protecting Gompers' leadership, it was more forthright and persuasive. In 1920, for example, an editorial declared: "Russia is precisely the only country in the world where the workers are not slaves, where they are full masters of their own destinies." [46] And occasionally Gompers himself earned direct attack, such as when he rebuked the International Federation of Trade Unions for opposing shipment of arms to Poland in her war with Russia. "Is an endeavor to prevent a government from dragging its people into a new world war tantamount to a subversion of the American republic and its supplanting by a Soviet regime?" an editorial demanded bitterly. It proceeded to ridicule "this ungodly fear" of the Soviet government.[47] However earnest its lip-service loyalty to its union superiors, therefore, the true devotion of the ILGWU was obvious. The resolutions by its own conventions, urging official trade relations with Russia and recognition of the Soviet government, translated that devotion into official policy.[48]

But editorials and resolutions are only devitalized vehicles for attitudes, simplifying and diluting the experience that produces them. In the comments of Benjamin Schlesinger, returning in 1920 from the same visit to his homeland that Sidney Hillman would make a year later, the ambivalence of the ILGWU appears in dramatic fashion. Five weeks of observation had convinced him, Schlesinger said, that Bolshevism was the best form of government for Russia in her present condition; any alternative would simply release the forces of chaos. He emphasized that he had not been converted to Bolshevism, but only to a recognition of the needs and desires of the Russian people. The general atmosphere was oppressive, he conceded, "but what would you have? It is a revolution. Russia finds itself in the midst of a struggle against a world of enemies. Can there be freedom of speech under such circumstances?"

Such questions hint, by their defensiveness, that Schlesinger was not merely a disinterested observer. And in fact, when describing his experience at an opera performance in Moscow, he frankly exposed the emotional quality of his perception. Sitting in the tsar's box among thousands of working men and women, "I realized the meaning of the Russian Revolution with all my five senses. Every doubt vanished like thin smoke. My heart throbbed with joy, and . . . a thought was hammering away in my mind: If it was possible for workmen to take their proper place in society, at work and at play, in Russia, why should not this be possible all over the world?" Surely such a reaction indicates a sympathy perilously close to the very conversion to Bolshevism he had denied. Yet his next statement prohibits that inference: "you can hardly imagine what a deep breath of relief I drew when I left Russia" and its suffocating atmosphere of oppression.[49]

Thus Hillman came away from Russia with a vision of a proletarian utopia; Gompers never went to the country, which he vilified as a barbaric tyranny; and Schlesinger returned with both ideas juxtaposed in bewildering illogic. Yet the ILGWU president was being the most honest of them all, because logic was both an inappropriate and an impossible means for an American unionist to evaluate Russia in the early 1920's. Undoubtedly, the Russian people were burdened with poverty and deprived of their rights. But the Soviet leaders themselves acknowledged these facts and, by introducing the NEP, sought to relieve them. Furthermore, the Bolsheviks judged their revolution by the future, not by the present vestiges of a tsarist past, and for them the future was described by a rhetoric of justice and freedom for the working class. A man like Gompers, who had succeeded within the capitalist framework, perceived only the present and hated it. But union leaders who were of Russian and Jewish birth and who, whether in explicit or tacit form, cherished a socialist faith could not be immune to the Soviet rhetoric. They conceived a hope which the recognition of Soviet oppression could only join, not nullify. Within this coexistence, a logic of emotions prevailed.

This ambiguity of attitude was adequate when dealing with the question of Communism in distant Russia. When Communism crossed the ocean and, in the mid-twenties, threatened to dominate American unions, however, the question suddenly was no longer abstract, but very tangible. Now the labor leaders and their organizations had to defend themselves against the seizure of power by a skillful and relentless faction. This drastic relocation of focus relegated Russia to an incidental role in the unions' debate over Communism, important only in terms of its connection with the Third International (Comintern) and the International of Labor Unions (Profintern). A study of American labor's attitudes toward Russia need not and cannot encompass the complex history of Communism in the labor movement. Only the necessary details will be given here.[50]

Moscow's domination and direction of the American Communist movement is an undeniable fact. To unionists like Gompers and William Green, that relationship automatically anathematized all Communists and Communist sympathizers, and made any cooperation with them intolerable. John L. Lewis, president of the United Mine Workers after 1919, was equally adamant as he ruthlessly suppressed the numerous Communist conspiracies which bred within his ranks during the twenties. He warned against the "gray wolves of a pernicious philosophy" who, under orders from the USSR, sought to swallow the American labor movement. *The United Mine Workers Journal* and the union conventions echoed him, opposing diplomatic recognition as an encouragement to the enemy. By April 1926, Lewis declared the Communist Party and all its affiliated organizations subversive and outlawed.[51]

Many unionists remained unconvinced, however, particularly because the American Communist movement in 1921 forsook its openly revolutionary policy — known as "dual unionism" — and adopted ostensibly cooperative tactics based on the principle labeled "boring from within." During the next two years, Communists penetrated deeply into the garment, railroad, mining, and metal unions, under the guidance of William Z. Foster's Trade Union Education League (TUEL). But in 1923, this success, along with the entire strategy that produced it, collapsed everywhere except among the garment workers. The occasion was the convention of the Farmer-Labor Party, the political organization led by the radical president of the Chicago Federation of Labor, John Fitzpatrick. The Communists had found Fitzpatrick to be an exceedingly useful ally whose cooperation lent respectability to their organization and facilitated their strategy of boring from within. Yet in 1922 he had become increasingly apprehensive of their purposes and they, in turn, increasingly impatient with his hesitation. Lagging negotiations in the spring of 1923 to unite Fitzpatrick's Farmer-Labor Party and the Communists' Workers' Party provoked the latter into breaking with the labor leader. At the convention in July they applied steamroller tactics to win approval for the immediate formation of a Federated Farmer-Labor Party. Fitzpatrick and his followers angrily walked out and disowned all affiliations with the Communists. Most unions began to expel Communists from their ranks as well as to outlaw membership in the TUEL. Necessarily, American Communism became an underground phenomenon again, dual-unionist despite itself, the pariah which Gompers' invective had always said it was.

Yet this debacle did not prevent the Communists from achieving enormous, though temporary, victories within the garment unions, especially the ILGWU. For at the beginning of the 1920's, Schlesinger's union was, despite its impressive success during the preceding decade, suffering from radical instability created by deteriorating conditions throughout the garment industry.[52] The TUEL quickly took advantage of this opportunity to infiltrate the ILGWU locals and to construct a force in opposition to the union leadership. Confronting this insurgency, President Schlesinger was immobilized, partly because of poor health and capricious temperament,

174

but just as much because he could not reconcile his idealistic hopes for the Bolshevik Revolution with the malevolent expression it was taking within his own organization. By 1923 he was replaced by Morris Sigman, a less attractive personality but a more vigorous, often ruthless leader.[53]

But even Sigman could not extirpate what *Justice* called "the cancer that is devouring the vitals of the organization." [54] He outlawed the TUEL as a dual union in August 1923, and the 1924 convention refused to seat TUEL delegates. But these were feeble gestures compared with the Communists' stunning capture of three New York locals in the fall of 1924. The columns in *Justice* emitted sound and fury which did nothing to prevent the radicals from gaining enough strength in local elections of early 1926 to control the joint board of the New York cloak unions. As Sigman's reprisals became more and more reckless, Communist popularity rose even higher.[55]

Again it was only the Communists' own excesses that defeated them. In July 1926, they forced Sigman to call a general strike of cloakmakers which, although initially supported by most of the union, soon was extended by Communist obduracy and political motivation beyond the point of reason. After six months without work, the only result was union demoralization. At this point, in December, the general executive board was able to oust the insurgents from the joint board, end the strike, and purge the union of TUEL agents.[56]

During this crisis, the ILGWU's ambivalence toward Soviet Russia split into frankly antagonistic fragments. No one doubted that the insurgents were tools of the Red International and therefore of Moscow. To *Justice* this meant that Russia was as guilty as the TUEL. Already dismayed in 1922 by the persecution of socialists in Russia, the newspaper reacted to Communist infiltration of the union with fierce attacks on the Bolshevik government, "the embodiment of the greatest tyranny of our day and the most outspoken violator of the ideal of human freedom." [57] The union conventions, however, never wavered in their support of diplomatic recognition of the USSR. The sponsors of a prorecognition resolution in 1924, for example, emphatically stated that "the people of Russia are not to pay for the mistakes of their leaders in America," those "so-called friends of Soviet Russia." As a labor organization, they continued, "we shall only act in a spirit of brotherly love, of solidarity to the workers and people in Russia." [58] Despite the shocking and almost fatal collision with American Communism, a majority of the delegates in every convention but one, during the decade before recognition, reaffirmed this faith.[59]

The Amalgamated Clothing Workers, meanwhile, were forced to wage a similar struggle with Communist insurgents, although their union never came so close to jeopardy. In the early years of the decade, Hillman's relationship with both the Workers' Party and the TUEL was cordial, for they shared a hostility to the AF of L and a desire for industrial unionism. The formation of the Russian-American Industrial Corporation expanded this friendship still more. But it was a fragile amity; two Amalgamated policy decisions were enough to shatter it. First, the union refused to intercede on behalf of Workers' Party delegates expelled from the Cleveland convention of the Conference for Progressive Political Action in July 1924; and then the union remained a supporter of Robert La Follette's subsequent presidential campaign, despite the Communists' break with the Progressive leader. Quickly the Communist movement turned on Hillman as an enemy. The TUEL intensified its attempts to bore from within the Amalgamated, infiltrating locals, calling mass meetings to denounce the policies of the union officialdom, even breaking windows and furniture in the union's New York office. But by 1926, the same year as the general strike in the ILGWU, William Foster's radical group encountered failure and expulsion.[60]

The logistics of the struggle within the Amalgamated are less relevant than their effect on the union's attitude toward Russia. With the same sort of evidence as that which led *Justice* to condemn the Bolshevik regime, *The Advance* instead distinguished the Communist enemies of their union from the Communist leaders of the Revolution. In the midst of the crisis, in fact, the union's official newspaper declared: "The Amalgamated wages no battle against communism or communists. As an organization we do not concern ourselves with the political convictions of the members of the union." The subversive aims of the Workers' Party were intolerable, it agreed. But that party was not to be confused with Russian Communism. "Soviet Russia is a phenomenon of a larger order." The editorial now addressed those readers whose perspective may have been distorted by the recent turmoil: "The outstanding matter to remember . . . is that Russia, one of the largest countries of the world, is governed by the working class of Russia. One who accepts this fact has no escape but — either to support the Soviet Government, or to fight it. The Amalgamated has made its choice long ago." [61]

However implacably the union had to fight insurgents within its ranks, therefore, it never let that fact sully its vision of the USSR as the proletariat's promised land. Like the ILGWU, its conventions regularly repeated the demand for recognition of the Soviet Union.[62] Hillman himself did not amend the laudatory and expectant attitude he had always held toward the Bolshevik Revolution, even after he visited Russia for a third time in 1925, after the TUEL threatened his leadership, and after the Soviets canceled the contract of the Russian-American Industrial Corporation.[63] On the contrary, he continued to argue for recognition of a regime which, he said, had proved trustworthy in commercial and financial matters and successful in its economic recovery. He harshly criticized the leftist insurgents whose excesses had forced him to put aside the union's traditional tolerance of dissent. Yet he in no way related those insurgents to the Kremlin leaders.[64]

Curiously, the union's first doubts about Russia were prompted not by the struggle within its own ranks, but by the struggle within the Soviet hierarchy between Stalin and Trotsky. Already in the 1926 editorial quoted above, *The Advance* recognized the possibility of questioning the methods by which the Bolshevik leaders maintained themselves in power. But at the time it only hinted hesitantly at the problem and quietly skirted around it. By January 1929, only a few days before Trotsky was finally exiled from Russia, the probable author of that editorial emerged from anonymity and circumlocution. J. B. S. Hardman, editor of *The Advance* since 1925 and a life-long socialist, now permitted no doubt about his attitude. Calling the persecution of Trotsky and his supporters a deed of "disgrace" and "criminality," Hardman uttered a protest burdened with the despair of a betrayed believer:

For if these men are guilty of a crime, that is not against the Revolution, the working class, or the labor state. It's a crime of insubordination to the canonized truth of the leadership of the Russian Communist Party at present in power, a truth which will automatically become an untruth when another set of leaders gain the seat of power. The working class is more generous than the parties of the working class.[65]

Yet like Schlesinger nine years before, like Hillman, like Trotsky himself, Hardman struggled to reconcile the distressing behavior of the Soviet regime with the inspiring promise of the Revolution. In the same issue in which this article appeared, he wrote an editorial praising American businessmen who sought to deal with the USSR and criticizing those politicians who still awaited the demise of the Soviets.[66] In 1926 he had warned that, in judging Russia, there was no middle ground between advocacy and opposition, yet here he was attempting to occupy that no-man's land. Schlesinger's fate had been immobilization, Trotsky's had been exile, Hardman's was moral compromise. In an editorial marking the thirteenth anniversary of the Revolution, he tried to answer those who criticized Soviet oppression. Yes, dictatorship was repulsive, he agreed, but one could not condemn the vital aim of the Revolution simply because of "specific details" necessary to its accomplishment. "Freedom is a relative thing," he insisted.[67]

Hardman's retreat to relativism embodies the pathetic and inevitable intellectual journey of those who could not discard the vision of October 1917.[68] Challenged by the distasteful facts of deprivation, injustice, and cruelty under Soviet rule, they averted their mind's eye to the future where facts had not yet taken place, where the old hopes survived unbruised by circumstance or compromise. Because the Bolshevik Revolution claimed to be a deed in the name of all workers of the world, it necessarily involved the attention of American labor leaders. For men such as Gompers, Green, or John L. Lewis, whose success was achieved within the capitalist structure which the Communists wished to destroy, the Soviet regime was an enemy to be relentlessly opposed and toppled. For those like Schlesinger and Hillman, who had become revolutionary socialists in disgust at a reactionary tsardom and who retained that heritage even while recognizing its irrelevance to the progress of American unionism, the issue of Soviet Russia was not so easily settled. Rather, they found themselves caught between contradictory attitudes which did not resolve but simply coexisted uneasily.

The result was an illogic, such as that of Schlesinger, or — much worse — a series of reluctant distinctions. Gompers and Green, in unison with the American government, distinguished the Russian people from the Russian rulers and opposed the latter. But Hillman, Hardman, and Schlesinger made a more refined and perilous distinction between the Bolshevik Revolution and the Bolshevik Party, between the future and the necessary transition to it, between the ends and the means. When the Revolution was still young, and particularly after the NEP was introduced, this seemed a satisfactory mode of analysis. As Soviet Russia grew older and more unhappy under Stalin's rigidifying rule, the disjunction between the two parts of the facile formula widened; the peril of the distinction became enormous. By the early 1930's, it was less and less likely that sympathetic labor leaders could maintain ambivalence except at the cost of amorality, at the cost of confessing that freedom was "a relative thing." After the autocratic Five-Year Plan replaced the quasi-capitalist NEP, after the consumer became subordinate to industrialization, after workers were denied the right to change jobs and were pressured into joining shock brigades in their free time, after "the liquidation of the kulaks" and the trials of factory managers who had not filled their quotas — in short, after the Revolution was resumed in its most relentless form, many American unionists began to admit that perhaps the oppressive means allowed only oppressive ends.

Events forced upon them the fundamental doubts they had resisted earlier; in many cases, these doubts became frank opposition to Stalin's regime. The break emerges clearly in the pages of *The Advance*. Hardman's editorials stubbornly retained the original faith, even to the point of declaring late in 1932 — incredibly without sarcasm — that Russia is "a nation which is starving itself into social greatness." [69] Already in 1930, however, Charles W. Ervin, the regular political correspondent, had lost patience with such paradoxes. The Soviet drive against the kulaks and the ejection of bourgeois children from school shared, in his opinion, the Inquisition's theory "that by showing mercy to the unorthodox, the salvation of the orthodox is menaced and that cruelty shown today will diminish the amount of suffering in the years to come. To me this is a most damnable doctrine." A few months later, Ervin remarked: "I fail to understand some of my Radical and Liberal friends who condone things happening in Russia which they condemn when they happen here." [70]

The year 1930 was one of doubt for others in the left wing of American labor. On November 23, in response to an invitation by the Joint Socialist and Labor Committee against Political Terrorism and Capital Punishment in Soviet Russia, more than 350 delegates from 165 national and local unions, Socialist Party branches, Workingmen's Circle branches, and progressive fraternal societies met in New York to form a permanent body opposing Soviet political repression. Their resolution uttered an "indignant protest against the reign of terror which prevails in Soviet Russia." Benjamin Schlesinger, president of the ILGWU again and one of the signers of the invitation, was too ill to attend, but he sent his assurances that his union would support the Committee. About the same time, the editor of *Justice* was writing an indictment against the forced labor practiced in the USSR.[71]

The Soviet charisma for American labor sympathizers was fading. But events at home precluded endorsement of capitalism as the alternative to Communism. For the Depression had created an "army of the unemployed" of dimensions hardly contemplated even in the bitterest Marxian prophecies. In Russia, meanwhile, the Five-Year Plan had created more jobs than the labor force could fill. Taking advantage of this coincidence, Amtorg, the Soviet commercial representative in the United States, advertised for applicants to work in the USSR. By September of 1931, 2,000 skilled workers already had gone, 6,000 skilled workers were about to leave, and more than 100,000 had applied for the remaining 4,000 vacancies.[72]

Ironically, just when Stalin's policies were dissuading labor leaders from their lingering hopes for Russia, the American economic collapse was encouraging a similar hope among their followers. The antithetical nature of the two groups' motivations — idealism and necessity — does not mar the symmetry. Rather, it implicitly repeats the earlier point that Russia in the early thirties no longer represented an idealistic future, but an expedient present.

Because of obvious practical difficulties, the vast majority of American workers never regarded emigration to the USSR as a serious possibility. Yet neither did they seek a solution to their plight in domestic Communism. Numerous intellectuals may have thought that the Communists had the answer,[73] but organized labor remembered too keenly the activities of the TUEL ever to have such notions. Moreover, the Communists themselves prevented the workers from forgetting: the 1929 congress of the Profintern, acting on the resolution of the Comintern a year earlier, reintroduced the policy of dual unionism that had been discarded in 1921. Despite large and well-founded doubts about the new line, William Foster and his TUEL (renamed as the Trade Union Unity League) obediently began to implement it in the eight unions suggested to them as targets. The result was a failure still more decisive than in the preceding decade.[74]

Yet even if Stalinist Russia had disillusioned labor leaders and was impractical for the rank and file, it demanded attention simply because it was experiencing a shortage of labor while millions of American workers were being laid off. For most observers, the key to the difference was economic planning. David Dubinsky, Schlesinger's successor as president of the ILGWU, returned from a visit to the Soviet Union in July 1931 with mixed reactions — impressed by the enthusiasm of the Russian masses, critical of the industrial inefficiency and the political distatorship. But of one thing he was sure: because the Communists were working with a plan, their experiment was important.[75] Dubinsky was preaching to the converted. Already *The Advance* emphatically and *Justice* timidly had taken up the same theme of planning.[76] Even the conservative executive committee of the AF of L was aroused, in the fall of 1931, into urging President Hoover to convene a national economic conference as a means for devising a remedy to the unequal distribution of income.[77]

In view of the fact that people as ideologically separated as George Soule and Gerard Swope were endorsing "economic planning" as the solution to depression, labor's advocacy is not surprising. The significant point, however, is that most leftist union leaders, with the exception of Hardman, carefully divorced the idea of planning from the Five-Year Plan and restricted it to nonrevolutionary terms. They, and probably most of the rank and file, sought satisfaction to their exigency neither in distant Russia nor in the programs of domestic Communism. The Depression aroused them to a sense of possibility within the given system, not to a drastic alienation.[78] Sidney Hillman, for example, urged upon labor the need for cooperative and vigorous attack on its problems. To wait for a revolution to sweep away the problems and to sweep in an ideal system was, he insisted, an easy excuse for doing nothing. "While building with the future always in mind, we live in the present." [79] To the nation as a whole, meanwhile, he presented the need and virtue of planning, but almost ostentatiously ignored the Soviet Five-Year Plan as a model. The unemployment-compensation plan, cooperative housing, and cooperative banks of his own union provided more appropriate models.[80] An editorial in *Justice* echoed Hillman's plea for planning and invoked, not Gosplan, but the precedent of the War Industries Board.[81]

Economic planning required the cooperation of government and employers. While that was being sought, and as a stimulus to it, labor had to make itself a strong force on the national scene. During the 1920's, business aggressions and the TUEL had weakened labor organization; the early years of the Depression had accelerated that deterioration. Now labor leaders recognized the desperate need to reverse the trend. They preached unionization, not an October Revolution, as the way to labor's revitalization.

The New Deal provided the initial outlet for realizing these aspirations. The National Industrial Recovery Act not only instituted a form of planning but, in the famous Section 7a, sanctioned the right of labor to organize and bargain collectively. During the next few years, union membership swelled impressively; and as an appropriate symbol of labor's new outlook, the Amalgamated, in October 1933, finally rejoined the AF of L. Sidney Hillman was an important participant both in drafting the NRA law and then in administering it. "We are going to support it whole-heartedly," he announced at a mid-1933 hearing on the code for the men's clothing industry. In his opinion, NRA was "the only thing through which most of us can see anything ahead." [82] William Green, David Dubinsky, *The Advance,* and *Justice* emphatically concurred.[83] Even J. B. S. Hardman — the unconverted apologist for the Soviet Union, the dreamer of socialist dreams — exultantly foresaw "days of storm and upsurge." Apathy was gone, adventure had come, he declared. "Let it be stated: there has not been a more interesting time than this in a decade or longer." [84]

This enthusiastic unanimity was, in great part, a thing of rhetoric. Many cautioned that, for full economic justice, the workers required a New Game rather than a New Deal.[85] Moreover, the AF of L's tenacious adherence to craft unionism incited the secession of John L. Lewis, Hillman, and others, who formed the Congress of Industrial Organization in 1935. But the crucial fact remains that Hillman and other

184

liberal unionists no longer looked to the Soviet Union as labor's promised land. Stalin had destroyed that hope; the New Deal and then the CIO provided an alternative. The Russian-born visions had become Americanized at last.

The radical *New Masses* lyrically portrays here a dynamic Five-Year-Plan universe populated by an idealistic, almost cherubic youth.

TOWARD A CLASSLESS SOCIETY

by William Gropper

VII / Dissident Responses during the Five-Year Plan

Our pioneering days in this Republic are over. The frontier has been reached and the stream backs up.

— Stuart Chase, "You and I and the Big Idea,"
Survey, LXVII (March 1, 1932), 568

In mid-1930 Lincoln Steffens wrote to his wife that "the Youth school of writers lack and need" Soviet Russia to save them from cynicism and drink.[1] As the Depression worsened within the next three years, this prescription was to be adopted more fully than Steffens could have foreseen. Those writers who had retreated from politics to art after the World War now sought renewed engagement with the social problems of their country. The pace of their conversion is as startling as the manner in which they performed it. Matthew Josephson, for example, in 1931 discovered the constructive possibilities in the "vast standardization of human needs and movements" which had characterized American life in the twenties and had so thoroughly repelled artists. He declared: "The question of finally consecrating this character of uniformity, through grafting upon it the inspiring collective principle, is one of new tactics and interpretations. The driving power, as in all great social adventures, must come from the high quantity of moral certainty and moral passion."[2] This surely seems a strange sentiment for a former Dadaist who had fled to Paris in order to escape the American mob and to enjoy a great private, not social, adventure.

187

The transformation of Theodore Dreiser was equally sudden and extreme. "I don't care a damn about the masses," he exclaimed in a 1922 interview for the *Los Angeles Times*. "It is the individual that concerns me." [3] Until 1930 he continued to uphold vehemently his belief in survival of the fittest and his disdain for reformers who, as he told the Communist writer, Mike Gold, deludedly "regard humanity . . . as a very kindly and much imposed upon organism" rather than "a predatory organism." [4] Yet by 1931 he had completely discarded these ideas, imploring the American people to recognize the bankruptcy of individualism and the need for social control to ensure equity for all.[5]

Josephson and Dreiser were not undergoing a peculiar and eccentric experience, however drastic the change that was involved. After polling sixteen writers on their attitudes toward social problems early in 1932, the editors of *The Modern Quarterly* announced: "Politics and literature are no longer viewed as separate and conflicting categories. If the American writer has not become class conscious yet, he at least has become social-conscious." Just as the writers had been radical in their alienation from the New Era, now they were radical in their approach to the Depression. As *The Modern Quarterly* pointed out, almost all respondents regarded communism, not socialism, as the only effective solution to the crisis. At the same time, however, seven of the sixteen, including John Dos Passos, Edwin Seaver, John Chamberlain, and Malcolm Cowley, opposed joining the Communist Party, while six others were noncommittal.[6] Apparently, artistic intellectuals were turning leftward in response to the social crisis, not to Communist doctrine, although the latter provided the most convenient and outspoken articulation of their dissent.[7]

This radicalization of the writers inevitably entailed a change in their attitudes toward the Soviet Union. As bohemians and rebels they had scorned or ignored it because they were uninterested in the problems of material welfare in any form, whether Soviet or American; as ostensible left-wing revolutionaries, they looked to the Five-Year Plan for practical guidance and general inspiration. In the same way that they adopted Communist ideas as the most satisfactory outlet for their protest, while avoiding the commitment of party membership, they used the Soviet phenomenon as the most convenient weapon for their protest. Sympathy with the USSR was a symptom, not a cause, of their radicalism. In another of those increasingly fashionable symposia of authors, this one on "How I Came to Communism," only Mike Gold, a party veteran for many years, mentioned the Soviet Union as a determining factor; Waldo Frank, Clifton B. Fadiman, Granville Hicks, Sherwood Anderson, and Edmund Wilson mentioned it incidentally, if at all.[8]

The intellectual itinerary of Theodore Dreiser clearly exemplifies the forces at work among literary intellectuals. After a Soviet trip in 1928, Dreiser returned with mixed feelings, a predominant confidence in the Moscow regime competing with dismay at the dictatorship, terror, and the turgid banality of propagandist art. He also became caught in a tangled analysis which admired the Communists' ascetic idealism, argued that they ought to relax their grim materialism by "a little luxury," and predicted that they might go unprecedentedly far in solving "the strange mystery of our being here at all."[9] After the Crash, however, Dreiser looked at the Soviet Union in a new perspective. By 1931 he was praising its individualism and artistic creativity. But by then this was only a secondary reassurance to his main concern that Americans should look to the Five-Year Plan as an instructive model for obtaining economic and social justice.[10] In effect, his troubled tension over individual freedom versus mass

189

conformity and over creativity versus materialism had broken under the pressure of national crisis. The mystery of being here at all became almost frivolous in the face of the hunger, poverty, and disease that Dreiser discovered while leading a delegation of writers to Harlan and other Kentucky mining counties in November 1931.[11] Now the mystery was how to save human lives, and the clue seemed to lie in Communism. Thus, three years after actually going to Russia, Dreiser arrived ideologically via Kentucky.

This intellectual route soon was traveled by other literary pilgrims to radicalism. Malcolm Cowley, a member of Waldo Frank's delegation to Harlan County in February 1932, talked to hungry, haggard, hopeless miners and thought of the vigorous, smiling workers photographed in the Soviet publication, *USSR in Construction*. The former expatriate writer and occasional Dadaist became a revolutionary.[12]

Waldo Frank himself physically articulated the literary leftward movement by visiting the Soviet Union shortly after leaving Harlan County. For over a decade and a half he had been seeking a reconciliation between the aesthetic and the revolutionary, seeking the personal and social "wholeness" that capitalism precluded or destroyed.[13] The search had led him from the United States to Spain to Latin America and then to Kentucky. In 1932, he set out for the USSR on an "unconscious pilgrimage" in which "the issues for myself are great." The Soviet drama, he believed, involved the "fate of the Person and of Culture, the fate of all that man has heroically and so briefly builded [*sic*] in the few thousand years of history." [14] There at last he found fulfillment. After waiting for thirteen hours on a Volga pier among a crowd of dirty, sleeping peasants, he came "close to this Russian human creature, close forever." He had perceived their sensibility, their struggle to become free and wholly human. In Leningrad,

190

watching the workers walk with pride and vitality, he sensed "the pulse of the proletarian Russian street." In the factories he was awed by the workers' happy dedication to the world-wide proletarian cause.[15] He joyously announced: "I am at home in Russia. . . . Russia has become a theatre of the spirit: a place where human will, human values are incarnate."[16] In Russia, where the falseness of capitalist culture was absent, the uncultured masses had hope and self-knowledge. The intellectual absolutism of the Soviet regime caused him some apprehension but, he argued, it was both traditional in Russia and preferable to "that flabby relativism" disguised as liberalism in the West.[17] He had no hesitations about where his loyalties lay: all believers in truly human culture must defend the Soviet Union with their spirit and, if necessary, even with their bodies.[18]

Frank's enthusiasm perplexes as it rhapsodizes. He had recaptured the original poetry of the Revolution which, as Floyd Dell remarked in 1922, had been diluted into NEP prose.[19] But the Soviet leaders were simultaneously translating the NEP into the statistics and smokestacks of the Five-Year Plan. In effect, two languages were being spoken, two sorts of realities were being described. The difference ultimately provokes the suspicion that Frank had imported into Russia a preconceived artifice and then added local coloring. In his determination to find "wholeness," he had seen only half — the half which allowed him to claim both that he adhered to Marxism and that he would "complete" it by providing "a methodology for the new culture." "To be a good Marxian," Frank declared after returning from Soviet Russia, "is to be creative enough to go beyond Marx."[20]

This kind of affirmation complemented rather than contradicted the antipathy which E. E. Cummings felt toward the Soviet Union after a brief visit in 1931. The poet had decided to make the trip not as an "unconscious pilgrimage," but simply "because I've never been there." [21] Everything he saw convinced him that the land of the proletariat had enthroned impersonality, mechanization, and dogma, all the enemies of self, sentiment, and spontaneity in which he believed. His final picture was grim:

USSR a USSR a night—USSR a nightmare USSR home of the panacea Negation haven of all (in life's name) Death-worshippers hopper of hates Becausemachine (U for un- & S for self S for science and R for -reality) how it shrivels: how it dwindles withers; how it wilts diminishes wanes, how it crumbles evaporates collapses disappears — the verily consubstantiated cauchemar of premeditated NYET.[22]

The vivid contrast between Frank's dawn and Cummings' nightmare should not obscure the fact that both men were deviating from the principles of Soviet Communism. Both were departing from the philosophy of historical materialism and the practice of industrialization on a class basis — Cummings in the direction of aesthetic anarchism and Frank in the direction of aesthetic organicism. If Cummings marked the point where the leftward movement of writers had begun in 1930, Frank showed that it tended to go "beyond Marx." For in turning to political radicalism, most of the artists had enlarged their set of values to include social concerns without intending to surrender those values. They postponed cultural creativity until after the social revolution, but creativity remained their ultimate goal. Thus they adopted Communism as a means without fully clarifying whether it also would satisfy their ends. In the necessity of the American Depression, they could defer that dilemma, although ultimately, as the literary history of the later thirties reveals, they had to confront it with uncertainty and anguish.[23] In their return from exile, these writers had swept past the liberals' hesitations about Soviet Russia and Communism. But the apparent reassurance offered by radicalism only led, at a later date, to an even more acute intellectual discomfort than that which liberals were suffering early in the decade.

In March 1930, less than five months after the Wall Street crash, Oswald Garrison Villard asked a plaintive question of his fellow editor, Ellery Sedgwick of *The Atlantic Monthly*: "Why is it that in the greatest crisis in our history we are absolutely destitute of men and programs?" [24] Confronting the economic shambles of what had been the New Era, the critical liberals were at first as confounded as its ardent boosters were. They may have been certain of the destruction that had occurred, but, as Villard and others revealed, they were uncertain about what they wanted to build on the ruins.[25] The American future had suddenly become a question mark.

At the very time that Villard was confessing his bewilderment, however, the Moscow correspondent of his journal, *The Nation*, was writing in a strikingly different tone. Louis Fischer returned to Russia, after a vacation, to find "not only new achievements, radically new policies, and a new social atmosphere, but a powerful, all-enveloping, newly released wave or wall of energy and enthusiasm." In the second year of the Five-Year Plan, Fischer described the mood with excitement: "Everything moves here. Life, the air, people are dynamic. When I watch these recently unsealed reservoirs of energy I am sometimes carried away and think that nothing is impossible in the Soviet Union." [26]

Since 1917, American liberals had been citing the Soviet experiment to document their critique of the United States, but in the booming prosperity of the twenties their arguments made only a thin, almost wistful sound which few people heard. The Crash changed all this. When the American half of the Soviet-American comparison suddenly collapsed, the liberals seemed to have been freed from their dilemma. Now they could praise the USSR with the exuberant conviction that they had been right all the time. The American prosperity had proved to be a disguise for inner decadence, while the Russian people were striving to fulfill the production quotas of the Five-Year Plan with a stirring fervor. This became the incessant theme for American sympathizers: the Soviet Union was young, vital, ardent, and dedicated. As Bruce Bliven, a *New Republic* editor, wrote in 1931: "Russia . . . is a land of hope; it strikes you almost with the force of a blow, as soon as you are across the border." Comparing the energy and enthusiasm of young Russians to the attitudes of American college students, Bliven felt the impulse "to weep for my countrymen." [27] When Raymond Robins revisited Soviet Russia in 1933, fifteen years after completing his diplomatic and Red Cross service, he exclaimed over the "NEW ORDER OF THINGS visible, vital and vibrant, clashing ruthlessly with the old order — YOUTH in the saddle and riding hard." [28]

After 1929, the liberals' moral mode of discourse acquired particular force because of the material failure that the United States had undergone. The Russian standard of living was low, food and housing were scarce, luxuries were unobtainable — but liberals pointedly emphasized that there was no unemployment and, more important, that there was a purpose to the harsh conditions. The Plan demanded temporary sacrifices in order to build the foundation for socialism, which would provide equal comforts for all. Russians were suffering for reasons they understood and willingly accepted. Americans, on the other hand, were suffering simply because their system had broken down and their leaders did not know how to repair it. Harry F. Ward, a professor at Union Theological Seminary in New York, declared that the Plan "gives the masses that which our liberals are so afraid of, that which life has not had since the break up of the Middle Ages — a central purpose." [29] Ella Winter, the wife of Lincoln Steffens,

194

reached the same conclusion during a Soviet visit in 1932: "Is a woman happy when she is giving birth to a longed-for child? They are bringing to birth a new world with a new *Weltanschauung,* and in the process questions of personal contentment become secondary." [30]

Thus liberals glossed over the cruelties of agricultural collectivization, involving liquidation of the kulaks by terror or deportation to labor camps, over the increased persecution of intellectuals, over the reinvigorated activities of the secret police — in short, over the general intensification of harsh dictatorship that accompanied the Plan. The liberals were silent partly because they did not yet know the facts. Partly too, however, they were silent because they did not want to know. For one thing, they feared conceding even minimal validity to their conservative opponents at home who denounced the Soviet regime in such extreme terms. More fundamental, the USSR seemed to liberals to satisfy their long search for the hope which they had lost since the World War. To them, Soviet Communism was an essentially idealistic, not materialistic, doctrine because it was grappling with basic principles of human relationships and social justice. Jerome Davis frankly called it "a spiritual force." [31]

This terminology seems singularly inappropriate to an atheistic creed of historical materialism. Yet the liberals were discussing the mood and method of striving toward material goals rather than the goals themselves. It is likely that they would have disapproved of these goals when attained, just as they had objected to them in the frivolous and intolerant form they took during the New Era. But in the USSR, which was struggling against adversity, that eventuality was hypothetical because attainment still lay in the future. In the United States, after the Crash, the attainment suddenly lay in the past. Suddenly, both societies were ones of want, ones in which the practical problem of bread was prior to all others. Now the liberals could evade the troubling question of whether prosperity and idealism were compatible values; with the destruction of American prosperity, that question could be conveniently postponed, just as it was in the Soviet Union. Ironically, the liberals were ideologically comfortable because of adversity. Lincoln Colcord, for example, perceived a stimulating and daring climate of thought, in the fall of 1931, which induced him to consider a return from his decade of self-imposed exile in Maine.[32]

Even if the Depression renewed the liberals' sense of opportunity at home, they could not escape the fact that idealism alone, however inspiring, was a mood rather than a program. If the Communist leaders aroused "a spiritual faith," President Herbert Hoover also was calling for faith — in capitalism. The liberals had to specify their ideals. It was not enough merely to be men of strong faith, calling for followers; one had to have a substantive solution as well. *That* could not be conveniently postponed.

The question of solutions formed the focus of Edmund Wilson's "Appeal to Progressives" in the January 14, 1931, issue of *The New Republic,* an article of impressive lucidity that produced enormous effect. The free-lance writer described the Depression as a probable turning point in American history because it seemed to entail not only an economic breakdown, but a loss of "our conviction of the value of what we were doing." Those liberals who had sought to achieve reforms within the capitalist system were guilty, therefore, of both economic and ideological inadequacy. If the liberal program of social planning and control meant anything at all, Wilson continued, it had to mean socialism. This line of reasoning led to the crux of his appeal: "I believe that if the American radicals and progressives who repudiate the Marxian dogma and the strategy of the Communist Party hope to accomplish anything valuable, they must take Communism away from the

Communists, and take it without ambiguities or reservations, asserting emphatically that their ultimate goal is the ownership of the means of production by the government." [33]

Here was an answer to Villard's plaintive question of the year before. Wilson was telling the liberals, in effect, that they had to bring to fruition the Soviet-American comparison they had been making throughout the twenties. By 1930, that juxtaposition had become more vivid than ever before, for while the American Depression deepened, the Soviet regime was implementing its First Five-Year Plan, which promised enormous industrialization and agricultural collectivization under the direction of Gosplan, the central government agency. The symmetry seems obvious and portentous: as laissez-faire crumbled under its inherent and inescapable fallacies, Soviet Communism was proving the strength of its contrary economic principles. The liberals' ideological retreat now turned out to be, as Lincoln Steffens had predicted, a step into the future. Appropriately, in 1931 Steffens' *Autobiography* became a bestseller and the subject of planning became a great vogue.

But retrospective symmetry simplifies the situation. Those liberals who sympathized with the Soviet Union before 1930 had stressed its social and psychological rather than its economic virtues. In fact, they had generally ascribed the Soviet economic recovery to the NEP, which impressed them as a sound, pragmatic approach. By the time of Edmund Wilson's appeal, however, the Depression and the Plan had subordinated the cultural questions on which liberals had focused. Thus, Wilson was demanding not simply that liberals import their Soviet sympathy, but that they develop a new kind of sympathy. Spokesmen like the editors of *The Nation* and *The New Republic*, despite their decade of strenuous tolerance for the Soviets, could not negotiate the conversion. Both journals vigorously supported the need for American planning in or-

197

der to overcome the Depression and they praised the Five-Year Plan as a success, but they never fused the two themes into a single program. On the contrary, *The New Republic* congratulated Stalin for permitting greater individual incentives and rewards in 1931 and, a year later, firmly announced: "We must have planning, but it ought to be good planning, based on democratic assumptions." [34] Meanwhile, Villard was writing in *The Nation* that the United States should imitate the Soviet emphasis on general welfare, but that the American economic crisis derived from the faults of its leaders, not from its economic and political structure.[35] Ironically, then, at the very time that the Soviet Union was winning favorable attention from left-wing Americans, some of its earliest and most steadfast friends found that the terms of their friendship were irrelevant. They seemed to have been outmoded rather than vindicated.

A group of economists that visited the USSR during the late 1920's and early 1930's came closer to answering Wilson's appeal because their professional interests predisposed them to examine the economic significance of their experience. Even before the introduction of the Five-Year Plan in October 1928, Scott Nearing, Rexford G. Tugwell, Stuart Chase, and others were pointing to Soviet planning as the explanation for Russia's economic stabilization since 1920 and as the source for further progress in the future. Tugwell was both surprised and impressed by the "experimentalism" demonstrated by the Communist planners. The future member of the New Deal brain trust concluded in 1928: "Perhaps the time is not far off when we shall, in spite of doctrinaire differences, begin to ask ourselves whether there are not some lessons that even we dominant Americans can learn there." [36]

Under the combined impact of the Plan and the Depression, economists developed avid interest in the Soviet experiment. Predictably, some criticized it as a rigid, overcentralized, inadequate mechanism for obtaining economic growth, and others cited statistics to prove its success and to warrant adoption of a similar approach to the American economy.[37] By 1931, Tugwell went so far as to warn the American Economic Association that, while conservatives were creating a situation ripe for violence in the United States, the "future is becoming visible in Russia." [38] This may have been more of a polemical than an academic statement, however. Certainly it does not justify any claim that Tugwell's interest in planning was caused by his Soviet visit in 1927. On the one hand, that interest was firmly developed before then and, on the other hand, in a book published in 1933 he argued for economic planning without any reference to the Soviet precedent.[39]

William Trufant Foster, another early and notable advocate of planning, was more explicit: "Must we follow the plan of Russia? I think not." [40] This was the prevailing response among most social scientists as they outlined programs under which the United States could plan its way out of economic disaster. They stressed coordination and voluntary participation, explicitly denying the feasibility of a dictatorial system like that administered by Gosplan. Charles A. Beard even claimed that the Five-Year Plan was an afterthought at the end of a series of economic improvisations and that its success still had to be demonstrated. Moreover, he said, it was not Russian in origin but was borrowed from American capitalist and technocrat techniques. The only un-American feature was the tyranny with which it was applied. Beard therefore recommended "a 'Five-Year Plan' for America" under which syndicates of corporations would cooperatively analyze the economic situation and voluntarily adjust their production and distribution to predicted needs. Although an economic determinist with Marxist leanings before the war, Beard now demanded an ethical and democratic focus for

199

his economic solutions.[41] Others shared the general emphasis, even if not the particular tenets, of his plan.[42] As the radical economist George Soule remarked, while making his suggestions in *A Planned Society,* the American precedent of the War Industries Board in 1917–1918 seemed much more relevant than the Five-Year Plan to advocates of planning. This was a shrewd insight confirmed by later historians.[43] The Soviet model had provoked Americans to devise more palatable and familiar alternatives.

Slightly more than a year after his original "Appeal to Progressives," Edmund Wilson evaluated the liberals' accomplishments during the interim. He was profoundly dismayed. Instead of taking Communism away from the Communists, he complained, they had merely perpetuated their outworn beliefs under new guises. Wilson scornfully criticized their schemes for a planned economy as being "designed to preserve the capitalist system while eliminating some of its worst features — though so far as one can tell from what they write, they haven't the ghost of an idea of an agency to put even these into effect." In Wilson's opinion, Beard, Stuart Chase, Walter Lippmann, and others deserved only rebuke for their foolish belief that capitalism could reform itself. Apparently, he said, the liberals had forgotten the lesson of Wilsonian progressivism: if capitalists did the planning, "they would plan to save their own skins at the expense of whoever had to bleed." When Beard objected to the Five-Year Plan because it was dictatorial, he was overlooking the fact that Americans outside of the "owning-class orbit" also were subject to tyranny. If the United States was to be reformed, Edmund Wilson concluded, it had to become a socialist society — not a replica of the USSR, of course, but like it with respect to the abolition of social classes as well as private enterprise and profit.[44] These were harsh words and drastic ideas. In effect, Wilson announced the futility of his appeal to liberals, who were irretrievable prisoners of their middle-class premises. Thus he moved closer to the strict Communist conviction that, as *The New Masses* put it, "social economic planning is impossible without a proletarian revolution." [45]

In their moment of apparent opportunity, then, the liberal ranks were being depleted by defectors to Communist doctrines. Lincoln Steffens bluntly announced that "we liberals, the world over, have had our day," doomed by the failure to have aims that were more than "vague and various." [46] Their neighbors to the left, the socialists, suffered a similar fate during the early thirties. In the first five years of the greatest economic crisis since its birth, the American Socialist Party barely managed to double its membership, attaining the pitiful total of 15,000. At the same time, it split into angry factions, the Old Guard under Morris Hillquit, the national chairman, resisting the younger Militants who wanted to emphasize the principle of class struggle and thereby to seize the drama and initiative from the Communists. The acid test inevitably was the Soviet Union's version of socialism. At the 1930 convention of New York socialists, for example, both groups demanded American recognition of the USSR and disapproved of Soviet intolerance toward dissent. But the Militants advocated "a definitely friendly attitude toward Soviet Russia" and minimized the dictatorship, whereas the Old Guard asked only for normal diplomatic and commercial relations and extensively criticized the "governmental terrorism, and . . . ruthless suppression of all dissenting opinion." Hillquit termed the Soviet regime "a travesty of socialism." [47]

However laudable this position was in moral terms, it proved quite unsatisfactory in practice. High-minded qualms held little appeal for those hungry, hopeless workers or restless intellectuals who were ready for immediate and vigorous solutions. The right to dissent on an empty stomach was, in comparison with the full employment in Russia, a luxury.

Norman Thomas, the party's nominee for President in 1928 and again in 1932, perceived this fact. Although he shared the Old Guard's denunciation of the Soviet dictatorship and insisted that his party must seek strictly democratic planning in the United States, he also warned readers of the party's official newspaper, *The New Leader*: "We have done ourselves much harm by what has looked like carping and indiscriminate criticism of Russia. Just because there are things in Russia that need to be criticized for the good of workers everywhere — as well as a great deal to praise — we want to be extremely careful to make our criticism sound and convincing." [48] The national convention of 1932 passed a resolution which translated the Socialist perplexity into clumsy ambivalence. First applauding the Soviet economic effort and then rebuking the Soviet dictatorship, the resolution was, according to one socialist, the most unsatisfactory one ever adopted by the party.[49]

John Dos Passos spoke for many others when he caustically quipped that "becoming a socialist right now would have just the same effect on anybody as drinking a bottle of near-beer." [50] He joined Edmund Wilson, Lincoln Steffens, and fifty other intellectuals in subscribing to an "open letter," written in September 1932, which declared their support for the Communist Party and scoffed at the reformism of other parties. A month later they expanded the letter into a pamphlet, *Culture and the Crisis,* and institutionalized their feelings into the League of Professional Writers for Foster and Ford, the Communist candidates for President and Vice-President.[51]

The company of unregretful mourners at the grave of liberalism was growing. In the crisis of the early thirties they rejected liberal legalism and moralism as a code of gentlemanly conduct which the Crash had outdated along with

202

capitalism. The old truths — economic as well as moral — had collapsed, they said; the times were ripe for new men with new and stronger truths, among which traditional freedom was secondary. George S. Counts sounded a typical note in 1932: "The genuinely free man is not the person who spends the day contemplating his own navel, but rather the one who loses himself in a great cause or glorious adventure." [52] And in 1932 the scene for adventure and glory was among the builders of the Five-Year Plan. One reader of *The Nation* advised all forward-looking individuals to emigrate to Russia where progress was taking place under the stimulus of cooperation, not the profit motive. "Today freedom and democracy are phantoms," she exclaimed, while the Soviets offered the real freedom of an enlightened, efficient, and humanitarian oligarchy.[53] In other words, results alone mattered now.

Nevertheless, the perspective from the far left distorts the condition of liberalism after the Crash. Its adherents were neither clinging desperately to the fragments of shattered shibboleths nor brooding impotently upon their navels. Instead, they were attempting to formulate political positions that went beyond the capitalist status quo but short of Communist revolution. Just as during the twenties they had visited Russia to observe reform, rather than visiting Paris to enjoy rebellion, now they wanted to rehabilitate American society rather than to uproot its foundations and begin from the beginning. They had heard Edmund Wilson's appeal and were trying to take Communism away from the Communists. According to many of them, the best vehicle was a third party. The economist Paul Douglas had organized the League for Independent Political Action in 1929, two years after visiting the USSR. As the Depression set in, he regarded the League as the germ of a new party espousing doctrines of governmental economic planning and public ownership of utilities.

John Dewey served as the League's chairman, while Stuart Chase, Villard, Reinhold Niebuhr, and Norman Thomas were among the members of the national committee. Significantly, all of them except Thomas had traveled to the Soviet Union.[54]

The position taken by Dewey is particularly interesting because, in 1928, he had been so tempted to compromise his commitment to liberty after observing the constructive role offered to intellectuals by the Soviet regime. The Depression conceivably might have overcome his hesitations, just as it overcame those of so many of his fellow intellectuals. Yet he resisted the comforts of dogma; even though he developed new social programs, he built upon a loyalty to pragmatism and intelligence. As he explained in 1930, in *Individualism Old and New*, the United States had entered a collective age in which conventional individualism had lost its meaning. Now the issue was the "utilization of the realities of a corporate civilization to validate and embody the distinctive moral element in the American version of individualism: Equality and freedom expressed not merely externally and politically but through personal participation in the development of a shared culture." A year later he was echoing Douglas' call for a new party to implement economic planning without subjection to Moscow's command and without the dictatorial aspects of the Five-Year Plan.[55]

George S. Counts, his colleague at Columbia Teachers' College, was much more tolerant of Soviet practices and romantically inclined to immersion in a "glorious adventure." Ultimately, however, he defined collectivism in terms parallel to Dewey's. He, too, sought to integrate the traditional American ideal of democracy into the rationalized economic machinery which he urged as the means to recovery.[56] Counts was most eloquent and most successful when he applied these principles to American education. Before 1929 his enthusiasm for the Soviet blending of school and society had aroused little response among his fellow educators. Progressive education had come to mean a child-centered, not a society-centered, school. By comparison, Counts's ideas bore ominous implications of conformism or even political indoctrination. When the Depression began, educational as well as economic individualism lost its persuasiveness, and Counts's programs seemed cogent. At the 1932 convention of the Progressive Education Association, he issued a challenge: "Dare Progressive Education Be Progressive?" Only if education overcame fears of indoctrination and developed a theory of social welfare, a "vision of human destiny," he exclaimed, would it attain genuine meaning.

This call to intellectual adventure provoked the formation of a committee whose report was as radical as Counts could have wished — but too radical for the cautious Association to endorse. Nonetheless, a fundamental reassessment in progressive education had begun.[57] The collection of essays by Dewey, William H. Kilpatrick, and others, published in 1933 under the vivid title, *The Educational Frontier*, epitomized the transformation. With frequent side glances at the Soviet example, the authors renewed the radical social character which originally pervaded progressive education as conceived by Dewey.[58] But this social radicalism acquired a spirit of indoctrination which Dewey's original theories — instrumental and open-ended — did not have.

Thus, despite the scorn of its critics from the left, liberalism was changing in order to present constructive alternatives to the American crisis. More decisively than ever before, numerous liberals turned their backs on orthodox laissez-faire and demanded the deliberate, vigorous intervention of the government into the economy. At the same time, they hoped to preserve the framework of political democracy. Clearly exemplary of this ideological position was the decision by the League for Independent Political Action to support

Norman Thomas for President in 1932.[59] In short, more than a decade after first turning to the USSR as a potentially purer example of American ideals, these and other liberals were returning home to Americanize their Soviet experience. They implicitly acknowledged that the dynamic force in the world had shifted eastward, but they returned as they had left — fellow travelers.

Despite basic ideological reservations, however, they defended the Soviet Union more vehemently than at any time since 1920. During the popular outcry against the anti-religious campaign by the Moscow government, liberal spokesmen derided the American hysteria as political rather than religious in motive and minimized the significance of the Soviet actions.[60] When the Soviets staged their various trials of engineers accused of sabotage, *The Nation* angrily objected to the principle of class justice, but *The New Republic* had no hesitation in condoning the trials.[61] The latter journal even asserted in 1932 that Stalin had never been a dictator like Mussolini or others because the Communist Party could depose him at any time.[62] Throughout the early 1930's, these two liberal organs praised the growing economic stability under the Five-Year Plan and demanded resumption of Soviet-American trade relations.[63]

Inevitably the focal point of liberal sympathy for the USSR became the issue of diplomatic recognition. During the Hoover Administration the liberals had dutifully repeated their advocacy of recognition, adding the new argument that such a move would increase Soviet purchases in the United States and thereby help to ease the Depression. But they realized that the President was unalterably opposed to any such gesture of appeasement toward his old enemies, the "Bolshevik murderers." [64] The election of Franklin D. Roosevelt in November 1932 signaled the hope of ending the impasse. Already during his campaign, the new President had expressed his open-mindedness on the question of recognition.[65] On the day after the election, Senator William E. Borah wrote to Alexander Gumberg, his old ally in the struggle for Soviet-American diplomatic relations, that "those who profess to know" were convinced that the President-elect favored the cause.[66] By the spring of 1933, the triumvirate of Borah, Gumberg, and Raymond Robins was reviving the campaign which they had allowed to lapse during the previous unpromising decade. Joined by Jerome Davis and their former adversary, Samuel N. Harper, they arranged conferences and luncheons with Washington officials in a spirit of bounding optimism. It was like old times, like the halcyon days of 1917–1918. Indeed, as if to complete the sense of *déjà vu*, their old friend, William Bullitt, had returned from retirement and was serving as Special Assistant to the Secretary of State.[67]

Their lobbying behind the scenes was complemented by an unprecedented deluge of public support from liberal and radical circles. In January 1933, 800 college professors, including several college presidents, sent a petition to Roosevelt in favor of recognition. In March, representatives of the American Women's Committee for Recognition of Soviet Russia presented a resolution to the White House and State Department, the list of 170 signers being headed by the name of Jane Addams. In May, 35 economists, educators, and engineers sent a similar petition to the President. Meanwhile, the Independent Committee for the Recognition of Soviet Russia had been formed, its advisory council including Lincoln Steffens, William Allen White, George S. Counts, John Haynes Holmes, and other notable figures.[68]

These groups had advantages which previous proponents of recognition had lacked. First of all, the Depression provided an emotional, if not a strictly economic, basis for the argument that recognition would encourage Soviet-American trade and thereby give jobs to some of the millions of unemployed. Second, the diplomatic tensions in the Far East, deriving mainly from Japanese aggressions in Manchuria, endowed recognition with the possibility of contributing to world peace by bolstering the Soviet Union as a counterweight to Japan. Finally, and less tangible, the passage of sixteen years since the Revolution had removed much of the combustible quality of the issue. Recognition seemed more like a tardy concession to irrevocable facts than a sanction of Communism. The question of Soviet repudiation of debts had become particularly anomalous because of the European countries' default on repayments of American war loans.[69]

On November 17, 1933, following lengthy negotiations with Maxim Litvinov, Commissar for Foreign Affairs, President Roosevelt announced American recognition of the Soviet regime. Borah immediately sent a telegram which, by chance, was the first to be opened at the White House: "CONGRATULATIONS STOP IT WAS THE FINE BIG COURAGEOUS THING TO DO." [70] *The New Leader* welcomed the end of what it called seventeen years of official duplicity.[71] *The Nation* hailed the action as a major accomplishment of the New Deal, a contribution to world peace, and "the return of common sense after the long reign of fantasy and fear." [72] But the editors of *The New Republic* perceived even greater significance:

Twenty years hence, historians looking back on the present day might easily decide that the resumption of diplomatic relations between the United States and Russia is one of the two or three outstanding events of the fifteen years after the end of the War.[73]

This excitement expressed the satisfaction of long-frustrated desires, but it also expressed more. Recognition had been elevated far above diplomatic formality by the sixteen years of rhetoric lavished upon it from all sides. It had become a symbol of the fact that, to Americans, the Soviet government represented not simply a political regime, but a challenge to their values. Consequently, Roosevelt's action aroused elation among liberals because they interpreted it as a tacit admission of the validity of Soviet principles. The normalization of diplomatic relations seemed to endorse the ideological relationship which liberals had been sustaining since the Revolution. Now the United States would learn from the Soviet experiment instead of blindly denouncing it. Recognition of the USSR, which repealed one of the most negative inheritances of "normalcy," symbolized to liberals that at last they could see in the United States the future which Steffens had seen only in Russia. Their intellectual exile seemed to be ended and vindicated by the New Deal.

Early in the Depression, many Americans warned that fiendish economic dumping by the USSR was endangering the business community's brave effort to uphold not only fair prices, but also the American trinity of home, church, and property.

"AM I GOING TO LET THAT BIRD CRAB MY ACT?"

VIII / Business Leaders and the Plan

Russia is beginning a new civilization, and the attention of the world is riveted on her.

— Elisha M. Friedman, *Russia in Transition: A Business Man's Appraisal* (New York, 1932), p. 487

At one point during his presidential address to the 1930 convention of the National Association of Manufacturers, John E. Edgerton declared with unremitting emphasis: *"Certainly nothing has happened to weaken the confidence of understanding minds in the essential parts of our American economic system and in its adaptability to the highest ends of progress, nor in our scheme of government."* [1] But something had happened — the stock market and then the New Era had crashed — and all the italics of the NAM could not put the pieces together again. Edgerton's talk about unweakened confidence only revealed more acutely and pathetically the doubts which assailed him and his colleagues.

A year later, Albert H. Wiggin, chairman of the governing board of the Chase National Bank in New York, was more frank as he spoke to a very different group, the subcommittee of the Senate Committee on Manufactures. Summarizing Wiggin's argument against the creation of a national economic council, Senator Robert La Follette, Jr., in charge of the hearings, said: "Your counsel is really one of despair, then. We are going to suffer these terrible dislocations and the suffering that goes with them on the part of the people generally?"

211

"I think you are looking for a superman," Wiggin replied, "and there is no such thing. Human nature is human nature. Lives go on. So long as business activity goes on we are bound to have conditions of crisis once in so often."

La Follette probed still further: "You think, then, that the capacity for human suffering is unlimited?" Wiggin responded simply: "I think so." [2]

Although the bank executive was willing to recognize the crisis which, in 1930, the NAM president still attempted to disguise under bravado, neither apparently had surrendered the complacent assurance that their economic beliefs were still valid. The economic circumstances had changed drastically since the 1920's, but the thinking of these business spokesmen remained essentially the same. Noisy confidence had merely quieted into apathetic resignation to the fickle economic cycle. Like Lenin in the dark days when the NEP began, American capitalists executed a "strategic retreat" and, unlike Lenin, settled into irresponsibility.[3]

But this portrait alone is misleading, for another mood — a more active and alarmed one — also spread through the business community in these first years of the Depression. William Allen White described it to Frederick Lewis Allen in December 1931: "And, oh boy, you are right when you say that Babbitt 'thinks civilization is headed for economic doom.' I was in a meeting a few weeks ago in which were one of the heads of the Steel Trust, Radio Corporation, General Motors, Standard Oil, and a half a dozen industrial corporations, and the way those lads are dreaming of barricades in the street this winter would raise your hair." [4] Even if one makes adequate compensation for White's customary effervescence, the central apocalyptic quality survives. Like most Americans, business leaders were apprehensive of the future. But their fears had a special intensity which reached into the awesome dimension of "civilization" in an encounter with "economic doom." Surely this was only verbal extravagance. But was it?

Businessmen in the 1920's habitually reminded themselves and others of the unprecedented prosperity which American capitalism had created and which they interpreted, under the inflating prod of pride, as the mark of a superior civilization. Both the pride and the civilization were manufactured from a material base which, at the end of 1929, suddenly dissolved. Soon the boast of New Era spokesmen became parody in the hands of hostile and disillusioned critics.[5] And curiously it underwent a somewhat similar transmutation in the minds of its own perpetrators, for businessmen quickly began to talk of the trial and doom of civilization. The millennium now became Last Judgment as their attitudes swerved from one extreme to the other. Given that the economic standard by which they had measured all other values — moral and political as well as economic — had failed them, this reaction is understandable.

Thus *Business Week* editorialized in the following fashion:

It is one thing for men to lose their jobs; another for them to lose their faith.

In that light, this depression is more than a passing circumstance in our history; it is a crucial turning point in industrial civilization, not only for the United States, but for the world. . . . It is not too much to say [that] the philosophy of individual and organized private initiative upon which our business system is founded and operated under the leadership of business men, economists, and engineers who have replaced the kings and statesmen of the past, is definitely on trial today, more decisively than it ever has been before.

But the editorial did not conclude here. It went on to make a prediction.

Unless the United States can effectively resume its leadership in world economic affairs and demonstrate by its own success in meeting this crisis the superiority of the philosophy of which it now stands as practically the sole exponent, outright communism will

213

be knocking at the gates of Berlin and London within the next decade, and the echoes of that summons will be heard across the wide seas.[6]

Thus the fate of the world depended on the success of American capitalism's struggle with the forces of depression. Like the talk of "civilization," this analysis was an inversion of business attitudes in the preceding decade. Whereas earlier these American economic leaders had looked to the Soviet Union with enthusiasm, paternally proud of its progress from communist ruin to capitalist success, by 1930 they looked with fear. In part, this again was a reflex incited by their excessive reliance on superlatives. But it was a response to conditions of the world as well as of the mind. For as observers ceaselessly pointed out, Soviet Russia was suffering from a shortage of workers in her drive to meet the ambitious schedule of the Five-Year Plan. The United States, meanwhile, had no Plan and millions of unemployed. By some cruel trick, the Soviet-American relationship had turned inside out, the child becoming father to the man. The New World was suddenly an old, decadent economy exactly fulfilling the dooming prophecies of Marxian dogma, preached now by "a new civilization" whose success was astounding the world.[7] It is hardly surprising that American capitalists assumed an apocalyptic tone as they confronted this scene. The editor of *The Journal of the American Bankers' Association* not only articulated this attitude, but also perceived the tragic irony of the situation. In 1931 he excoriated the American engineers and industrialists who, by aiding Russia, were repeating "what the Roman governors did for Alaric and his crew of Goths." Their profit seeking could mean the suicide of capitalist civilization.[8]

Not even this vivid sense of doom, however, stifled the contrary instinct to survive and struggle back to equilibrium. Few businessmen could accept Wiggin's "counsel of despair."

214

In the search for a way out of the Depression, many began to examine and then adopt the solution offered by intellectuals. " 'ECONOMIC PLANNING' recently has become the epigrammatic program of practically every economic interest group in our Nation," one commentator exclaimed in mid-1932. "In a measure, it is a dogma of faith into which many have compressed their hope that the economic hereafter will be more pleasant than the economic present." [9] Broadly speaking, he was correct. Reluctantly but increasingly, businessmen were acknowledging that unrestrained laissez-faire had been partly responsible for the economic collapse and that recovery depended on some sort of restraint. This fact provokes two crucial questions: first of all, how far and how fast did business thinking move toward economic planning; and, second, to what degree was that movement caused by the Soviet example?

As could be easily inferred from a general knowledge of their economic premises in the twenties, businessmen only gradually accepted the validity of planning, and then never as thoroughly as liberal or radical intellectuals did. Yet without having admitted it, they had been partly acting from a related view long before the Depression. The development of trusts in the late nineteenth and early twentieth centuries was an expression of the desire and necessity to rationalize production. When the Progressive movement sought to subjugate these economic giants to government control, businessmen diverted the threat to their autonomy by developing a system of self-rule. The creation of the Chamber of Commerce in 1912 was one outstanding expression of this policy. Another was the growth of trade associations, which became exceedingly numerous during the postwar decade and which were sanctioned by the Supreme Court in two decisions of 1925.[10]

Economic planning, however, signified practices and concepts more radical than these. It not only demanded conscious intervention in the economic system but also, according to most exponents, required the active participation of the federal government. Businessmen hitherto had been distinctly intolerant of all of these tenets. When they began to take up the slogan of economic planning in these early Depression years, therefore, they did so with caution and with the firm intention of stopping far short of the socialist territory occupied by the strongest advocates of planning. The editorials of the relatively liberal *Business Week* furnish a useful gauge of the rate at which some businessmen approached planning. In November 1929, the journal focused on the individuals who, it said, really constituted "business" and whose talent, having once created prosperity, soon would recreate it. By mid-1930, however, it was criticizing the "recklessness" of the New Era and investing its hope in "the individual and *collective* human intelligence and ability" to guide business. Soon it was confessing the necessity for government action unless private business met the crisis with the vigor that *Business Week* urged. By June 1931, it no longer was backing into the inevitable but, under the title of "Do You Still Believe in Lazy-Fairies?", was stating it forthrightly: "to plan or not to plan is no longer the question. The real question is, who is to do it." [11]

In the course of the Depression's second year, innumerable business leaders and groups joined the campaign for planning.[12] The first comprehensive plan was that of Gerard Swope, president of the General Electric Company, which he presented to the National Electric Manufacturers' Association on September 16, 1931.[13] Immediately famous as the Swope Plan, it accelerated the conversion of the business community. The Chamber of Commerce itself, after appointing a Committee on Continuity of Business and Employment to study the situation, admitted that the period of extreme individualism had yielded to one in which "a proper coordination of production and consumption" was necessary.[14]

But *Business Week* had asked an important question: who was to do the planning? Henry I. Harriman, chairman of the Chamber of Commerce's Committee on Continuity and president of the Chamber itself in 1932, gave the answer of most businessmen when, in his testimony before La Follette's subcommittee on the bill to establish a national economic council, he said that the council should be "appointed by business and supported by business." [15] In other words, business spokesmen were unable or unwilling to discard the model of trade associations and business self-government. They stressed relaxation of antitrust laws as a major stimulus to constructive action and cooperation by business firms.[16] With vehemence they distinguished between economic planning and economic control; to them, the latter meant government control, and that was anathema. It was contrary to the American tradition of individualism and democracy, they argued. *American* planning was from the bottom up. Matthew Woll, vice-president of the American Federation of Labor, summoned all his rhetorical artillery in defense of this theme. As acting president of the National Civic Federation, he urged his organization to convoke a "great American congress of industry" whose research would "begin that march toward permanence of machinery without which we cannot infuse into industry that democratic urge and authority vital to its life as a field of human endeavor and vital to its salvation from an onslaught of state political control that cannot be avoided in the absence of self-control." In short: "We need . . . to meet the cold-blooded communist five-year plan, with a warm-blooded ten-year plan of democratic idealism woven into the very pattern of our national fabric." [17]

These remarks prompt examination of the relationship between American and Soviet versions of planning. Clearly,

Woll considered them to be two totally disparate and antagonistic species. Yet they *did* share the genus of planning, and the Soviet Union's Five-Year Plan *had* preceded American businessmen's suggestions by several years. Did it not only precede but also cause business interest in planning? President Hoover, who himself proposed "an American plan" in mid-1931, insisted that "the 'plan' idea is an infection from the slogan of the 'five-year plan' through which Russia is struggling to redeem herself from the ten years of starvation and misery." In caustic terms he warned against the adoption of "economic patent medicines from foreign lands." [18] At the other end of the political spectrum, Louis Fischer, the left-wing journalist who reported on and still sympathized with Russia, also claimed that the American bourgeoisie was imitating the Soviet discovery.[19]

This theme was not original. After having developed the habit in the 1920's of viewing the USSR as a precocious student of American success, many American capitalists, in the despair born of Depression, naturally were prone to reverse the relationship.[20] Yet the political commitments of Hoover and Fischer predisposed them to a distorted judgment. American businessmen may have realized that the USSR had survived the collapse of American prosperity, yet none became Communists or even fellow travelers; most, in fact, nostalgically clung for a long time to the void that had been the New Era. Many attributed the continued Soviet progress to the Five-Year Plan (for what else, after all, could have been responsible?) ; yet none was willing to recommend the same sort of plan for the United States. Certainly the opportunities for such a recommendation were ripe, particularly as "planning" became the watchword for the business community. Senator La Follette's bill to create a national economic council, for example, was a direct response to the growing public tolerance for the idea of a rationalized economic process. For two months his subcommittee heard testimony stretching over 750 closely typed pages. At the end of it all, however, only two businessmen and three others had mentioned the Soviet Union, four of them in order to make it clear that the Five-Year Plan was irrelevant to the American situation, and only one at any length and with any approval.[21]

The argument from silence is always a delicate one. The conclusion that the businessmen were in fact repressing the humiliating admission of Soviet success has some undeniable merits. A more valid conclusion, however, is that American businessmen honestly saw nothing worthy of imitation in the Five-Year Plan. The United States had joined Russia in being one of the "two great experiments in human existence face to face in the world," but the point was that they were face to face.[22] They shared an economic jeopardy but not a set of moral or political values. That was clear after Americans learned of the autocratic features and inefficient results of the Plan. Although businessmen discarded the joyful propaganda they had built around the NEP, now that Stalin obviously had turned toward authoritarian communism, they still cherished the democratic beliefs from which the propaganda had sprung. They were unwilling to subject their own nation to the harsh consequences of a communist system. They supported a national economic council without any tolerance for a Gosplan. Rather, they were ready, as William Allen White said, to raise "barricades in the street" against any radicals anxious to overthrow capitalism.[23]

The model for business ideas about planning lay, if anywhere, in the domestic experience of the War Industries Board during the First World War. Two witnesses at the La Follette hearings explicitly mentioned this organization.[24] Other businessmen invoked the same precedent as they groped their way toward a tolerance of planning. Indeed the author of the Swope Plan was a veteran of the board.[25] Added to this precedent were the concepts and practices developed by the trade associations of the preceding decade. The eventual institutional product of the planning discussion was, of course, the National Recovery Administration, which borrowed directly from the form of trade associations and which borrowed former War Industries Board personnel such as Hugh Johnson, Bernard Baruch, Leo Wolman, and Swope. In the phrase of Arthur Schlesinger, Jr., the NRA was the "child of the War Industries Board." [26]

In the radically different circumstances after 1929, therefore, American businessmen ceased to exclaim enthusiastically about the ideological convergence of the United States and the USSR. That had been a tendency they had converted into a certainty in order to justify their economic interest in the Soviet Union. The Five-Year Plan made the idea untenable. But the purely economic interest survived strongly, as will be shown later in the chapter. Moreover, the ideological enthusiasm was maintained in qualified form by another group of Americans: the engineers working on the scene of the Five-Year Plan.

American technical assistance provided one of the most interesting by-products of the Soviet-American economic entente, for it required the actual presence of Americans in Russia. After businessmen had for so many years condemned Communism because it did not or could not work, here were Americans brought to the Soviet Union to make it work better. These engineers had to evaluate Communists and Communism at first hand, without the American environment and without a distance of thousands of miles to introduce distortion. They had only their own senses and, of course, their own preconceptions as a means of observation. No factors such as claims to confiscated oilfields or, on the other hand, ambitions to monopolize those fields precluded them from discovering both the virtues and failings of the great Red experiment. Their perspective was unique.

As of 1931, more than one thousand American technicians were working for the Soviets.[27] By 1933, six hundred engineers were working in automobile and tractor plants alone.[28] Why did they go? Probably for most, the decision was made by the firms which employed them and which, like the Ford Motor Company, made technical-assistance contracts with the USSR. Many were free agents, however, whose outstanding work in the United States induced Soviet planners to offer them attractive salaries; as hard times became harder in the Depression, these salaries seemed even more attractive.[29] In addition, sheer curiosity impelled many to overcome apprehensions about living in a strange and, according to most travelers, uncomfortable country. None went because of an ideological commitment to Communism, according to William H. Chamberlin, the *Christian Science Monitor*'s Soviet correspondent.[30]

On their arrival in the Soviet Union, most engineers found themselves to be the center of attention. Government officials invariably gave them special accommodations in Moscow, took them to theaters and the opera, made sure that they traveled to the site of their job in comfort (luxury was unobtainable in Russian trains of the early 1930's), and generally treated their guests as industrial diplomats of high rank. Colonel Hugh L. Cooper, directing construction of the Dneiperstroy hydroelectric project, and John Calder, supervising work on the Stalingrad tractor plant, even had the rare distinction of personal conferences with Stalin himself. The majority of engineers had less extraordinary but equally satisfying conditions, such as food denied to the average Russian, liquor (in contrast to Prohibition America), and, if they were bachelors, the interest of Russian women desiring food, clothing, and a warm apartment.[31] Although these privileges never made life in the USSR as comfortable as it had been at home, they did compensate in large part for unavoidable inconvenience and strangeness.

Much more dominant and interesting than these personal circumstances was the industrial scene itself. Yet it was a human rather than a technical phenomenon which first impressed many of these visitors. "There is something akin to religious fervor behind every pick and shovel in Russia," exclaimed the vice-president of the Bundy Engineering Company with significant hyperbole after his return in 1930.[32] Walter A. Rukeyser, who twice visited the USSR during 1929–1930 as a consultant mining engineer for the asbestos mining and milling industry, made a similar observation about "the fanatical pride of all workers from the head director down to the lowliest 'mop' " toward their factories and jobs.[33] At a time when *Business Week* saw the need for a "moral regeneration" in the United States, the Soviet spirit was particularly striking to these American visitors.[34]

Other nontechnical themes appeared in the engineers' reactions. John D. Littlepage, a mining engineer who left the Soviet Union in 1937 after nine years there, explained that the attraction for him had not been Communism or the Russian people, but "the great open spaces of the Russian East." More important to him than the political system was this great geographical expanse, the last such undeveloped area in the world.[35] Twenty years earlier, another mining engineer, William Boyce Thompson, had been equally stirred by the wild Siberian country, which had reminded him of his native Montana.[36] If America had lost its fervor after 1929, it certainly had lost most of its wilderness long before. In Russia many engineers found a new frontier and revived their desire for adventure of vast dimensions. The personal motives which the Soviet Union satisfied were clearly expressed in an engineer's letter to *Mining and Metallurgy* in 1930: "There is no reason why a spirited and self-reliant American cannot come over here and do himself and Russia some good, if he but have a sympathetic attitude toward the struggle of Russia to attain higher things." [37] A self-reliant American! This vocabulary, borrowed from Emerson's century, implied the kind of emotional need which "civilized" America had left unfulfilled, had rendered anachronistic. The irony is that anyone could stress self-reliance in the context of Communist Russia, the country of selfless service to the Plan, to the Revolution, to History. Such disparity proves the strength of the preconceptions with which even hardheaded engineers surveyed the Soviet scene.

A few, however, achieved an emotional view which only Soviet Russia itself could have created. The experience of Walter A. Rukeyser is worth quoting at length because of its vivid detail. He was attending a performance of the propaganda ballet, *Krasny mak* (The Red Poppy), at the Bolshoi Theater, sitting in what had been the imperial box.

A peasant next to me, his elbows on the faded plush of the rail, head in hands, his beard bobbing slowly up and down as he masticated an apple in perfect synchronization with the music, seemed perfectly absorbed in the beauty of the performance. . . .

How the shade of the last of the Romanovs must have been revolted by the simple but dirty peasant munching an apple in the imperial box!

A great light began to dawn on me. . . . There came to me the realization that here was history — living history. And I was watching it. Not reading about it from the sidelines, but living it! I had but to reach over and I could even touch it. Before me was a new kind of czar, who, multiplied by one hundred and fifty million, spelled a new order of things. And I realized something else. This lousy boor beside me was a human being; he liked the same things I liked, the same things the Czar of all the Russias had liked. . . .

And then I realized the power of Soviet propaganda! I swore at myself for a sloppy sentimentalist. But the thought lingered in my mind: "If I, with all the advantages of education, feel myself, even for a moment, encompassed by this insidious propaganda of music,

223

dance, and spectacle, what must be the effect upon these ignorant masses?"[38]

The fervor and mystique of the Revolution, the challenge of Soviet reconstruction, the search for adventure — the role of such themes in the engineers' thinking indicates the uniform terms in which Americans from all backgrounds reacted to Soviet Russia. The impressions of the engineers are novel, however, because they were part of a larger set of very critical attitudes. These technical experts, working with Russians on the "Red experiment," ultimately attained a more balanced, objective view than did distant observers or short-term tourists. For the engineers were in the USSR to do a job and, as experts, they intended to do it well, reforming Soviet techniques whenever necessary. Rukeyser, for example, did not allow his romantic insight into the meaning of the Revolution to blur his disapproval of Soviet industrial practices. In unison with most of his American colleagues in Russia, he criticized the excessive Soviet penchant for theory and statistics. Soviet engineers loved to resort to conferences and reams of data, preferring an office to the field. American engineers, by contrast, used slide rule and handbook only for occasional calculations, generally relying instead on practical experience and common sense as they personally supervised the workers. Results proved the superiority of American methods. When American engineers echoed the Soviet boasts of unprecedented production of tractors, the construction of the largest dam in the world, and other such feats, they were praising their own techniques as much as Soviet achievements.[39]

Although some described the Russian theorizing habit as almost a racial characteristic, most correctly regarded it as a function of the pressures imposed by the Moscow planners. In the USSR after 1928, the Plan was everything and everywhere: it was in the minds of every Soviet official, manager, engineer, and worker; it was written in newspapers, posted on walls, and blaring from radio loudspeakers. Necessarily it impressed itself on the American engineers, too, most of whom were victims of its infectious exhortations to build bigger and faster.[40] They were also aware, however, of the Plan's serious shortcomings. Without political centralization and relentless pressure on every participant in the economic system, the mobilization of supplies and human energy would have been impossible. But the costs were high. First of all, no one was willing to take responsibility for decisions, because a mistake was interpreted as a counterrevolutionary act. The consequence was a plethora of red tape, which was intended to doublecheck and depersonalize each decision but which introduced its own disconcerting inefficiency. Second, centralization required Moscow planners to have knowledge and foresight which they could not always have. Often, to overcome one error, the Gosplan would issue a directive which disrupted other parts of the interconnected economy. As a result, almost every American engineer could tell stories of his project being halted by dilatory action on the part of his Russian colleagues or by clumsy haste to meet a production deadline, by the lack of some necessary machine or by the delivery of the wrong one, and so on.[41] Even more harassing was the constant fear among Americans that criticism of a Soviet manager or engineer could lead to his imprisonment or even execution as a saboteur.[42] *Mining and Metallurgy* and the American Chemical Society went so far as to warn that foreign engineers might become scapegoats in the event of failure in the Five-Year Plan.[43]

Complementing the engineers' criticisms of white-collar inefficiency was their frequent reference to the workers' inadequacy, particularly in comparison with American productivity. The Soviet laborers usually adjusted to high-speed industrial techniques with great difficulty, particularly since so many of them were peasants recruited from the farms. Mistreatment of machines because of ignorance or carelessness provided constant exasperation for American supervisors.[44] A special problem was insubordination, originating in the propaganda about proletarian superiority and encouraged by the workers' right to obtain the dismissal of their superiors if the latters' incompetence or counterrevolutionary intentions could be proved.[45] The thrilling fact of a proletarian munching an apple in the imperial box also had its less appealing side.

Few engineers left the USSR without an awareness of the complexity (and, frequently, the duplicity) of the Soviet scene and without a corresponding ambivalence toward the Communist experiment. George A. Burrell, for example, concluded his account in 1932 of his experience in the Soviet petroleum industry by juxtaposing the unemployment, poverty, crime, and political corruption in the United States with their absence in the USSR. But the engineer quickly added another contrast. Also absent in Russia, he noted, was American freedom of thought and action. "I suppose one lesson that we can draw from the comparison," he concluded, "is that we cannot afford to be too critical of the Soviet Union. . . . But we have a long way to sink to approximate Russian conditions." [46] The postscript was significant. However respectful he may have become toward the industrial progress under the Five-Year Plan, he still could not countenance its autocratic methods.

Rukeyser reached a similar resolution of his ambivalence. In 1929 he had entered the USSR in anticipation of a huge experiment using men and machines to create a unique, humane society. Subsequently, as was quoted above, he had experienced an exhilarating communion with the meaning of the Revolution. Nevertheless, he left Russia in 1930 with "the feeling that I was living again. I had been sick and now

I was well again. Here was normalcy, cleanliness, plenty. I had left the Communist Utopia behind me — I was again in the world of Capitalistic Depression." [47]

Thus fervor, slogans, construction of some of the largest industrial projects in the world, flattering admiration of American expertise and American techniques — none of these compensated for suppression of personal liberties and consumers' rights. Many of the American engineers were persuaded by personal contact with the Soviet Union to discard prejudices of the sort circulated in the United States by anti-Soviet groups. But their fundamental set of values was unchanged or, if anything, was reinforced. They returned home as capitalists and patriots.[48] Although the Soviet slogans may have been contagious to Americans so recently departed from the New Era, the ideology behind the slogans definitely remained distasteful.[49]

In the United States, meanwhile, business attitudes toward the Soviet Union were undergoing a complex transformation during which the opposition between the pro-Soviet and anti-Soviet camps took on new terms. In fact, unlike the platitudes and virtual monologues which, from 1918 until 1930, constituted the so-called debate over Soviet trade and recognition, the two sides now began to engage in a genuine dialogue. Those who supported the Administration's policy of non-intercourse continued to work from essentially moral reasons. But after 1930 they increasingly replaced them with more empirical analysis of the economic arguments which their opponents used to justify their dealings with the USSR. In these last few years before diplomatic recognition, the business community finally was discussing the Soviet questions in terms appropriate to their special interests, namely, economic ones.

Hostile spokesmen and journals, using the reports of tourists, journalists, and engineers, laid dark emphasis on the numerous signs of Soviet failure to fulfill the Five-Year Plan. The shortages and rationing of basic consumer goods, particularly food; industrial inefficiency, amplified by the forced rate of development and the errors of Soviet planners; the surly or desperate resistance by peasants to collectivization — these were the favorite themes of critics of the Soviet experiment.[50] Yet this line of attack, although generally accurate, was ineffectual in competing with the more persuasive fact of a rising level of American trade with and investment in the USSR. Few businessmen, caught in the apparently ceaseless whirlpool of depression, dared disdain a market which in 1930 increased the value of its purchases by 35 per cent over the preceding year.[51] In fact, the USSR was the only important nation, the Department of Commerce reported, which increased its American purchases during the first nine months of 1930 as compared with the same period in 1929.[52] The number of technical-assistance contracts with the Soviets now totaled forty-five, second only to Germany.[53] As *Business Week* bluntly conceded, the Soviet Union was coming to the rescue of American industry.[54]

The rescue was not one of benevolence, needless to say. The Five-Year Plan created a sudden and spectacular need in Russia for machinery, tools, and motor vehicles.[55] The most natural source for such imports was the United States, the leading industrial nation of the world. With the Wall Street crash, a year after the Plan's initiation, the Soviet task of purchasing American goods was at first greatly simplified. The capitalists' own overindulgence suddenly solidified what Soviet propagandists and their few American friends had begun with such difficulty: the attraction of American businessmen to the Soviet marketplace. *Business Week* inadvertently revealed the terrific impact of the Depression on Soviet-American economic relations as early as January 1930. In directing attention to Ivy Lee's argument for official trade relations with the USSR, the editorial explained: "For what Mr. Lee had to say about Russia and about its interest for us, Americans, at this particular easeless moment in our history went straight home quite simply like so much common sense." [56] Yet Lee had made his views public in 1926. Apparently they became common sense only four years later, when capitalism entered a time of troubles and businessmen sought new silver linings of commerce.[57]

Business interest in Soviet trade began as early as the mid-twenties. Yet that had been speculation with a tinge of ideological motives. In 1930, the interest was closer to desperation and was strictly economic. As conditions worsened, moreover, it often threatened to change from a tendency to a tide. Already in 1930, a poll reported that leading bankers, manufacturers, exporters, and importers generally believed that: Soviet credit was good; the Communist regime had secretly compensated American industrialists whose property it had nationalized; nonrecognition was irrelevant; and the Soviet demand for American goods was large.[58] Spokesmen as influential as the manager of the National Association of Manufacturers' trade department praised Soviet economic progress and potential.[59] In the same generous spirit, the editors of *American Machinist* temporarily interrupted their skepticism of the Five-Year Plan to remark that such a program was "as startling to the twentieth century as was the American Republic to the eighteenth." [60] Thus, even if American goods contributed to Soviet survival and even if that survival involved the eventual death of capitalism, an impressive segment of the business community ignored eventualities and attended to the immediate need for the profits of Soviet-American commercial exchange. Distant doom was preferable to the tortured dying of American capitalism.[61]

The standpatters had not surrendered, however. Until the

middle of 1930, their dissent still was in the New Era's mode of moral outrage which, in the context of depression, was simply irrelevant.[62] But in July the anti-Soviet camp found a solid economic issue on which to fight, an issue which ironically was created by the same circumstances that had caused the recent rise in Soviet-American trade. For the Depression not only increased American willingness to trade, but also lowered world price levels — especially of commodities — thereby forcing Russia to sell more and more of her primarily agricultural and raw-material goods in order to buy the same amounts of the machinery she needed. The Soviets bitterly complained of their plight. Yet capitalist nations replied not with sympathy, but with accusations of "dumping," that is, the sale of exports at prices below domestic levels and below cost in an effort to destroy competitors rather than merely to compete with them.[63] As the Soviet Union began to increase the volume of its exports to the United States, many American businessmen, joined by political and other figures, raised a cry of alarm. Here, they warned, was the economic vanguard of the political revolution always promised by the Communist regime.

Suddenly the weapons brandished by advocates of Soviet-American trade were turned against them. The Soviet progress they had advertised in order to encourage timid American investors was being described as an insidious threat to American stability. In short, the terms were inside out. It is true, of course, that critics of Soviet export policy overlooked the fact that prices and costs in a socialized economy do not have the same relation as in a capitalist system, for a socialist government can balance a loss in the sale of one good by raising the price of another good. Second, critics did not distinguish between the Soviets' need to set low prices in order to sell goods and the intention to monopolize a market; the latter is dumping and the Soviets were not guilty of it.[64] Finally, it is both true and ironic that those who objected to Soviet dumping were guilty of complaining that the Communist system, which they had predicted would never succeed, suddenly was *too* successful. Yet these intellectual acrobatics were unnoticed in the hysteria over the Soviet menace. Conservatives of varied economic interests converged on the issue of dumping and consolidated their once faltering ranks around it.

The issue swept into notoriety on July 25, 1930, when the Assistant Secretary of the Treasury, Seymour Lowman, prohibited the entry of a shipment of Soviet paper pulpwood, claiming that it had been made by convict labor and therefore violated provisions of the Tariff Act of 1930. The reasoning behind the provisions was that the use of convict labor created, in effect, a politically authorized sweatshop which allowed a nation to sell its products at rates too low for any private producer, paying fair wages, to compete with. To protect the American economy, therefore, the Assistant Secretary banned the pulpwood and proposed an investigation of Soviet manganese ore, coal, and timber on similar grounds.[65]

Public reaction was immediate and noisy. J. Carson Adkerson, president of the American Manganese Producers' Association, not only applauded the Treasury's action, but announced that the association was planning an appeal to Washington for an embargo against alleged Soviet dumping of manganese. Approval also came from Matthew Woll. Speaking for the Wage Earners' Protective Conference and its 500,000 members, Woll promised proof that the entire economic system of the Soviets depended, at least partly, upon forced labor. On the other hand, numerous groups protested strongly against the pulpwood decision. These included the large financial and business interests who were exporting to the USSR, as well as the British, Norwegian, and Danish governments whose citizens owned the ships carrying the cargoes in question. Pressure was so intense that the Treasury virtually reversed itself a week later when it allowed the pulpwood to enter. In November, though, it added the impossible condition that importers submit proof against convict labor for each challenged cargo they brought to American ports.[66]

But the heat only rose to greater intensity as industrialists, the Chicago Board of Trade, and even a Congressional committee joined the furor. Among the most vociferous was Adkerson's Manganese Producers' Association, persistently demanding government action against Soviet strangulation of their infant industry.[67] The American Iron and Steel Institute, in a brief filed with the customs bureau of the Treasury Department, angrily dismissed the manganese producers' plea for special treatment. Despite its many sophisticated arguments, the institute neglected to include the most obvious and basic one, namely that the production of iron and steel required manganese ore and that the Soviet ore was superior to any other.[68]

Other industries became aroused. To textile producers, Soviet cotton exports seemed to portend a debilitating threat.[69] Anthracite mine owners and operators joined with the United Mine Workers in a terrified and incongruous alliance against supposed dumping of Soviet anthracite, despite denial by the coal dealers that the USSR was doing any such thing and despite evidence that the sale price was above the American levels.[70] The oil industry also was shocked into action when, in 1931, Soviet petroleum production spurted to second place in the world market. But this action took constructive, not retaliatory, form. In 1932 the president of Vacuum Oil called together the leading international oil companies in order to meet with Soviet representatives and to reach agreement on mutual limitation of exports by means of his so-called world-stabilization plan. Although the conference failed to overcome Soviet objections, Vacuum's gesture indicated the growing economic status accorded the USSR.[71] A more belligerent indication was Adkerson's organization, in October 1930, of a pressure group and information agency known as the Joint Conference on Unfair Russian Competition. Membership included the manganese, lumber, match, glue, coal, and sausage-casing industries, with fur and wheat expected to join soon.[72]

Wheat, in fact, was the focus of particularly feverish excitement. In the early 1930's, the USSR relied upon grain as a crucial source of foreign revenue to finance its purchases for the Five-Year Plan. As commodity prices declined throughout the world, the Soviet regime was forced to increase its exports of grain, particularly wheat.[73] In September 1930, the Secretary of Agriculture, Arthur M. Hyde, accused the Soviets of selling short in Chicago approximately 7.5 million bushels of wheat in order to depress American wheat prices and thereby sabotage the market. Because wheat prices already had fallen to the lowest level in twenty-five years, people were apprehensive; Hyde's announcement provoked a near-panic. Not even the assurances by the Chicago Board of Trade that the Soviets had engaged only in legitimate hedging could subdue the commotion.[74] In fact, Congressman Hamilton Fish of New York, conducting an investigation into domestic Communism, saw here a rich opportunity for expanding his scope. Already he had been probing into the activities of the Amtorg Trading Corporation, so inclusion of the Chicago wheat market was only a slight detour.[75] Fish uncovered nothing new, but his decision dramatized the fact that dumping was a controversial issue of political and moral as well as economic overtones. The publishing house of Dodd, Mead & Company gauged public interest shrewdly when, in 1931, it published H. R. Knickerbocker's account of his trip to Russia under the title of *The Red Trade Menace:*

233

Progress of the Soviet Five-Year Plan; the English version of the same year was sedately entitled *The Soviet Five-Year Plan and Its Effect on World Trade.*

It would be misleading, however, to give predominance to those who were the noisiest. True, the alarmists were numerous and often prestigious. Hugh Bancroft, the publisher of *Barron's Weekly* and the *Wall Street Journal*, for example, warned that the Soviet Union undoubtedly was maneuvering "to destroy all western civilization by economic warfare." [76] But other business spokesmen, no less committed to the capitalist system, rejected this view. In part, their dissent derived from annoyance that their colleagues were condemning Russia for not playing by the rules of the capitalist game when, in fact, Russia was playing only too well. The editors of *Barron's* toyed with this inconsistency when, after rebuking the Fish committee for investigating Amtorg's perfectly proper activities, they declared: "Our government cannot be undermined by profitable trade." [77] The less theoretical side of the same point was expressed by *Business Week* when it reported that businessmen did not care about Red propaganda, but cared greatly about the recent diversion of Amtorg's purchase orders to European competitors. Fish, Woll, and Adkerson were justly alarmed about dumping, the journal conceded, but they had not met the question intelligently or persuasively.[78] Significantly, however, *Business Week* did not propose an alternative solution, thereby suggesting inadvertently that perhaps the proponents of Soviet-American trade had the strongest argument of all: profits.

As has been noted, the Depression incited many businessmen to esteem the Soviet market and to accelerate the already strong increase in Soviet-American trade. Although that trade still constituted only a little more than 1 per cent of total American commerce in 1930, its favorable balance and its growing domination of the Soviet market held pleasing promise for the future. In 1930, the United States exceeded all other nations in exports to the USSR, furnishing 25 per cent of total Soviet purchases.[79] In 1931, American exporters esteemed this trade even more strongly when they found it slipping through their fingers. For the Soviet Union had decided to teach a lesson to the nation which had levied accusations of dumping, had imposed some embargoes and threatened more, and — perhaps most crucial — had stubbornly withheld long-term credits.[80] The Soviet regime retaliated by cutting back its orders of American goods from $4.5 million in August 1931 to $600,000 in September and then to $300,000 in October. In all, the value of Soviet-American exchange in the first ten months of the year was half of that in the corresponding period of 1930.[81] This cutback was part of a general reduction in Soviet trade, in response to growing industrial self-sufficiency and to the pressure of a large foreign debt.[82] But it also was declared by Amtorg officials to be an anti-American measure.[83] This boycott continued relentlessly throughout 1932, causing the value of American exports to Russia to drop 90 per cent from 1931 totals. As the American share of Soviet imports fell to a feeble 4.5 per cent, Germany's share swelled to 46.5 per cent.[84]

Consternation spread among those business groups that had invested money and hope in the Soviet market. Apparently, all their effort was to be defeated by the antidumping campaign. With renewed vigor, impelled by anxiety, they publicized the virtues of trading with the USSR. To refute the argument that dumping proved the connection between Soviet economic progress and Soviet strategy for world revolution, they revived the New Era theme that trade would in fact convert the Soviets to capitalist notions. To alleviate a major cause of Soviet reluctance to trade with the United States, these businessmen emphasized the reliability of the Soviet Union as a creditor and urged extension of long-term credits. And finally, for those who, like Othello, required "ocular proof," the American-Russian Chamber of Commerce and the American Express Company arranged for forty-three representatives of thirty-two manufacturing concerns to tour Russia in the summer of 1931.[85] Apparently these efforts were effective, for in the spring of 1933 *Business Week* discerned among businessmen the evolution of "a curious kind of hushed unanimity" that the way out of the Depression was via Soviet trade channels.[86]

The tacit boycott by the USSR also produced reaction of another sort: a renewed agitation for diplomatic recognition of the Communist regime. Following a brief and uncoordinated flurry of interest in recognition in the mid-1920's, businessmen had ignored that prickly question, since Soviet-American trade began to grow without diplomatic settlement. By 1929, according to *The Magazine of Wall Street*, all pressure for recognition had ceased.[87] The dumping controversy of the next year changed the situation, creating a slight revival of support for recognition as a means of stabilizing economic relations with the Soviets.[88] In 1931, when the Soviet retaliation became evident, concern developed into more explicit and serious form. A member of the State Department reported to the Under Secretary of State that "representatives of highly conservative commercial and financial institutions" were markedly impressed with the progress of the Soviet Union and were opposed to any interference by the American government.[89] Jerome Davis reported that his poll of fifty of the largest and best-known firms doing business with the USSR revealed that twenty-two favored immediate recognition and another eleven wanted President Hoover to send a trade commission to explore the economic and political situation. Only four flatly opposed recognition.[90]

A trend was becoming evident and developments during

the next two years confirmed it. In response, skeptical business spokesmen persistently dared advocates of recognition to explain how the diplomatic action would create commercial effects: why would a recognized Russia buy more or enlarge her small niche in the total American economy? [91] But the advocates evaded the challenge. They did not need facts for their appeal to businessmen increasingly crushed by the Depression, and therefore they did not need to contradict facts either. They only needed confidence and a program, and they had both.[92] Such were the motives at work within the American-Russian Chamber of Commerce, for example. Since reaffirming its traditional adherence to nonrecognition in 1926, the organization had not commented officially on this issue. Seven years later, however, the Chamber formally reversed its stand after a canvass of members had revealed "overwhelming" support of recognition. In a press release on July 13, 1933, the Chamber offered two explanations for its members' change of mind: the Soviet Union had proved its stability (as if that had not been proved in 1926) and the United States would "enjoy the benefits of any substantial trade with the U.S.S.R." only by meeting European competition. The statement called attention specifically to the recent forecast by Maxim Litvinov, Soviet Commissar for Foreign Affairs, of one billion dollars of Soviet orders in foreign markets.[93] Clearly, to be at all substantial, the entire argument required the reason of trade.

Excitement began to reach a climax in the second half of 1933. In July the prospects for recognition greatly improved with the announcement that the Reconstruction Finance Corporation would grant a credit of $4 million to Amtorg for the Soviet purchase of 60,000 to 80,000 bales of cotton. Within a month, the RFC had received forty applications for loans to enable American manufacturers to sell goods to Russia on long-term credits.[94] In October, agitation intensified after President Roosevelt requested the Soviet President, Kalinin, to send an envoy to the United States. During November, as Litvinov discussed and completed terms with the Administration, predictions of Soviet-American trade exuberantly swelled: the American Foreign Credit Underwriters Corporation and the American-Russian Chamber of Commerce foresaw $50 million in Soviet merchandise orders during the first six months after recognition; the executive vice-president of the American Manufacturers Export Association foresaw $120 million to $150 million in the first year; and former Senator Smith Brookhart, who had become Special Adviser to the Agricultural Adjustment Administration, predicted $500 million of trade during the first year.[95]

On November 15, 1933, the President of the United States provided a successful climax to the campaign for recognition. Now the panacea of Soviet trade, advertised by business enthusiasts as a wonder drug against the Depression disease, would be tested. The evidence of the next decade was not merely anticlimactic; it was damning. Exports to the Soviet Union did steadily increase, it is true, but they began from a low level and regained the peak values of 1930–1931 only in 1941. Diplomatic normalization proved to be irrelevant to the political, economic, and technical considerations causing the Soviets to reduce foreign trade in their move toward autarchy.[96] Business recovered from the Depression, not by the patent medicine of recognition, but by the efforts of Dr. New Deal and, ultimately, Dr. Win-the-War.

If businessmen found little satisfaction in the aftermath of recognition, the historian of their attitudes toward the Soviet Union in the four years preceding recognition is even less satisfied. Although after the Crash the dismaying disjunction between the arguments of those for and against Soviet-American economic relations disappeared, it only resolved into an equally irrational debate over economic issues. One group, driven now by economic necessity rather than ideological pretensions, urged trade with the USSR as a partial means of alleviating the Depression. Undeniably the Soviet market was open to a large supply of American exports, but advocates of such trade inflated fact into incredible fantasy, which skeptics easily refuted. The skeptics were guilty of their own fantasy — the phobia they constructed around the dumping question. Both sides, preoccupied with their illusions, shirked the burden of empiricism. Neither came even close to the balanced, informed perspective attained by engineers who worked in Soviet Russia during these years. Most unfortunate of all, perhaps, both sides ignored the one Soviet export which *could* relieve the Depression: the concept of planning. Naturally, those businessmen who were biased against the Communist regime saw only brutal autocracy in the methods of the Five-Year Plan. Yet proponents of trade and recognition were equally blind to any lessons that the Plan might have offered to the United States.

The Soviet Union served, then, as a mirror for the prejudices and fears of American capitalists. But it was an expedient mirror, reflecting only selected facts. Businessmen saw nothing in it they did not want to see. They certainly did not see, or did not admit to seeing, the sketch for a utopian future which so many intellectuals wanted to transcribe for the United States. Instead, they clung grimly to the dead past of the New Era. Their admission that the Depression was a crisis, and that the crisis required "planning," was only a qualification of prejudice, not a new understanding of the world. The Soviet Union served them as a distant fragment of dogma, nothing more.

By 1933, the pro-recognition Scripps-Howard chain had turned the traditional scene inside out: now a disheveled and hungry Uncle Sam is looking longingly at Russian luxury.

Starving in the Midst of Plenty
—Talburt in the New York "World-Telegram."

IX / Popular Responses during the Five-Year Plan

Russia is the most interesting place on the planet.
— William Allen White to Harold Ickes, November 14, 1933

In 1929 approximately 2,500 Americans visited the Soviet Union. In 1930 that number doubled and, a year later, it climbed to perhaps as high as 10,000.[1] If charted and superimposed upon a graph of the numbers of books and articles on the subject of planning, the parallel would be striking:

Number of titles on planning[2]		Number of entries per month on planning listed in Readers' Guide to Periodical Literature[3]	
1928	112		
1929	188	Dec. 4, 1928–June 4, 1930	.2
1930	210	June 4, 1930–June 5, 1931	2.1
1931	365	June 5, 1931–Jan. 4, 1932	4.1
1932	401	Jan. 4, 1932–May 5, 1932	9.2

Perhaps it would be merely underlining the obvious to superimpose a third statistical trend, the stock-market averages after September 1929. The translation of attitudes into numbers is, at best, a crude sort of precedure, but the Crash was the crudest shock and the Depression the crudest sort of misery for millions of Americans. Consequently, the vivid pattern of a hypothetical graph offers an appropriately simplified introduction to the analysis of American attitudes toward Russia during those dark years.

Even before the Depression, the Five-Year Plan was arousing enormous interest among Americans. In October of 1929, a year after the Communist regime instituted its massive economic program, Samuel N. Harper described American concern as "quite keen" and claimed that "even the skeptical sit up and take notice" of the Soviet achievements.[4] A few days later, by chance, H. V. Kaltenborn, associate editor of the *Brooklyn Daily Eagle* and a recent visitor to the USSR, confirmed this impression in a letter to Harper. Audiences were "tremendously eager" to be told about Russia, he wrote, and they never tired of asking questions.[5] Oswald Garrison Villard of *The Nation,* who had been on the same Soviet tour as Kaltenborn, facetiously complained that he was not allowed to talk about anything else when invited to speak before groups and clubs. After a very successful series of five lecturers in the south, he exclaimed: "everyone who can talk on Russia is overwhelmed with invitations to do so." [6]

When the Wall Street crash plunged the United States into economic crisis, this initial interest in the Plan not only grew rapidly, but took on a shrill tone of intensity.[7] Speaking in June 1931, Nicholas Murray Butler, president of Columbia University, described the economic crisis as a historical turning point, in some ways more powerful than the fall of Rome, the Renaissance, and the English and French revolutions of the seventeenth and eighteenth centuries. Deploring the lack of constructive, courageous leadership in the United States, he envied the Soviet Union for the purposefulness of its Five-Year Plan, even if he could not admire the plan itself.[8] Ray Long, a magazine editor, visited the USSR late in 1930 and resorted to equally extreme analogies: "It is the most interesting journey one may make anywhere today . . . the experiment being made in Russia is the most fascinating human experiment — and certainly the most important — of our times. Indeed, in its effect on the world at large, it is probably the most important human step since the birth of Christianity." [9] Not since the early days of the Revolution had Americans been so intrigued with Russia as an experiment. Occasionally, the curiosity took such bizarre forms as the request to Harper, by the editor of *The Embalmers' Monthly and National Funeral Director*, for information on the embalming of Lenin's corpse.[10] But the living Plan, not the dead leader, was more exciting to most Americans. So startling in its use of political and economic power, so grandiose in design, it provoked Americans to superlatives. In the words of a *New York Times* correspondent, Russia was "the biggest human experiment now being made." [11]

In retrospect, one inevitably attributes this surge of interest in Soviet affairs to the context of economic depression in the United States. The Five-Year Plan exerted such impact upon the thinking of Americans because their own capitalist institutions had given way, undermining the certainties which had been so strenuously invested in them during the past decade. In effect, American interest in the Soviet experiment was a form of self-interest. For Americans saw their own spirit of boosterism, their own penchant for the grandiose, even their own industrial techniques and technicians being applied to an explicitly anticapitalist purpose. Their fascination was a morbid one; they knew that their economic future was under a double jeopardy, being tested at home and challenged in Russia.

Retrospect can illuminate the past, but it can also blur chronology — particularly the chronology of attitudes. The interesting fact is that, until the second half of 1930, this fateful economic relationship did not fully emerge from the shadow of the terms of the older Soviet-American relationship. Few outside the liberal and radical camps yet perceived the decisiveness of the Depression or admitted the feasibility of the Five-Year Plan. Instead, they continued to focus on aspects of the USSR other than the practice of economic planning.

This was particularly true of those Americans who visited the "experiment" in person. The official government agency, Intourist, tried to provide all possible convenience and comfort, including simplified visa arrangements, deluxe trains, a corps of young English-speaking guides, and, of course, showers in Moscow hotel rooms. By 1932 it had even purchased sixty Lincoln automobiles from the Ford Motor Company so that, in the big cities, the Americans could move around at "Amerikansky tempo." [12] The Soviet government took extraordinary pains for the 1929 tour which was arranged by the American-Russian Chamber of Commerce and the American Express Company and which included influential businessmen. For these potential creditors or customers of the USSR, Intourist provided a special train dating from the days of tsarist luxury and equipped with two dining cars, mahogany-paneled bedrooms, shower baths, unlimited vodka and caviar.[13] For the second tour in 1931, when food was desperately short everywhere and particularly at railroad-station buffets, Soviet officials attempted to furnish another special train so that, as the Moscow representative of the American-Russian Chamber of Commerce privately explained, the tour would not give a "black eye" to the USSR.[14]

These exertions achieved only limited success. In the first place, they prompted a few Americans to complain that they were being exposed to the virtues and insulated from the defects of Soviet society, although most stressed the freedom of travel they enjoyed.[15] Secondly, even the staunchest effort by Intourist could not eradicate or conceal the difficult living conditions under the Plan. Professor Harper might have worried about getting fat on the lavish Intourist menu in 1932, whereas two years earlier he had lost fifteen pounds and acquired innumerable bugs that accompanied him as far as Berlin; but in both cases he was keenly aware that the Russian people were shabby and hungry. Before Harper visited in 1932, Mrs. William Henry Chamberlin, wife of the *Christian Science Monitor*'s Moscow correspondent, asked him to bring socks, toothbrushes, quinine tablets, and chocolate for her family. Harper himself found it "heart-rending to see how some of my friends were living" in Moscow. But he also concluded that the populace was enthusiastic and that the Communist leaders would not press their sacrifices too far.[16] For Americans less familiar with traditional conditions in Russia, physical discomfort or disgust often tainted their general reaction.

Nevertheless, physical circumstances were ultimately less decisive than mental ones. On the one hand, those Americans who sought to document their political radicalism excused the severe living standard as transitory or admired the idealism it encouraged, while they exclaimed over the underlying principles of social justice.[17] On the other hand, for those who came without prior tolerance, showers and Lincoln cars were comforting but unpersuasive. Despite the inordinate luxury and attention devoted to the American-Russian Chamber of Commerce tour in 1929, for example, only a third of its members left the Soviet Union in favor of unconditional recognition and less than half were reassured that the USSR was a safe site for investment.[18] Even on full stomachs and lulled by vodka, most Americans did not forsake their ideological premises. They judged by their own standards because they believed in them, and interpreted relativism as betrayal of those standards. Moreover, in the first years of the Plan, when dictatorship and deprivation were so conspicuous, the Soviet scene offered little evidence to dilute this certainty. The report by one visiting newspaper correspondent clearly exemplifies the power of premises. Claiming that

245

she entered in 1930 with an open, even sympathetic mind, she found the autocracy and food shortages deplorable and concluded that the Soviets would not attain their aims except at the expense of the people. In the end, however, she revealed the individualistic axiom which had guided her observations and precluded her from understanding the socialist motives of the Communist experiment: "I ask you, what kind of a mass can you have unless it is made up of individuals, who are sound, intelligent and righteous." [19]

In the first years of the Depression, the preconceptions of the previous thirteen years continued to exert their effect. Most Americans still saw the Soviet Union as the distasteful antithesis to their values or, at best, a land of exotic adventure. Two New York society girls, for example, went there in 1930 to satisfy "curiosity and cussedness." Although failing to find any of the secret-police spies they were told to expect, the idea "made us feel important and dangerous." In this spirit they traveled throughout European Russia, avidly describing architecture, food, weather, trains, and occasionally the political and economic conditions. Because of indiscreet photography and the lack of valid passports, the police in one town took them to the station for questioning. "Prisoners of the Cheka in Red Russia," the girls exuberantly entitled their article in *Good Housekeeping*, although their grand inquisitor turned out to be a handsome and genial young man who released them after a slight scolding.[20]

The USSR also appealed to other sorts of desires. An American writer residing in Moscow told of the American professor, visiting the Soviet experiment in 1930, who wanted to confirm the reports of women publicly bathing nude in the traditional Russian manner. When the two men arrived at the beach, they found a fence and a boy with a whistle to summon his father, who fined loiterers at the knotholes. Most of those fined, the boy said, were foreigners.[21] Thus the American stereotypes of 1918 still prevailed: the Bolshevik rulers were bestial tyrants and the Russian people were childlike innocents. Although the myth of the nationalization of women had finally vanished, it was replaced by the theme that the Communist divorce laws attempted to destroy the family. Defenders of the Soviet legislation and of the Russians' broader sense of modesty could not diminish popular antagonism toward this foreign morality or, rather, immorality.[22]

This righteous antagonism erupted into a vituperative climax during the first three months of 1930. The stimulus was the intensified antireligious pressure by the Soviet government in 1929, after a period of relative restraint. Coinciding with accelerated expansion of the League of Militant Atheists, the Soviets forbade any activity by religious organizations except performance of divine services, prohibited anyone but parents from giving religious instruction to children, discriminated economically against the clergy, and began to demolish various cathedrals.[23] When Pope Pius XI issued an appeal, on February 8, 1930, for three days of prayers on behalf of the victims of Soviet religious persecution, religious and secular forces in the United States organized a massive anti-Soviet drive.[24] In the House of Representatives, Hamilton Fish of New York introduced a resolution condemning Soviet intolerance and reaffirming diplomatic nonrecognition. "I am convinced," he declared, "that civilization and Christianity are practically synonymous." [25] The American Committee on Religious Rights and Minorities, headed by the president of the Presbyterian Board of Foreign Missions, censured the Soviet actions in a statement signed by influential figures in public affairs. Lutheran, Presbyterian, Episcopalian, and Jewish organizations went on record with similar protests.[26] Meanwhile, the Reverend Edmund A. Walsh of Georgetown University issued a pamphlet documenting the papal position with statistics on the numbers of ecclesiastical victims murdered or imprisoned by the Moscow regime and with sacrilegious cartoons distributed by various atheistic groups in Russia.[27] During the three days in March designated by the Pope, prayer services in the churches and synagogues of New York were attended by overflowing crowds. In the opinion of Alexander Gumberg, it was "one of the biggest campaigns against Soviet Russia that we have ever witnessed." [28]

The surprising aspect of the organized indignation is neither that it occurred at all nor that it engaged the passions of so many Americans; the execution of Buchkavich in 1923 provoked, even without papal guidance, an outburst of similar intensity, though of less concerted quality. Rather, the campaign is notable because of the vigorous dissent it aroused in unexpected quarters. Naturally, radicals like Theodore Dreiser and liberals like the editors of *The Nation* decried the protests as a veiled capitalist drive against the Soviet Union.[29] But even such a moderate organ as *The Outlook* criticized the protests as futile, possibly self-defeating gestures. At the same time, the *New York Herald Tribune* remarked that not only had the Orthodox Church been a corrupt institution, but the Soviets still permitted church services. The *Galveston Tribune* bluntly argued that "if the Russian masses want their Church saved, they will save it." Meanwhile, *Time* rebuked Father Walsh for citing atrocities and an antireligious cartoon, which were at least seven years old, as if they were evidence of current Soviet persecutions.[30]

Religious ranks also split into disputing factions. Many Protestant and Jewish spokesmen stressed the evils of the Orthodox Church, the freedom of religion in Russia, and the dangerous international effects of reckless outrage. On March 6, seventy-seven student and faculty members of the Liberal Club of Union Theological Seminary divided their criticism between the Soviet persecution and the unconstructive, political nature of **American** protests. A few weeks later, eighty-seven leading New York City ministers signed a statement by the executive committee of the Conference of Younger Churchmen which urged that "whatever values may be born out of the Russian social experiment should be given the opportunity to mature." The best means of combating Communist antireligious policies, the statement added, would be to increase "our own efforts for a cooperative and just society." [31]

This last dissent did more than object to American hysteria or apologize for the Soviets; it deflected the dispute into an altogether different ideological territory. By a subtle and significant maneuver, the American social system, not Soviet religious policy, was at issue. The liberal Catholic journal, *The Commonweal,* followed the same path in an editorial of March 17. Although it had no tolerance for the "group of half-crazed fanatics" in the Kremlin, it was not content with one-sided accusation. "The record of socialized Russia," the editors declared, "is . . . strikingly like the record of unmoral capitalism." Both systems emphasized production and privilege at the expense of social justice; as for Communist immorality, it had a strong rival in the Western divorce rate, hedonism, and "pornographic festivals." In short: "We all have drifted toward the abyss in which unhappy Russia lies" and, the editorial concluded, we can defeat Soviet Communism only by first erecting a "triumphantly resurgent Christianity" at home.[32]

This conversion of criticism to self-criticism, amid the emotional turbulence of the anti-Soviet drive, foreshadowed a fundamental revision of Protestant and, to a lesser extent, Catholic attitudes toward the USSR. Throughout the postwar decade a large segment of Protestant spokesmen had steadfastly admired the beneficent aspects of the Soviet phenomenon. After the Depression began, they presented their views with increasing forcefulness. John Haynes Holmes, pastor of the Community Church of New York, revisited the USSR in 1931 after an interval of ten years. Although he still found widespread poverty, he was astounded by the improvement since 1922 and awed by the popular fervor. Russia, he told a Chicago audience, was "headed toward the building of a new society, upon a program of absolute economic equality and freedom." [33] Sherwood Eddy, a secretary for the Young Men's Christian Association and guide for numerous "seminars" of Americans to the USSR after 1925, echoed Holmes's elation. Although the Communists' tyranny and atheism distressed him, Eddy regarded the Soviet economic and social system as a challenge to the amorality, injustice, and ultimate ineffectuality of American capitalism.[34] Similarly, Harry F. Ward, a professor of Christian ethics at Union Theological Seminary, found in Soviet Russia the moral and cooperative society for which he had been searching since the World War. Here was "a new world," where social consciousness, not necessity or profit, motivated a people to work and where the government was fostering cultural democracy to replace its temporary dictatorship.[35]

The reaction by Reinhold Niebuhr was more probing and cogent than any of these. The socialist theologian, who was serving on the national committee of the League for Independent Political Action, recorded his on-the-scene impressions in four articles during September–October 1930. The first three brooded darkly upon the Soviet idolatry of the machine, the dedication to industrialization at the expense of spirituality and justice, the bureaucratization and brutality of the Five-Year Plan. Nevertheless, the last article introduced a broader perspective:

Nothing good can be said for the hypocrisy of our world which uses force covertly for the maintenance of social inequality and then professes itself horror stricken by the overt use of force for the maintenance of social equality. An ethical choice between these two theories and practices would be more favorable to the Russian scheme than our self-deceived western world can realize.[36]

From almost all denominations and from such unlikely places as Missoula, Montana, Protestant ministers traveled to the Soviet Union during 1930–1933 and discovered a society dedicated to moral principles and social action which, they said, were sadly lacking at home. By October 1931, *The Christian Register* was stating in an editorial:

American Protestantism has gone over in its sympathy to the Russian experiment and the basic idea of the Russian philosophy. . . . These ministers, true to the traditions of the prophets, are aware of the moral evil beneath our economic and social order, and are satisfied that Russia's fundamental principle of a non-profit making and cooperative commonwealth is true to the teachings of Jesus and square with the pretensions and professions of all the churches.[37]

Catholics also gave increasing, though grudging, recognition to the Soviet challenge. "Like everybody else I cannot stop thinking about Russia," a retired Baltimore pastor wrote in the June 1931 issue of *The Catholic World*. For despite its atheism and tyranny, the Soviet commitment to cooperative principles made him wonder whether it could not eventually offer a better social system than existed anywhere else in the world.[38] John La Farge, future editor of *America*, the Jesuit weekly, urged Americans to imitate the Five-Year Plan by reforming social evils if they wanted to overcome the otherwise evil philosophy of Communism.[39] Even the relentlessly anti-Soviet Father Walsh declared, in 1931, that the Russian phenomenon contained constructive aspects which Americans should carefully examine even as they condemned its odious materialism, dictatorship, and revolutionary doctrines.[40]

The growing emphasis on social and economic rather than moral concerns, in the debate over Soviet religious policies, discloses the irresistible primacy which the Five-Year Plan began to exert in the Soviet-American relationship. Indeed, only a few months after that furor subsided, the issue of Communist "dumping" and "convict labor" came into prominence. Already in February and March of 1930 the Congressional debate over tariff revision had touched upon these controversial questions. At one point, Representative Adam M. Wigant of Pennsylvania succinctly bridged the old and new themes by avowing: "Free men shall not compete with the slaves of a godless government." [41] When the Treasury imposed its ban on Soviet pulpwood in July, American attention decisively shifted from the religious to the economic sins of the Moscow regime. Immediately, conservatives like Ralph Easley and Matthew Woll of the National Civic Federation or the editors of the *Washington Post* called for total embargo.

But much of the nation's press voiced skepticism and even annoyance at this alarm. The *New York Herald Tribune*, for example, considered it "unwise to determine our whole trade policy toward Russia in the general atmosphere of emotion and dubious documents which has been stirred up for the moment." The *Newark News* said it was simply bored by the "sudden clamor of Red, Red, Red!" At the same time, the *Baltimore Sun* and other newspapers pointed out that an embargo would increase unemployment by further reducing American exports.[42] Secretary of Agriculture Hyde's accusations of Soviet shortselling of wheat aroused ridicule among many Democratic papers. It was " a tempest in a teapot," according to the *Cleveland Plain Dealer,* and even the *Wall Street Journal* mocked Hyde's "terrifying discovery." But again the *Washington Post,* along with other papers, gave worried credence to this "devilish plot" to impoverish American farmers and to foment international disorder.[43]

As Hamilton Fish extended the scope of his special investigating committee's already voluminous hearings to include not only Communist propaganda but Soviet dumping, the debate continued to boil. On January 15, 1931, Senator Tasker L. Oddie of Nevada praised Fish for alerting the nation to the Communist menace and introduced a bill to prohibit the importation of all goods from the USSR as well as goods manufactured in other countries from Soviet raw materials. Only a total embargo, he explained, would protect the United States from convict-made products.[44] Two days later, the Fish committee issued its final report, which vilified Communism as an atheistic, tyrannical, destructive, and subversive movement, deplored the "constant campaign of terrorism" within the USSR by the "perverted intellectuals and prostitutes" of the Soviet secret police, warned of the insidious dumping practiced by the Soviet government, and ominously declared: "The mystery and the horror of the convict labor camps is yet to be told in its lurid details." [45]

During the next six weeks, the outcry against the Red economic menace reached full volume. A resolution sent to the Senate by the junior committee of the National Patriotic Association in Chicago illustrates the phobia in its most vivid form. Urging passage of the proposed embargo, the resolution explained that "we see the beautiful structure of our civilization built so lovingly by those who made our great Nation blasted, torn apart, and consumed by the collective labor" in the USSR.[46] Meanwhile, the House Ways and Means Committee held two sets of hearings on bills designed to strengthen the 1930 Tariff Act's provisions against convict-made goods and to advance their effective date by nine months. The usual group of representatives from industrial, patriotic, and labor groups recorded their indictment of the Soviet trade menace. On February 21, the House approved the bill. The measure probably would have ended Soviet-American commerce, but it was defeated in the Senate Finance Committee by rubber, coffee, and tobacco interests whose imports would also have fallen under the forced-labor provisions.[47]

Although the issue of dumping survived this setback, interest and support gradually diminished. As late as March 1932, the indefatigable Senator Oddie presented to the Secretary of the Treasury a petition from ten senators, twenty-six congressmen, and a hundred patriotic and industrial organizations demanding enforcement of the prohibitory clauses in the 1930 Tariff Act.[48] But few new converts rushed to their ranks. In fact, *The World's Work* simultaneously changed editors and changed sides, joining the Scripps-Howard newspaper chain and numerous others in opposition to interference with Soviet-American trade.[49] For as unemployment inexorably mounted and hopes of swift economic recovery faded, the alleged threat from Soviet imports lost its urgency. During 1931, public concern began to focus not on how to protect the American economy, but on how to rehabilitate it. The warnings by anti-Soviet spokesmen not only seemed increasingly gratuitous, therefore, but — in an ironic twist — they inspired the very response they hoped to defeat. As Alexander Gumberg wrote to Walter Duranty in Moscow, on March 27, 1931: "Hamilton Fish and other enemies of the Soviets, who in their anxiety to injure them have advertised them as a great 'menace,' have done more to arouse interest and to make people believe that the Russian program is going to be a great success than could 100,000 propagandists."[50]

Midway through the second year of the Depression, the American public finally "discovered" the Five-Year Plan, as it were. By August, *The Saturday Evening Post* querulously remarked that "we all have a very bad case of too much Russia." According to the articles on the Soviet experiment, the editors complained, one was supposed to believe that "there is no country in the world which really matters or which is accomplishing anything at all except Russia." With varied enthusiasm, depending on their feelings toward the USSR, all observers corroborated the *Post*'s evaluation.[51] Curiosity about the Plan and economic planning in general was apparently insatiable, judging from the sudden spurt in books and articles on planning and the nearly quintupled output of American books on Russia from 1930 to 1931.[52] The career of M. Ilin's *New Russia's Primer* provides a particularly revealing index of popular interest. When George S. Counts translated this unpretentious explanation of the Plan, written for Russian schoolchildren, the Book-of-the-Month Club made it one of its selections for May 1931. The *Primer* not only was chosen by 46,000 members, exceeding the average distribution of other selections that year, but became a national bestseller for seven months. "This book is having a terrific run here," Samuel Harper wrote to a friend in June. Indeed, it ranked eighty-first on the *Publishers' Weekly* list of the hundred nonfiction bestsellers during 1921–1932, fifteen places above the only American book on Russia with similar success, Maurice Hindus' *Humanity Uprooted*.[53]

Interest does not imply advocacy, of course. Most Americans probably agreed with Thomas Edison's dictum during an interview in 1931: "The Reds have done pretty well, but they are cruel. And they are bucking human nature. Yes, perhaps they too can stimulate research, as private American industry does. But their experiment will end wrong, in my opinion. History says so." [54] Commentators assiduously pointed out Soviet failures to fulfill production quotas, explained that the apparent elimination of unemployment depended on the low productivity of Soviet labor, and stressed the personal hardship that the Plan entailed. When Stalin announced his reinstatement of piece work, bonuses, and greater autonomy by engineers and factory managers, many Americans proudly declared the superiority of capitalist techniques over socialist ones.[55]

Nevertheless, the familiar animosity resembled its pre-1930 antecedents in bitterness but little else. Now the prevailing tenor was defensive. The New Era days of smug condescension or dogmatic deprecation were gone. Antagonists of the Soviet system now had the burden of proving that their system could do better, and their suggestions increasingly cited the need for planning, non-Soviet planning. When the *New York Evening Post* hailed President Hoover's proposal of "an American plan" in a speech of June 1931 as "the first real American answer to Russia," the editors betrayed the new mental posture. "We cannot lie down and surrender before the brutal attack of Soviet economics," the *Post* continued. "Our own system is sounder, finer, happier, and we know it." [56] But this brave affirmation hardly concealed the crucial concession that the United States would fight the economic contest by Soviet rules — by better planning rather than by rigid laissez-faire. In effect, Americans far to the right of the liberals were following Edmund Wilson's advice to "take Communism away from the Communists." Even the conservative editors of *The Saturday Evening Post* saw the need, in 1931, "for a real five-year plan for America." [57]

This was the context of attitudes from which the thousands of American tourists departed for the Soviet Union during 1931 and 1932. As photographer Margaret Bourke-White explained her decision to make the long and novel trip: "I wanted to find out for myself why there was so much talk about that country." [58] Russian living conditions were harder than ever during this period. Miss Bourke-White, for example, lost the focusing cloth for her camera soon after her arrival, and during the remainder of her stay she looked in vain for a square yard of black cloth. When she left, she gave all her extra clothes, scraps of food, and soap to grateful Russian acquaintances. In comparison to the USSR, the stores and restaurants of Berlin, Paris, and cities in the United States, in the third year of the Depression, seemed overwhelmingly opulent to her.[59] Both hostile and sympathetic Americans were appalled by the shortages of food, clothing, manufactured goods, and housing throughout the Soviet Union.[60] Many of them also sensed the pervasive dulling impact of dictatorship and terror.[61]

Although the familiar themes in pre-1930 reports continued to play a dominant role, again the resemblance was incomplete. For many of these travelers went — or at least said that they went — with deep sympathy for the USSR, only to suffer enormous disillusionment by the time of their return. Their attitude underwent a much more drastic change, in other words, than those of previous tourists because the combined force of the Depression and the Plan made them unprecedentedly willing or even anxious to believe that the Soviet experiment offered the solution to the American crisis.

The occasions for disillusionment varied greatly, however. A Communist from Chicago stressed the general hardship and suppression of individuality as reasons for his defection from the faith. A doctor with radical political interests was repelled by the "intolerable tyranny." Will Durant, the celebrated author of *The Story of Philosophy*, seemed particularly preoccupied with physical discomfort, his own as well as that of the Russian people, and left within a month. After returning home, he urged diplomatic recognition but predicted the imminent failure of "this last bitter trial of an unnatural economy." The turning point in the sympathy of former heavyweight champion Gene Tunney occurred when he saw churchbells being melted down for use in factories. He had anticipated a public forum allowing freer speech than anywhere except England; the harsh actualities of the USSR transformed him into a bitter critic.[62]

The sequence of bright hope and dark disillusionment

257

formed one new characteristic in general American attitudes toward Soviet Russia. A second and complementary innovation was the extent to which many other visitors excused disquieting evidence in order to emphasize the positive features of the Soviet scene. By comparing the hunger and poverty to earlier Russian standards, they found an encouraging improvement. A former governor of Maine, traveling for a month under Intourist auspices, even claimed to have found no signs of distress at all, while another American ate ice cream in Rostov-on-Don and inferred that all Russian workers could enjoy this luxury.[63] In any case, these American sympathizers were much more interested in the future than the present and in the psychological rather than the physical conditions. Consequently, they described in detail the social-welfare legislation and institutions which provided the basis for equal distribution of privilege. Eventual well-being for all, they insisted, was more important than immediate benefits for a few. Indeed, they claimed that this vision of justice had inspired the Russian people to a self-sacrificing vigor that was awesome. The Plan was building a society on the basis of "a new type of citizen," as Samuel Harper said, a citizen dedicated to the common good by cooperative effort. In context, these American observers concluded, the issue of Soviet dictatorship almost vanished; a true social democracy would inevitably emerge from the moral and economic premises of the Five-Year Plan.[64]

Thus, partly because of apologist inclinations and partly because of an ignorance that Intourist encouraged, they ignored the liquidation of the kulaks, the terrorization of intellectuals, the suppression of dissenters, and the other stark cruelties which characterized the dictatorship as it sought to implement the Plan. Ultimately, the persuasiveness of this biased perspective derived from the economic crisis against which the United States was struggling with such apparent impotence. Whatever the political and physical defects of the Soviet experiment, at least the Russians had a purpose behind their sufferings. As Ray Long, editor of *Hearst's International and Cosmopolitan Magazine,* exclaimed in 1931: "What wouldn't a lot of Americans submit to today if they might exchange their unemployment for Hope?" [65]

As the United States entered its third year of Depression without any evidence of respite, this question became more and more compelling. The *New York Times* might insist, at the end of 1931, that the Plan had lost its dazzling fascination for the outside world, and it might join others in itemizing the extensive failures of the Soviet economy during the months thereafter.[66] But for a growing segment of the American public, the fact of full employment in the USSR meant more than intricate statistical critiques. In June of 1932, a professor at the University of Arizona reported that, during four cross-country trips in the last sixteen months, he discovered increasing admiration for Soviet economic progress. People saw in Russia an alternative to their present distress, he asserted. When William Henry Chamberlin returned from Moscow for a lecture tour in the winter of 1932–33, he was astonished at the glorification of the USSR. Americans, he found, believed that the Plan was some sort of magic and that Russians enjoyed a booming prosperity.[67] During that bleak winter of discontent, when the nation was poised between a repudiated Administration and an untried one, the image of the Soviet Union shimmered in many American minds with almost hypnotic intensity.

The growing partiality toward the USSR naturally reactivated the controversy over diplomatic recognition. When Herbert Hoover took office, he followed without change the established American refusal to recognize Soviet legitimacy. By the late 1920's the primary justification for this policy was the propaganda and revolutionary activities sanctioned by the Moscow regime; the Soviet repudiation of debts and uncompensated seizure of private property receded to secondary justifications.[68] Already on the eve of the Depression, some Americans were challenging nonrecognition as a detriment to American exporters. But defenders were adamant. According to the *Grand Rapids Herald*, the United States should not "sacrifice our national honor in favor of business." The *Indianapolis News* angrily opposed "compromising our integrity to increase our exports." There the matter remained, although many newspaper editors predicted that the logic of trade made recognition inevitable.[69]

The Crash provided that logic with an enormous momentum. Now the prospect of Soviet purchases became not merely a desirable addition to American profits, but a partial alleviation of accelerating failure. Even the clamor about alleged Soviet dumping did not dissuade those who demanded recognition as an economic relief measure. *The Outlook*, for example, bitterly derided those "paperweight politicians," Representative Fish, Senator Oddie, and Secretary of Agriculture Hyde, for obstructing the channel of Soviet-American commerce. "They and their followers forget," the editorial declared in October 1930, "that the United States needs the 150,000,000 Russian customers as much as Soviet Russia needs American goods." [70] During the first year of the Depression, influential conservative figures like Paul D. Cravath, a corporation lawyer, former New York Attorney General Albert Ottinger, and former World Court justice John Bassett Moore joined liberals like Senator Burton K. Wheeler of Montana in speaking out for recognition. Even H. Stanwood Menken, chairman of the board of the ultrapatriotic National Security League, changed sides. With bitter disgust, Ralph Easley, head of that other ultrapatriotic body, the National Civic Federation, ascribed this defection to the economic interests of some of Menken's law clients who sought Soviet contracts. But Menken held his ground, finally resigning from the League when its board reaffirmed support of nonrecognition.[71] Spokesmen for continued boycott of the Soviet government maintained their position with unabated vigor during 1930–1931, disputing the expectation of increased trade as a mirage and damning recognition as an endorsement of criminality. But the dissenting camp steadily enlarged.[72]

By the spring of 1932, the advocates of recognition became still bolder and more vociferous. On April 4, an editorial in the *Washington News* confidently asserted: "The dollar-and-cents argument for better relations with Russia is unanswerable." [73] At the same time, the Scripps-Howard newspaper chain began to agitate for recognition.[74] Arthur Krock, the *New York Times* columnist, noted "the sudden Senatorial activity" in favor of recognition as the means of strengthening the USSR and thus restraining Japanese aggression in the Far East.[75] On the other side of the nation, the Commonwealth Club of California concluded fifteen months of lectures and discussion with a vote strongly in favor of relations with Russia.[76] Discerning the trend of opinion, numerous Russian-American groups flooded the Senate Foreign Relations Committee, in mid-1932, with petitions against recognition.[77] But the future was clear, particularly after Franklin Roosevelt explicitly declared, one month before his election, that he had an open mind on the issue.[78] By January of 1933, the *New York Times* described "a growing disposition" among Congressional leaders toward approval of recognition. Of 51 senators who were polled, 22 were definitely in favor, 20 were noncommittal, and only 9 opposed. Of the 22 proponents, 16 were Democrats and 4 were insurgents or Progressives, while 5 of the 9 opponents were Republicans.[79]

The last nine months of official Soviet-American silence resounded with the clash of American opinions about the virtues of prolonging the sixteen-year-old policy. Warnings about Soviet propaganda vied with promises of lucrative trade and enlarged possibilities of world peace. (The issue of unpaid debts faded after the Allied nations defaulted on their war loans.[80]) All the themes and emotions that had developed around Soviet Russia since the Revolution were now invested in the question of establishing diplomatic relations. When Al Smith, the former governor of New York, advocated recognition during his testimony before the Senate Committee on Economics at the end of February, he made front-page news and great public agitation. The *Washington Post* rebuked him for supporting competition between American workers and Russian slaves, while the *Brooklyn Daily Eagle* congratulated him for rejecting "a stupid policy that has for all these years kept the Russian market closed to us." According to *The Literary Digest*, a majority of editors supported Smith.[81]

His fellow Catholics were less pleased, however. Under the title, "A Dent in the Brown Derby," *America* sadly remarked that Smith's argument "seems to rest on a principle entirely foreign to his humane and generous spirit." Commercial benefit, the editorial continued, does not justify dealing with a government in league with the Third International. A month later, the Jesuit publication exclaimed: "There are things more precious than trade, and one of them is decency." The USSR, it contended, stands for everything contrary to the Christian world and values. *The Commonweal* was equally adamant against committing "treason to our whole existing American social order." At the same time, various Knights of Columbus chapters were petitioning the Senate Foreign Relations Committee to maintain the boycott on the menace to Christian civilization.[82] Within organized Protestantism, opinion about recognition was more divided. On the one hand, the General Conference of the Evangelical Synod of North

America and leaders of the American Tract Society went on record against it, and a minister at the New Jersey Baptist convention in October deplored any endorsement of "a nation which has blasphemed God." On the other hand, 430 Protestant clergymen sent a petition to the President in favor of recognition, their petition being echoed by a score of church journals and hundreds of other ministers across the country.[83] One large Jewish group, the Central Conference of American Rabbis, also urged an end to the anomalous relationship between the United States and Russia.[84]

The fervor of Catholic and some Protestant opposition was matched by the innumerable patriotic societies which summoned their resources, in the spring of 1933, for a last stand. The tenor of their feelings is illustrated, perhaps, by the title of a newly formed group, the Paul Reveres. This organization included on its advisory board Hamilton Fish, Senator Clayton R. Lusk of New York, representatives of the Daughters of the American Revolution, and other notable anti-Communists.[85] No mere diplomatic arrangement was at stake, in their opinion, but rather the question of "opening wide our gates to a tremendous wave of poisonous propaganda," to use the words of an American Legion official. The Legion hoped to alert the nation by a vast rally in Washington on April 18. In the wake of this event, petitions to the House Foreign Affairs Committee and the Senate Foreign Relations Committee were sent by Legion chapters, the Daughters of the American Revolution, the United States Daughters of 1812, and similar groups around the country.[86] One of Senator George Norris' constituents in Omaha even tried to persuade him that recognition was a plot by "predatory elements" working within the government and in league with the Jewish "International Banking setup" that helped to finance the Russian Revolution.[87]

This anti-Semitic interpretation was exceptional rather

263

than typical, but it suggests the mounting hysteria of the anti-Soviet forces as their failure became increasingly imminent during 1933. After sixteen years, most of the American people seemed unalarmed by the likelihood of diplomatic relations. Even *The American Magazine* ended its thirteen years of neglect for Soviet Russia when, in April, it provided its 1.8 million readers with Paul Cravath's article explaining the advantages of recognition. Three months later, the equally popular *Hearst's International and Cosmopolitan Magazine* followed suit with an article by Senator Borah, only the third article on the USSR that it had published since 1924.[88] Recognition of Russia had finally graduated from a cause espoused by an esoteric band of liberals and radicals into a subject worthy of a place in family magazines. After the announcement in July of the $4 million credit arrangements between the Reconstruction Finance Corporation and Amtorg, even the patriotic groups lapsed into a noticeable silence born of futility.[89] They prepared for stolid resignation to the inevitable. Most of the press, on the contrary, prepared for a booming Soviet-American trade which would help to relieve the Depression and, according to the *Providence News-Tribune*, might incidentally tame the vicious aspects of the Communist system.[90]

By the time that Commissar Litvinov arrived in the United States, on November 7, to negotiate the terms of recognition, a large majority of the American press had clearly expressed its approval. A few stalwarts of the status quo, including the *Chicago Tribune,* the *Washington Star,* the *Seattle Times,* and the *Los Angeles Times,* remained hostile. But by now they were among a stubborn minority. Such a conservative bastion as the *New York Times* relented so far as to welcome the renewal of traditional Russian-American friendship, although it stressed that recognition would be "of the Russian people rather than of the Soviet Government." The *Baltimore*

Sun congratulated the Administration for its "move toward sanity and realism," while others happily predicted benefits to world peace and American trade.[91]

At the end of October, the Committee on Russian-American Relations of the American Foundation published the results of its questionnaire sent to more than 1,100 newspapers. When asked whether they approved of immediate American recognition of the USSR, followed by negotiations to settle outstanding disputes between the two nations, 63 per cent of the editors assented and 26.9 per cent opposed, the rest giving inconclusive or qualified replies. In geographical terms, the greatest sentiment for recognition came from the south and some of the large eastern states, while the midwest was divided and New England strongly opposed.[92] A simultaneous but much more limited study of press opinion by the State Department produced generally parallel results.[93] This two-thirds majority is particularly significant in view of the fact that the questionnaire specified subsequent, not prior, negotiation of terms. It also presents a marked contrast to the less extensive survey of editorial reactions prepared for Secretary of State Henry Stimson in March 1931, following his announcement that he had ordered a new study of the Soviet situation. The State Department's analysis of editorials in 183 newspapers revealed only 13 per cent of them in favor of recognition and 63 per cent against any change in diplomatic policy.[94] During the two-and-a-half-year interval between the two surveys, opinion had sharply reversed. In fact, early in November, the radical editors of *The World Tomorrow* noted with astonishment the "comparative unanimity" of public support for Roosevelt's move toward recognition.[95]

Explanations of this drastic change must rely on more impressionistic methods than a contemporary social scientist, equipped with the statistics of opinion polls, would ordinarily tolerate. Nevertheless, it is clear that editorial positions underwent a decisive shift within a short period of time, while Soviet policies remained fundamentally unchanged. The major changes during the early thirties took place in the United States, where the deepening Depression enlarged American interest in exports to the Soviet Union. At the same time, increasing Japanese aggression against Manchuria provoked a Far Eastern crisis in which by 1932 the United States became deeply involved. The threat of Nazi Germany, it should be noted, was rarely mentioned as a reason for Soviet recognition. The two themes of Soviet-American trade and international peace formed dominant motifs in editorial approval of recognition, although it is difficult to decide which was more important. The *Portland Oregonian* and *Cincinnati Enquirer,* for example, emphasized the inhibiting effect on Japan that would result from Soviet-American relations, while the *Dallas News* ran a front-page headline on November 18: "RECOGNITION AID TO SALE OF TEXAS COTTON IN RUSSIA." [96]

Two further conditions probably played a subterranean role in encouraging support for recognition. First of all, the Five-Year Plan not only aroused enormous interest among Americans, but induced them to regard the Soviet regime as a constructive and, in many ways, admirable agency for national welfare. Second — the most amorphous but perhaps most fundamental of all the reasons — once President Roosevelt decided to open the question of recognition, many Americans probably realized that sixteen years of aloofness had proved both ineffectual in changing Soviet policies and anomalous from a logical point of view. The agents of the October Revolution were obviously in control and were going to continue in control; by 1933 diplomatic denial of their existence had an aspect of fantasy.[97]

President Roosevelt attempted to appease American anxieties by engaging in ten days of negotiations with Litvinov in order to settle the various contentious issues separating the two nations. On November 16 they reached final terms in a formal exchange of notes. The USSR promised: not to interfere with the domestic affairs of the United States, including abstention from propaganda; to guarantee religious freedom and the right of a fair trial to American citizens in Russia; to negotiate a settlement of mutual claims with respect to debts and property. Even *The Commonweal* congratulated the President for protecting religion as much as possible and expressed hope that recognition would soften Soviet atheism and tyranny. Its sister periodical, *America,* was not reassured, however, nor were *The Saturday Evening Post,* the *Chicago Tribune,* and other traditional critics of the USSR.[98] But the *St. Louis Post-Dispatch* celebrated the agreement with revealing rhetoric. Its editorial of November 19 asserted that the end of the Soviet-American quarrel marked the acceleration of Russia's rise "in the scale of civilization" and the beginning of "one of the most spectacular chapters of history." Following this prediction, the editors exclaimed:

There is a destiny of nations which transcends all such immediacies as those which have estranged the United States from Russia. We bear a prophetic relation to the rest of the world, and so does Russia.[99]

This echo of Wilsonian messianism forms an appropriate conclusion to the long interlude of official silence which began in the same spirit under Wilson himself. Even more appropriate — and vividly indicative of the changes occurring over that interlude — the Soviet regime, so often indicted as the enemy of civilization, was regarded as a participant in the destiny of the world. In the minds of many Americans, Russia was once again "a fit partner in a league of honour."

X / In Retrospect

For more than sixteen years, while the governments of the
United States and Soviet Russia had no official relationship,
the American people expressed a multitude of highly colored
and deeply felt reactions to the Soviet regime. The virtual
unanimity of enthusiasm for the February Revolution, which
seemed to Americans to have created a "new democracy" and
a reinvigorated belligerent against Germany, soon disinte-
grated. By the time of the Bolsheviks' overthrow of the Provisional Government and especially after the conclusion of
the Russo-German peace treaty at Brest-Litovsk in March
1918, American opinions were bitterly divided. The majority,
impelled by the emotional drive for victory in the World War,
castigated the Bolsheviks as traitors to the Russian people
and to the Russian Revolution, while President Wilson withheld diplomatic recognition from the new regime. Popular
hostility quickly focused on military intervention as the
means by which to save Russia from German control and for
the Allied cause. When Wilson sent troops to Siberia and
northern Russia in mid-1918, most Americans applauded his
decision. At the same time, they created a malevolent portrait
of the Soviet leaders as immoral, brutal German agents, some
Americans even adding anti-Semitic hues.

A large number of liberals rejected this defamatory position, however. Their initial support for Wilson's war policy
gradually diminished in the face of an intolerant belligerence
at home and an increasingly vindictive pursuit of victory in

268

Europe. Instead of denouncing Soviet "betrayal," these liberals imitated Raymond Robins' criticism of the Administration for having misunderstood the essentially constructive aims of Lenin's regime. In their opinion, the Brest-Litovsk Treaty was a desperate step to save Russia from German aggression, a step they claimed the Allies could have prevented by accepting Trotsky's request for support and by redefining their war aims in emphatically democratic terms. Intervention in Russia accelerated the liberals' drift from Wilsonian loyalty and amplified their sympathy for the Soviet regime. The terms of the Versailles Treaty further confirmed their defection, driving Lincoln Steffens and others away from liberalism into a frankly pro-Soviet attitude. Most liberals stopped short of radicalism, however, still adhering to support of parliamentary rather than revolutionary methods and to individual freedom rather than class dictatorship.

By the spring of 1919, much of the American public shared the liberals' opposition to intervention, but for nonliberal reasons of disgust with the attempt to democratize Europe. This desire to surrender the international responsibility preached by Wilson also took the form of the Red Scare, a vehement drive against domestic radicalism, particularly Communism. During the next decade a new era in American history developed, one in which prosperity and parochialism fostered a complacent pride in capitalism and country. Nonrecognition of the Soviet government was a natural and almost unquestioned aspect of this national temper. But the original hostility toward the Bolsheviks became modified, partly by a decline in interest, partly by a surge of sympathy for the Russian people during the famine of 1921–1923, and primarily by the apparent turn toward capitalism signaled by Lenin's introduction of the New Economic Policy. Although some observers — notably the patriotic groups and the American Federation of Labor — retained unrelenting hostility, many others interpreted the NEP as the beginning of "normalcy" in Russia or even as the portent of Communist extinction. Among business leaders this confidence was especially strong; by the second half of the 1920's, such prestigious individuals as W. Averell Harriman and Henry Ford were arranging concessions with the Soviets, seduced by the promise of huge profits as well as by the belief that Russia was an adolescent capitalist version of the United States.

The execution of Monsignor Buchkavich in 1923 revived the animosities of the war years, but it did not displace the sanguine expectations aroused by the NEP. Stalin's victory over Trotsky, later in the decade, further persuaded many Americans that the USSR was retreating from the principles of rigid collectivism and world revolution. On the eve of the stock-market crash, popular American feeling was still distinctly antagonistic to Soviet rule, but a growing segment believed that the regime was evolving toward acceptable political and economic principles. Correspondingly, pressure for Soviet-American commercial relations and, to a lesser extent, for diplomatic relations had become quite strong, particularly among business circles.

The position of writers, liberals, and radicals during the twenties was one of exile, either physically on the part of the lost generation or intellectually on the part of those who despised the conformity and materialism of postwar America. Whereas most writers and some liberals turned away from political concerns, however, a large group sought solace in the Soviet experiment. A growing number of social workers, educators, social scientists, and political journalists visited the USSR during the decade, and an even larger number admired it at a distance. They praised its achievements in social justice while straining to overcome dismay at class dictatorship. Increasingly alienated from their own country, liberals tended to resolve this dilemma of welfare versus freedom in the Soviet favor and thereby subtly weakened the structure of their liberalism. Even the expulsion of Trotsky, first from the government and then from the Soviet Union, did not seriously shake the pro-Soviet loyalty of the liberals, with the exception of some labor sympathizers.

The combination of the First Five-Year Plan and the Crash drastically transformed the context and content of American attitudes toward Russia. Most of the apolitical writers now became strident radicals, looking to the USSR and advocating Communism as the means for obtaining social justice in the United States. Liberals also regained a sense of relevance to the American scene, but they refused to endorse the Plan without qualification, much less to adopt Communism. Instead, they urged economic planning without revolution and dictatorship, at the same time demanding diplomatic and commercial relations with the Soviets.

Meanwhile, the general public was revising its view of Russia. After an echo of earlier righteous outrage, in response to the Soviet campaign against religion, most Americans began to turn their attention to the Five-Year Plan. In 1930 the attention took the form of hysteria over dumping, fostered by the charges from business groups competing with Soviet products and from patriotic societies. As the Depression deepened, however, American feeling started to shift toward curiosity about economic planning in general and the Soviet Plan in particular. The numbers of tourists visiting the USSR and publications about the Red experiment soared in unison during the early thirties. At the same time, numerous engineers went to work for the Soviets. Both on the scene and at home, Americans remained predominantly critical of Soviet principles and achievements. Nevertheless they took up the slogan of "economic planning" with remarkable enthusiasm. Even many business spokesmen and the leaders of the AF of L conceded the failure of their laissez-faire premises, although their conversion was less related to the Soviet phenomenon than to domestic economic disaster.

The Depression also had a major role in ending the diplomatic impasse between the two nations. Increasingly desperate for buyers, business leaders urgently sought Soviet trade. When Soviet purchases suddenly dropped, following the dumping controversy, these businessmen claimed that recognition alone would open the Russian market to American exports and thereby help to relieve American unemployment. An enlarging chorus of agreement came from liberals, newspaper editors, Protestant ministers, and others, demanding recognition on behalf of American trade, world peace, and common sense. The patriotic groups, Catholics, business interests fearful of Soviet competition, and irreconcilable conservatives became an impotent minority during 1933. President Roosevelt's announcement on November 17 won the approval, varying from enthusiastic to resigned, of most Americans.

The President's enactment of recognition, accompanied by support from most of the American people, concluded the acrimonious years of the Soviet-American "nonrelationship." Yet this expression of official and popular cordiality leaves a basic question unanswered: Had American attitudes toward the USSR decisively turned away from the predominant hostility of the preceding decade and a half? Had a reconciliation in emotional and intellectual as well as diplomatic terms taken place? In order to formulate an answer, one must probe beneath the evidence of events and opinions to the underlying attitudes, evaluating these attitudes in the three dimensions of direction for or against, content, and intensity.

The sweeping generalization that most Americans by 1933 finally approved of Soviet Russia must be quickly and strongly qualified in several respects. First of all, despite the fact that recognition reversed traditional policy, it was granted on traditional terms. The Soviets won American legitimization only by promising to respect American principles of religious freedom and national integrity, and to arrange for a settlement of debts. Thus, Wilson and his Republican successors were vindicated, at least nominally. Second, despite an unprecedented amount of tolerance or frank sympathy for the Soviet regime among liberals, Protestant ministers, writers, economists, newspaper editors, and others, there remained many dissidents even on the left. Those labor leaders who had defended the USSR were retreating toward a more critical position, while liberals of the *New Republic–Nation* variety firmly balanced admiration for the Communist social experiment with antagonism toward its dictatorial methods. As for some business leaders' advocacy of diplomatic and commercial relations with the USSR, that was a form of economic need more than genuine tolerance. Third, the outbursts of indignation over religious persecution and commercial dumping by the Moscow regime revealed a fund of continuing hostility, even if on a smaller scale than during the Red Scare of 1919.

Generalization disintegrates into a mosaic of exceptions, therefore, incorporating the heterogeneity of American society. Yet the complexity still does not defeat the suspicion that the preponderant tenor of American feeling toward Soviet Russia in 1933 was decidedy more benign than at any time during the twenties and, of course, 1918–1919. The impulse to describe, from a distant perspective, a shift in prevailing attitudes still insists on being satisfied. To state the case in its starkest form: a decade earlier, Roosevelt could not have acted so easily, or would not have even dared to act, because of an inevitable deluge of popular protest. He took the bold step only because, by the early thirties, open-mindedness had finally surpassed hostility toward the USSR. This is a persuasive argument, valid in its broad outlines of the period. Yet it also is insufficient, not only because it blurs the important variations in American feelings, but also because it defines the *direction* of attitudes while ignoring their *content*. When the dimension of content is added, the argument becomes more intricate and more interesting.

Theodore Dreiser, for example, expressed serious reservations about Soviet dictatorship, collectivism, and rigid materialism when he visited Russia in 1928; three years later, he praised the collectivist and materialist Five-Year Plan for suggesting how to create prosperity and working-class freedom in the United States. At the same time, Sidney Hillman gradually neutralized his initial admiration for the purposefulness of workers under Soviet "iron discipline" until, by the 1930's, he had come to endorse a distinctly liberal form of planning. This juxtaposition is striking less because of its contrast of direction than its similarity of content. Although passing each other in opposite directions, Dreiser and Hillman were on the same path. That is to say, the basic components in the attitudes of both men were identical: a commitment to social justice and individual freedom. Only the arrangement of those components distinguishes the two men's views of Russia.

This is more than an isolated and peculiar instance. Throughout the period between the Revolution and recognition, the ingredients in most American attitudes toward Russia remained constant, being rearranged rather than transformed when those attitudes took a new direction. For the majority of Americans, "democracy" as a salient value during the World War receded, during the twenties, before "individualism" and "capitalism." After the Crash, these two became subordinate to "planning," although they and "democracy" persisted as restraints on those who sought centralized direction of the economy. Thus American attitudes toward Russia always included the same set of values, but with the order of priorities revised in response to the varying situations of war, prosperity, and depression. The sequence differed from group to group and often differed within groups, of course, but the differences derived from disagreement on priority of values rather than the values themselves. Samuel Gompers and Sidney Hillman, Father Walsh and John Haynes Holmes, William Allen White and John Dewey, Hamilton Fish and William Borah, J. Carson Adkerson and Hugh L. Cooper, all adhered to American rather than to Communist principles. The only exceptional group (other than the Communists) were the writers who adopted after 1929 a new value — social concern — and otherwise continued to dissent from most of the American creed.

This plurality within the American value scheme, giving it a chameleon character of adaptability to national circumstances, leads to an explanation of why American attitudes toward the Soviet Union were so fickle and also so self-contradictory. Russia's manifold identities as the newest democracy and a bestial tyranny, or as an adolescent capitalism and a laboratory in social justice, were masks which suited American observers at the moment. They were replaced because Americans' concerns changed in accordance with their own national situation. They were applied simultaneously because various individuals or groups had differing conceptions of the American scene. And they all fitted because the Soviet Union was a heterogeneous phenomenon. The "truth" about Russia was really "truths," with the particular emphasis depending on the observer's preconceptions. Thus, Scott Nearing could praise the effectiveness of Soviet economic planning in 1926 while the editor of the *New York Journal of Commerce* described the USSR as a great capitalistic experiment. E. E. Cummings could despise it as the kingdom of the pitiless machine while Waldo Frank was enraptured by the humanity and wholeness he discovered. In the manner which social psychologists have found to be characteristic

275

of all attitudes, Americans saw what they wanted to see in Soviet Russia, and its diversity encouraged them to do so.

Thus the content of American attitudes toward the Soviet Union refines the fact of their direction. Yet it also emphasizes the self-interested sources and fickle nature of those attitudes. Can one nonetheless discover, amidst their chameleon qualities, any pattern of attitude formation and reformation which would indicate a stronger causal relationship between Soviet facts and American assessment? The case histories of four American journalists assigned to the "Soviet beat" — Anna Louise Strong, William Henry Chamberlin, Louis Fischer, and Eugene Lyons — provide an interesting vehicle for testing this suggestion. Insulated from the milieu of their own country, their attention constantly focused on portraying the Russian scene, they most closely approximated the undistracted, unself-seeking scientist in the laboratory.

The first to arrive in the USSR was Anna Louise Strong. Born in 1885 in Nebraska and soon moving to Ohio, she was both the oldest of the four and the only one who did not grow up in the eastern part of the United States. Her Mayflower ancestry (on both sides of the family) and a strong religious heritage also distinguished her from the other three. Miss Strong soon proved to be intellectually precocious, very ambitious, and quite restless. By the age of twenty-three, having acquired a doctoral degree in philosophy at the University of Chicago, she was proud, lonely, and, according to her recollection in 1935, hungry "for a world where I might create and be wanted." [1] Soon she began seven years of successful work in child welfare, during which time she was converted to socialism. In 1915 she joined her father in Seattle, took up part-time politics and journalism, and campaigned against military preparedness.

276

By the end of 1917 she was a radical, deeply distraught by American entry into the war and admiring the Bolshevik Revolution without fully understanding Marxism. Inevitably she became involved in the Seattle general strike; almost as inevitably, a casual suggestion by Lincoln Steffens inspired her to go to Russia. Under the auspices of the American Friends Service Committee relief mission, she arrived via Poland in 1921, ready to begin her final career as free-lance writer, journalist, Communist, and, eventually, wife of a Soviet official.[2] Three years later she catalogued the stirring qualities of the USSR: "The heroism, the sacrifice, the comradeship, and the joy that went with it. The joy of pioneers who, in the midst of hardship, exult to believe that they are creating something new." [3]

William Henry Chamberlin was a quite different sort of person, although his early biography closely resembled Miss Strong's. Born in Brooklyn in 1897 and educated at Haverford, a Quaker college, his intellectual adolescence was shaped by antagonism to American entry into the war and by the glowing phenomenon of the October Revolution. Like Miss Strong, he drifted into radicalism with only vague comprehension of socialist, much less Marxian, theory. In 1922, accompanied by his Russian-born wife, he too undertook a pilgrimage to the Soviet Union, soon obtaining a position as regular correspondent for the *Christian Science Monitor*.[4] At first, his admiration for the idealism of the Communist Party as well as the "new spirit of fraternity" and freedom among the workers easily discounted the vulgarity of the NEP speculators, the red tape, and the evidence of careerism among some party members.[5] But gradually his ardor diminished; by 1924, according to his recollection sixteen years later, he had settled into "disenchantment and neutrality." [6] Thereafter, he impressed fellow correspondents in Moscow as a diligent, dispassionate, and reliable student of the Soviet scene.[7]

Louis Fischer and Eugene Lyons came from lower-class rather than middle-class backgrounds. Fischer was born amid the Philadelphia slums in 1896, son of a factory laborer who eventually turned to selling fish and fruit. Personal hardship and deprivation made him naturally sympathetic with the Bolshevik defense of the underdog, although he later remembered that the 1917 revolutions had produced inexplicably little impact on him at the time. He first became keenly aware of Russia while working as a journalist in Europe during 1921–1922. In September of the latter year, he and his Russian-born wife went to the land of the proletariat, impelled by high hopes rather than utopian illusions. By 1924 he was becoming the regular correspondent for *The Nation,* intimately acquainted with such top officials as Foreign Minister Chicherin and mixing only occasional criticism into his predominantly laudatory accounts of Soviet progress.[8]

Lyons grew up amid the poverty of New York's lower east side, a first-generation American who became involved in socialist activities almost before puberty. The Russian Revolution flared like a bright and guiding star on his intellectual horizon. During the next decade he worked on American Communist publications, briefly visited Italy on the eve of the Fascist coup, then returned home to write and fight for Sacco and Vanzetti and to take a job in the American office of Tass, the Soviet news agency. The opportunity to visit Russia in 1928, as a United Press correspondent, seemed like the culmination of his political and emotional loyalties.[9]

Thus, all four journalists came to the Soviet Union from varying personal backgrounds but with a common enthusiasm which differed in intensity rather than kind. Even if their Communist sympathy might have been unpredictable at their births, it is certainly explicable in retrospect. Their later destinies are much more startling, however. Lyons, the last to arrive and the most strongly predisposed in political terms, was the first to become disillusioned. The "concentrated terror" of agricultural collectivization and anti-kulak pressure during the winter of 1930–31 jeopardized all the justifications he had constructed for the Soviet system. Particularly appalling to him were the tortures applied by the secret police to citizens suspected of concealing foreign currency. At first he kept silent about the cruelties, hesitant to give ammunition to the enemies of the USSR and fearful of losing his friends. But soon he became ashamed of his hypocrisy. During the final three years of his tenure in Moscow, his bitterness steadily mounted into outright hostility. After his departure in 1934, he became an ardent foe of the Stalin regime and a venomous critic of American fellow travelers.[10] There may also have been less ideological reasons for his defection. In his autobiography of 1941, Louis Fischer remarks that Lyons limited his Russian experience to Moscow social circles, rather than studying villages or factories, and that he was resentful at not receiving special attention from the Soviet leaders as reward for his Communist activities at home.[11]

Chamberlin soon followed Lyons's retreat from the faith, although at a different rate. Early in the thirties he still tended to apologize for Soviet defects and to emphasize constructive and idealistic potentialities. But this balance gave way in 1932 when he interpreted the widespread famine as a deliberate tactic by the regime for defeating peasant opposition to collectivization. This famine, which reporters like Walter Duranty of the *New York Times* concealed in accord with governmental policy, was the pivotal event in Chamberlin's evolution from "neutrality" to hostility. By 1934 he left the USSR as a determined opponent and, during subsequent years, became a frank, wholly orthodox conservative.[12]

Fischer also became disillusioned with the USSR, but not until 1938, after watching the purge trials and participating in the Spanish Civil War — and then never with the rancor of his two colleagues. By 1941, three years after leaving Russia, he was sure that "the maintenance of personal freedom should be the primary consideration of every human being. It is never a choice between freedom and a full stomach. No dictatorship has given either," whereas democracy at least seeks to satisfy both.[13] But the original member of the quartet, Anna Louise Strong, held firmly to her faith.

The composite study of four sympathizers with the Soviet experiment presents a variety resisting generalization. Although all of them were informed and intelligent observers of the same facts, they reacted in different ways. Lyons and Fischer were the most "proletarian" in origin, but their dissimilar temperaments produced different modes of response. Lyons swung swiftly from extreme engagement to extreme disengagement during his firsthand exposure to Soviet realities, while Fischer pursued a more circumspect course. Chamberlin, also less fanatical, defected at almost the same time as Lyons and followed him into bitter conservatism. Meanwhile, the earliest and the most sentimental adherent, Miss Strong, remained steadfast.

In short, attitudes toward the Soviet Union, even if in response primarily to Russian rather than to American circumstances, were so implicated in personal temperament that they defied both predictability and empiricism. Moreover, firsthand experience did not impose, either on these resident Americans or on the transient American tourists, a unifying effect. Those who visited the USSR reacted in totally heterogeneous ways, usually asserting their prejudices with more firmness, frequently losing sympathy, occasionally acquiring tolerance, but always exhibiting responses which require explanation in terms of personal backgrounds and professional interests rather than the facts of the Soviet phenomenon. Only the engineers working for the Plan formed a generally uniform and disinterested set of attitudes.[14]

This picture of apparently wild flux is misleading, however, since it deals with individuals as if they were isolated and autonomous observers of the Red experiment. In fact, most Americans not only never visited the USSR, but responded to it (if they responded at all) as members of a group. In a manner that recent studies of opinion formation have found to be typical, Americans took up their positions toward Soviet Russia under the influence of people whom they ordinarily respected or, on the other hand, whom they ordinarily disparaged.[15] That is to say, they took sides not only for or against Russia, but for or against other Americans. The editors of *The New Republic* exemplified this behavior when they remarked in 1918: "We sympathize with them [the Bolsheviks] . . . because of the enemies they have made." This formation of attitudes according to the cues of "reference groups" introduced a large degree of stability — often rigidity — into the intellectual situation. Because a person valued the reassurance and approval of his peers and feared to gratify those he had always defined as "enemies," he usually suppressed his disagreements. That reflex accounts for the discomfort of Eugene Lyons, Chamberlin and other incipient dissenters from the radical camp. Only when they decided that hypocrisy was even more intolerable than loneliness and disgrace did they break away.

The majority of Americans never faced the alternatives in quite so painful a way, since the Soviet Union did not serve them as the prime criterion — the acid test — of social acceptability. It had lower salience among their concerns. Most citizens were uninterested in foreign affairs, and presumably they could differ about Russia without alienating everyone whose approval they valued. On the other hand, since the

Soviet question was not their prime standard of group respectability, they cared less about studying it and taking a position autonomously. As a result, they accepted the view of the conventional "opinion leader," thus again reinforcing the stability of attitudes.

Still another dimension must be added to direction and content, for these two alone leave unanswered the question of why so many Americans were so passionately concerned about the Soviet Union in the first place. What was responsible for the almost unrelieved intensity of American attitudes toward Russia throughout this long period? Social psychologists again have drawn suggestive conclusions from recent studies. Bernard Berelson, Paul Lazarsfeld, and William N. McPhee examined attitudes of residents in Elmira, New York, during the presidential campaign of 1948. They not only found a bias of perceptions in line with the respondents' particular political loyalties, but they discovered a tendency to distort in order to obtain "psychic protection," that is, to reduce internal conflicts and to avoid intellectual inconsistencies that otherwise would be obvious.[16]

In 1917–1918, the intensity of American feelings toward Russia can be explained by the context of the war spirit, which aroused such extreme fervor. During the postwar decade, however, the intensity persisted despite a decline in the amount of interest. The Red Scare is the most obvious example, but the furor over the execution of Buchkavich as well as the extravagance of optimism concerning Russia's drift to capitalism under the NEP are equally pertinent proofs. Supplementing these examples by such phenomena as the Scopes trial, the resurgence of the Ku Klux Klan, the passage of restrictive immigration laws, and the occasionally strained spirit of patriotic and capitalist boosterism, one can see a constant theme of anxiety throughout the ostensibly confident New Era. As Henry F. May has so acutely argued, the intellectual character of the twenties was one of "disintegration" in which "common values and common beliefs were replaced by separate and conflicting loyalties." [17]

The decade and a half following American entry into the war was indeed a period of drastic change. Having decisively entered the world arena in a messianic spirit, Americans discovered by 1920 that Europe was stagnant rather than saved. At the same time, the Soviet Revolution was issuing a strident challenge to the morality of the war, the Western concept of democracy, and the American premise of capitalism. American claims to political, moral, and economic leadership had not only fallen short of success, but now confronted a rival. Had the rivalry been simply physical, it would not have earned so much attention, for Russia in the 1920's was barely recovering from six years of continuous disruption. But it was ideological — in fact, it involved opponents whose values tended to overlap at crucial points. The Soviets preached un-American atheism, collectivism, and class dictatorship, but they also preached efficiency, progress, and democracy of a sort — and did so with the messianic fervor and invocation of historical destiny which had become characteristic of American ideals. This overlapping relationship was largely responsible for American dissension and consternation about the Soviet regime during the 1920's. When regarded in one perspective, the Communists were demoniacal enemies; in another perspective, they were harsher but more effective Progressives or even capitalists.

In addition to mixed concern, however, many Americans felt an emotional intensity which implies more than pure competitiveness. Elihu Root, for example, wrote to Ivy Lee in March 1926:

The Russian Bolsheviks hold to their communistic doctrines with a fierce religious fervor. They have a missionary spirit like the

283

early followers of Mohammed. If the American people lose their sincere belief in their own institutions and fall into a weak milk and water attitude towards the principles upon which our government is based, we are going to have very serious troubles ahead of us.[18]

The abrupt transition from Communist fervor to possible American loss of faith suggests the connection that Root saw between them. He betrayed the same insecurity about national integrity which the State Department and the patriotic groups expressed in their alarm about subversion by Communist agents. Rivalry became phobia because many Americans lacked confidence in the strength of their own ideals.

This latent anxiety, constantly submerged by the reassurance of a booming economy, developed into explicit stress after the Crash of 1929. The failure to make the world safe for democracy was amplified by the failure to make America safe for prosperity. At the same time, the Soviet Union became a competitor of proportions more ominous than ever, not only in the physical sense of being able to dump goods on the American market, but in the ideological sense that the Plan had pre-empted the claim to progress which Americans had so noisily asserted as their exclusive endowment. Basically, then, the opponents of recognition were correct: the establishment of diplomatic relations, even with face-saving conditions, represented an endorsement by the United States. But rather than an endorsement of the devil, it was a humble acknowledgment that two missionaries inhabited the world, and that the conflict of their doctrines would not be settled by the swift expiration or surrender of the Soviets. The long silence was ended but, as subsequent decades were to prove, it was only the prologue to a larger and more momentous drama.

Appendices / Bibliography / Notes / Index

Appendix A / Number of Books on Russia by American Authors and
Outstanding Soviet-American Events, 1917–1933

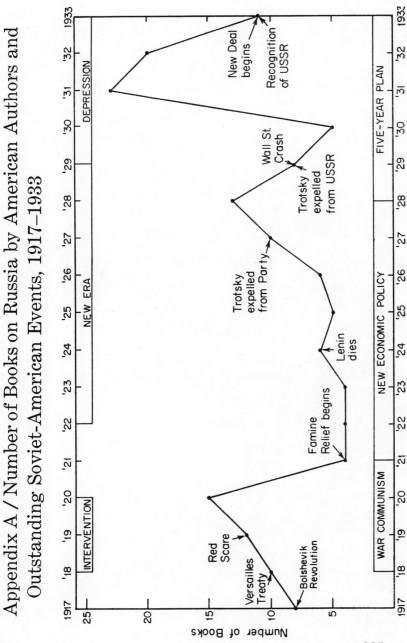

Appendix B / Circulation of Major Periodicals, 1920 and 1930

	1920		1930	
1.	Saturday Evening Post	2,108,923	Saturday Evening Post	2,924,363
2.	Ladies' Home Journal	1,972,189	Woman's Home	
3.	American Magazine	1,441,080	Companion	2,606,123
4.	Woman's Home		Ladies' Home Journal	2,581,942
	Companion	1,392,218	McCall's	2,505,088
5.	McCall's	1,350,067	American Magazine	2,279,108
6.	Collier's	1,042,570	Collier's	2,257,290
7.	Literary Digest	900,000	Good Housekeeping	1,767,380
8.	National Geographic	743,386	Literary Digest	1,602,397
9.	Good Housekeeping	682,823	Hearst's International	
			and Cosmopolitan	1,590,840
10.	Review of Reviews	172,552	National Geographic	1,291,082
11.	World's Work	126,043	Time	300,172
12.	Atlantic Monthly	107,776	Review of Reviews	160,005
13.	Outlook	105,340	Atlantic Monthly	129,798
14.	Independent	100,589	World's Work	127,774
15.	Scribner's	97,748	Harper's	120,947
16.	Harper's	85,896	Outlook and Independent	85,536
17.	Current History	49,350	Business Week	75,238
18.	Liberator	40,000	Scribner's	73,517
19.	New Republic	35,000	Current History	61,830
20.	Nation	28,960	Survey	37,217
21.	Survey	13,686	Nation	37,127
22.	Dial	7,466	New Republic	25,000
23.			New Masses	25,000

Source: N. W. Ayer & Son, *American Newspaper Annual & Directory: A Catalogue of American Newspapers* (Philadelphia, 1921), and *Directory of Newspapers and Periodicals* (Philadelphia, 1931).

Appendix C / Editorial Opinion on Recognition of Russia: Newspaper Circulation, 1931 and 1933

	For recognition		Against recognition	
	March 1931	October 1933	March 1931	October 1933
NEW ENGLAND	60,400(4)ᵃ	481,847 (27)	619,300(12)	480,826(33)
Me.	–	–	65,000 (2)	82,989 (5)
N.H.	–	9,359 (2)	23,800 (2)	43,759 (4)
Vt.	–	6,845 (2)	3,800 (1)	28,016 (3)
Mass.	21,800(1)	240,534 (13)	405,500 (3)	208,432(13)
R.I.	–	–	50,000 (2)	11,869 (2)
Conn.	38,600 (3)	225,109 (10)	71,200 (2)	105,941 (6)
MIDDLE ATLANTIC	634,300 (4)	3,518,821(110)	933,800(13)	1,029,354(41)
N.Y.	634,300 (4)	1,779,449 (44)	510,300 (8)	767,285(17)
N.J.	–	536,061 (14)	53,400 (1)	60,472 (4)
Pa.	–	1,203,311 (52)	426,500 (4)	201,597(20)
SOUTH	267,400(5)	3,336,027(230)	301,300 (9)	408,502(55)
Wash. D.C.	61,400(1)	65,644 (1)	73,900 (1)	–
Va.	46,200(1)	192,426 (7)	13,700 (2)	22,830 (5)
W. Va.	–	64,462 (8)	34,100 (2)	59,926 (9)
N.C.	–	143,974 (12)	48,000 (1)	27,677 (6)
Fla.	38,300(1)	177,459 (20)	47,800 (1)	23,639 (6)
Ala.	45,100(1)	284,953 (15)	–	–
La.	–	94,570 (3)	9,900 (1)	12,416 (2)
Texas	23,400(1)	578,415 (59)	73,900 (1)	73,384 (2)

EAST NORTH				
CENTRAL	498,900(6)	2,303,939(123)	1,003,000(20)	1,866,742(86)
Ohio	264,800(2)	1,103,147(47)	295,400(3)	293,157(16)
Ind.	–	200,574(22)	132,600(4)	213,652(23)
Ill.	9,200(1)	551,156(26)	115,000(5)	902,113(20)
Mich.	–	99,825(15)	433,500(7)	356,899(16)
Wisc.	234,900(3)	349,237(13)	27,500(1)	91,931(11)
WEST NORTH				
CENTRAL	95,900(2)	2,122,898(91)	614,300(6)	662,079(52)
Minn.	91,700(1)	366,148(15)	193,200(2)	133,652(4)
Iowa	–	488,921(19)	122,100(1)	88,962(10)
Mo.	–	887,578(18)	268,300(1)	346,020(14)
Neb.	4,200(1)	185,881(10)	9,300(1)	4,163(1)
Kansas	–	167,487(22)	21,400(1)	35,809(1)
FAR WEST &				
PACIFIC	40,300(1)	1,156,516(137)	114,900(6)	583,364(40)
Col.	40,300(1)	64,714(11)	–	7,090(3)
Mont.	–	42,524(7)	16,600(1)	5,487(2)
N.M.	–	42,795(5)	1,400(1)	8,956(3)
Wash.	–	146,223(9)	55,000(2)	187,161(10)
Calif.	–	462,103(63)	41,900(2)	294,138(12)

Note: Because the purpose of this table is to make comparisons, I have not itemized those states for which the 1931 survey gave no data, even though the 1933 survey did cover these states. The regional totals for 1933 include these unlisted states, however, and therefore exceed the sum of the given state totals.

Sources: 1931: "Stimson Study of Russia: Analysis of Editorial Comments," March 13, 1931–April 1, 1931, in Herbert Hoover Archives, The Hoover Institution on War, Revolution and Peace, Stanford University. 1933: Survey of the Committee on Russian-American Relations of the American Foundation, October 1933, in Meno Lovenstein, *American Opinion of Soviet Russia* (Washington, D.C., 1941), pp. 139–143.

[a] Number of newspapers is in parentheses.

Bibliography

PRIMARY SOURCES

PERSONAL PAPERS

William E. Borah Papers, Library of Congress
Alexander Gumberg Papers, Wisconsin Historical Society
Samuel N. Harper Papers, University of Chicago
Edward M. House Papers, Yale University
George W. Norris Papers, Library of Congress
John Reed and Louise Bryant Papers, Harvard University
Raymond Robins Papers, Wisconsin Historical Society
Elihu Root Papers, Library of Congress
Norman Thomas Papers, New York Public Library
William B. Thompson Papers, in Hermann Hagedorn Papers, Library of Congress
Oswald Garrison Villard Papers, Harvard University
William Allen White Papers, Library of Congress

NEWSPAPERS

Arizona Republic
Atlanta Constitution
Chicago Tribune
Cincinnati Enquirer
Des Moines Register
Hartford Courant
New Orleans Times-Picayune

New York Times
Norfolk Virginian-Pilot
St. Louis Post-Dispatch
Seattle Post-Intelligencer
Seattle Times
Washington Post

(With the exception of the *New York Times,* the above newspapers were read only for the following selected periods: August 10–14, 1920; July 24–August 23, 1921; December 16–January 11, 1923–24; January 21–25, 1924; November 3–10, 1927; November 23–December 5, 1927; January 26–February 15, 1929; November 16–20, 1933.)

293

BIBLIOGRAPHY

GOVERNMENT DOCUMENTS

Bolshevik Propaganda: Hearings before a Subcommittee of the Committee on the Judiciary, United States Senate, pursuant to S. Res. 439 and 469, 65th Congress, 3rd Session (February 11–March 10, 1919). Washington, D.C.: Government Printing Office, 1919.

Committee on Public Information, *The German-Bolshevik Conspiracy*, War Information Series, no. 30. n.p., October 1918.

Embargo on Soviet Products: Hearings before the Committee on Ways and Means, House of Representatives, 71st Congress, 3rd Session, on H.R. 16035 (February 19, 20, and 21, 1931). Washington, D.C.: Government Printing Office, 1931.

Establishment of a National Economic Council: Hearings before a Subcommittee of the Committee on Manufactures, United States Senate, 72nd Congress, 1st Session, on S. 6215 (71st Congress), A Bill to Establish a National Economic Council (October 22–December 19, 1931). Washington, D.C.: Government Printing Office, 1932.

Investigation of Communist Propaganda: Report no. 2290 (pursuant to H. Res. 220) from the Special Committee to Investigate Communist Activities in the United States, House of Representatives, 71st Congress, 3rd Session (January 17, 1931). n.p., n.d.

National Archives, Record Group 59 (State Department); Record Group 46 (Petitions to the Senate Foreign Relations Committee); Record Group 233 (Petitions to the House Foreign Affairs Committee).

Papers Relating to the Foreign Relations of the United States: 1920–1933. Washington, D.C.: Government Printing Office, 1935–1948.

Papers Relating to the Foreign Relations of the United States: The Lansing Papers, 1914–1920, 2 vols. Washington, D.C.: Government Printing Office, 1940.

Papers Relating to the Foreign Relations of the United States: 1918, Russia, 3 vols. Washington, D.C.: Government Printing Office, 1931–1932.

Papers Relating to the Foreign Relations of the United States: 1919, Russia. Washington, D.C.: Government Printing Office, 1937.

Prohibition of Importation of Goods Produced by Convict, Forced or Indentured Labor: Hearings before the Committee on Ways and Means, House of Representatives, 71st Congress, 3rd Session, on H.R. 15597, H.R. 15927, and H.R. 16517 (January 27
294

and 28, 1931). Washington, D.C.: Government Printing Office, 1931.

Recognition of Russia: Hearings before a Subcommittee of the Committee on Foreign Relations, United States Senate, 68th Congress, 1st Session, pursuant to S. Res. 50 (January 21 to 23, 1924). Washington, D.C.: Government Printing Office, 1924.

Treaty of Peace with Germany: Hearings before the Committee on Foreign Relations, United States Senate, 66th Congress, 1st Session, Senate Document no. 106, X. Washington, D.C.: Government Printing Office, 1919, pp. 1161–1297.

BOOKS, PAMPHLETS, AND MAGAZINES

BUSINESS AND ENGINEERING

American Industries
American Machinist
The Annalist
Automotive Industries
Barron's: The National Financial Weekly
Business Week
The Commercial and Financial Chronicle
Electrical World
Engineering and Mining Journal
Engineering News-Record
Fortune

Harvard Business Review
The Iron Age
Iron Trade Review
Journal of the American Bankers Association
The Magazine of Wall Street
Mining and Metallurgy
The Nation's Business
The Oil and Gas Journal
Printers' Ink
Printers' Ink Monthly
Railway Age
Railway Review
Textile World

American-Russian Chamber of Commerce, *Russia, The American Problem.* New York: n.p. n.d. [1920?].

Bron, Saul G. *Soviet Economic Development and American Business: Results of the First Year under the Five-Year Plan and Further Perspectives.* New York: Horace Liveright, 1930.

Burrell, George A. *An American Engineer Looks at Russia.* Boston: Stratford Company, 1932.

Campbell, Thomas D. *Russia: Market or Menace?* New York: Longman's, Green and Co., 1932.

Chamber of Commerce, of the United States. *Annual Meetings.*

Donham, Wallace Brett. *Business Adrift.* New York: Whittlesey House, McGraw-Hill, 1931.

―――― *Business Looks at the Unforeseen.* New York: Whittlesey House, McGraw Hill, 1932.

BIBLIOGRAPHY

Fay, Charles Norman. *Business in Politics: Considerations for Leaders in American Business.* Cambridge, Mass.: Cosmos Press, 1926.

Ford, Henry. *My Life and Work.* Garden City, N.Y.: Garden City Publishing, 1922.

——— *My Philosophy of Industry: A Series of Authorized Interviews Written by Fay Leone Faurote.* London: George G. Harrap, 1929.

——— *Today and Tomorrow.* Garden City, N.Y.: Doubleday, Page, 1926.

Friedman, Elisha M. *Russia in Transition: A Business Man's Appraisal.* New York: Viking Press, 1932.

"Henry Ford," *Bolshaya sovetskaya entsiklopediya.* Moscow: State Institute of the Soviet Encyclopedia, 1936, LVIII, 128–130.

Javits, Benjamin A. *Business and the Public Interest: Trade Associations, the Anti-Trust Laws and Industrial Planning.* New York: Macmillan, 1932.

Lee, Ivy. *Present-Day Russia.* New York: Macmillan, 1928.

Littlepage, John D., and Demaree Bess. *In Search of Soviet Gold.* New York: Harcourt, Brace, 1937.

Morgan, Thomas A. *Trade with Soviet Russia: Address Delivered at a Meeting of the Coastal States Coordinated, Columbia, S.C., (February 16, 1932).* n.p. n.d.

Muldavin, Albert. *The Red Fog Lifts.* New York: Appleton, 1931.

National Association of Manufacturers of the United States. *Proceedings of Annual Meetings.*

Rukeyser, Walter Arnold. *Working for the Soviets: An American Engineer in Russia.* New York: Covici-Friede, 1932.

Scott, John. *Behind the Urals: An American Worker in Russia's City of Steel.* Cambridge, Mass.: Houghton Mifflin, 1942.

Sibley, Robert. *America's Answer to the Russian Challenge.* San Francisco: Farallon Press, 1931.

LABOR

The Advance   *Locomotive Engineers Journal*
American Federationist   *United Mine Workers Journal*
Justice

Amalgamated Clothing Workers of America. *Documentary History.*

American Federation of Labor. *Report of Proceedings of Annual Conventions.*

Gompers, Samuel, and William English Walling. *Out of Their Own Mouths: A Revelation and Indictment of Sovietism.* New York: E. P. Dutton, 1921.

296

Green, William. *Reports on Communist Propaganda in America, as Submitted to the State Department, United States Government.* Washington, D.C.: American Federation of Labor, 1934.

Hardman, J. B. S., ed. *American Labor Dynamics, in the Light of Post-War Developments: An Inquiry by Thirty-Two Labor Men, Teachers, Editors, and Technicians.* New York: Harcourt, Brace, 1928.

International Association of Machinists. *Proceedings of Conventions.*

International Ladies' Garment Workers' Union. *Report and Proceedings of Conventions.*

Russia after Ten Years: Report of the American Trade Union Delegation to the Soviet Union. New York: International Publishers, 1927.

Schlossberg, Joseph. *The Workers and Their World: Aspects of the Workers' Struggle at Home and Abroad, Selected Essays by Joseph Schlossberg.* New York: A.L.P. Committee, 1935.

United Mine Workers of America. *Attempt by Communists to Seize the American Labor Movement.* Washington, D.C.: Government Printing Office, 1923.

——— *Proceedings of Conventions.*

EDUCATION

Educational Review   *Progressive Education*
The Parents' Magazine   *School and Society*

Counts, George S. *The American Road to Culture: A Social Interpretation of Education in the United States.* New York: John Day, 1930.

——— *Dare the School Build a New Social Order?* New York: John Day, 1932.

——— *A Ford Crosses Soviet Russia.* Boston: Stratford, 1930.

——— *Secondary Education and Industrialism: The Inglis Lecture, 1929.* Cambridge, Mass.: Harvard University Press, 1929.

——— *The Social Foundations of Education* (part 9 of the *Report of the American Historical Association Commission on the Social Studies*). New York: Charles Scribner's Sons, 1934.

——— *The Soviet Challenge to America.* New York: John Day, 1931.

Dewey, John. *See* Books, Pamphlets, Magazines, general.

Kilpatrick, William H., ed. *The Educational Frontier: Written in Collaboration by William H. Kilpatrick, Boyd H. Bode, John L. Childs, H. Gordon Hullfish, John Dewey, R. B. Raup, V. T. Thayer.* New York: Century, 1933.

BIBLIOGRAPHY

Nearing, Scott. *Education in Soviet Russia.* New York: International Publishers, 1926.
Pinkevitch, Albert P. *The New Education in the Soviet Republic.* New York: John Day, 1929.
Wilson, Lucy L. W. *The New Schools of New Russia.* New York: Vanguard Press, 1928.
Woody, Thomas. *New Minds: New Men? The Emergence of the Soviet Citizen.* New York: Macmillan, 1932.

RELIGION

America
The American Friend
The American Hebrew
The Catholic World
The Christian Century
The Commonweal

The Congregationalist
The Lutheran Witness
The Missionary Review of the World
The World Tomorrow
Zion's Herald

American Jewish Committee. *Annual Reports.*
American Jewish Yearbook.
Billikopf, Jacob, and Maurice B. Hexter. *The Jewish Situation in Eastern Europe Including Russia and the Work of the Joint Distribution Committee: Joint Report as Delivered at the National Conference of the United Jewish Campaign and the Joint Distribution Committee (Chicago, October 9–10, 1926).* n.p., n.d.
Central Conference of American Rabbis. *Yearbook.*
Cooke, Richard J. *Religion in Russia under the Soviets.* New York and Cincinnati: Abingdon Press, 1924.
Eddy, Sherwood. *The Challenge of Russia.* New York: Farrar & Rinehart, 1931.
———— *Everybody's World.* New York: George H. Doran, 1920.
———— *Russia Today: What Can We Learn from It?* New York: Farrar & Rinehart, 1934.
Emhardt, William Chauncey. *Religion in Soviet Russia: Anarchy.* Milwaukee: Milwaukee Publishing Co., 1929.
Rosenberg, James N. *On the Steppes: A Russian Diary.* New York: Alfred A. Knopf, 1927.
Spinka, Matthew. *The Church and the Russian Revolution.* New York: Macmillan, 1927.
Walsh, Edmund A. *The Last Stand: An Interpretation of the Soviet Five-Year Plan.* Boston: Little, Brown, 1931.
———— *Why Pope Pius XI Asked Prayers for Russia on March 19,*

1930: A Review of the Facts in the Case Together with Proofs of the International Program of the Soviet Government. New York: Catholic Near East Welfare Association, 1930.

Ward, Harry F. *In Place of Profit: Social Incentives in the Soviet Union.* New York: Charles Scribner's Sons, 1933.

—— *The New Social Order: Principles and Programs.* New York: Macmillan, 1919.

Yarmolinsky, Avrahm. *The Jews and Other Minor Nationalities Under the Soviets.* New York: Vanguard Press, 1928.

GENERAL

The American Economic Review
The American Magazine
The American Mercury
The American Socialist Quarterly
Annals of the American Academy of Political and Social Science
Asia
The Atlantic Monthly
The Bookman
The Century Magazine
Collier's
The Crisis
Current History
Current Opinion
The Dial
The Family
Foreign Affairs
The Forum
The Freeman
Good Housekeeping
Harper's Magazine
Hearst's International and Cosmopolitan
The Independent
The Journal of Political Economy
The Ladies' Home Journal
The Liberator
The Literary Digest

The Little Review
McCall's
The Modern Quarterly
The Nation
The National Geographic Magazine
National Republic
The New Leader
New Masses
The New Republic
North American Review
Opportunity
The Outlook
Political Science Quarterly
The Public
The Publishers' Weekly
The Review of Reviews
Russian Review
The Saturday Evening Post
The Saturday Review of Literature
The Sewanee Review
Scribner's Magazine
Social Science
Struggling Russia
The Survey
Time
Transition
Woman's Home Companion
The World's Work
The Yale Review

BIBLIOGRAPHY

Acheson, Judy. *Young America Looks at Russia.* New York: Frederick A. Stokes, 1932.

Ackerman, Carl W. *Trailing the Bolsheviki: Twelve Thousand Miles with the Allies in Siberia.* New York: Charles Scribner's Sons, 1919.

Albertson, Ralph. *Fighting without a War: An Account of Military Intervention in North Russia.* New York: Harcourt, Brace & Howe, 1920.

American Legion. *Reports to Annual Conventions.*

American Relief Administration. *Bulletins.*

Baedeker, Karl. *Russia with Teheran, Port Arthur and Peking: Handbook for Travellers.* New York: Charles Scribner's Sons, 1914.

Baldwin, Roger N. *Liberty under the Soviets.* New York: Vanguard Press, 1928.

Batsell, Walter Russell. *Soviet Rule in Russia.* New York: Macmillan, 1929.

Beard, Charles A., ed. *America Faces the Future.* Boston: Houghton Mifflin, 1932.

———— *Cross Currents in Europe Today.* Boston: Marshall Jones, 1922.

Beatty, Bessie. *The Red Heart of Russia.* New York: Century, 1918.

Berkman, Alexander: *The Bolshevik Myth (Diary, 1920–1922).* New York: Boni & Liveright, 1925.

Beury, Charles E. *Russia after the Revolution.* Philadelphia: George W. Jacobs, 1918.

Borders, Karl. *Village Life under the Soviets.* New York: Vanguard Press, 1927.

Bourke-White, Margaret. *Eyes on Russia.* New York: Simon & Schuster, 1931.

Brown, Jr., William Adams. *The Groping Giant: Revolutionary Russia as Seen by an American Democrat.* New Haven: Yale University Press, 1920.

Bryant, Louise. *Mirrors of Moscow.* New York: Thomas Seltzer, 1923.

———— *Six Red Months in Russia: An Observer's Account of Russia before and during the Proletarian Dictatorship.* New York: George H. Doran, 1918.

Bullard, Arthur. *The Russian Pendulum: Autocracy — Democracy — Bolshivism.* New York: Macmillan, 1919.

Bullitt, William C. *The Bullitt Mission to Russia: Testimony before the Committee on Foreign Relations, United States Senate.* New York: B. W. Huebsch, 1919.

———— *It's Not Done.* New York: Harcourt, Brace, 1926.

Butler, Nicholas Murray. *The Faith of a Liberal: Essays and Addresses on Political Principles and Public Policies.* New York: Charles Scribner's Sons, 1924.

—— *Greetings to the New Russia: Address at a Meeting Held at the Hudson Theater, N.Y., April 23, 1917, under the Auspices of the National Institute of Arts and Letters.* Washington, D.C.: Carnegie Endowment for International Peace, 1917.

—— *Is America Worth Saving? Addresses on National Problems and Party Policies.* New York: Charles Scribner's Sons, 1920.

—— *The Path to Peace: Essays and Addresses on Peace and Its Making.* New York: Charles Scribner's Sons, 1930.

—— *A World in Ferment: Interpretations of the War for a New World.* New York: Charles Scribner's Sons. 1917.

Chamberlin, William Henry. *Russia's Iron Age.* Boston: Little, Brown, 1934.

—— *The Soviet Planned Economic Order.* Boston: World Peace Foundation, 1931.

—— *Soviet Russia: A Living Record and a History.* Boston: Little, Brown, 1930.

Channing, C. G. Fairfax. *Siberia's Untouched Treasure: Its Future Role in the World.* New York: G. P. Putnam's Sons, 1923.

Chase, Stuart. *A New Deal.* New York: Macmillan, 1932.

—— Robert Dunn, and Rexford Guy Tugwell, eds. *Soviet Russia in the Second Decade: A Joint Survey by the Technical Staff of the First American Trade Union Delegation.* New York: John Day, 1928.

Clark, Evans. *Facts and Fabrications about Soviet Russia.* New York: Rand School of Social Science, 1920.

Colton, Ethan T. *The XYZ of Communism.* New York: Macmillan, 1931.

Comerford, Frank. *The New World.* New York: Appleton, 1920.

Committee on Russian-American Relations of the American Foundation. *The United States and the Soviet Union: A Report on the Controlling Factors in the Relations between the United States and the Soviet Union.* New York: American Foundation, 1933.

Cowles, John. *Glimpses of Soviet Russia in September and October, 1923.* n.p.: reprinted in *Des Moines Register,* n.d.

Crosley, Pauline S. *Intimate Letters from Petrograd.* New York: E. P. Dutton, 1920.

Cumming, C. K. and Walter W. Pettit, eds. *Russian-American Relations, March, 1917–March, 1920: Documents and Papers.* New York: Harcourt, Brace & Howe, 1920.

Cummings, E. E. *EIMI*. New York: Covici, Friede, 1933.

Darling, Jay N. *Ding Goes to Russia*. New York: Whittlesey House, McGraw-Hill, 1932.

Davis, Jerome, ed. *The New Russia between the First and Second Five-Year Plans*. New York: John Day, 1933.

Davis, Malcolm W. *Open Gates to Russia*. New York: Harper & Brothers, 1920.

Dennis, Alfred L. P. *The Foreign Policies of Soviet Russia*. New York: E. P. Dutton, 1924.

Dewey, John. *Characters and Events: Popular Essays in Social and Political Philosophy*, ed. Joseph Ratner, 2 vols. New York: Henry Holt, 1929.

––––––– *Impressions of Soviet Russia and the Revolutionary World: Mexico — China — Turkey*. New York: New Republic, 1932.

––––––– *Individualism Old and New*. New York: Minton, Balch, 1930.

––––––– *The Public and Its Problems*. New York: Henry Holt, 1927.

Dobbert, Gerhard, ed. *Red Economics*. New York: Houghton Mifflin, 1932.

Dos Passos, John. *In All Countries*. New York: Harcourt, Brace, 1934.

Douglas, Paul H. *The Coming of a New Party*. New York: Whittlesey House, McGraw-Hill, 1932.

Dreiser, Theodore. *Dreiser Looks at Russia*. New York: Horace Liveright, 1928.

––––––– *Harlan Miners Speak: Report on Terrorism in the Kentucky Coal Fields Prepared by Members of the National Committee for the Defense of Political Prisoners*. New York: Harcourt, Brace, 1932.

––––––– *Letters of Theodore Dreiser: A Selection*, ed., Robert H. Elias, 3 vols. Philadelphia: University of Pennsylvania Press, 1959.

––––––– *Tragic America*. New York: Horace Liveright, 1931.

Duncan, Irma, and Alan Ross Macdougall. *Isadora Duncan's Russian Days, and Her Last Years in France*. New York: Covici, Friede, 1929.

Dunn, Robert W. *Soviet Trade Unions*. New York: Vanguard Press, 1928.

Durant, Will. *The Tragedy of Russia: Impressions from a Brief Visit*. New York: Simon & Schuster, 1933.

Eastman, Max. *Leon Trotsky: The Portrait of a Youth*. New York: Greenberg, 1925.

––––––– *Marx and Lenin: The Science of Revolution*. New York: Albert & Charles Boni, 1927.

——— *Since Lenin Died*. New York: Boni & Liveright, 1925.

Eaton, Richard. *Under the Red Flag*. New York: Brentano's, 1924.

Eyre, Lincoln. *Russia Analyzed*. New York: World, 1920.

Fairburn, William Armstrong. *Russia the Utopia in Chains*. New York: Nation Press, 1931.

Fanning, C. E., ed. *Selected Articles on Russia: History, Description and Politics*. New York: H. W. Wilson, 1918.

Farson, Negley. *Black Bread and Red Coffins*. New York: Century, 1930.

Field, Alice Withrow. *Protection of Women and Children in Soviet Russia*. New York: E. P. Dutton, 1932.

Fischer, Louis. *Machines and Men in Russia*. New York: Harrison Smith, 1932.

——— *Oil Imperialism: The International Struggle for Russian Petroleum*. New York: International Publishers, 1926.

——— *The Soviets in World Affairs: A History of Relations Between the Soviet Union and the Rest of the World*, 2 vols. New York: Jonathan Cape & Harrison Smith, 1930.

——— *Why Recognize Russia? The Arguments for and against the Recognition of the Soviet Government by the United States*. New York: Jonathan Cape & Harrison Smith, 1931.

Foreign Policy Association, *Pamphlets*.

Francis, David R. *Russia from the American Embassy: April, 1916–November, 1918*. New York: Charles Scribner's Sons, 1921.

Frank, Waldo. *Dawn in Russia: The Record of a Journey*. New York: Charles Scribner's Sons, 1932.

——— *Our America*. New York: Boni & Liveright, 1919.

——— *The Re-Discovery of America: An Introduction to a Philosophy of American Life*. New York: Charles Scribner's Sons, 1929.

Freeman, Joseph. *The Soviet Worker: An Account of the Economic, Social and Cultural Status of Labor in the U.S.S.R.* New York: Liveright, 1932.

——— Joshua Kunitz, and Louis Lozowick. *Voices of October: Art and Literature in Soviet Russia*. New York: Vanguard Press, 1930.

Gibbons, Floyd. *The Red Napoleon*. New York: Jonathan Cape & Harrison Smith, 1929.

Golder, Frank Alfred and Lincoln Hutchinson. *On the Trail of the Russian Famine*. Stanford: Stanford University Press, 1927.

Goldman, Emma. *My Disillusionment in Russia*. Garden City, N.Y.: Doubleday, Page, 1923.

———— *My Further Disillusionment in Russia.* New York: Doubleday, Page, 1924.

———— *The Truth about the Boylsheviki.* New York: Mother Earth Publishing Association, n.d [1918].

Grady, Eve Garrette. *Seeing Red: Behind the Scenes in Russia Today.* New York: Brewer, Warren & Putnam, 1931.

Haan, Hugo. *American Planning in the Words of Its Promoters: A Bird's Eye Survey Expressed in Quotations Collected.* Philadelphia: American Academy of Political and Social Science, March 1932.

Haines, Anna J. *Health Work in Soviet Russia.* New York: Vanguard Press, 1928.

Hard, William. *Raymond Robins' Own Story.* New York: Harper & Brothers, 1920.

Harper, Florence MacLeod. *Runaway Russia.* New York: Century, 1918.

Harper, Samuel Northrup. *Civic Training in Soviet Russia.* Chicago: University of Chicago Press, 1929.

———— *Making Bolsheviks.* Chicago: University of Chicago Press, 1931.

Harrison, Marguerite E. *Marooned in Moscow: The Story of an American Woman Imprisoned in Russia.* New York: George H. Doran, 1921.

———— *Unfinished Tales from a Russian Prison.* New York: George H. Doran, 1923.

Heller, A. A. *The Industrial Revival in Soviet Russia.* New York: Thomas Seltzer, 1922.

Hibben, Paxton. *Reconstruction in Russia: An Address before the Forum of the Community Church of New York City, Easter Sunday, 1925.* New York: n.p., 1925.

Hindus, Maurice. *Broken Earth.* New York: International Publishers, 1926.

———— *The Great Offensive.* New York: Harrison Smith & Robert Haas, 1933.

———— *Humanity Uprooted.* New York: Jonathan Cape & Harrison Smith, 1929.

———— *Red Bread.* New York: Jonathan Cape & Harrison Smith, 1931.

Hodgkin, Henry T., ed. *Seeing Ourselves through Russia: A Book for Private and Group Study.* New York: Ray Long & Richard R. Smith, 1932.

Hoover, Calvin B. *The Economic Life of Soviet Russia.* New York: Macmillan, 1931.

Hopper, Bruce. *Pan-Sovietism: The Issue before America and the World.* New York: Houghton Mifflin, 1931.

Ilin, M. *New Russia's Primer: The Story of the Five-Year Plan.* Boston and New York: Houghton Mifflin, 1931.

"John Dewey," *Bolshaya sovetskaya entsiklopediya.* Moscow: State Institute of the Soviet Encyclopedia, 1931, XXIII, 719.

Johnson, John. *Russia in the Grip of Bolshevism: A Vivid Story of a Trip to the Land of the Soviets.* New York: Fleming H. Revell, 1931.

Kingsbury, Susan M., and Mildred Fairchild. *Factory, Family and Woman in the Soviet Union.* New York: G. P. Putnam's Sons, 1935.

Knickerbocker, H. R. *The Red Trade Menace: Progress of the Soviet Five-Year Plan.* New York: Dodd, Mead, 1931.

Krutch, Joseph Wood. *The Modern Temper: A Study and a Confession.* New York: Harcourt, Brace, 1929.

Lamont, Corliss, and Margaret Lamont. *Russia Day by Day: A Travel Diary.* New York: Covici, Friede, 1933.

Letters from Russian Prisons: Consisting of Reprints of Documents by Political Prisoners in Soviet Prisons, Prison Camps and Exile, and Reprints of Affidavits Concerning Political Persecution in Soviet Russia, Official Statements by Soviet Authorities, Excerpts from Soviet Laws Pertaining to Civil Liberties, and Other Documents. New York: Albert & Charles Boni, 1925.

Levine, Isaac Don. *The Man Lenin.* New York: Thomas Seltzer, 1924.

────── *Red Smoke.* New York: Robert M. McBride, 1932.

────── *Stalin.* New York: Cosmopolitan Book Corporation, 1931.

Lipphard, William Benjamin. *Communing with Communism: A Narrative of Impressions of Soviet Russia.* Philadelphia: Judson Press, 1931.

Long, Ray. *An Editor Looks at Russia: One Unprejudiced View of the Land of the Soviets.* New York: Ray Long & Richard R. Smith, 1931.

Long, Robert Crozier. *Russian Revolution Aspects.* New York: E. P. Dutton, 1919.

McBride, Isaac. *Barbarous Soviet Russia.* New York: Thomas Seltzer, 1920.

McCormick, Anne O'Hare. *The Hammer and the Scythe: Communist Russia Enters the Second Decade.* New York: Alfred A. Knopf, 1928.

Magnes, Judah L. *Russia and Germany at Brest-Litovsk: A Doc-*

umentary History of the Peace Negotiations. New York: Rand School of Social Science, 1919.

Moore, Frederick F. *Siberia To-Day.* New York: Appleton, 1919.

Mowrer, Paul Scott. *Red Russia's Menace: How the Communist Dictators of Moscow Have Constructed a Militant Monster for Armed Aggression and Are Plotting World Conquest.* Chicago: Chicago Daily News, 1925.

Moyer, George S. *Attitude of the United States towards the Recognition of Soviet Russia.* Philadelphia: University of Pennsylvania, 1926.

Nearing, Scott, and Jack Hardy. *The Economic Organization of the Soviet Union.* New York: Vanguard Press, 1927.

────── *Glimpses of the Soviet Republic.* New York: Social Science Publishers, 1926.

Newman, E. M. *Seeing Russia.* New York: Funk & Wagnalls, 1928.

Nurenberg, Thelma. *This New Red Freedom.* New York: Wadsworth Press, 1932.

Poole, Ernest. *The Dark People: Russia's Crisis.* New York: Macmillan, 1918.

────── *The Village: Russian Impressions.* New York: Macmillan, 1918.

Porter, Anna. *A Moscow Diary.* Chicago: Charles M. Kerr, 1926.

Price, George M. *Labor Protection in Soviet Russia.* New York: International Publishers, 1929.

Reed, John. *Ten Days That Shook the World.* New York: Boni & Liveright, 1919.

Robinson, William J. *Soviet Russia as I Saw It: Its Accomplishments, Its Crimes and Stupidities.* New York: International Press, 1932.

Rogers, Will. *There's Not a Bathing Suit in Russia and Other Bare Facts.* London: Brentano's, n.d. [1927]

Root, Elihu. *The United States and the War: The Mission to Russia, Political Addresses.* Cambridge, Mass.: Harvard University Press, 1918.

Ross, Edward Alsworth. *Russia in Upheaval.* New York: Century, 1918.

────── *The Russian Soviet Republic.* New York: Century, 1923.

Russell, Charles Edward. *Bolshevism and the United States.* Indianapolis: Bobbs-Merrill, 1919.

────── *Unchained Russia.* New York: Appleton, 1918.

Saloman, Samuel. *The Red War on the Family.* New York: J. J. Little & Ives, 1922.

Sayler, Oliver M. *Russia White or Red.* Boston: Little, Brown, 1919.

———— *The Russian Theatre under the Revolution*. Boston: Little, Brown, 1920.

Schuman, Frederick L. *American Policy toward Russia since 1917: A Study of Diplomatic History, International Law and Public Opinion*. New York: International Publishers, 1928.

Seldes, George. *World Panorama, 1918–1933*. Boston: Little, Brown, 1933.

Seldes, Gilbert. *The Years of the Locust: America, 1929–1932*. Boston: Little, Brown, 1933.

"Should the United States Recognize Soviet Russia?" *The Commonwealth: Official Journal of the Commonwealth Club of California*, VIII, no. 18, pt. 2 (May 3, 1932), 69–112.

Smith, Jessica. *Woman in Soviet Russia*. New York: Vanguard Press, 1928.

Soule, George. *A Planned Society*. New York: Macmillan, 1932.

Spargo, John. *Bolshevism: The Enemy of Political and Industrial Democracy*. New York: Harper & Brothers, 1919.

———— *The Greatest Failure in All History: A Critical Examination of the Actual Workings of Bolshevism in Russia*. New York: Harper & Brothers, 1920.

———— *The Psychology of Bolshevism*. New York: Harper & Brothers, 1919.

———— *Russia as an American Problem*. New York: Harper & Brothers, 1920.

Spewack, Samuel. *Red Russia Revealed: The Truth about the Soviet Government and Its Methods*. New York: World, 1923.

Stearns, Harold E. *America and the Young Intellectual*. New York: George H. Doran, 1921.

———— ed. *Civilization in the United States: An Inquiry by Thirty Americans*. New York: Harcourt, Brace, 1922.

———— *Liberalism in America: Its Origin, Its Temporary Collapse, Its Future*. New York: Boni & Liveright, 1919.

Steffens, Lincoln. *The Letters of Lincoln Steffens*, ed. Ella Winter and Granville Hicks, 2 vols. New York: Harcourt, Brace, 1938.

———— *Moses in Red: The Revolt of Israel as a Typical Revolution*. Philadelphia: Dorrance, 1926.

Stekoll, Harry. *Through the Communist Looking-Glass*. New York: Brewer, Warren & Putnam, 1932.

Stewart, George. *The White Armies of Russia: A Chronicle of Counter-Revolution and Allied Intervention*. New York: Macmillan, 1933.

Strong, Anna Louise. *Children of Revolution: Story of the John Reed Children's Colony on the Volga, Which Is as Well a Story*

of the Whole Great Structure of Russia. Seattle: Piggott, 1925.
—— *The First Time in History: Two Years of Russia's New Life (August, 1921, to December, 1923).* New York: Boni & Liveright, 1924.
—— *Peasant Life in Soviet Russia.* Girard, Kansas: Haldeman–Julius, 1927.
Sumner, Malcolm. *The Russian Evolution: Address Delivered November 22, 1922, before the Society of the Arts and Sciences, New York City.* n.p., n.d.
Terpenning, Walter A. *To Russia and Return.* n.p.: Terpenning, n.d. [1922].
Thompson, Donald C. *Donald Thompson in Russia.* New York: Century, 1918.
Thompson, Dorothy. *The New Russia.* New York: Henry Holt, 1928.
Tobenkin, Elias. *Stalin's Ladder: War and Peace in the Soviet Union.* New York: Minton, Balch, 1933.
Tugwell, Rexford G. *The Industrial Discipline and the Governmental Arts.* New York: Columbia University Press, 1933.
Varney, John. *Sketches of Soviet Russia: Whole Cloth and Patches.* New York: Nicholas L. Brown, 1920.
Villard, Oswald Garrison. *Russia from a Car Window.* New York: Nation Press, 1929.
Walling, William English. *Russia's Message: The People Against the Czar.* New York: Alfred A. Knopf, 1919 (1st ed. 1908).
—— *Sovietism: The ABC of Russian Bolshevism — According to the Bolshevists.* New York: E. P. Dutton, 1920.
Walter, Ellery. *Russia's Decisive Year.* New York: G. P. Putnam's Sons, 1932.
White, William C. *These Russians.* New York: Charles Scribner's Sons, 1931.
Williams, Albert Rhys. *Lenin: The Man and His Work, and the Impressions of Col. Raymond Robins and Arthur Ransome.* New York: Scott & Seltzer, 1919.
—— *The Russian Land.* New York: New Republic, 1927.
—— *Through the Russian Revolution.* New York: Boni & Liveright, 1921.
Williams, Frankwood E. *Russia, Youth and the Present-Day World: Further Studies in Mental Hygiene.* New York: Farrar & Rinehart, 1934.
Wilson, Edmund. *The Shores of Light: A Literary Chronicle of the Twenties and Thirties.* New York: Farrar, Straus & Young, 1952.

Winter, Ella. *Red Virtue: Human Relationships in the New Russia.* New York: Harcourt, Brace, 1933.
Wright, Russell. *One-Sixth of the World's Surface.* Hammond, Ind.: [published by author], 1932.
Wrightman, Orrin Sage. *The Diary of An American Physician in the Russian Revolution, 1917.* Brooklyn: Brooklyn Daily Eagle Commercial Printing Department, 1928.
Zelie, John Sheridan. *The Russian Relief Work of the Federal Council of Churches.* New York: n.p., 1922.

SECONDARY SOURCES

THESES

Cheslaw, Irving G. "An Intellectual Biography of Lincoln Steffens." Unpub. diss., Columbia University, 1952.
Gronert, Bernard. "The Impact of the Russian Revolution upon the A.F. of L., 1918–1928." Unpub. master's thesis, University of Wisconsin, 1948.
Roberts, Beth Alene. "A Study of American Opinion Regarding Allied Intervention in Siberia." Unpub. master's thesis, University of Hawaii, 1938.
Solberg, Winton U. "The Impact of Soviet Russia on American Life and Thought, 1917–1933." Unpub. diss., Harvard University, 1952.
Wieland, D. F. "American Labor and Russia, 1917–1925." Unpub. master's thesis, University of Wisconsin, 1948.

BOOKS

MEMOIRS, AUTOBIOGRAPHIES

Chamberlin, William Henry. *The Confessions of an Individualist.* New York: Macmillan, 1940.
———— *The Evolution of a Conservative.* Chicago: Henry Regnery, 1959.
Colton, Ethan T. *Forty Years with Russians.* New York: Association Press, 1940.
Cowley, Malcolm. *Exile's Return: A Narrative of Ideas.* New York: W. W. Norton, 1934.
Du Bois, W. E. Burghardt. *Dusk of Dawn: An Essay toward an Autobiography of a Race Concept.* New York: Harcourt, Brace, 1940.
Duranty, Walter. *I Write as I Please.* New York: Halcyon House, 1935.

BIBLIOGRAPHY

Eastman, Max. *Love and Revolution: My Journey through an Epoch*. New York: Random House, 1965.
Eddy, Sherwood. *Eighty Adventurous Years: An Autobiography*. New York: Harper & Brothers, 1955.
—————— *A Pilgrimage of Ideas or the Re-Education of Sherwood Eddy*. New York: Farrar & Rinehart, 1934.
Ervin, Charles W. *Homegrown Liberal: The Autobiography of Charles W. Ervin*, ed. Jean Gould. New York: Dodd, Mead, 1954.
Fischer, Louis. *Men and Politics: An Autobiography*. New York: Duell, Sloan & Pearce, 1941.
Freeman, Joseph. *An American Testament: A Narrative of Rebels and Romantics*. New York: Farrar & Rinehart, 1936.
Goldman, Emma. *Living My Life*, 2 vols. New York: Alfred A. Knopf, 1931.
Gompers, Samuel. *Seventy Years of Life and Labor: An Autobiography*, 2 vols. New York: E. P. Dutton, 1925.
Graves, William S. *America's Siberian Adventure, 1918–1920*. New York: Jonathan Cape & Harrison Smith, 1931.
Harper, Paul V., ed. *The Russia I Believe In: The Memoirs of Samuel N. Harper, 1902–1941*. Chicago: University of Chicago Press, 1945.
Hoover, Herbert. *An American Epic*, 4 vols. Chicago: Henry Regnery, 1959–1964. Vol. III, *Famine in Forty-Five Nations: The Battle on the Front Line, 1914–1923*.
Lyons, Eugene. *Assignment in Utopia*. New York: Harcourt, Brace, 1937.
Sisson, Edgar. *One Hundred Red Days: A Personal Chronicle of the Bolshevik Revolution*. New Haven: Yale University Press, 1931.
Steffens, Lincoln. *The Autobiography of Lincoln Steffens*, 1 vol. ed. New York: Harcourt, Brace, 1931.
Strong, Anna Louise. *I Change Worlds: The Remaking of an American*. New York: Henry Holt, 1935.
Winter, Ella. *And Not to Yield: An Autobiography*. New York: Harcourt, Brace & World, 1963.

GENERAL

Aaron, Daniel. *Writers on the Left: Episodes in American Literary Communism*. New York: Harcourt, Brace & World, 1961.
Agar, Herbert. *The Saving Remnant: An Account of Jewish Survival*. New York: Viking Press, 1960.
Anderson, Paul H. *The Attitude of the American Leftist Leaders*
310

toward the Russian Revolution, 1917–1923. Notre Dame: University of Notre Dame Press, 1942.

Bailey, Thomas A. *America Faces Russia: Russian-American Relations from Early Times to Our Day.* Ithaca: Cornell University Press, 1950.

Baykov, Alexander. *The Development of the Soviet Economic System: An Essay on the Experience of Planning in the U.S.S.R.* New York: Macmillan, 1947.

———— *Soviet Foreign Trade.* Princeton: Princeton University Press, 1946.

Beard, Charles A. and Mary T. *The American Spirit: A Study of the Idea of Civilization in the United States* (vol. IV of *The Rise of American Civilization*). New York: Macmillan, 1942.

Bereday, George Z. F., William W. Brickman, and Gerald H. Read, eds. *The Changing Soviet School: The Comparative Education Soviety Field Study in the U.S.S.R.* Boston: Houghton Mifflin, 1960.

Bernstein, Irving. *The Lean Years: A History of the American Worker, 1920–1933.* Boston: Houghton Mifflin, 1960.

Black, Cyril E., ed. *The Transformation of Russian Society: Aspects of Social Change since 1861.* Cambridge, Mass: Harvard University Press, 1960.

Borning, Bernard C. *The Political and Social Thought of Charles A. Beard.* Seattle: University of Washington Press, 1962.

Browder, Robert Paul. *The Origins of Soviet-American Diplomacy.* Princeton: Princeton University Press, 1953.

Burns, Edward McNall. *The American Idea of Mission: Concepts of National Purpose and Destiny.* New Brunswick: Rutgers University Press, 1957.

Carter, Paul A. *The Decline and Revival of the Social Gospel: Social and Political Liberalism in American Protestant Churches, 1920–1940.* Ithaca: Cornell University Press, 1956.

Chapman, Charles C. *The Development of American Business and Banking Thought, 1913–1936.* New York: Longmans, Green, 1936.

Childs, Harwood Lawrence. *Labor and Capital in National Politics.* Columbus: Ohio State University Press, 1930.

Childs, Marquis, and James Reston, eds. *Walter Lippmann and His Times.* New York: Harcourt, Brace, 1959.

Cremin, Lawrence A. *The Transformation of the School: Progressivism in American Education, 1876–1957.* New York: Alfred A. Knopf, 1961.

Curti, Merle. *American Philanthropy Abroad: A History.* New Brunswick: Rutgers University Press, 1963.

BIBLIOGRAPHY

Curtiss, John Shelton. *The Russian Church and the Soviet State, 1917–1950*. Boston: Little, Brown, 1953.

Danish, Max D. *The World of David Dubinsky*. Cleveland: World, 1957.

Deutscher, Isaac. *The Prophet Armed: Trotsky, 1879–1921*. New York: Oxford University Press, 1954.

———— *The Prophet Unarmed: Trotsky, 1921–1929*. London: Oxford University Press, 1959.

Dobb, Maurice. *Soviet Economic Development since 1917*. New York: International Publishers, 1948.

Draper, Theodore. *American Communism and Soviet Russia*. New York: Viking Press, 1960.

Drinnon, Richard. *Rebel in Paradise: A Biography of Emma Goldman*. Chicago: University of Chicago Press, 1961.

Dulles, Foster Rhea. *The American Red Cross: A History*. New York: Harper & Brothers, 1950.

———— *Road to Teheran: The Story of Russia and America, 1781–1943*. Princeton: Princeton University Press, 1945.

Egbert, Donald Drew, and Stow Persons, eds. *Socialism and American Life*, 2 vols. Princeton: Princeton University Press, 1952.

Elias, Robert H. *Theodore Dreiser: Apostle of Nature*. New York: Alfred A. Knopf, 1949.

Epstein, Melech. *Jewish Labor in U.S.A., 1914–1952: An Industrial, Political and Cultural History of the Jewish Labor Movement*. New York: Trade Union Sponsoring Committee, 1953.

Fisher, H. H. *The Famine in Soviet Russia, 1919–1923: The Operations of the American Relief Administration*. New York: Macmillan, 1927.

Forbes, John. *The Quaker Star under Seven Flags: 1917–1927*. Philadelphia: University of Pennsylvania Press, 1962.

Gerschenkron, Alexander. *Economic Relations with the U.S.S.R.* New York: Committee on International Economic Policy in cooperation with the Carnegie Endowment for International Peace, 1945.

Green, Marguerite. *The National Civic Federation and the American Labor Movement, 1900–1925*. Washington, D.C.: Catholic University of America Press, 1956.

Hagedorn, Hermann. *The Magnate: William Boyce Thompson and His Time (1869–1930)*. New York: Reynal & Hitchcock, 1935.

Halliday, E. M. *The Ignorant Armies*. New York: Harper & Brothers, 1960.

Hicks, Granville. *John Reed: The Making of a Revolutionary*. New York: Macmillan, 1936.

Higham, John. *Strangers in the Land: Patterns of American*

312

Nativism, 1860–1925. New Brunswick: Rutgers University Press, 1955.

Hoffman, Frederick J. *The Twenties: American Writing in the Postwar Decade.* New York: Viking Press, 1955.

Hopkins, C. Howard. *History of the Y.M.C.A. in North America.* New York: Association Press, 1951.

Howe, Irving, and Lewis Coser. *The American Communist Party: A Critical History (1919–1957).* Boston: Beacon Press, 1957.

Jessup, Philip C. *Elihu Root,* 2 vols. New York: Dodd, Mead, 1938.

Johnson, Claudius O. *Borah of Idaho.* New York: Longmans, Green, 1936.

Johnson, William H. E. *Russia's Educational Heritage.* Pittsburgh: Carnegie Press, 1950.

Jones, Mary Hoxie. *Swords into Ploughshares: An Account of the American Friends Service Committee, 1917–1937.* New York: Macmillan, 1937.

Josephson, Matthew. *Sidney Hillman: Statesman of American Labor.* Garden City, N.Y.: Doubleday, 1952.

Kennan, George F. *Soviet-American Relations, 1917–1920,* 2 vols.: *Russia Leaves the War* and *The Decision to Intervene.* Princeton: Princeton University Press, 1956, 1958.

La Follette, Bella Case, and Fola La Follette. *Robert M. La Follette,* 2 vols. New York: Macmillan, 1953.

Lasch, Christopher. *The American Liberals and the Russian Revolution.* New York: Columbia University Press, 1962.

Leavitt, Moses A. *The JDC Story: Highlights of JDC Activities, 1914–1952.* New York: American Jewish Joint Distribution Committee, 1953.

Leuchtenberg, William E. *Franklin D. Roosevelt and the New Deal, 1932–1940.* New York: Harper & Row, 1963.

—— *The Perils of Prosperity, 1914–1932.* Chicago: University of Chicago Press, 1958.

Lovenstein, Meno. *American Opinion of Soviet Russia.* Washington, D.C.: American Council on Public Affairs, 1941.

Lynd, Robert S., and Helen Merrell Lynd. *Middletown: A Study in American Culture.* New York: Harcourt, Brace, 1929.

Lyons, Eugene. *The Red Decade: The Stalinist Penetration of America.* New York: Bobbs-Merrill, 1941.

McKenna, Marian C. *Borah.* Ann Arbor: University of Michigan Press, 1961.

Madison, Charles A. *American Labor Leaders: Personalities and Forces in the Labor Movement,* 2nd ed. New York: Frederick Ungar, 1962.

May, Henry F. *The End of American Innocence: A Study of the*

BIBLIOGRAPHY

First Years of Our Own Time, 1912–1917. New York: Alfred
A. Knopf, 1959.

Maynard, Sir John. *Russia in Flux.* New York: Macmillan, 1951.

Meiburger, Anne Vincent. *Efforts of Raymond Robins Toward the
Recognition of Soviet Russia and the Outlawry of War, 1917–
1933.* Washington, D.C.: Catholic University of America Press,
1958.

Merk, Frederick. *Manifest Destiny and Mission in American
History: A Reinterpretation.* New York: Alfred A. Knopf,
1963.

Miller, Robert Moats. *American Protestantism and Social Issues,
1919–1939.* Chapel Hill: University of North Carolina Press,
1958.

Murray, Robert K. *Red Scare: A Study in National Hysteria,
1919–1920.* Minneapolis: University of Minnesota Press, 1955.

Nevins, Allen, and Frank Ernest Hill. *Ford: Expansion and Challenge, 1915–1933.* New York: Charles Scribner's Sons, 1957.

Prothro, James Warren. *The Dollar Decade: Business Ideas in the
1920's.* Baton Rouge: Louisiana State University Press, 1954.

*Recent Social Trends in the United States: Report of the President's
Research Committee on Social Trends,* 2 vols. New York:
McGraw-Hill, 1933.

Reed, Louis S. *The Labor Philosophy of Samuel Gompers.* New
York: Columbia University Press, 1930.

Saposs, David J. *Left Wing Unionism: A Study of Radical Policies
and Tactics.* New York: International Publishers, 1926.

Schlesinger, Jr., Arthur M. *The Age of Roosevelt,* 2 vols.: *The
Crisis of the Old Order, 1919–1933* and *The Coming of the
New Deal.* Boston: Houghton Mifflin, 1957, 1958.

Schneider, David M. *The Workers' (Communist) Party and American Trade Unions.* Baltimore: Johns Hopkins Press, 1928.

Schwarz, Solomon M. *The Jews in the Soviet Union.* Syracuse:
Syracuse University Press, 1951.

Shannon, David A. *The Socialist Party of America: A History.*
New York: Macmillan, 1955.

Soule, George. *Prosperity Decade: From War to Depression, 1917–
1929* (vol. VIII of *The Economic History of the United States*).
New York: Rinehart, 1947.

—————— *Sidney Hillman, Labor Statesman.* New York: Macmillan,
1939.

Strakhovsky, Leonid I. *American Opinion about Russia, 1917–
1920.* Toronto: University of Toronto Press, 1961.

—————— *The Origins of American Intervention in North Russia
(1918).* Princeton: Princeton University Press, 1937.

Taft, Philip. *The A.F. of L., from the Death of Gompers to the Merger.* New York: Harper & Brothers, 1959.

———— *The A.F. of L. in the Time of Gompers.* New York: Harper & Brothers, 1957.

Tupper, Eleanor, and George E. McReynolds. *Japan in American Public Opinion.* New York: Macmillan, 1937.

Unruh, John D. *In the Name of Christ: A History of the Mennonite Central Committee and Its Service, 1920–1951.* Scottsdale, Pa.: Herald Press, 1952.

Unterberger, Betty Miller. *America's Siberian Expedition, 1918–1920: A Study of National Policy.* Durham: Duke University Press, 1956.

White, John Albert. *The Siberian Intervention.* Princeton: Princeton University Press, 1950.

Williams, William Appleman. *American-Russian Relations, 1781–1947.* New York: Rinehart, 1952.

Woodward, Julian Lawrence. *Foreign News in American Morning Newspapers: A Study in Public Opinion.* New York: Columbia University Press, 1930.

ARTICLES

Boller, Jr., Paul F. "The 'Great Conspiracy' of 1933: A Study in Short Memories," *Southwest Review,* XXXIX (Spring 1954), 97–112.

Brickman, William W. "John Dewey's Foreign Reputation as an Educator," *School and Society,* LX (October 22, 1949), 257–265.

Brooks, Evelyn C. and Lee M. "A Decade of 'Planning' Literature," *Social Forces,* XII (March 1934), 427–459.

Coben, Stanley. "A Study in Nativism: The American Red Scare of 1919–20," *Political Science Quarterly,* LXXIX (March 1964), 52–75.

Feuer, Lewis S. "Travelers to the Soviet Union, 1917–32: The Formation of a Component of New Deal Ideology," *American Quarterly,* XIV (Summer 1962), 119–149.

Fike, Claude E. "The Influence of the Creel Committee and the American Red Cross on Russian-American Relations, 1917–1919," *Journal of Modern History,* XXXI (June 1959), 93–109.

Handy, Robert T. "The American Religious Depression, 1925–1935," *Church History,* XXIX (March 1960), 3–16.

Hart, Hornell. "Changing Opinions about Business Prosperity: A Consensus of Magazine Opinion in the United States, 1929–

315

BIBLIOGRAPHY

32," *American Journal of Sociology*, XXXVIII (March 1933), 665–687.

Hicks, Granville. "Lincoln Steffens: He Covered the Future; The Prototype of a Fellow-Traveler," *Commentary*, XIII (February 1952), 147–155.

Hook, Sidney. "Communism and the Intellectuals," *American Mercury*, LXVIII (February 1949), 133–144.

Lasch, Christopher. "American Intervention in Siberia: A Reinterpretation," *Political Science Quarterly*, LXXVII (June 1962), 205–223.

May, Henry F. "Shifting Perspectives on the 1920's," *Mississippi Valley Historical Review*, XLIII (December 1956), 405–427.

Mohrenschildt, Dimitri von. "American Intelligentsia and Russia of the N.E.P.," *Russian Review*, VI (Spring 1947), 59–66.

———— "The Early American Observers of the Russian Revolution, 1917–1921," *Russian Review*, III (Autumn 1943), 64–74.

Parry, Albert. "Charles R. Crane, Friend of Russia," *Russian Review*, VI (Spring 1947), 20–37.

———— "Washington B. Vanderlip, the 'Khan of Kamchatka'," *Pacific Historical Review*, XVII (August 1948), 311–330.

Rollins, Jr., Alfred B. "The Heart of Lincoln Steffens," *South Atlantic Quarterly*, LIX (Spring 1960), 239–250.

Widmayer, Ruth. "The Evolution of Soviet Educational Policy," *Harvard Educational Review*, XXIV (Summer 1954), 159–175.

METHODOLOGICAL AIDS

Albig, William. *Modern Public Opinion*. New York: McGraw-Hill, 1956.

Berelson, Bernard. *Content Analysis in Communication Research*. Glencoe, Ill.: Free Press, 1952.

———— Paul F. Lazarsfeld, and William N. McPhee. *Voting: A Study of Opinion Formation in a Presidential Campaign*. Chicago: University of Chicago Press, 1954.

Buchanan, William, and Hadley Cantril. *How Nations See Each Other: A Study in Public Opinion*. Urbana: University of Illinois Press, 1953.

Gottschalk, Louis, ed. *Generalization in the Writing of History: A Report of the Committee on Historical Analysis of the Social Science Research Council*. Chicago: University of Chicago Press, 1963.

Hovland, Carl I, Irving L. Janis, and Harold H. Kelley. *Communication and Persuasion: Psychological Studies of Opinion Change*. New Haven: Yale University Press, 1953.

Katz, Elihu, and Paul F. Lazarsfeld. *Personal Influence: The Part*

Played by People in the Flow of Mass Communications. Glencoe, Ill.: Free Press, 1955.

Klineberg, Otto. *Tensions Affecting International Understanding: A Survey of Research* (Social Science Research Council Bulletin 62). New York: Social Science Research Council, 1950.

Maccoby, Eleanor E., Theodore M. Newcomb, and Eugene L. Hartley, eds. *Readings in Social Psychology,* 3rd ed. New York: Holt, Rinehart & Winston, 1958.

Newcomb, Theodore M. *Social Psychology.* New York: Dryden Press, 1950.

Pool, Ithiel de Sola, Suzanne Keller, and Raymond A. Bauer, "The Influence of Foreign Travel on Political Attitudes of American Businessmen," *Public Opinion Quarterly,* XX (Spring 1956), 161–175.

Potter, David M. *People of Plenty: Economic Abundance and the American Character.* Chicago: University of Chicago Press, 1954.

Schramm, Wilbur, ed. *The Process and Effects of Mass Communication.* Urbana: University of Illinois Press, 1954.

Bibliographical Aids

American Economic Association. *Index of Economic Journals,* 5 vols. Homewood, Ill.: Richard D. Irwin, 1961–1962.

Grierson, Philip. *Books on Soviet Russia, 1917–1942: A Bibliography and a Guide to Reading.* London: Methuen, 1943.

The Industrial Arts Index: Subject Index to a Selected List of Engineering, Trade and Business Periodicals, Books and Pamphlets, with a List of Important Technical Societies. New York: H. W. Wilson, 1914–.

Smith, Bruce Lannes, and Chitra M. Smith. *International Communication and Political Opinion: A Guide to the Literature.* Princeton: Princeton University Press, 1956.

——— Harold D. Lasswell, and Ralph D. Casey. *Propaganda and Promotional Activities: An Annotated Bibliography.* Minneapolis: University of Minnesota Press, 1935.

——— *Propaganda, Communication, and Public Opinion: A Comprehensive Reference Guide.* Princeton: Princeton University Press, 1946.

Notes

For purposes of convenience, I have not listed all the evidence for each conclusion in the text; in most cases I have mentioned typical examples only. As a result, what may appear to be a generalization based on one or two instances is in fact more broadly based. Any reader who is interested in the full documentation may consult my dissertation, which is deposited in the Archives of Widener Library, Harvard University.

ON METHOD AND MATTER

1. Wilbur Schramm, ed., *The Process and Effects of Mass Communication* (Urbana, Ill., 1954), p. 209.

2. Eugene L. Hartley, Ruth E. Hartley, and Clyde Hart, "Attitudes and Opinions," in *ibid.*, pp. 229–230.

3. Bernard Berelson, *Content Analysis in Communication Research* (Glencoe, Ill., 1952), pp. 95–98, alludes to problems of analyzing mass media.

4. Several analysts of public opinion have recently suggested that most Americans model their views on those of respected acquaintances ("opinion leaders") who in turn take their views from the mass media. If this hypothesis is valid then my study of written data would be dealing with an accurate sample of American opinion during 1917–1933. Thus the latest findings of mass-media analysts justify at least a tentative confidence in the value of studying attitudes before the era of opinion polls. See, for example: Bernard R. Berelson, Paul F. Lazarsfeld, and William N. McPhee, *Voting: A Study of Opinion Formation in a Presidential Campaign* (Chicago, 1954), pp. 93–115; Elihu Katz and Paul F. Lazarsfeld, *Personal Influence: The Part Played by People in the Flow of Mass Communication* (Glencoe, Ill., 1955), chap. 14 and pp. 32–33, 325.

5. For a cogent discussion of the "culture" concept, see David M. Potter, *People of Plenty: Economic Abundance and the American Character* (Chicago, 1954), pp. 36–37.

6. Thomas C. Cochran, "The Historian's Use of Social Role," in *Generalization in the Writing of History: A Report of the Committee on Historical Analysis of the Social Science Research Council*, ed. Louis Gottschalk (Chicago, 1963), p. 104. On p. 103, Cochran defines social role as "the part played by an individual in response to an understand-

ing shared by members of a group as to the attitudes and behavior that should normally follow from his occupation of a given position or status."

I. TWO REVOLUTIONS AND ONE BETRAYAL

1. "The Russian Revolution" (editorial), *Zion's Herald*, XCV (March 21, 1917), 356–357. It should be noted at the outset that all dates in this book are given in New Style (Western) form, but that the descriptive designations for the two phases of the 1917 Revolution (February and October) are kept in accordance with their more common Old Style (Russian) form.

2. "The Russian Revolution," *Literary Digest*, LIV (March 24, 1917), 799–800; "Democratic Russia as Our Ally," *ibid.*, LIV (March 31, 1917), 885–887; *New York Times* (editorials), March 16, 10:1 [p. and col.], March 26, 4:2, April 13, 8:1, April 14, 12:6, April 17, 10:7 — all 1917; "The Opportunities of Democracy" (editorial), *Christian Century*, XXXIV (August 2, 1917), 7; "Russia in Revolt" (editorial), *Congregationalist and Advance*, CII (March 22, 1917), 371. The welcome by Samuel Gompers, president of the American Federation of Labor, as conveyed to the Petrograd Duma, is reprinted in Secretary of State to Ambassador Francis, April 3, 1917, *Papers Relating to the Foreign Relations of the United States* [hereafter cited as *Foreign Relations*], *1918, Russia* (3 vols., Washington, D.C., 1931–1932), I, 18.

3. Cited in Leonid I. Strakhovsky, *American Opinion about Russia, 1917–1920* (Toronto, 1961), p. 6.

4. *New York Times*, March 26, 1917, 4:2.

5. *Ibid.*, April 13, 1917, 8:1.

6. Thomas A. Bailey, *America Faces Russia: Russian-American Relations from Early Times to Our Day* (Ithaca, N.Y., 1950), pp. 121–126, 179–184, 214–223; Foster R. Dulles, *Road to Teheran: The Story of Russia and America, 1781–1943* (Princeton, N.J., 1945), pp. 95–96; George F. Kennan, *Soviet-American Relations, 1917–1920* (2 vols., Princeton, N.J., 1956, 1958), I, *Russia Leaves the War*, pp. 12–13.

7. Bailey, *America Faces Russia*, pp. 126–133; Kennan, *Russia Leave the War*, pp. 12–13; Kennan, *Soviet-American Relations, 1917–1920*, II, *The Decision to Intervene*, p. 325.

8. Henry F. May, *The End of American Innocence: A Study of the First Years of Our Own Time, 1912–1917* (New York, 1959), pp. 243–244; Bailey, *America Faces Russia*, pp. 136–140.

9. For a few comments of Jewish leaders, see *New York Times*, April 29, 1917, 16:1, May 2, 1917, 6:4; "Russian Jewry Liberated" (editorial), *American Hebrew and Jewish Messenger* [hereafter cited as *American Hebrew*], C (March 23, 1917), 616–617; *American Jewish Year Book* (1917–1918), XX, 238–239.

10. *Foreign Relations: 1918, Supplement I, The World War* (2 vols., Washington, D.C., 1933), I, 200.

11. See citations in n. 2 above. Also *New York Times* (editorial),

320

March 23, 1917, 8:2; Gerald Morgan, "The New Russia," *North American Review*, CCV (April 1917), 503–505, 508–509; "New Russia and the War" (editorial), *Nation*, CIV (March 22, 1917), 330; *New Republic* (editorial), X (April 21, 1917), 332; Samuel N. Harper, "Zemstvo Russia," *Independent*, XC (April 2, 1917), 22–23.

12. Kennan, *Russia Leaves the War*, pp. 24–25.

13. George Kennan, "The Victory of the Russian People," *Outlook*, CXV (March 28, 1917), 546.

14. For example, "Russia in Revolt" (editorial), *Congregationalist and Advance*, CII (March 22, 1917), 371; *Nation* (editorial), CIV (March 22, 1917), 327; Paul Wharton, "The Russian Ides of March," *Atlantic Monthly*, CXX (July 1917), 30.

15. *New York Times*, March 16, 10:1, 1917, and April 12, 10:3, 1917.

16. For example, "The Secret of the Revolution," *Literary Digest*, LIV (April 7, 1917), 1000; Hamilton Fyfe, "The Russian State of Mind," *Saturday Evening Post*, CXC (November 3, 1917), 22, 97–98; "Russia's Revolution" (editorial), *Public*, XX (March 30, 1917), 297–298; Charles Edward Russell, *Unchained Russia* (New York, 1918), pp. 221–224, 245–249; Ernest Poole, *The Dark People: Russia's Crisis* (New York, 1918), p. 122; "The Russian Evolution" (editorial), *Collier's*, LIX (April 14, 1917), 10–11.

17. "Russia and Democracy" (editorial), *Outlook*, CXVI (August 29, 1917), 643.

18. *American Hebrew*, C (March 23, 1917), 611.

19. *New York Times*, March 26, 1917, 4:2.

20. Quoted in David R. Francis, *Russia from the American Embassy: April, 1916–November, 1918* (New York, 1921), p. 125.

21. Edward McNall Burns, *The American Idea of Mission: Concepts of National Purpose and Destiny* (New Brunswick, N.J., 1957), portrays the theme in broad outline. For more profound analyses, see Frederick Merk, *Manifest Destiny and Mission in American History: A Reinterpretation* (New York, 1963), esp. chap. 12; and Christopher Lasch, *The American Liberals and the Russian Revolution* (New York, 1963), pp. 218–220.

22. "Russia on the Threshold of — What?" (editorial), *Missionary Review of the World*, XL (May 1917), 323. *The Leader* is cited in "Russia and Ourselves," *Literary Digest*, LV (August 25, 1917), 15; *Nation* (editorial), CIV (March 29, 1917), 355.

23. "Effect of Russian Chaos on the War," *Literary Digest*, LIV (May 26, 1917), 1577–1578. For examples of apprehension, see "The Greater Victory" (editorial), *New Republic*, XI (May 19, 1917), 65–67; *ibid.* (editorial), XI (July 28, 1917), 342.

24. Cited in "A Dictator for the Slav Republic," *Literary Digest*, LV (August 4, 1917), 25.

25. Secretary of State to Ambassador Francis, May 1 and May 11, 1917, *Foreign Relations, 1918, Russia*, I, 108–109.

26. Lasch, *American Liberals*, pp. 42–46.

27. Elihu Root, *The United States and the War: The Mission to Russia, Political Addresses* (Cambridge, Mass., 1918), p. 99.

28. Address before the Union League Club, N.Y., August 15, 1917, *ibid.*, p. 50; address in Seattle, August 4, 1917, *ibid.*, pp. 149–150.

29. Root to Lansing, June 17, 1917, *Foreign Relations, 1918, Russia,* I, 122.

30. *Ibid.*, pp. 131–146, esp. p. 143. Lansing, incidentally, was highly skeptical of this optimism: Lasch, *American Liberals*, p. 44.

31. Quoted by Philip C. Jessup, *Elihu Root* (2 vols., New York, 1938), II, 361.

32. For evidence of reassurance, see "Russia and Ourselves," *Literary Digest*, LV (August 25, 1917), 14–15; "Russia and Democracy" (editorial), *Outlook*, CXVI (August 29, 1917), 643.

33. *New York Times*, July 22, II, 2:1; July 24, 10:1; August 2, 8:1; September 11, 12:1; September 12, 10:1: all 1917.

34. Lasch, *American Liberals*, p. 92.

35. "Russia" (editorial), *Collier's*, LX (October 30, 1917), 11.

36. Stanley Washburn, "The Changes in Russia," *Review of Reviews*, LVI (September 1917), 279; Herman Bernstein, "New Russia as I Saw It," *American Hebrew*, CI (September 28, 1917), 578; "Russia Finding Herself," *Literary Digest*, LV (September 8, 1917), 16–17; "The Russian Army" (editorial), *Saturday Evening Post*, CXC (September 29, 1917), 24; *New York Times*, October 27, 1917, 3:5.

37. Lansing to Francis, *Foreign Relations, 1918, Russia*, I, 214–215; Edgar Sisson, *One Hundred Red Days: A Personal Chronicle of the Bolshevik Revolution* (New Haven, 1931), pp. 3, 31.

38. Kennan, *Decision to Intervene*, pp. 190–192.

39. "The Bolsheviki" (editorial), *Public*, XX (October 5, 1917), 954–955; Bernstein, "New Russia as I Saw It," p. 577; *New York Times* (editorials), July 30, 1917, 8:3, and September 27, 1917, 12:2.

40. Charles Johnston, "Russia's Danger: Its Cause and Cure," *North American Review*, CCVI (September 1917), 386, 389; "Bolsheviki at Russia's Throat," *Literary Digest*, LV (November 17, 1917), 10–11; Donald C. Thompson, *Donald Thompson in Russia* (New York, 1918), pp. 159–160.

41. Kennan, "Will the Russian Political I.W.W.'s Succeed?" *Outlook*, CXVII (November 21, 1917), 455; "Bolsheviki at Russia's Throat," *Literary Digest*, LV (November 17, 1917), 9; *New York Times* (editorials), November 11, 1917, II, 2:1, and November 22, 1917, 12:2; "Russia in Convulsions" (editorial), *American Hebrew*, CII (November 16, 1917), 42.

42. Cited in "The Peril of a Bolshevik Peace," *Literary Digest*, LV (December 8, 1917), 15.

43. "Russia's Catastrophe" (editorial), *Outlook*, CXVII (December 5, 1917), 551.

44. *Public* (editorial), XXI (January 11, 1918), 36; "The Bolsheviki" (editorial), *ibid.*, XX (October 5, 1917), 954–955.

45. Lasch, *American Liberals*, pp. 74–79; "Has Russia a Tomorrow?" (editorial), *Collier's*, LX (January 12, 1918), 10.

46. Kennan, *Decision to Intervene*, p. 334; Harper, "Is Russia Play-

ing Germany's Game?" *Independent*, XCII (December 15, 1917), 535; Mott, "A View of the Situation in Russia," *Missionary Review of the World*, XLI (March 1918), 173.

47. C. E. A. Winslow, "Problems of Social Relief in Russia," *Survey*, XXXIX (December 1, 1917), 247–249; *New York Times*, December 7, 1917, 15:2; January 15, 11:3; February 4, 2:3 and 7:5; March 10, 6:3 — all 1918; "The Church in Russia" (editorial), *Congregationalist and Advance*, CIII (June 13, 1918), 743; "Evangelizing Russia" (editorial), *Zion's Herald*, XCVI (May 8, 1918), 579.

48. Lansing to Wilson, January 10, 1918, *Foreign Relations: The Lansing Papers, 1914–1920* [hereafter cited as *Lansing Papers*], (2 vols., Washington, D.C., 1940), II, 350.

49. "America for No Makeshift Peace," *Literary Digest*, LVI (January 12, 1918), 7–9; "Bolshevik Amazement at Germany's Cloven Hoof," *ibid.*, LVI (February 9, 1918), 12–14; Frank H. Simonds, "Russia's Mutilation — Germany Unmasked," *Review of Reviews*, LVII (April 1918), 366–374; "Russia" (editorial), *World's Work*, XXXV (April 1918), 586–587; "What Has Become of Russia?" (editorial), *Outlook*, CXVIII (March 6, 1918), 358–359.

50. Lansing to Wilson, January 2, 1918, *Lansing Papers*, II, 348–349.

51. Roger Lewis, "Russia's Enemy Within," *Collier's*, LX (December 22, 1917), 8.

52. *Congressional Record* [hereafter cited as *Cong. Rec.*], 65th Cong., 2nd Sess. (February 25, 1918), p. 2590; *New York Times* (editorial), December 8, 1917, 14:1; Charles Johnston, "Russia on the Edge of the Abyss," *North American Review*, CCXVIII (February 1918), 186; "Utopians Both" (editorial), *American Hebrew*, CII (March 22, 1918), 538; William Roscoe Thayer, "Despotism by the Dregs," *Saturday Evening Post*, CXC (May 4, 1918), 23, 126; John G. Holme, "The Break Up of Russia," *Asia*, XVIII (March 1918), 184; "Russia at Germany's Mercy," *Literary Digest*, LVI (March 2, 1918), 16–17.

53. Johnston, "Russia on the Edge of the Abyss," p. 195; *New York Times* (editorial), February 21, 1918, 10:1; Florence MacLeod Harper, *Runaway Russia* (New York, 1918), pp. 249–251, 285; A. G. Talfree, "The Russian Character," *Atlantic Monthly*, CXXI (May 1918), 598–600; Thayer, "Despotism by the Dregs," pp. 23–24; Charles E. Beury, *Russia after the Revolution* (Philadelphia, 1918), p. 62; William T. Ellis, "The Tavarish," *Saturday Evening Post*, CXC (February 9, 1918), 78.

54. William T. Ellis, "The Overflowing Melting Pot: Why the Americanization of America Must Begin," *Saturday Evening Post*, CXC (March 2, 1918), 22.

55. *Cong. Rec.*, 65th Cong., 2nd Sess. (January 18, 1918), pp. 1031–1032.

56. Lasch, *American Liberals*, p. ix.

57. This phrase appeared in his Fourteen Points address, January 8, 1918, *Foreign Relations, 1918, The World War*, I, 15.

58. *Nation* (editorial), CV (September 13, 1917), 279; "Russian

Cross Currents" (editorial), *ibid.*, CV (November 1, 1917), 476–477; "The Salvation of Russia" (editorial), *New Republic*, XII (September 22, 1917), 202–204.

59. Lincoln Steffens to Mrs. J. James Hollister, in *The Letters of Lincoln Steffens*, ed. Ella Winter and Granville Hicks (2 vols., New York, 1938), I, 416.

60. "Saving Russia" (editorial), *New Republic*, XIII (December 29, 1917), 230.

61. *Ibid.* (editorial), XIII (November 17, 1917), 57.

62. Robins to his wife, December 20, 1917, Robins Papers, Box 13, Wisconsin Historical Society.

63. For Francis' position, see Arthur Bullard to Colonel Edward M. House, December 12, 1917, House Papers, Drawer 3, Yale University. For information on Robins, see Claude E. Fike, "The Influence of the Creel Committee and the American Red Cross on Russian-American Relations, 1917–1919," *Journal of Modern History*, XXXI (June 1959), 93–109; Kennan, *Russia Leaves the War*, pp. 388–396; Lincoln Colcord, "The Basis of Our Russian Policy," *Freeman*, III (March 16, 1921), 9; William Appleman Williams, *American-Russian Relations, 1781–1947* (New York, 1952), pp. 80–82, 89–90, 147.

64. Robins to his wife, August 18, 1917, Robins Papers, Box 13.

65. Robins to his wife, October 7, 1917, and November 20, 1917, Robins Papers; *Bolshevik Propaganda*, Hearings before a Subcommittee of the Committee on the Judiciary, United States Senate, pursuant to S. Res. 439 and 469, 65th Cong., 3rd Sess., February 11–March 10, 1919 [hereafter cited as *Bolshevik Propaganda*] (Washington, D.C., 1919), pp. 826–828.

66. "Some Observations on the Present Conditions in Russia," n.d. [c. September 1917], MS in Robins Papers, Box 14.

67. *Bolshevik Propaganda*, pp. 782–784; Sister Anne Vincent Meiburger, *Efforts of Raymond Robins toward the Recognition of Soviet Russia and the Outlawry of War, 1917–1933* (Washington, D.C., 1958), pp. 26–27, 185.

68. Kennan, *Russia Leaves the War*, pp. 500–505, states the case thoroughly.

69. *Bolshevik Propaganda*, pp. 800–807.

70. Lasch, *American Liberals*, p. 89. For Francis' paraphrase of the Trotsky memorandum, see Francis to Lansing, March 12, 1918, *Foreign Relations, 1918, Russia*, I, 397–398. Because of delays, the verbatim proposal arrived only after the treaty was ratified but, contrary to Kennan's discussion (see n. 68 above), the State Department knew the general terms of the proposal from Francis' telegram, which was received the day before ratification.

71. Robins to Lenin, April 25, 1918, Robins Papers, Box 14.

72. Hermann Hagedorn, *The Magnate: William Boyce Thompson and His Time (1869–1930)* (New York, 1935), pp. 182–263; *Cong. Rec.*, 65th Cong., 2nd Sess. (January 31, 1918), pp. 1408–1409.

73. Kennan, *Russia Leaves the War*, pp. 48–49. Bullard professed his

admiration for Robins in a letter to Creel, December 9, 1917, cited by Lasch, *American Liberals*, p. 69.

74. Bullard to House, December 12, 1917, and memorandum by Bullard, January 1918, House Papers, Drawers 3, 34.

75. Lasch, *American Liberals*, pp. 70-74.

76. For an incisive analysis of the war aims debate, see George Kennan, "Walter Lippmann, the *New Republic*, and the Russian Revolution," in *Walter Lippmann and His Times*, ed. Marquis Childs and James Reston (New York, 1959), pp. 43-45. Christopher Lasch, agreeing with Kennan, goes into more detail: *American Liberals*, pp. 35-56, 63-77. For examples of the liberals' attitudes, see Steffens to House, June 20, 1917, *Letters*, I, 399-400; Steffens to Allen H. Suggett, October 15, 1918, *ibid.*, I, 431; "Saving Russia" (editorial), *New Republic*, XIII (December 29, 1917), 229-230; *ibid.* (editorial), XIV (February 16, 1918), 68; William C. Bullitt to House, February 3, 1918, House Papers, Drawer 3.

77. Bullard to House, March 7, 1918, House Papers, Drawer 34; Lasch, *American Liberals*, pp. 87-88.

78. Charles Johnston, "The Russian's Immense Inertia," *North American Review*, CCVI (November 1917), 730.

79. *New Republic*, XIII (November 17, 1917), 58.

80. "Russia and Democracy" (editorial), *Nation*, CVI (March 7, 1918), 252; "Not to Despair of Russia" (editorial), *ibid.*, CVI (March 21, 1918), 310; "How Not to Help Russia" (editorial), *ibid.*, CVI (June 1, 1918), 639; "Russia and Recognition" (editorial), *ibid.*, CVI (June 22, 1918), 727-728.

81. "For and Against the Bolsheviki" (editorial), *New Republic*, XIV (April 6, 1918), 280-281.

82. Reed to Robins, January 11, 1918 [misdated 1917], Robins Papers, Box 13.

83. Louise Bryant, *Six Red Months in Russia: An Observer's Account of Russia before and during the Proletarian Dictatorship* (New York, 1918), p. 45. For examples of other radical views, see *Liberator* (editorial), I (March 1918), 5; Bessie Beatty, *The Red Heart of Russia* (New York, 1918); Beatty, "Russian Bolshevism — Tyranny or Freedom," *Public*, XXII (January 25, 1919), 84-86; "The News from Russia" (editorial), *New World*, I (March 1918), 53; "Has Idealism Failed?" (editorial), *ibid.* [this journal soon changed its name to *The World Tomorrow*]; Emma Goldman's anarchist view is given in her pamphlet, *The Truth about the Boylsheviki* (New York, n.d. [1918]); the pacifists' reaction is exemplified in *New York Times*, February 17, 1918, 14:1.

84. Harper to Lippmann, January 18, 1918, Harper Papers, Cabinet 1, Drawer 2, University of Chicago.

85. Acting Secretary of State Polk to Consul General Summers at Moscow, March 11, 1918, *Foreign Relations, 1918, Russia*, I, 395-396.

86. Quoted by Kennan, *Russia Leaves the War*, pp. 512-513.

II. INTERVENTION AND WITHDRAWAL

1. Lansing to Wilson, December 10, 1917, *Lansing Papers*, II, 343–344.

2. For example, Charles Johnston, "Russia and the War after the War," *North American Review*, CCVII (March 1918), 378–387.

3. *Cong. Rec.*, 65th Cong., 2nd Sess. (June 20, 1918), p. 8064. For other remarks, see *New York Times* (editorial), April 29, 1918, 12:1; William T. Ellis, "The Tavarish," *Saturday Evening Post*, CXC (February 9, 1918), 11, 74–78; Robert Crozier Long, *Russian Revolution Aspects* (New York, 1919), p. 103; Russell, *Unchained Russia*, pp. 77–78, 255; Beury, *Russia after the Revolution*, pp. 59, 62, 66–68, 106–115; Herman Bernstein, "Russia under Bolshevik Rule," *American Hebrew*, CIII (June 28, 1918), 172–175, 185; William Franklin Sands, "Salvaging Russia," *Asia*, XVIII (August 1918), 628.

4. "Democracy Must Win" (editorial), *Saturday Evening Post*, CXCI (July 6, 1918), 20.

5. "Can Russia Recover?" (editorial), *Outlook*, CXIX (August 21, 1918), 612; "Liberty and License in Russia," *Missionary Review of the World*, XLI (March 1918), 163.

6. *New York Times* (editorials), January 1, 1918, 16:6, and February 26, 1918, 12:1.

7. For surveys of press opinion, see "Japan's Proposed Entry into Siberia — An Invasion or a Rescue?" *Current Opinion*, LXIV (April 1918), 233–234; "Armed Japanese Intervention in Russia," *Literary Digest*, LVI (March 16, 1918), 13–15. For anti-Soviets' warnings, see Charles H. Boynton, "An American Policy and Russia," *Asia*, XVIII (April 1918), 288; *New York Times*, March 7, 1918, 2:4. The *Times* discussed Japan in an editorial of March 3, 1918, 2:1. On American opinion of Japan, see Eleanor Tupper and George E. McReynolds, *Japan in American Public Opinion* (New York, 1937), pp. 81–140.

8. "A Year of the Russian Revolution" (editorial), *Congregationalist and Advance*, CIII (April 25, 1918), 520. Also "Help for Russia" (editorial), *Outlook*, CXIX (June 12, 1918), 251–252; Jackson Fleming, "A Counter-Thrust for Russia," *Asia*, XVIII (July 1918), 537–541.

9. George Kennan, "Can We Help Russia?" *Outlook*, CXIX (May 22, 1918), 141; MS of article by Samuel Harper, entitled "The Bolsheviki — The Final Conclusion, No Cooperation with Them Possible," printed on July 9, 1918, in *Christian Scence Monitor*, located in Harper Papers, Cabinet 2, Drawer 3; also comments by Herman Bernstein, who just returned from Russia, in *New York Times*, June 24, 1918, 3:5.

10. *Cong. Rec.*, 65th Cong., 2nd Sess. (August 22, 1918), p. 9348.

11. For example, *New York Times*, June 6, 13:6; June 9, III, 2:1; June 11, 3:1, 7 — all 1918.

12. Kennan, *Decision to Intervene*, pp. 345–346 and chap. 4.

13. Betty Miller Unterberger, *America's Siberian Expedition, 1918–1920: A Study of National Policy* (Durham, N.C., 1956), pp. 28–29, 63–64; Consul General Summers at Moscow to Secretary of State, Feb-

ruary 22, 1918, *Foreign Relations, 1918, Russia*, I, 385; Huntington's report, conveyed by DeWitt C. Poole to Lansing, May 22, 1918, *ibid.*, II, 165.

14. Francis to Lansing, May 2 and June 22, 1918, *ibid.*, I, 519–521, and II, 220–223; Kennan, *Decision to Intervene*, pp. 212–215.

15. Kennan, *Decision to Intervene*, pp. 349, 354–357; *Foreign Relations, 1918, Russia*, II, 160; *Lansing Papers*, II, 360–361.

16. Kennan, *Decision to Intervene*, pp. 74–82; *Cong. Rec.*, 65th Cong., 2nd Sess. (June 20, 1918), pp. 8064–8065; *ibid.* (July 13, 1918), p. 9123. The observers' report is reprinted in C. K. Cumming and Walter W. Pettit, eds., *Russian-American Relations, March, 1917–March, 1920: Documents and Papers* (New York, 1920), pp. 177–184.

17. Kennan, *Decision to Intervene*, chap. 4 and pp. 388–395; Wilson to Lansing, June 17, 1918, *Lansing Papers*, II, 363. The aide-mémoire is reprinted in Kennan, *Decision to Intervene*, appendix, pp. 482–485. The question of the British and French role in the Czech uprising has been much debated: *ibid.*, pp. 136, 146–147, 153–160; John Albert White, *The Siberian Intervention* (Princeton, N.J., 1950), pp. 237–255; Oliver M. Sayler, *Russia White or Red* (Boston, 1919), pp. 222, 229–233; Albert Rhys Williams, *Through the Russian Revolution* (New York, 1921), pp. 244–245; John Varney, *Sketches of Soviet Russia: Whole Cloth and Patches* (New York, 1920), pp. 80–81.

18. *New York Times*, August 4, 1918, 1:1.

19. The *Tribune* and other newspapers are cited in "New Forces in Russia," *Literary Digest*, LVIII (August 24, 1918), 8–9; for a few of many other examples, see "Our First Step in Siberia," *ibid.*, LVIII (August 17, 1918), 10–11; "The New East Front," *ibid.*, LVIII (August 31, 1918), 12; "The Renascence of Russia" (editorial), *North American Review*, CCVII (September 1918), 340–341; "America in Russia" (editorial), *Congregationalist and Advance*, CIII (August 22, 1918), 207.

20. *Cong. Rec.*, 65th Cong., 2nd Sess. (August 22, 1918), p. 9348; "Our First Step in Siberia," *Literary Digest*, LVIII (August 17, 1918), 10–11; "Our First Steps in Russia" (editorial), *World's Work*, XXXVI (September 1918), 445.

21. For an interpretation of intervention as anti-Japanese, see White, *Siberian Intervention*, pp. 4–5, 126–139, 259; Unterberger, *America's Siberian Expedition*, p. 232. Those who argue for an anti-Bolshevik interpretation include Williams, *American-Russian Relations*, p. 106, and E. M. Halliday, *The Ignorant Armies* (New York, 1960), pp. 22–29, 218. Significantly, so did William B. Graves, commander of American forces in Siberia: Graves, *America's Siberian Adventure, 1918–1920* (New York, 1931), pp. 191–195. Kennan, *Decision to Intervene*, pp. 400–402, and Lasch, *American Liberals*, p. 109, point out the inconsistencies in the intervention statement. Lasch, in *ibid.*, pp. 110–112, and "American Intervention in Siberia: A Reinterpretation," *Political Science Quarterly*, LXXVII (June 1962), 205–223, refutes the historians' interpretations and outlines the view which Americans held of intervention at the time.

22. *New York Times*, October 26, 1918, 5:5; *Cong. Rec.*, 65th Cong., 3rd Sess. (January 24, 1919), pp. 1970–1971; also, Roger Simons of the Department of Commerce, testifying in *Bolshevik Propaganda*, pp. 354–356.

23. Johnson to Robins, April 3, 1919, Robins Papers, Box 15. Robins denied the myth in *Bolshevik Propaganda*, p. 797. So did Bessie Beatty, in *ibid.*, p. 708; Oliver M. Sayler, "Bolshevik or Anarchist?" *New Republic*, XVIII (March 15, 1918), 210–212.

24. Vera Verunova, "In Red Russia," *Woman's Home Companion*, XLV (August 1919), 10–11, 81; "Nationalization of Women in Russia: New Documentary Evidence," *Current History*, XIII (October 1920), 169–171; Samuel Saloman, *The Red War on the Family* (New York, 1922), pp. 69–82, 85–89. George Seldes says that Lincoln Eyre traced the myth back to the office of the London *Times*, where it was first invented: Seldes, *World Panorama, 1918–1933* (Boston, 1933), p. 111.

25. Harper to William Allen White, July 15 [1918], White Papers, Box 51, Library of Congress. Harper denied being anti-Semitic but also shared the apprehension held by his friend, Charles R. Crane, of pro-Soviet machinations by American Jews: see Harper to Wright, July 17, 1918, and Harper to Allen J. Carter, November 18, 1919, Harper Papers, Cabinet 1, Drawer 2. For Crane's views, see Lasch, *American Liberals*, p. 7, fn.

26. *Bolshevik Propaganda*, pp. 112–116, 142. The fact is that those Bolsheviks of Jewish descent were fully assimilated and that, in terms of urban population, Jews constituted a disproportionately small percentage of the party membership: Solomon M. Schwarz, *The Jews in the Soviet Union* (Syracuse, N.Y., 1951), pp. 92–93, 261.

27. For Marshall, see *Bolshevik Propaganda*, pp. 378 381. For one of many similar statements, see "The Week in Review," *American Hebrew*, CV (June 6, 1919), 8. For a rebuke to liberal Jews, see *ibid.*, CV (July 11, 1919), 202.

28. Sisson, *One Hundred Red Days*, pp. 357–366; Kennan, *Russia Leaves the War*, chap. 22; Committee on Public Information, *The German-Bolshevik Conspiracy*, War Information Series, No. 30 (October 1918).

29. *Current History*, IX, pt. 1 (November 1918), 291. Other typical examples: "Proof of Russia's Betrayal," *Literary Digest*, LVIII (September 28, 1918), 16–17; J. T. M., "Advertise Bolshevism and You Destroy It," *Printers' Ink*, CVI (January 30, 1919), 3–4. Among the dissenters: Ernest Poole, *The Dark People*, pp. 92–93; John Spargo, *Bolshevism: The Enemy of Political and Individual Democracy* (New York, 1919), pp. 150–152; Arthur Bullard, *The Russian Pendulum: Autocracy — Democracy — Bolshivism* (New York, 1919), pp. 97–104.

30. Kennan, *Russia Leaves the War*, pp. 454, 456.

31. Harper to Guy Stanton Ford, November 15, 1918; Harper to Page, September 19, 1918; MS entitled "The Bolshevist Documents: What Do They Prove?" dated "c. 1919 [November or December]," with a notation on the top "Confidential, not published" — Harper Papers,

Cabinet 1, Drawer 2. In a letter to Richard Crane, May 15, 1920, Harper still denied the possibility of forgery.

32. Steffens to James H. McGill, October 31, 1918, *Letters*, I, 438.

33. Harold Stearns, "A Year of Mistakes," *Dial*, LXIV (March 28, 1918), 294.

34. Bullitt to Polk, March 2, 1918, House Papers, Drawer 34.

35. Bullitt to House, June 24, 1918, *ibid.*

36. "Japan and Russia" (editorial), *Nation*, CVI (March 7, 1918), 252–253; "How Not to Help Russia" (editorial), *ibid.*, CVI (June 1, 1918), 639–640; "Alternative Policies in Russia" (editorial), *New Republic*, XV (July 20, 1918), 329–331; "Standing by Russia" (editorial), *ibid.*, XV (May 25, 1918), 100–101; Lasch, *American Liberals*, pp. 99–103, carefully analyses the liberals' position. A letter from H. R. Mussey to Samuel Harper, May 23, 1918, exemplifies the liberals' vacillation between fear of intervention and of Germany: Harper Papers, Cabinet 1, Drawer 2.

37. *New Republic* (editorials), XVI (August 10 and 31, 1918), 30, 120.

38. "Russia and Intervention" (editorial), *Nation*, CVII (August 24, 1918), 192.

39. Bullitt to House, September 20, 1918, House Papers, Drawer 3.

40. *New Republic* (editorial), XVI (October 5, 1918), 260; "The Rescue of Russia" (editorial), *ibid.*, XVI (October 12, 1918), 301–304; "Intervention vs. Economic Help to Russia" (editorial), *ibid.*, XVII (November 9, 1918), 31–33.

41. "Black Prospects for Russia" (editorial), *ibid.*, XVII (December 28, 1918), 240. Also "Withdraw from Russia!" (editorial), *Dial*, LXV (December 14, 1918), 525–528; "Justice to Russia" (editorial), *Nation*, CVIII (January 4, 1919), 6–7; Oswald Garrison Villard to Earl B. Barnes, November 14, 1918, Villard Papers, Harvard University.

42. Harper to Herbert L. Carpenter, **October** 7, 1918, Harper Papers, Cabinet 1, Drawer 2.

43. Quoted in Unterberger, *America's Siberian Expedition*, p. 103.

44. For example, "Russia, the Skeleton at the Feast," *Literary Digest*, LX (January 11, 1919), 13–14; Alva W. Taylor, "Soviets and Bolsheviki," *Christian Century*, XXXVI (February 6, 1919), 13–14; "The Danger of Social Hysteria" (editorial), *ibid.*, XXXVI (April 3, 1919), 3–4; "The Acid Test of Russia" (editorial), *Independent*, XCVII (February 1, 1919), 139–140.

45. Bryant to Reed, March 13–April 16, 1919, Reed-Bryant Papers, Harvard University.

46. Polk to the Commission to Negotiate Peace, January 7, 1919, *Foreign Relations, 1919, Russia*, p. 461.

47. *Cong. Rec.*, 65th Cong., 3rd Sess. (December 30, 1918), p. 864; *ibid.* (February 10, 1919), p. 3105; *ibid.* (February 12, 1919), p. 3242.

48. *Ibid.* (January 22, 1919), p. 1880; *ibid.* (January 4, 1919), p. 1060.

49. For Johnson's speeches and resolutions, see *ibid.* (January 29,

1919), pp. 2261–2270 (quotations on pp. 2261 and 2263); (December 12, 1918), pp. 342–346; (January 13, 1919), p. 1313. La Follette's speech is in *ibid.* (January 7, 1919), p. 1101. Borah explained his support of entry into the war in *ibid.*, 1st Sess. (July 26, 1917), p. 5497; he favored intervention in *ibid.*, 2nd Sess. (July 13, 1918), pp. 9054–9055; he opposed it in *ibid.*, 3rd Sess. (January 9, 1919), p. 1166. The votes on Johnson's resolution are in *ibid.* (February 7, 1919), p. 2878, and 66th Cong., 1st Sess. (June 27, 1919), p. 1864. For evidence of Robins' aid, see Belle Case and Fola La Follette, *Robert M. La Follette* (2 vols., New York, 1953), II, 890, 921; Lasch, *American Liberals*, pp. 92–93.

50. Robins was a leading spokesman for this argument: *Bolshevik Propaganda*, pp. 807–808, and Williams, *American-Russian Relations*, pp. 131–157. For other proponents, see "The Acid Test of Russia" (editorial), *Independent*, XCVII (February 1, 1919), 139–140; Jerome Davis, "What We Can Do for Russia," *ibid.*, XCVII (February 8, 1919), 190–191, 196–199; "Bolshevism on Trial" (editorial), *New Republic*, XVIII (February 15, 1919), 70–72.

51. See Chapter One.

52. Robins states his views in *Bolshevik Propaganda*, p. 816. For agreement, see Lincoln Colcord, "Soviet Russia and the American Revolution," *Dial*, LXV (December 28, 1918), 592; Bullard, *Russian Pendulum*, pp. 217–222; Malcolm W. Davis, *Open Gates to Russia* (New York, 1920), chap. 4; *Nation* (editorial), CVIII (February 15, 1919), 239; Lewis S. Gannett, "Toward International Cooperatives," *Survey*, XLII (August 9, 1919), 709.

53. Colcord, "Soviet Russia and the American Revolution," pp. 591–595; "Withdraw from Russia!" (editorial), *ibid.*, LXV (December 14, 1918), 525.

54. For examples of the radicals' views, see "Bolshevik Problems" (editorial), *Liberator*, I (April 1918), 8; "The Nature of the Choice" (editorial), *ibid.*, I (February 1919), 5–6; Max Eastman, "November Seventh, 1918," *ibid.*, I (December 1918), 22–23; John Reed, "Recognize Russia," *ibid.*, I (July 1918), 18–20; Bryant to Reed, March 24, [1919], Reed-Bryant Papers; "Making Russia Safe for Capital" (editorial), *World Tomorrow*, II (July 1919), 191–192; *New York Times*, June 9, 1919, 10:1. For details of the Socialist Party split, see David A. Shannon, *The Socialist Party of America: A History* (New York, 1955), p. 127 and chap. 6.

55. "Theorizing While They Perish" (editorial), *New Republic*, XVIII (April 19, 1919), 364–365.

56. Colcord to House, March 8, 1919, House Papers, Drawer 5.

57. Lasch, *American Liberals*, pp. 176–193, thoroughly discusses these events and the liberal reactions to them. The text of Bullitt's reports is in *Foreign Relations, 1919, Russia*, pp. 81–86; information on the Bullitt mission also appears in Bullitt, *The Bullitt Mission to Russia: Testimony before the Committee on Foreign Relations, United States Senate* (New York, 1919), pp. 68–95.

58. "Peace at Any Price" (editorial), *New Republic*, XIX (May 24, 1919), 101.

59. Bullitt to Wilson, May 17, 1919, House Papers, Drawer 3. This letter, along with the reports by Bullitt, Steffens, and Pettit of their mission to Russia in April, were made public in Bullitt's testimony before the Senate Foreign Relations Committee: see *Bullitt Mission*, which is an extract from his full testimony in *Treaty of Peace with Germany:* Hearings before the Committee on Foreign Relations, United States Senate, 66th Cong., 1st Sess., Sen. Doc. No. 106, X (Washington, D.C., 1919), 1161–1297.

60. Steffens to Allen H. Suggett, April 13, 1919, *Letters*, I, p. 466.

61. Gertrude Atherton, "Time as a Cure for Bolshevism," *New York Times*, March 16, 1919, VII, p. 3.

62. *Current History*, IX, pt. 2 (February 1919), 334. For other instances, see *Cong. Rec.*, 65th Cong., 3rd Sess. (January 24, 1919), p. 1971; Frederick F. Moore, *Siberia Today* (New York, 1919), p. 71; Pauline S. Crosley, *Intimate Letters from Petrograd* (New York, 1920), p. 220. See also the survey by Charles A. and Mary R. Beard, *The American Spirit: A Study of the Idea of Civilization in the United States* (vol. IV of *The Rise of American Civilization;* New York, 1942).

63. For example: "The Russian Chaos" (editorial), *Review of Reviews*, LVIII (October, 1918), 349; Nicholas Murray Butler, address before the Commercial Club of Cincinnati, April 19, 1919, *Is America Worth Saving?: Addresses on National Problems and Party Policies* (New York, 1920), pp. 13–14; Charles Edward Russell, *Bolshevism and the United States* (Indianapolis, 1919), pp. 153–165; W. C. Huntington, "What the Russian Situation Means to America," *Scribner's Magazine*, LXV (March 1919), 370.

64. Walter Lippmann and Charles Merz, "A Test of the News: An Examination of the News Reports in the New York *Times* on Aspects of the Russian Revolution of Special Importance to Americans: March 1917–March 1920," *New Republic*, XXIII, pt. 2 (August 4, 1920), 10–11.

65. *New York Times* (editorial), January 13, 1919, 10:3; Mark Sullivan, "Peace or Bolshevism?" *Collier's*, LXIII (February 22, 1919), 5–6; Butler, address to the Chamber of Commerce, Utica, N.Y., May 16, 1919, *Is America Worth Saving?*, pp. 33–34.

66. Acting Secretary of State to the Commission to Negotiate Peace, March 29, 1919, *Foreign Relations, 1919, Russia*, pp. 200–201; Ambassador Morris to Acting Secretary of State, April 19, 1919, *ibid.*, pp. 333–336; Consul David B. Macgowan to Secretary of State, October 19, 1919, *ibid.*, pp. 532–533; Chargé in Russia DeWitt C. Poole to Acting Secretary of State, May 7, 1919, *ibid.*, pp. 342–344; Acting Secretary of State to the Commission to Negotiate Peace, May 6, 1919, *ibid.*, pp. 339–341; Lansing to Polk, November 4, 1919, *ibid.*, p. 443. But some State Department representatives described Kolchak as cruel and illiberal: Ambassador Morris to Secretary of State, July 27, 1919,

ibid., p. 400; Bullard's views, as conveyed by Chargé in Japan to Acting Secretary of State, January 23, 1919, *ibid.*, p. 327. For typical domestic views, see " 'Conquering' Russia" (editorial), *Outlook*, CXXI (April 30, 1919), 730–731; Charles W. Holman, "How Siberia Got Rid of Bolshevism," *World's Work*, XXXVIII (June 1919), 135–147.

67. *Cong. Rec.*, 65th Cong., 3rd Sess. (January 24, 1919), p. 1081.

68. The contributions by dozens of newspaper editors to a special anti-Bolshevik issue of *Struggling Russia* form a particularly striking example of this "populist" attitude: "Editors and Their Messages to the Russian People," *Struggling Russia*, I (November 22, 1919), 538–547. For one of many reports of anti-Bolshevik sentiment in Russia, see Gregory Mason, "Let Russia In," *Outlook*, CXXII (July 23, 1919), 472.

69. Lawrence F. Abbott, "Bolshevism versus Americanism," *Struggling Russia*, I (November 22, 1919), 518.

70. Moore, *Siberia Today*, pp. 76–77, 260–261; *New York Times*, January 12, 1919, III, 5:1; Huntington, "What the Russian Situation Means to America," *Scribner's*, LXV (March 1919), 372–373.

71. White to Miss A. M. Hoit, October 2, 1919, Harper Papers, Cabinet 1, Drawer 2.

72. *Cong. Rec.*, 65th Cong., 3rd Sess. (December 12, 1918), p. 342.

73. The best analysis of the Scare is by Robert K. Murray, *Red Scare: A Study in National Hysteria, 1919–1920* (Minneapolis, 1955).

74. "Both Ends and the Middle," *Saturday Evening Post* (editorial), CXCII (November 1, 1919), 28; and quoted by Murray, *Red Scare*, pp. 64–65.

75. *Bolshevik Propaganda*, pp. 5–6.

76. John Higham, *Strangers in the Land: Patterns of American Nativism, 1860–1925* (New Brunswick, N.J., 1955), chaps. 8 and 9, puts the Scare into the context of nativism and antiradicalism. Stanley Coben, "A Study in Nativism: The American Red Scare of 1919–20," *Political Science Quarterly*, LXXIX (March 1964), 52–75, presents a provocative discussion of these larger themes.

III. POPULAR RESPONSES DURING THE NEP

1. Secretary of State to Italian Ambassador, August 10, 1920, *Foreign Relations, 1920*, III, 463–468.

2. Julian Lawrence Woodward, *Foreign News in American Morning Newspapers: A Study in Public Opinion* (New York, 1930), pp. 67, 72, 76. The complete list of papers and percentages is in table 4, p. 72, of Woodward's book.

3. Adapted from Hornell Hart, "Changing Social Attitudes and Interests," in *Recent Social Trends in the United States: Report of the President's Research Committee on Social Trends* (2 vols., New York, 1933), I, 430. Hart excluded 54 magazines from consideration; he lists them on pp. 383–384, n. 2.

4. See Appendix A.

5. *Cong. Rec.*, 66th Cong., 2nd Sess. (April 28, 1920), p. 6208.

6. For earlier uses, see Chapter Two. For later examples, see *New York Tribune*, cited in *Norfolk Virginian-Pilot*, August 13, 1920; *Seattle Times* (editorial), July 28, 1921; Francis, *Russia from the American Embassy*, pp. 335, 349; *New York Times*, September 20, 1925, 29:1, and June 18, 1923, 15:6.

7. The quotation is from a speech at the Church of the Good Shepherd in Augusta, Georgia: *New York Times*, March 22, 1920, 14:8. For examples of Butler's usage, see Butler, *Is America Worth Saving?* pp. 5, 89, 137, 147, 153; Butler, *The Faith of a Liberal: Essays and Addresses on Political Principles and Public Policies* (New York, 1924), pp. 68, 188; Butler, *The Path to Peace: Essays and Addresses on Peace and Its Making* (New York, 1930), pp. 137, 144, 234.

8. This outline is necessarily somewhat impressionistic, but supporting evidence is plentiful. See, for example, the study of Muncie, Indiana, by Robert S. and Helen Merrell Lynd, *Middletown: A Study in American Culture* (New York, 1929), esp. pp. 177, 198, 204–205. Also Sinclair Lewis' *Main Street* (New York, 1920) and *Babbitt* (New York, 1922), *The National Republic* is also informative in its hysterical Americanism: for example, "Intelligentsia vs. Commonsensia" (editorial), *National Republic*, XIII (October 1925), 20; "Commerce and Civilization" (editorial), *ibid.*, XV (March 1928), 16–17. A General Electric advertisement in *Literary Digest*, LXXV (November 25, 1922), 49, includes the interesting remark: "Light is a civilizer — a power that works for law, order and progress."

9. For example, Eleanor Franklin Egan, "Sacrifice for Sacred Principles," *Saturday Evening Post*, CXCV (July 8, 1922), 88; Walter Russell Batsell, *Soviet Rule in Russia* (New York, 1929), p. 238. Floyd Gibbons' *The Red Napoleon* (New York, 1929) is a novel pervaded with racist antagonism to the USSR.

10. White to Ralph Easley (head of the vehemently anti-Bolshevik National Civic Federation), January 5, 1923, White Papers, Box 70.

11. A partial exception must be made for religion, which suffered a "depression" during the postwar period: Robert T. Handy, "The American Religious Depression, 1925–1935," *Church History*, XXIX (March 1960), 3–16. Nevertheless, it is clear that most Americans were still religious in at least a formal sense.

12. Joseph T. Klapper, "Mass Media and Persuasion," in *The Process and Effects of Mass Communication*, ed. Wilbur Schramm, (Urbana, Ill, 1954), pp. 303–307; Herbert H. Hyman and Paul B. Sheatsley, "Some Reasons Why Information Campaigns Fail," in *Readings in Social Psychology*, ed. Eleanor E. Maccoby, Theodore M. Newcomb, and Eugene L. Hartley, 3rd ed. (New York, 1958), pp. 164–173; Bernard Berelson, Paul Lazarsfeld, and William N. McPhee, "Political Perception," *ibid.*, pp. 72–85; William Albig, *Modern Public Opinion* (New York, 1956), pp. 335–340.

13. For example, Evans Clark, *Facts and Fabrications about Soviet Russia* (New York, 1920); Joseph Freeman, *An American Testament: A Narrative of Rebels and Romantics* (New York, 1936), pp. 199–200.

14. Barton, "Just What Would Bolshevism Do to Me? An Interview

with John Spargo," *American Magazine*, XC (December 1920), 110. For information on Middletown, see Lynd, *Middletown*, p. 239.

15. For example, *Washington Post* (editorial), August 11, 1920; *Chicago Tribune* (editorial), August 12, 1920; *New York Times*, May 14, 1920, 17:8; Alonzo Englebert Taylor, "Views of a Layman on Bolshevism," *Saturday Evening Post*, CXCII (January 17, 1920), 77; Cody Marsh, "Glimpses of Siberia, The Russian 'Wild East,' " *National Geographic*, XXXVIII (December 1920), 513; Maude Radford Warren, "Bolshevik Women," *Ladies' Home Journal*, XXXVII (December 1920), 176; John A. Gade, "Inside Red Russia," *World's Work*, XL (July 1920), 232; Frank Comerford, *The New World* (New York, 1920), chaps. 13–14; Spargo, *Russia as an American Problem*, p. 344. Some dissenters, significantly all of them recent visitors to Russia, insisted that order prevailed: Marguerite E. Harrison, *Marooned in Moscow: The Story of an American Woman Imprisoned in Russia* (New York, 1921), p. 65; Isaac McBride, *Barbarous Soviet Russia* (New York, 1920), p. 58; Lincoln Eyre, *Russia Analyzed* (New York, 1920), p. 24.

16. The *Sun* and other papers are cited in "To Cure Russia by 'Absent Treatment,' " *Literary Digest*, LXVIII (February 5, 1921), 5–7. Also "After Wrangel, What?" *ibid.*, LXVII (November 27, 1920), 14–15; *New York Times*, August 14, 1920, 2:2, November 12, 1920, 17:4, and January 23, 1921, II, 3:1; Samuel N. Harper to "Pa Bolshy" [Frederick M. Corse], November 1, 1920, Harper Papers, Cabinet 1, Drawer 2.

17. The *News* and other papers are cited in "Lenine's Gold Declined," *Literary Digest*, LXIX (April 9, 1921), 12 13. Also "Morality of Trading with Lenine," *ibid.*, LXV (May 15, 1920), 28–29; "To Trade with the Bolsheviki," *ibid.*, LXVI (July 24, 1920), 18–19; William English Walling, *Sovietism: The ABC of Russian Bolshevism — According to the Bolshevists* (New York, 1920), pp. 122–124; John Spargo, "Shall We Trade with Soviet Russia?" *Independent*, CV (April 9, 1921), 368–369.

18. *Cong. Rec.*, 66th Cong., 3rd Sess. (January 22, 1921), pp. 1861–1868.

19. The only invocations of populist democracy appear to be in four books published in 1920 and written by people who had left Russia by September 1919 or before. Their ideas, then, were lingering echoes of an earlier period. William Adams Brown, Jr., *The Groping Giant: Revolutionary Russia as Seen by an American Democrat* (New Haven, 1920), pp. 49, 62, 191; Varney, *Sketches of Soviet Russia*, p. 163; Ralph Albertson, *Fighting without a War: An Account of Military Intervention in North Russia* (New York, 1920), p. 137; Davis, *Open Gates to Russia*, chap. 4.

20. "The Menace of Russian Propaganda," *Review of Reviews*, LXI (February 1920), 121.

21. "Peace with the Bolsheviki" (editorial), *World's Work*, XXXIX (April 1920), 535. Optimists included A. M. Kliefoth, a foreign-trade adviser to the State Department and an anti-Bolshevik friend of Har-

per's — *New York Times*, February 12, 1921, 17:1; Clyde Davis, "The Economic Possibilities of Russia," *World's Work*, XXXVI (October 1918), 666; Davis, *Open Gates to Russia*, pp. 12, 14–15, chaps. 4–10; George Norris to C. E. Hopping, December 30, 1920, Norris Papers, Tray 8, Box 7, Library of Congress; William Allen White to William S. Culbertson, March 28, 1921, White Papers, Box 59.

22. Maurice Dobb, *Soviet Economic Development since 1917* (New York, 1948), pp. 123–148; Alexander Baykov, *The Development of the Soviet Economic System: An Essay on the Experience of Planning in the U.S.S.R.* (New York, 1947), pp. 49–52.

23. *Chicago Tribune*, August 2, 1921; *New York Times*, August 1, 1921, 1:1.

24. "The Situation in Russia" (editorial), *Review of Reviews*, LXVII (April, 1923), 358; "Europe at Work, and Russian Progress" (editorial), *ibid.*, LXVIII (December 1923), 580–581; Abraham Epstein, "Russia's Industrial Collapse," *Current History*, XVII (October 1922), 100–107; Malcolm Sumner, *The Russian Evolution* (address delivered on November 22, 1922, before the Society of Arts and Sciences, New York), pamphlet (n.p., n.d.); James P. Goodrich, "Can Russia Come Back?" *Outlook*, CXXX (March 1, 1922), 341–344; John Hays Hammond, "Russia of Yesterday and Tomorrow," *Scribner's*, LXXI (May 1922), 526; C. G. Fairfax Channing, *Siberia's Untouched Treasure: Its Future Role in the World* (New York, 1923), pp. 25-26, 315, 320–445; Edwin W. Hullinger, "The Death of Communism in Russia; What Has Taken Its Place," *Outlook*, CXXXIV (June 27, 1923), 263–265; Duranty's comments are in *New York Times*, October 5, 1921, 19:4, and October 7, 1921, 1:4.

25. "Emigrés and Soviets," *World's Work*, XLIII (November 1921), 16–17; "For a Talk with Lenin," *ibid.*, XLIII (February 1922), 348–349.

26. Eleanor Franklin Egan, "Exposed to Bolshevism," *Saturday Evening Post*, CXCIV (June 17, 1922), 3–4, 45–53; Egan, "Different Shades of Rose," *ibid.*, CXCIV (June 24, 1922), 10–11, 114–120; Egan, "Sacrifice for Sacred Principles," *ibid.*, CXCV (July 8, 1922), 23, 81–91; Egan, "Utopian Nightmares," *ibid.*, CXCV (July 15, 1922), 14–15, 41–46; Robert C. Long, "Europe's Brass El Dorado," *ibid.*, CXCV (October 7, 1922), 21, 134–137.

27. Root to Princess Cantacuzène, August 3, 1921, Root Papers, Box 138, Library of Congress.

28. *New York Times*, November 11, 1921, 17:1; Root to Princess Cantacuzène-Speransky, April 17, 1933, and to Bainbridge Colby, May 24, 1933, Root Papers, Box 149.

29. Kennan, "Finance, Trade, and Agriculture in Russia," *Outlook*, CXXXV (October 10, 1923), 242–244.

30. Harper's initial skepticism is evidenced in letters to DeWitt C. Poole, October 25, 1921, and January 19, 1922; for his later optimism, see Harper to Bakhmetiev, November 20, 1922, and to Sherwood Eddy, November 26, 1923 — all in Harper Papers, Cabinet 1, Drawers 2 and 3.

31. For Frear, see *Cong. Rec.*, 68th Cong., 1st Sess. (December 13,

1923), pp. 256–276; Wheeler's views are in *ibid.* (December 10, 1923), p. 143; Brookhart's are in *New York Times,* June 16, 1923, 12:4, and July 20, 1923, 2:6, and in *Locomotive Engineers Journal,* LVII (October, 1923), 791–792. La Follette recorded his impressions in "What I Saw in Europe," *La Follette's Magazine,* XVI (January, 1924), 4–6. Britten is quoted in *New York Times,* September 26, 1923, 8:1. Beedy's remarks are in *ibid.,* July 26, 1923, 21:1, and *Cong. Rec.,* 68th Cong., 1st Sess. (January 8, 1924), p. 1712. King's earlier comments are in *ibid.,* 65th Cong., 3rd Sess. (January 24, 1919), p. 1971; *ibid.,* 66th Cong., 3rd Sess. (December 20, 1921), pp. 567–568, and (January 22, 1921), pp. 1861–1868; his later speech is in *ibid.,* 68th Cong., 1st Sess. (April 24, 1924), pp. 7032–7056.

32. Hoover to Wilson, March 28, 1919, *Foreign Relations, 1919, Russia,* p. 101. The full memorandum is in H. H. Fisher, *The Famine in Soviet Russia: The Operations of the American Relief Administration* (New York, 1927), pp. 10–14.

33. *Ibid.,* pp. 23–27.

34. Hoover to Wilson, June 21, 1919, *Foreign Relations, 1919, Russia,* p. 118.

35. For example, the American Central Committee for Russian Relief, created in 1919 and sponsored by former Ambassador Francis, Princes Cantacuzène, Root, Gompers, Mott, Charles E. Russell, Charles R. Crane, and others: Executive Committee to Mrs. Eaton, November 5, 1919, Harper Papers, Cabinet 1, Drawer 2; Valentine Ugbet to William B. Thompson, n.d. [c. 1920], Robins Papers, Box 17. Pro-Soviet groups included an advisory committee to the All-Russian Jewish Public Committee at Moscow, with support given by Norman Thomas, Judah Magnes, Sidney Hillman, Francis Hackett, and others: "Relief to Russia," *Survey,* XLV (January 8, 1921), 527–528. There was also the American Relief for Russian Women and Children, of which Jane Addams was chairman, and the American Friends Service Committee gave some aid.

36. "The Ring around Lenine," *Literary Digest,* LXI (May 10, 1919), 14–15; *Cong. Rec.,* 65th Cong., 3rd Sess. (January 18, 1919), p. 1660.

37. Fisher, *Famine,* pp. 52–53; Hoover to London Office of ARA, June [July] 23, 1921, *Foreign Relations, 1921,* II, 807–808; London Office of ARA to Hoover, July 31, 1921, *ibid.,* p. 809. The full text of the Riga Agreement is in a letter from Commissioner at Riga to Secretary of State, August 23, 1921, *ibid.,* pp. 813–817.

38. Fisher, *Famine,* pp. 105, 111–113, 161–162. On YMCA relief work, see Ethan T. Colton, *Forty Years with Russians* (New York, 1940), pp. 40–47, 51–59, 60–95, 98–101, 110–112. On the AFSC, see Mary Hoxie Jones, *Swords into Ploughshares: An Account of the American Friends Service Committee: 1917–1937* (New York, 1937), pp. 43–45, 69–71; John Forbes, *The Quaker Star under Seven Flags, 1917–1927* (Philadelphia, 1962), pp. 149–154, 156–157, 165–167, 190; "Help Uphold the Standard!" (editorial), *American Friend,* X (October 26, 1922), 865; Wilbur K. Thomas, "Facts about Friends' Service

in Russia This Winter," *ibid.*, X (December 7, 1922), 979; Murray S. Kenworthy, "Conditions in the Russian Famine Area," *ibid.*, X (July 20, 1922), 574–575, 582. On Catholic relief, see Edmund A. Walsh, *The Last Stand: An Interpretation of the Soviet Five-Year Plan* (Boston, 1931), pp. 215–216. On the Federal Council of Churches, see John Sheridan Zelie, *The Russian Relief Work of the Federal Council of Churches* (New York, 1922); Colton, *Forty Years*, p. 102. On the Mennonites, see John D. Unruh, *In the Name of Christ: A History of the Mennonite Central Committee and Its Service, 1920–1951* (Scottsdale, Pa., 1952), pp. 13–24.

39. For example, Hoover to John C. Groome, Director of the ARA Mission to the Baltic Region, June 14, 1919, quoted in American Relief Administration, *Bulletin*, no. 15 (June 27, 1919), 17.

40. Isaac F. Marcosson, "American Relief—And After: An Interview with Herbert Hoover," *Saturday Evening Post*, CXCIII (April 30, 1921), 36.

41. See, for example, his arguments with the AFSC: Forbes, *Quaker Star*, p. 150.

42. Hoover to Hughes, December 6, 1921, *Foreign Relations, 1921*, II, 787–788. Merle Curti, *American Philanthropy Abroad: A History* (New Brunswick, N.J., 1962), pp. 284–285, discusses Hoover's motives, mentions the practical but incidental purpose of decreasing American agricultural surplus, and generously concludes that Hoover's motives were primarily disinterested and humanitarian. The evidence paints a much less altruistic picture.

43. The *Herald* is quoted in "The Third Horseman Rides in Russia," *Literary Digest*, LXX (August 13, 1921), 7–9. For examples of similar views, see "Millions Starving in Lenine's Paradise of Atheism," *ibid.*, LXX (August 6, 1921), 32–33; *New York Times* (editorial), August 10, 1921, 12:4; *Washington Post* (editorial), July 24, 1921; *Seattle Post-Intelligencer* (editorial), August 14, 1921; *Norfolk Virginian-Pilot*, August 2, 1921. *Collier's*, which almost totally ignored Soviet Russia during the 1920's, printed an article presenting the famine in poignant terms: Arthur Ruhl, "What I've Just Seen in Russia," *Collier's*, LXXI (April 7, 1923), 9, 24. So did the bitterly hostile *Saturday Evening Post* and *Current History*: Eleanor Franklin Egan, "Utopian Nightmares," *Saturday Evening Post*, CXCV (July 15, 1922), 14–15, 41–46; "The Russian Famine Tragedy," *Current History*, XVI (April 1922), 145–159, and "Russian Famine Studies from the Field," XVI (May 1922), 303–308.

44. Robert Moats Miller, *American Protestantism and Social Issues, 1919–1939* (Chapel Hill, 1953), p. 40, cites 22 Protestant journals in favor and none opposed. See also *Congregationalist* (editorial), CVI (August 11, 1921), 175; "Religious Currents in Russia" (editorial), *Missionary Review of the World*, XLIV (October 1921), 745–747.

45. *Cong. Rec.*, 67th Cong., 1st Sess. (August 11, 1921), p. 4855. Another bitter anti-Bolshevik, Charles R. Crane, also favored relief: *Chicago Tribune*, August 12, 1921.

46. *Seattle Times*, July 27, 1921. Similarly, *New Orleans Times-*

Picayune, July 20, 1921; *Norfolk Virginian-Pilot,* August 2, 1921; *Cincinnati Enquirer,* August 12, 1921.

47. Root to Princess Cantacuzène, July 14, 1921, Root Papers, Box 138.

48. Charles W. Eliot, quoted in *New York Times,* May 22, 1922, 14:7; Jerome Landfield, "The Relief of Starving Russians," *Review of Reviews,* LXIV (September, 1921), 267–271.

49. *Chicago Tribune,* July 29 and August 2, 1921.

50. *Cong. Rec.,* 67th Cong., 2nd Sess. (December 17, 1921), pp. 452–458, 468–479.

51. *Ibid.* (December 20, 1921), pp. 566–570, 574–581.

52. *Ibid.* (December 17, 1921), p. 471.

53. Fisher, *Famine,* appendices B and C, pp. 553–567.

54. Haskell to Hoover, August 28, 1923, cited in ARA, *Bulletin,* no. 41 (October 1923), 2–3.

55. John S. Curtiss, "Church and State," in *The Transformation of Russian Society: Aspects of Social Change since 1861,* ed. Cyril E. Black (Cambridge, Mass., 1960), pp. 405–425; Curtiss, *The Russian Church and the Soviet State, 1917–1950* (Boston, 1953), pp. 45–46, 76, 104–115, 119–121.

56. "The Drifter," *Nation,* CXVI (February 21, 1923), 217; "Russia's Internal Struggle," *Current History,* XVII (October 1922), 156.

57. For example, Ellsworth Huntington, "The Suicide of Russia," *Scribner's,* LXXVII (February 1925), 157; Lothrop Stoddard, "1917 — Red Russia Turns Pink — 1927," *World's Work,* LV (November 1927), 18.

58. For the *Evening Journal* and other newspapers, see "Bolshevism's 'Public Challenge to God,'" *Literary Digest,* LXXVI (April 14, 1923), 7–9. Also: "Mirrors of Blood," *Time,* I (April 14, 1923), 12.

59. "The Russian Experiment" (editorial), *America,* XXVII (May 27, 1922), 136; *New York Times,* August 29, 1924, 13:2; Walsh, "No Longer a Nation But an Idea," *Journal of the American Bankers' Association,* XVIII (July 1925), 25 — on Walsh's relief work, see Walsh, *Last Stand,* pp. 306–307; "Russia Passes into History" (editorial), *Commonweal,* II (July 8, 1925), 218.

60. For typical antipathy, see "Religion in Soviet Russia" (editorial), *Missionary Review,* XLIV (July 1921), 511–512.

61. Frederick J. Libby, "The Open Mind for Russia," *American Friend,* IX (February 17, 1921), 132. Reverend Mills and Bishop Nuelson, both Methodists, reported their findings in Mills, "The Truth about Soviet Russia: The Bolsheviks and the Churches," *Zion's Herald,* C (December 20, 1922), 1610. John R. Voris, a leader of interdenominational activities, wrote a series of articles in *Christian Century,* XXXVIII (November 17, 1921), 15–18; (November 24, 1921), 10–14; (December 1, 1921), 11–15; (December 8, 1921), 15–19; (December 29, 1921), 14–18. The views of John Haynes Holmes, pastor of Community Church of New York, are reported in *New York Times,* September 11, 1922, 9:1.

62. "The Wide-Open Door of Russia" (editorial), *Christian Century,*

XL (January 18, 1923), 68–69; "Lenine Learns Wisdom" (editorial), *Congregationalist*, CVI (June 16, 1921), 728. The quoted comment comes from Miller, *American Protestantism*, p. 39; in chap. 2 of his book, Miller describes Protestant liberalism of this period. Paul A. Carter, *The Decline and Revival of the Social Gospel: Social and Political Liberalism in American Protestant Churches, 1920–1940* (Ithaca, N.Y., 1956), chaps. 2–4, discusses the subject even more fully.

63. "The Tragedy of Moscow" (editorial), *Congregationalist*, CVIII (April 12, 1923), 454; "Russia and Religion" (editorial), *Christian Century*, XL (May 10, 1923), 581–583; Jerome Davis, "America and the Butchkavitch Execution," *ibid.*, XL (May 10, 1923), 586–589; John Haynes Holmes, "Religion in Revolutionary Russia," *Nation*, CXVI (May 9, 1923), 541–544; "Conviction of Russian Prelates" (editorial), *Zion's Herald*, CI (April 11, 1923), 461.

64. Princess E. M. Almedingen, "A Futile Russian Self-Acquittal," *America*, XXXI (May 3, 1924), 56–57. For evidence of the evangelists' hopes, see Norman J. Smith, "The Evangelical Christians in Russia," *Missionary Review*, XLVIII (July 1925), 525–532.

65. Quoted in Miller, *American Protestantism*, p. 29.

66. "The Religious Melée in Russia," *Literary Digest*, LXXVII (May 26, 1923), 32–33; Miller, *American Protestantism*, p. 41; "Bishop Blake's Address at Moscow," *Christian Century*, XL (June 21, 1923), 791, 798 — all give some details of this incident.

67. For example, "England's Recognition of Russia" (editorial), *Congregationalist*, CIX (May 1, 1924), 550; "Shall We Recognize Russia?" (editorial), *Christian Century*, XLIII (October 7, 1926), 1222–1223; "Still Another Witness," *Zion's Herald*, CII (October 8, 1924), 1306.

68. For background information, see Schwarz, *Jews in the Soviet Union*, pp. 24–28, 241–253, 274–284; and Avrahm Yarmolinsky, *The Jews and Other Minor Nationalities under the Soviets* (New York, 1928), pp. 24–33. Melech Epstein, *Jewish Labor in U.S.A., 1914–1952: An Industrial, Political and Cultural History of the Jewish Labor Movement* (New York, 1953), pp. 64–67, describes reactions of Russian and American Jews. For examples of sympathy, see *New York Times*, March 5, 1928, 14:2; David Abarbanel, "Woes of Jews in Soviet Russia," *American Hebrew*, CXI (May 19, 1922), 24, 42.

69. Schwarz, *Jews in the Soviet Union*, pp. 99–101, 112.

70. For example, see the section on Russia in the *Annual Reports* of the executive committee of the American Jewish Committee, 1920–1929. See also the attack by the American Jewish Congress: *New York Times*, June 11, 1928, 21:1. Also "Communist Jews of Soviet Russia," *American Hebrew*, CXXV (November 1, 1929), 755–756.

71. Schwarz, *Jews in the Soviet Union*, pp. 117–121, 162, 271; Moses A. Leavitt, *The JDC Story: Highlights of JDC Activities: 1914–1952* (New York, 1953), pp. 4, 9, 10; James N. Rosenberg, *On the Steppes: A Russian Diary* (New York, 1927), pp. x–xi; Curti, *American Philanthropy*, pp. 365–369; "Rehabilitating Russian Jews in Russia," *American Hebrew*, CXVII (May 22, 1925), 81, 100; "Mr. Marshall

Does Not Mince Words," *ibid.*, CXVII (September 11, 1925), 493; "Mr. Marshall and Dr. Wise Return," *ibid.*, CXVII (September 11, 1925), 496.

72. For example, Jacob Billikopf and Dr. Maurice B. Hexter, *The Jewish Situation in Eastern Europe Including Russia and the Work of the Joint Distribution Committee: Joint Report as Delivered at the National Conference of the United Jewish Campaign and the Joint Distribution Committee* (Chicago, October 9–10, 1926); "Judaism on the Russian Prairies," *American Hebrew*, CXIX (September 3, 1926), 451; Lewis Browne, "Around the World with a Portable," *ibid.*, CXX (November 26, 1926), 79, 84; "Brainin Reaffirms Faith in Russian Colonization," *ibid.*, CXX (November 12, 1926), 35; Bernard Edelhertz, "The Russian Oasis," *ibid.*, CXXII (March 30, 1928), 722, 732.

73. Meiburger, *Efforts of Raymond Robins*, pp. 62–65, 75–76. For examples of their pressure, see Petition to the Senate Committee on Foreign Relations by the WILPF (Chicago Branch), May 1, 1922, in National Archives, Record Group 46; *New York Times*, March 16, 1923, 2:7.

74. Gumberg to William Henry Chamberlin, March 15, 1923, Gumberg Papers, Box 3, Wisconsin Historical Society. For information on Gumberg, see William Henry Chamberlin, *The Confessions of an Individualist* (New York, 1940), pp. 56–58.

75. Robins to Borah, December 9, 1922, Borah Papers, Box 234, Library of Congress; Williams, *American-Russian Relations*, pp. 178–179.

76. For one of Hughes's many statements, see *New York Times*, May 2, 1922, 1:6. For Coolidge, see his message to Congress, December 6, 1923, *Foreign Relations, 1923*, I, viii ix. A typical American Legion resolution, this one from the Cuyahoga County Council in Ohio, May 17, 1922, is reprinted in *Cong. Rec.*, 67th Cong., 2nd Sess. (May 22, 1922), pp. 7354–7355. For the National Civic Federation, see *New York Times*, March 29, 1920, 12:7. For Gompers, see *New York Times*, May 1, 1922, 1:2, and Chapter 6 below.

77. Robert Paul Browder, *The Origins of Soviet-American Diplomacy* (Princeton, N.J., 1953), p. 16.

78. The *Post* is cited in "Russia Approaching Recognition," *Literary Digest*, LXXIII (April 15, 1922), 10–11.

79. Robins is quoted in *Advance*, VIII, no. 5 (March 28, 1924), 8.

80. Robins to Gumberg, April 9, 1922; also Gumberg to Robins, April 21, 1922; Robins to Gumberg, May 13, 1922; Robins to Gumberg, October 23, 1922 — all in Gumberg Papers, Box 2; Gumberg to Robins, December 5, 1922, Robins Papers, Box 18.

81. Gumberg to Robins, January 12, 1923, Robins Papers, Box 19.

82. Harper to Bernard Pares, January 15, 1923, Harper Papers, Cabinet 1, Drawer 2.

83. Gumberg to Robins, April 1, 1923, Robins Papers, Box 19. In 1935, Walter Duranty wrote that the execution "did more than anything else to retard American recognition of the U.S.S.R. for ten years." Duranty, *I Write as I Please* (New York, 1935), p. 205.

84. Robins to James P. Goodrich, May 31, 1923, and June 4, 1923,

Gumberg Papers, Box 3. Williams, *American-Russian Relations*, pp. 203–204, claims that Robins was in Berlin, at the time of Harding's death, in order to go to Moscow. Meiburger, *Efforts of Raymond Robins*, p. 90, claims that he was in Europe to promote outlawry of war and was disgusted with Harding's refusal to commit himself on recognition. Evidence does not decisively exclude either argument.

85. Robins to Gumberg, December 1, 1923, Gumberg Papers, Box 3.

86. Message to Congress, December 6, 1923, *Foreign Relations, 1923*, I, viii–ix; Commissar for Foreign Affairs to Coolidge, December 16, 1923, *ibid.*, II, 787; Hughes to Consul at Reval, December 18, 1923, *ibid.*, II, 788.

87. "No Rush to Know Russia," *Literary Digest*, LXXX (January 5, 1924), 10–11; *Atlanta Constitution*, December 22, 1923; *Hartford Courant*, December 21, 1923; *Cincinnati Enquirer*, December 22, 1923; *Arizona Republic*, December 21, 1923. Some found fault with Hughes's stand: for example, *Des Moines Register*, December 21, 1923; *Norfolk Virginian-Pilot*, December 20, 1923; *St. Louis Post-Dispatch*, January 9, 1924.

88. The debate is in *Cong. Rec.*, 68th Cong., 1st Sess. (January 7, 1924), pp. 592–626. The hearings are in *Recognition of Russia, 1924:* Hearings before a Subcommittee of the Committee on Foreign Relations, United States Senate, 68th Cong., 1st Sess., pursuant to S. Res. 50 [hereafter cited as *Recognition*] (Washington, D.C., 1924).

89. Borah to Robins, December 20, 1923, and to John Haynes Holmes, December 28, 1923, Borah Papers, Box 245. See also the comment by A. W. Kliefoth to Samuel Harper, February 4, 1924, Harper Papers, Cabinet 1, Drawer 3.

90. See n. 88 above: pp. 592–614 of *Cong. Rec.*, and pp. 161–530 of *Recognition*.

91. Williams, *American-Russian Relations*, p. 207; Borah to Jerome Davis, February 21, 1924, Borah Papers, Box 245.

92. *Cong. Rec.*, 68th Cong., 1st Sess. (January 8, 1924), p. 709.

93. For typical examples, see Petition to the Senate Foreign Relations Committee from the Rotary International of Uhrichsville, Ohio, March 2, 1926, in National Archives, Record Group 46; "Russian Recognition" (editorial), *Saturday Evening Post*, CXCIX (January 1, 1927), 20; "The Threat of Soviet Russia" (editorial), *Outlook*, CXLVI (June 29, 1927), 277–278.

94. All the comments are cited in "Lenin," *Literary Digest*, LXXX (February 2, 1924), 8–9, except for *Chicago Tribune*, January 23, 1924.

95. See the appellation of "boss" in a Duranty article, *New York Times*, July 31, 1926, 4:5, and "Flame But No Fire," *Time*, VIII (November 8, 1926), 17.

96. *New York Times*, January 23, 1924, 3:4. Also *Chicago Tribune* (editorial), January 23, 1924; *Washington Post* (editorial), January 23, 1924; *St. Louis Post-Dispatch* (editorial), January 22, 1924.

97. For example, *Des Moines Register* (editorial), December 21, 1923; *Atlanta Constitution* (editorial), January 6, 1924; *Cincinnati Enquirer* (editorial), January 23, 1924; *New York Times*, January 22,

1924, 16:4; May 6, 1924, 3:3; November 8, 1925, II, 4:2; "'Newest' E. P.," *Time*, V (April 13, 1925), 8; "The Soviet Spider and the Capitalistic Fly," *Literary Digest*, LXXXV (April 25, 1925), 15.

98. Sir John Maynard, *Russia in Flux* (New York, 1951), p. 254.

99. *Chicago Tribune* (editorial), November 1, 1927.

100. Chamberlin, "Soviet Russia's First Steps toward Democracy," *Current History*, XX (April 1924), 28–34.

101. "The Split in Russia" (editorial), *Outlook*, CXLII (February 17, 1926), 241–242; "Trend of World Affairs," *National Republic*, XV (September 1927), 12–13, 64; Jerome Landfield (a director of the American-Russian Chamber of Commerce and associate editor of *Independent and Weekly Review*) to Samuel N. Harper, December 23, 1924, Harper Papers, Cabinet 1, Drawer 3; *Cincinnati Enquirer* (editorial), November 25, 1927.

102. *Arizona Republic* (editorial), January 28, 1929.

103. *New York Times* (editorial), September 25, 1926, 16:2; "Russia and Recognition" (editorial), *Independent*, CXVI (January 30, 1926), 119–120.

104. "Why Britain Breaks with Moscow," *Literary Digest*, XCIII (June 4, 1927), 9–10; "Trying to Tame the Bolshevik Bear," *ibid.*, XCIV (July 2, 1927), 8–10; "Great Britain and Russia" (editorial), *Saturday Evening Post*, CC (July 16, 1927), 26.

105. *Cincinnati Enquirer* (editorial), December 2, 1927. For examples of tolerance, see *New Orleans Times-Picayune*, December 2, 1927; "The Bolshevik 'Peace Bomb,'" *Literary Digest*, XCV (December 17, 1927), 12–13; "Russia's Thorny Olive Branch," *ibid.*, XCVII (April 7, 1928), 11. Typical hostility was expressed by editorials in *Chicago Tribune*, December 2, 1927; *Washington Post*, December 1, 1927; *St. Louis Post-Dispatch*, December 5, 1927; *Hartford Courant*, December 1, 1927.

106. "The Bitter Lesson in Russia" (editorial) *Saturday Evening Post*, CXCIX (January 15, 1927), 26.

107. Maynard, *Russia in Flux*, pp. 263–264.

108. *New York Times*, February 22, 1926, 16:7; Robert Crozier Long, "Peasant Renovators of Russia," *Saturday Evening Post*, CXCVI (January 26, 1924), 134.

109. For typical views, see James P. Goodrich, "The True Communists of Russia," *Current History*, XVI (September 1922), 927–932; Manya Gordon Strunsky, "Democratic Forces in Russia," *North American Review*, CCXV (February 1922), 155–166; "A 'Groundswell' That Will Redeem Russia" (editorial), *Review of Reviews*, LXVIII (July 1923), 13.

110. Isaac F. Marcosson, "After Lenine — What? The Future of Russia," *Saturday Evening Post*, CXCVII (February 14, 1925), 141.

111. For example, Charles W. Merriam to Paul Harper, August 13, 1926, written in Berlin after visiting Russia with Paul's brother Samuel, Harper Papers, Cabinet 1, Drawer 3; Samuel N. Harper, *Civic Training in Soviet Russia* (Chicago, 1927), p. xiv; Anna Porter, *A Moscow Diary* (Chicago, 1926), p. 9.

112. *New York Times*, September 22, 1929, II, 5:3; July 7, 1927, 11:6.
113. Fred A. Britten, "Russia's Reign of Terror," *National Republic*, XIII (January 1926), 51, 59.
114. Karl Baedeker, *Russia with Teheran, Port Arthur, and Peking: Handbook for Travellers* (New York, 1914), pp. xiv, xxvi.
115. Eleanor Franklin Egan, "Communist Accommodations," *Saturday Evening Post*, CXCV (July 1, 1922), 71.
116. Anne O'Hare McCormick, *The Hammer and the Scythe: Communist Russia Enters the Second Decade* (New York, 1928), pp. 18, 21–23, 27–29; Dorothy Thompson, *The New Russia* (NewYork, 1928), pp. 16–17, 22–23; Junius B. Wood, "Russia of the Hour," *National Geographic*, L (November 1926), 564; Anna Louise Strong, "When the Reds Get Down to Business," *Collier's*, LXXIII (February 16, 1924), 10; Paxton Hibben, "Russia's Restoration as a World Power," *Current History*, XXIII (February 1926), 633–640; Porter, *Moscow Diary*, p. 12; Jacob Billikopf, "Present-Day Russian Conditions as Viewed by an Impartial Observer," *Annals of the American Academy of Political and Social Science* [hereafter cited as *Annals*], CXXXII (July 1927), 32–36.
117. A confidential MS entitled "Three Months in the Soviet Union," n.d., written after leaving the USSR on October 15, 1926, in Harper Papers, Cabinet 2, Drawer 2. Years later, Harper admitted that he had gone on "a somewhat overenthusiastic search for those constructive features which I had not at first seen in Bolshevism but which I felt must be there": Paul V. Harper, ed., *The Russia I Believe In: The Memoirs of Samuel N. Harper, 1902–1941* (Chicago, 1945), p. 234.
118. Thompson, *New Russia*, p. 256.
119. McCormick, *Hammer*, pp. 6–7. For comments on the frontier character, see Strong's remarks in Alfred L. P. Dennis, Stanley High, Maurice Hindus, and Anna Louise Strong, *Russia in Transition: An American Symposium. A Stenographic Report of the 77th New York Luncheon Discussion, February 28, 1925, of the Foreign Policy Association* (Pamphlet 34, July 1925; New York, 1925), p. 6; Thompson, *New Russia*, p. 6; McCormick, *Hammer*, pp. 226–227.
120. On fervor, see McCormick, *Hammer*, pp. 40, 66–67, 208–212; Thompson, *New Russia*, chap. 4 and pp. 214–244. On morality, see Maurice Hindus, *Broken Earth* (New York, 1926), pp. 124–125; "A Woman Resident in Russia" and "The Russian Effort to Abolish Marriage," *Atlantic Monthly*, CXXXVIII (July 1926), 108–114; Thompson, *New Russia*, pp. 45, 261–268; McCormick, *Hammer*, pp. 155, 161, 173–177.

IV. BUSINESS LEADERS AND THE NEP

1. William Feather, "A Fourth of July Speech — *New Style*," *Nation's Business*, XIV (July 1926), 13–14.
2. 34th Annual Convention, *Proceedings of the Annual Meetings of the National Association of Manufacturers of the United States of*

America [hereafter cited as *Proceedings of NAM*] (October 14–16, 1929), p. 342.

3. James Warren Prothro, *The Dollar Decade: Busines Ideas in the 1920's* (Baton Rouge, 1954), pp. 81–90, 209–211; Charles Norman Fay, *Business in Politics: Considerations for Leaders in American Business* (Cambridge, Mass., 1926), pp. 49, 82; "Business Declares Its Principles," *Nation's Business*, IX (June 1921), 48.

4. 27th Annual Convention, *Proceedings of NAM* (May 8–10, 1922), p. 115.

5. For example, 28th Annual Convention, *ibid.* (May 14–16, 1923), p. 115; *16th Annual Meeting of the Chamber of Commerce of the United States* (May 7–10, 1928), pp. 43–44.

6. "The Great Communistic Experiment" (editorial), *Engineering and Mining Journal*, CXII (August 27, 1921), 321.

7. Fay, *Business in Politics*, p. 91.

8. Royal R. Keely, "An American Engineer's Experiences in Russia," *American Machinist*, LV (November 17, 1921), 788–789.

9. For example, "The Russian Situation" (editorial), *Railway Age*, LXVII (October 3, 1919), 723–724; E. A. Macmillan, "The Railroad Transportation Situation in Soviet Russia," *Railway Review*, LXX (February 18, 1922), 218–223; Leo Pasvolsky, "The Railroad Situation in Soviet Russia," *Annalist*, XVIII (December 5, 1921), 532.

10. Oswald F. Schuette, "Bolshevik Ruin of Metal Industries," *Iron Age*, CVI (August 26, 1920), 525–526; H. A. Kursell, "Economic Aspects of Present-Day Russian Mining," *Mining and Metallurgy*, IV (July 1923), 337–339.

11. Keely, "An American Engineer's Experiences in Russia," *American Machinist*, LV (December 8, 1921), 919–921; Leo Pasvolsky, "Industrial Management, Soviet Russia's Unsolved Problem," *Annalist*, XVII (March 21, 1921), 353.

12. "The Trend Toward Private Ownership of Land in Russia," *Commercial and Financial Chronicle* [hereafter cited as *Comm. Fin. Chronicle*], CXV (October 19, 1922), 1671–1672.

13. "Notes from Deluded Russia," *Nation's Business*, XI (February 1923), 27; "Where the Cost of Living is High," *ibid.*, 24.

14. Herbert Hoover, "Russia — An Economic Vacuum," *ibid.*, X (June 5, 1922), 14–16; Hughes to Samuel Gompers, April 5, 1921, *Foreign Relations, 1921*, II, 769.

15. Julius H. Barnes (president of the Chamber of Commerce), "The Facts That Answer Trotsky," *Nation's Business*, XIII (November 1925), 20.

16. *New York Times*, March 22, 1921, 1:2.

17. For example, letter of Hoover to C. V. Hibbard (associate general secretary of the Young Men's Christian Association), March 23, 1923, quoted in Fisher, *Famine*, appendix A, pp. 541–542.

18. "Latvian Correspondent" and "Trade Conditions in Russia," *American Machinist*, LV (December 29, 1921), 1058a.

19. Frederick L. Schuman, *American Policy toward Russia since 1917: A Study of Diplomatic History, International Law and Public*

Opinion (New York, 1928), p. 194; Browder, *Origins of Soviet-American Diplomacy*, pp. 26–27.

20. "Comprehensive Electrical Projects in Russia" (editorial), *Electrical World*, LXXX (September 30, 1922), 701. For one of many examples, see "Why We Cannot Open Up Russia," *Journal of the American Bankers' Association*, XV (September 1922), 126–128.

21. *New York Times*, October 26, 19:5; October 27, 3:5; November 21, 1:3; November 26, 15:6; November 29, 1:4; November 30, 1:1; December 12, 1:3; December 14, 3:1 — all 1920; *ibid.*, August 7, 1921, 3:6; Schuman, *American Policy toward Russia*, pp. 251–252; "Lenine and Washington B. Vanderlip" (editorial), *Engineering and Mining Journal*, CX (December 25, 1920), 1201–1202; Washington B. Vanderlip, "Side-Lights on Soviet Moscow," *Asia*, XXI (May 1921), 402–405. For the full story, see Albert Parry, "Washington B. Vanderlip, the 'Khan of Kamchatka,'" *Pacific Historical Review*, XVII (August 1948), 311–330.

22. Williams, *American-Russian Relations*, pp. 195–196; Memorandum by the Economic Adviser of the Department of State, May 3, 1922; Ambassador in Italy to the Secretary of State, May 3 and 4, 1922; Secretary of State to the Ambassador in Italy, May 4, 1922; A. C. Bedford to the Secretary of State, May 5, 1922 — all in *Foreign Relations, 1922*, II, 773–776, 786; Louis Fischer, *Oil Imperialism: The International Struggle for Russian Petroleum* (New York, 1926), pp. 55–59.

23. *Ibid.*, pp. 93–95, 155–161.

24. Dobb, *Soviet Economic Development*, pp. 123–148; Baykov, *Development of the Soviet Economic System*, pp. 49–52.

25. Hoover to Hughes, December 6, 1921, *Foreign Relations, 1922*, II, 787–788.

26. *Ibid.* Note that Hoover referred to Russia as an "economic vacuum" in June 1922, more than a year after the NEP began.

27. *New York Times*, March 26, 1921, 1:8; April 24, 1921, II, 3:1.

28. "What of Russia?" (editorial), *Iron Age*, CXII (September 6, 1923), 619–620.

29. "Mr. H. G. Wells and Russia," *Comm. Fin. Chronicle*, CXI (November 20, 1920), 1991–1992, sec. 1.

30. "The Hope for the Future of Russia," *ibid.*, CXIII (November 12, 1921), 2025–2026; Review of *Reforging of Russia*, by E. W. Hullinger, *ibid.*, CXX (March 7, 1925), 1138–1139, 1142–1143.

31. "The Electrification of Soviet Russia" (editorial), *Electrical World*, LXXX (August 26, 1922), 412.

32. For example, Eugene M. Kayden, "Russia's Home Trade Reviving," *Annalist*, XXII (August 27, 1923), 287.

33. Emil Lengeyl, "'Americanization' The Watchword in Russia," *Annalist*, XXIX (February 18, 1927), 270, 276.

34. Schuman, *American Policy toward Russia*, pp. 300, 249.

35. Frank L. Partik, "Solving the Russian Trade Puzzle," *Magazine of Wall Street*, XXX (May 13, 1922), 15; Martin Golden, "The Recovery of Economic Vitality in Russia," *ibid.*, XXXII (August 18, 1923), 700–701, 772–774; *New York Times*, January 26, 1922, 25:6; "Extent

of Russia's Ruin and Chances of Recovery," *Railway Age*, LXXII (May 6, 1922), 1073-1074.

36. For example, R. Estcourt, "Our Underlying Economic Difference with Russia," *Annalist*, XIX (May 22, 1922), 557-558; "Saving Russia with Tractors," *Automotive Industries*, XLVI (February 2, 1922), 237; R. D. Adams, "Conditions Improving for Mining Ventures in Siberia," *Engineering and Mining Journal-Press*, CXVI (November 10, 1923), 815-816.

37. "Latvian Correspondent" and "Industrial Russia Today," *American Machinist*, LVI (January 26, 1922), 124.

38. *New York Times*, January 16, 1922, 23:5.

39. Williams, *American-Russian Relations*, p. 184.

40. Browder, *Origins of Soviet-American Diplomacy*, pp. 23-24.

41. Jonathan Mitchell, "Trade with Russia Becomes Respectable," *Outlook*, CLII (July 10, 1929), 406-407; Schuman, *American Policy toward Russia*, p. 249. Dobb, *Soviet Economic Development*, p. 172, identifies Nogin.

42. Williams, *American-Russian Relations*, pp. 211-212.

43. American-Russian Chamber of Commerce, *Russia, The American Problem* (New York, n.d. [1920?]); *New York Times*, January 20, 1920, 3:3, and June 24, 1926, 44:2.

44. *New York Times*, July 9, 1923, 3:3, and February 17, 1923, 13:1; *Advance*, VIII (March 7, 1924), 5.

45. "British-American Interests Get Rich Gold Concessions," *Engineering and Mining Journal-Press*, CXIX (May 9, 1925), 778; "Announce Details of Lena Goldfields-Soviet Agreement," *ibid.*, CXIX (June 6, 1925), 938.

46. Williams, *American-Russian Relations*, pp. 212-213; "Harriman Interests Get Russian Manganese Concession Worth Millions," *Engineering and Mining Journal-Press*, CXIX (June 20, 1925), 1021.

47. "Mining Concessions in Russia" (editorial), *Engineering and Mining Journal*, CXI (January 29, 1921), 209; "The Russian Manganese Concession," *ibid.*, CXIX (June 27, 1925), 1033-1034.

48. Williams, *American-Russian Relations*, pp. 212-213; *New York Times*, September 3, 1930, 12:3.

49. "Russia — A Growing Field for American Business," *Magazine of Wall Street*, XXXVI (October 10, 1925), 1077; Schuman, *American Policy toward Russia*, p. 248; Browder, *Origins of Soviet-American Diplomacy*, appendix A, pp. 223-224, table 1.

50. Schuman, *American Policy toward Russia*, p. 253.

51. Theodore M. Knappen, "The Apogee of Strange Partnerships — Soviet Socialists and American Capitalists," *Magazine of Wall Street*, XLIII (January 26, 1929), 591.

52. "Vacuum Oil Defends Trade with Soviet Russia," *Comm. Fin. Chronicle*, CXXV (July 23, 1927), 470-471, 533; also Fischer, *Oil Imperialism*, pp. 125-135.

53. *New York Times*, March 28, 1926, 1:2.

54. Knappen, "Apogee of Strange Partnerships," *Magazine of Wall Street*, XLIII (January 26, 1929), 550-551; Cooper's speech of June

1927 is quoted by Senator Brookhart: *Cong. Rec.*, 70th Cong., 2nd Sess. (January 11, 1929), p. 1571; Charles M. Muchnic, "A Business Man's View of Russia: Letters from an American Executive," *Harper's Magazine*, CLIV (September 1929), 449.

55. H. Parker Willis' article, appearing originally in *New York Journal of Commerce*, inserted into *Cong. Rec.*, 69th Cong., 1st Sess. (June 9, 1926), p. 10985.

56. Isaac Deutscher, *The Prophet Unarmed: Trotsky, 1921–1929* (London, 1959), pp. 222–471. The facts are presented more concisely by Dobb, *Soviet Economic Development*, pp. 181–207.

57. For example, "American Engineers in Russia, and The Claims of Russo-Asiatic Against the Soviet Government" (editorial), *Engineering and Mining Journal*, CXXVIII (November 16, 1929), 761; Joseph Newburger (president of the Newburger Cotton Co. in Memphis, Tenn.) to William E. Borah, November 17, 1924, a letter reprinted in *Cong. Rec.*, 68th Cong., 2nd Sess. (January 7, 1925), p. 1198; *New York Times*, August 20, 1926, 7:2.

58. Henry Ford, *Today and Tomorrow* (Garden City, N.Y., 1926), p. 24; Ford, *My Life and Work* (Garden City, N.Y., 1922), p. 4.

59. Eventually about 200 Russians came to the Rouge plant for training; a somewhat smaller number of Americans went to the USSR, some of them staying five or six years. The first automobile rolled off the Nizhni-Novgorod assembly lines in the early winter of 1933: Allen Nevins and Frank Ernest Hill, *Ford: Expansion and Challenge: 1915–1933* (New York, 1957), pp. 675–683.

60. *Ibid.*, pp. 255, 673–675.

61. Ford, "Why I Am Helping Russian Industry," *Nation's Business*, XVIII (June 1930), 22. He had expressed similar views three years earlier: *New York Times*, November 21, 1927, 15:1.

62. See Curti, *American Philanthropy*, passim.

63. Ford, *Today and Tomorrow*, p. 78, for example.

64. Ford, *My Philosophy of Industry: A Series of Authorized Interviews Written by Fay Leone Faurote* (London, 1929), p. 84; Ford, *Today and Tomorrow*, p. 254.

65. Ford, *My Philosophy of Industry*, pp. 34–35.

66. Ford, *Today and Tomorrow*, p. 167.

67. Bernhard Knollenberg, "American Business in Russia," *Nation's Business*, XVIII (May 1930), 266.

68. Nevins and Hill, *Ford*, p. 603; Maurice Hindus, "Ford Conquers Russia," *Outlook*, CXLVI (June 29, 1927), 280–282; "Henry Ford," *Bolshaya sovetskaya entsiklopediya* (Great Soviet Encyclopedia; Moscow, 1936), LVIII, 128–130.

69. Nevins and Hill, *Ford*, p. 684.

70. Ford, *Today and Tomorrow*, p. 252.

71. *American Industries*, XXX (October 1929), 9. For a discussion of business elitism, see Prothro, *Dollar Decade*, pp. 49–50, 55–59.

72. See, for example, the significant title of William Henry Chamberlin's article: "Missionaries of American Techniques in Russia," *Asia*, XXXII (July–August 1932), 422–427, 460–463.

73. Even the conservative *Comm. Fin. Chronicle* voiced this view: "Broadening of Russia's Concession Policy to Foreigners Viewed as Need for Soviet Capital from Abroad," *Comm. Fin. Chronicle*, CXXVII (September 22, 1928), 1599.

74. For example, Muchnic, "A Business Man's View of Russia," *Harper's*, CLIV (September 1929), 452–453.

75. *14th Annual Meeting of the Chamber of Commerce* (May 11–13, 1926), p. 80. Hoover's statement is in *New York Times*, March 22, 1921, 1:2.

76. Ivy Lee, *Present-Day Russia* (New York, 1928), p. 202. An earlier privately published edition appeared in 1927; its contents was revised in the later edition. Significantly, Muchnic, "A Business Man's View of Russia," *Harper's*, CLIV (September 1929), 441, uses almost identical language.

77. For example, "Soviet Contradictions," *Nation's Business*, XVII (June 1929), 27.

78. See the interesting comments in a debate on the morality of American engineers working mines confiscated from British owners: "American Engineers in Russia" (editorial), *Mining and Metallurgy*, X (December 1929), 551; "American Engineers in Russia . . ." (editorial), *Engineering and Mining Journal*, CXXVIII (November 16, 1929), 761; "A Question of Ethics" (editorial), *Iron Age*, CXXIV (December 12, 1929), 1613–1614.

79. Feather, "A Fourth of July Speech — *New Style*," pp. 13–14.

80. *New York Times*, March 22, 1921, 1:2.

V. DISSIDENT RESPONSES DURING THE NEP

1. Harold Stearns, "The Unending Revolution," *Dial*, LXVI (March 22, 1919), 303.

2. Stearns, "Liberalism Invincible," *ibid.*, LXVI (April 19, 1919), 409.

3. Stearns, *Liberalism in America: Its Origin, Its Temporary Collapse, Its Future* (New York, 1919), esp. pp. 25–31, chaps. 5 and 10.

4. Stearns, *America and the Young Intellectual* (New York, 1921), esp. p. 155 and the chapter entitled "What Can a Young Man Do?" which originally appeared in *Freeman*, I (August 4, 1920), 488–491.

5. Stearns, ed., *Civilization in the United States: An Inquiry by Thirty Americans* (New York, 1922), p. vii.

6. Waldo Frank, *Our America* (New York, 1919), p. 135. Wescott's remark appears in an article in *Transatlantic Review*, II (October 1924), 447, cited by Daniel Aaron, *Writers on the Left: Episodes in American Literary Communism* (New York, 1961), p. 111; Josephson, "American Letter: Some Contemporary Themes," *Transition*, no. 14 (Fall 1928), 63; [Brooks], "A Reviewer's Notebook," *Freeman*, I (May 5, 1920), 191, and "A Reviewer's Notebook," *ibid.*, VIII (March 5, 1924), 623. On the prewar rebellion, see Henry F. May, *The End of American Innocence: A Study of the First Years of Our Own Time, 1912–1917* (New York, 1959). On the lost generation, see William E.

Leuchtenberg, *The Perils of Prosperity, 1914–1932* (Chicago, 1958), esp. pp. 7, 147, 174–76; Frederick J. Hoffman, *The Twenties: American Writing in the Postwar Decade* (New York, 1955); Malcolm Cowley, *Exile's Return: A Narrative of Ideas* (New York, 1934). On the preoccupation with machines, see Leuchtenberg, *Perils of Prosperity*, pp. 151–152; Freeman, *American Testament*, pp. 288–289; Stearns, *America and the Young Intellectual*, pp. 59, 130; Waldo Frank, *The Re-Discovery of America: An Introduction to a Philosophy of American Life* (New York, 1929), pp. 39–43; Eugene Jolas and Elliot Paul, "A Review," *Transition*, no. 12 (March 1928), 139–147. An exception to the general hostility toward machines was the organization, by the editors of *The Little Review*, of the Machine-Age Exposition in 1927, which displayed Soviet architecture: Jane Heap, "Machine Age Exposition," *Little Review*, XI (Spring 1925), 22–24; *New York Times*, May 29, 1927, II, 1:7.

7. Floyd Dell, "The Russian Idea," *Liberator*, V (January 1922), 26.

8. Aaron, *Writers on the Left*, pp. 93–95. For Dell's comment, see Dell, "A Psycho-Analytic Confession," *Liberator*, III (April 1920), 8.

9. Leigh Hoffman, answer to questionnaire, *Transition*, no. 14 (Fall 1928), 100–101.

10. White to Ray Stannard Baker, December 28, 1920, White Papers, Box 57.

11. Colcord to Edward M. House, May 17, 1922, House Papers, Drawer 5.

12. Croly, "The Eclipse of Progressivism," *New Republic*, XXIV (October 27, 1920), 210–216; Croly, "La Follette," *ibid.*, LX (October 26, 1924), 221–224; "Realistic Liberalism" (editorial), *ibid.*, LIII (November 23, 1927), 4–7.

13. From Baldwin's contribution to a symposium entitled "Where Are the Pre-War Radicals?" *Survey*, LV (February 1, 1926), 560.

14. "Back to Russia" (editorial), *Nation*, CXXIX (July 10, 1929), 32. For other examples of liberal opposition, see *New Republic* (editorial), XLII (April 15, 1925), 194; Lincoln Colcord to William E. Borah, December 28, 1920, Borah Papers, Box 209; Oswald Garrison Villard to I. A. A. Kittin, October 20, 1927, Villard Papers.

15. "The Status of Russian Relief," *Survey*, XLIV (June 26, 1920), 431; "Mr. Hoover, Feed Russia!" (editorial), *Nation*, CXII (February 16, 1921), 255; *New York Times*, July 26, 1921, 17:6; "Mr. Hoover's Ultimatum to Russia" (editorial), *World Tomorrow*, IV (August 1921), 228–229.

16. A copy of Magnes' address is in the Robins Papers, Box 17. Copies of his correspondence are also there: Perrin C. Galpin (acting secretary to Hoover) to Magnes, January 8 and 12, 1921; Magnes to Galpin, January 5 and 11, 1921; Wilbur K. Thomas (executive secretary of AFSC) to Magnes, January 12, 1921; Magnes to Norman Davis (Acting Secretary of State), January 14 and 15, 1921; Davis to Magnes, January 20, 1921. *Survey*, XLV (January 22, 1921), 591–592, fully reported Magnes' contentions.

17. Gregory, "Overthrowing a Red Regime," *World's Work*, XLII

(June 1921), 153-164; "Bread and Intervention" (editorial), *Freeman*, III (August 17, 1921), 533.

18. Wilbur K. Thomas to Raymond Robins, September 19 and October 22, 1921; Wardwell to Robins, October 22, 1921: Robins Papers, Box 17. Among the members of the executive committee were Lewis S. Gannett, Joseph Schlossberg, Wilbur K. Thomas, Alexander Trachtenberg. Among the members of the national committee were Jane Addams, Max Danish, Malcolm Davis, Norman Hapgood, Judah Magnes, Gifford Pinchot, Raymond Robins, Julius Rosenwald, Al Smith, Norman Thomas, Oswald Garrison Villard.

19. Forbes, *Quaker Star*, p. 173.

20. *Nation* (editorial), CXIV (February 22, 1922), 208. For background information on Hoover's charges, see G. B. Snell (of the Division of Russian Affairs, State Department) to Samuel N. Harper, January 24, 1922, Harper Papers, Cabinet 1, Drawer 2; *New York Times*, February 9, 1922, 1:6.

21. "Mr. Hoover Stabs Russia" (editorial), *Nation*, CXVI (March 21, 1923), 327; *Survey* (editorials), XLIX (March 1, 1923), 734, and L (April 1, 1923), 49-50.

22. Fisher, *Famine*, pp. 395-396; Forbes, *Quaker Star*, p. 185.

23. *Nation* (editorial), CXVII (November 7, 1923), 501.

24. For example, "The Revival of the Russian Industry," *ibid.*, CXXI (November 11, 1925), 554; "The Stability of the Soviets" (editorial), *New Republic*, XXXVI (February 6, 1924), 272-273; "Russia and the Future" (editorial), *Freeman*, VI (February 28, 1923), 581-582; Scott Nearing, *Glimpses of the Soviet Republic* (New York, 1926), pp. 6-8, 14-15.

25. Steffens to Fremont Older, October 5, 1923; Steffens to G. [Gussie Nobbe], September 11, 1923, in *Letters*, II, 627, 622.

26. "Cerebro-Leninites" (editorial), *Freeman*, III (April 6, 1921), 76.

27. "Ten Years of a Communist State" (editorial), *New Republic*, LII (November 2, 1927), 275; "Communist Theory vs. Russian Fact" (editorial), *ibid.*, LIV (May 16, 1928), 367.

28. John Dewey, *Impressions of Soviet Russia and the Revolutionary World: Mexico — China — Turkey* (New York, 1932), p. 31. The Russia articles originally appeared in *The New Republic* during November–December 1929. They also are reprinted in: Dewey, *Characters and Events: Popular Essays in Social and Political Philosophy*, ed. Joseph Ratner (2 vols., New York, 1929), II, 378-431.

29. George S. Counts, *The American Road to Culture: A Social Interpretation of Education in the United States* (New York, 1930), p. ix.

30. *Nation*, CXXVIII (January 16, 1929), 86.

31. For example, George M. Price, *Labor Protection in Soviet Russia* (New York, 1929); Anna J. Haines, *Health Work in Soviet Russia* (New York, 1928), p. 14; Oswald Garrison Villard, "Russia from a Car Window: V. The Soviets and the Human Being," *Nation*, CXXIX (December 4, 1929), 654-657; Paul H. Douglas, "Labor Legislation and Social Insurance," and Douglas and Robert Dunn, "The Trade

Union Movement," in *Soviet Russia in the Second Decade: A Joint Survey by the Technical Staff of the First American Trade Union Delegation*, ed. Stuart Chase, Robert Dunn, and Rexford Guy Tugwell (New York, 1928), chaps. 9, 8.

32. *New York Times*, December 15, 1927, 31:7.

33. Lillian D. Wald, "Public Health in Soviet Russia," *Survey*, LIII (December 1, 1924), 270–274; Jessica Smith, *Women in Soviet Russia* (New York, 1928); Alice Withrow Field, *Protection of Women and Children in Soviet Russia* (New York, 1932); Haines, *Health Work;* Susan M. Kingsbury and Mildred Fairchild, *Factory, Family and Woman in the Soviet Union* (New York, 1935).

34. Paul Blanshard, "Sex Standards in Moscow," *Nation*, CXXII (May 12, 1926), 522; V. F. Calverton, "Red Love in Soviet Russia," *Modern Quarterly*, IV (November 1927 — February 1928), 180–191; Theodore Dreiser, *Dreiser Looks at Russia* (New York, 1928), pp. 19–21.

35. Maurice B. Hindus, *Humanity Uprooted* (New York, 1929), p. 210; Rose Brisken, "A Case Worker in Russia," *The Family*, XIII (April 1932), 59–62.

36. Sherwood Eddy, *The Challenge of Russia* (New York, 1931), p. 141.

37. Du Bois, "Russia, 1926," *Crisis*, XXXIII (November 1926), 8; Du Bois, "Judging Russia," *ibid.*, XXXIII (February 1927), 189–190. His earlier views appear in Du Bois, "The Negro and Radical Thought," *ibid.*, XXII (July, 1921), 103. In his autobiography, Du Bois declared: "Since that trip my mental outlook and the aspect of the world will never be the same." *Dusk of Dawn: An Essay Toward an Autobiography of a Race Concept* (New York, 1940), p. 287.

38. For example, Villard, "Russia from a Car Window," *Nation*, CXXIX (December 4, 1929), 654–657; Douglas and Dunn, "The Trade Union Movement," and George S. Counts, "Education in Soviet Russia," in *Soviet Russia in the Second Decade*, pp. 193–194, 281–282; Scott Nearing in *Advance*, IX (January 29, 1926), 6–7.

39. John Dos Passos, *In All Countries* (New York, 1934), pp. 59–60. The chapter on Russia assembles scattered articles written during and after his Russian visit of 1928.

40. Lucy L. W. Wilson, "The New Schools in New Russia," *School and Society*, XXIII (March 17, 1926), 316–317.

41. *New York Times*, November 27, 1927, III, 3:5.

42. On illiteracy, see William H. E. Johnson, *Russia's Educational Heritage* (Pittsburgh, 1950), tables 26 and 27, pp. 282–283. On Soviet education generally, see George Z. F. Bereday, William W. Brickman, and Gerald H. Read, eds., *The Changing Soviet School: The Comparative Education Society Field Study in the U.S.S.R.* (Boston, 1960), pp. 51–54, 56; Ruth Widmayer, "The Evolution of Soviet Educational Policy," *Harvard Educational Review*, XXIV (Summer, 1954), 159–175; Abraham Epstein, "The Schools in Soviet Russia," *School and Society*, XVI (October 7, 1922), 393–403. On poor school conditions, see Frank Alfred Golder and Lincoln Hutchinson, *On the Trail of the*

Russian Famine (Stanford, 1927), pp. 232, 242; Leo Pasvolsky, "Education under Communism: The Results of Soviet Education," *Educational Review*, LXII (November 1921), 324–331.

43. William W. Brickman, "John Dewey's Foreign Reputation as an Educator," *School and Society*, LXX (October 22, 1949), 260; Widmayer, "Evolution of Soviet Educational Policy," p. 162. For the views of a high Soviet official in charge of education, see Albert P. Pinkevitch, *The New Education in the Soviet Republic* (New York, 1929), pp. 163–164, 173, 280–285.

44. Wilson, *The New Schools of New Russia* (New York, 1928), p. xiv; Wilson, "New Schools in New Russia," *School and Society*, XXIII (March 13, 1926), 323–324.

45. Dewey, *Impressions of Soviet Russia*, pp. 86, 104–108.

46. George S. Counts, *Secondary Education and Industrialism: The Inglis Lecture, 1929* (Cambridge, Mass., 1929), pp. 4–5. Counts visited Russia in 1927 and again in 1929 for a total of ten months.

47. An address given on December 28, 1916, published as "The Need for Social Psychology" in *Psychological Review* (July 1917), and reprinted in *Characters and Events*, II, 719.

48. Wilson, "New Schools in New Russia," p. 319; *New Schools of New Russia*, pp. 34–35.

49. Counts, "Education in Soviet Russia," in *Soviet Russia in the Second Decade*, pp. 268–270, 274; Counts, *The American Road to Culture*, pp. 186–189; Counts, *The Soviet Challenge to America* (New York, 1931), pp. 322–330.

50. Dewey, *Impressions of Soviet Russia*, pp. 52–54, 128–129.

51. *Ibid.*, pp. 4–10.

52. "John Dewey," *Bolshaya sovetskaya entsiklopediya* (Moscow, 1931), XXIII, 719.

53. The quotation is in Steffens to Marie Howe, January 8, 1926, *Letters*, II, 724. Also Steffens to Jack Hollister, February 21, 1920; to Laura Suggett, March 29, 1920; to Daniel Kiefer, June 21, 1920; to Ella Winter, June 12, 1922; to Gilbert E. Roe, April 16, 1925 — *ibid.*, II, 536, 539–540, 545, 590, 692–693. Steffens, *Moses in Red: The Revolt of Israel as a Typical Revolution* (Philadelphia, 1926).

54. Steffens to Matthew Schmidt, July 20, 1926, *Letters*, II, 758–759.

55. Irving G. Cheslaw, "An Intellectual Biography of Lincoln Steffens," unpub. diss., Columbia University, 1952, pp. 264–265, 186. I have gained many insights into Steffens' thought from this study as well as from Alfred B. Rollins, Jr., "The Heart of Lincoln Steffens," *South Atlantic Quarterly*, LIX (Spring 1960), 239–250.

56. Emma Goldman, *The Truth about the Boylsheviki* (New York, n.d. [1918]), pp. 4, 5, 11.

57. Goldman, *My Disillusionment in Russia* (Garden City, N.Y., 1923), and *My Further Disillusionment in Russia* (Garden City, N.Y., 1924), passim. The quoted phrases appear in the former volume, pp. 73, v. For Berkman's parallel reaction, see Berkman, *The Bolshevik Myth* (*Diary, 1920–1922*) (New York, 1925).

58. Goldman, *My Disillusionment*, p. 132.

59. From a letter to *Humanité* in Autumn 1921, cited in Irma Duncan and Alan Ross Macdougall, *Isadora Duncan's Russian Days and Her Last Years in France* (New York, 1929), p. 66.

60. Henry G. Alsberg, "Tyranny by Prophets," *Nation*, CXI (September 4, 1920), 269.

61. Paxton Hibben, *Reconstruction in Russia: An Address before the Forum of the Community Church of New York City, Easter Sunday, 1925* (New York, 1925), pp. 16–17.

62. Jerome Davis, "The System of Government in Soviet Russia," *Current History*, XXVII (December 1927), 382.

63. Villard to Frank E. Gannett, May 15, 1925, Villard Papers.

64. For example, James G. McDonald, in McDonald, Stuart Chase, and Rev. Edmund A. Walsh, *Soviet Russia After Ten Years: A Stenographic Report of the 99th New York Luncheon Discussion, November 19, 1927, of the Foreign Policy Association* (Pamphlet 47, December, 1927; New York, 1927); Harry F. Ward, "Civil Liberties in Russia," *Nation*, CXX (March 4, 1925), 236–237.

65. Roger Baldwin, *Liberty under the Soviets* (New York, 1928), p. 4.

66. *Ibid.*, p. 4.

67. *New Republic* (editorial), XXXIV (April 18, 1923), 197.

68. "Lenin — and After" (editorial), *Nation*, CXVI (March 28, 1923), 354; *ibid.* (editorial), CXVI (April 11, 1923), 403–404.

69. *Ibid.* (editorial), CXX (February 11, 1925), 132.

70. *New Leader* (editorial), IV (November 26, 1927), 8; "Dictatorship or Democracy in Russia" (editorial), *New Republic*, LI (August 10, 1927), 295–296.

71. *New York Times*, October 18, 1926, 1:2, 5:4. For further information on Eastman, see Aaron, *Writers on the Left*, pp. 121–125.

72. "Something New in the World" (editorial), *Nation*, CXXV (November 9, 1927), 494–495.

73. Brent Dow Allinson, "From the Cultural Front in Russia," *Dial*, LXXXV (September 1928), 245.

74. Phrases are taken from "Ten Years of a Communist State" (editorial), *New Republic*, LII (November 2, 1927), 276; Stuart Chase, "Industry and the Gosplan," in *Soviet Russia in the Second Decade*, p. 49; Dewey, *Impressions of Soviet Russia*, p. 120; Baldwin, *Liberty*, p. 60; Marguerite Tucker, "Are People in Russia Happy?" *New Masses*, IV (November 1928), 9. Dewey's statement is from *Impressions of Soviet Russia*, p. 38.

75. Dewey, *Impressions of Soviet Russia* p. 121.

76. Villard, "Russia from a Car Window," *Nation*, CXXIX (December 4, 1929), 654.

77. Heywood Broun, "It Seems to Heywood Broun," *ibid.*, CXXXI (July 16, 1930), 59.

78. Joseph Wood Krutch, *The Modern Temper: A Study and a Confession* (New York, 1929), pp. 240–245.

VI. LABOR AND PROLETARIAN RUSSIA

1. Quoted from a letter by Gompers to William Mitch (secretary, District No. 11, United Mine Workers). The letter is reprinted in *American Federationist*, XXVII (May 1920), 437–438.

2. Philip Taft, *The A.F. of L. in the Time of Gompers* (New York, 1957), pp. 233, 362.

3. Louis S. Reed, *The Labor Philosophy of Samuel Gompers* (New York, 1930), chap. 4. Its startling resemblance to Henry Ford's insistence on industrial autonomy indicates just how moderate Gompers' theory was. See Chapter Four for a discussion of Ford's ideas.

4. Marguerite Green, *The National Civic Federation and the American Labor Movement, 1900–1925* (Washington, D.C., 1956), passim; Taft, *A.F. of L. in the Time of Gompers*, pp. 225–231.

5. Reed, *Labor Philosophy*, p. 153. Also Samuel Gompers, *Seventy Years of Life and Labor: An Autobiography* (2 vols., New York, 1925), II, 405; Shannon, *Socialist Party*, pp. 81–122.

6. Gompers, *Seventy Years*, II, 400.

7. Samuel Gompers and William English Walling, *Out of Their Own Mouths: A Revelation and Indictment of Sovietism* (New York, 1921).

8. Reed, *Labor Philosophy*, pp. 168–169. The quotation is from Gompers and Matthew Woll, "The European Brainstorm," *American Federationist*, XXVII (October 1920), 919–920.

9. Gompers and Walling, *Out of Their Own Mouths*, pp. 224–225.

10. Gompers, *American Federationist* (editorial), XXXI (June 1924), 481. Taft, *A.F. of L. in the Time of Gompers*, p. 231, seeks to minimize Gompers' intolerance toward dissenters, but his case is not convincing.

11. For example, Gompers' speech at the 43rd Annual Convention, *Report of the Proceedings of the Annual Conventions of the American Federation of Labor* [hereafter cited as *Proceedings of AF of L*] (October 1–21, 1923), pp. 300–302.

12. Gompers, *Seventy Years*, II, 402; Gompers, *American Federationist* (editorial), XXVI (December 1919), 1131; Reed, *Labor Philosophy*, p. 36; Gompers and Walling, *Out of Their Own Mouths*, pp. 14–15, 79, 134.

13. Philip Taft, *The A.F. of L., from the Death of Gompers to the Merger* (New York, 1959), p. 2. Irving Bernstein, *The Lean Years: A History of the American Worker, 1920–1933* (Boston, 1960), pp. 83–90, 97–108, fully describes the decline.

14. Harwood Lawrence Childs, *Labor and Capital in National Politics* (Columbus, Ohio, 1930), pp. 54–55.

15. For example, 45th Annual Convention, *Proceedings of AF of L* (October 5–16, 1925), pp. 336–337; 47th Annual Convention, *ibid.* (October 3–14, 1927), p. 193.

16. 43rd Annual Convention, *ibid.* (October 1–12, 1923), pp. 296–302; 44th Annual Convention, *ibid.* (November 17–25, 1924), pp. 287–

293; 45th Annual Convention, *ibid.* (October 5–16, 1925), pp. 334–337; 46th Annual Convention, *ibid.* (October 4–14, 1926), pp. 262–279.

17. J. O. Holderman to Borah, March 5, 1918, Borah Papers, Box 191.

18. *New York Times*, January 27, 1921, 17:6.

19. Resolution by Local Union No. 702, Brotherhood of Painters, Decorators and Paperhangers of America, Taft, California, April 19, 1921; H. H. Freedheim, Central Labor Union, Twin Falls, Idaho, to Borah, February 27, 1921; James N. Jody [? — signature illegible] (secretary-treasurer of Pensacola, Florida, Trades and Labor Council) to Borah — Borah Papers, Box 209. Also, petitions to the Senate Foreign Relations Committee from Wisconsin State Federation of Labor, Milwaukee, August 9, 1922, and from United Cloth Hat and Cap Makers of North America, Local No. 10, St. Paul, Minnesota, December 12, 1922 — National Archives, Record Group 46.

20. 16th Convention, *Proceedings of the Conventions of the International Association of Machinists* (September 20 — October 6, 1920), pp. 272–275.

21. For example, 39th Annual Convention, *Proceedings of AF of L* (June 9–23, 1919), pp. 332–334.

22. 42nd Annual Convention, *ibid.* (June 12–14, 1922), pp. 420–437 (quotation on p. 430). Hayes was a prominent socialist, and Healy was head of the American Labor Alliance for Trade with Russia: David J. Saposs, *Left Wing Unionism: A Study of Radical Policies and Tactics* (New York, 1926), p. 34; Green, *National Civic Federation*, pp. 464–465.

23. 42nd Annual Convention, *Proceedings of AF of L* (June 12–14, 1922), pp. 459–462.

24. Joseph Schlossberg, *The Workers and Their World: Aspects of the Workers' Struggle at Home and Abroad, Selected Essays by Joseph Schlossberg* (New York, 1935), p. 179. For information on Schlossberg, see Matthew Josephson, *Sidney Hillman: Statesman of American Labor* (New York, 1952), pp. 105, 138, 453.

25. Josephson, *Hillman*, p. 136.

26. *Ibid.*, chap. 4, esp. pp. 105–110; Epstein, *Jewish Labor in U.S.A.*, pp. 40–47.

27. *Advance*, V (August 12, 1921), 4.

28. Epstein, *Jewish Labor in U.S.A.*, pp. 64–68; Schwarz, *Jews in the Soviet Union*, p. 98.

29. Josephson, *Hillman*, pp. 70, 80–82, 89, 93, 190–192, 317–324; also George Soule, *Sidney Hillman, Labor Statesman* (New York, 1930), pp. 213–214.

30. *Advance*, VI (May 26, 1922), 5.

31. *Ibid.*, V (November 18, 1921), 2.

32. 5th Biennial Convention, *Documentary History of the Amalgamated Clothing Workers of America* [hereafter cited as *Documentary History*] (May 8–13, 1922), pp. 366–367; reprinted in *Advance*, VI (May 26, 1922), 5.

33. For comments on human nature, see *Advance*, V (December 9, 1921), 5.

34. Neither Josephson nor Epstein perceives the persistence of this side of Hillman's character during the 1920's: for example, Josephson, *Hillman*, chap. 13; Epstein, *Jewish Labor in U.S.A.*, pp. 392–393.

35. 5th Biennial Convention, *Documentary History* (May 8–13, 1922), p. 366. Also in *Advance*, VI (May 26, 1922), 5.

36. *Ibid.*, VI (May 19, 1922), 5; *New York Times*, May 12, 1922, 11:2.

37. *Advance*, VI (February 2, 1923), 1. But the total never exceeded $300,000: Josephson, *Hillman*, p. 262.

38. *New York Times*, December 5, 1922, 1:2; Josephson, *Hillman*, pp. 60–64.

39. *New York Times*, December 6, 1922, 6:1.

40. *Advance*, VI (December 8, 1922), 8.

41. 6th Biennial Convention, *Documentary History* (May 12–17, 1924), pp. 278–279; 7th Biennial Convention, *ibid.* (May 10–15, 1926), p. 237; 8th Biennial Convention, *ibid.* (May 14–18, 1928), p. 238.

42. For example, *Advance*, VIII (November 7, 1924), 4; XI (November 26, 1926), 6–7; XV (January 25, 1929), 1, 3.

43. Charles A. Madison, *American Labor Leaders: Personalities and Forces in the Labor Movement*, 2nd ed. (New York, 1962), pp. 212–213.

44. *Justice*, I (August 9, 1919), 5.

45. *Ibid.*, II (June 25, 1920), 4. Actually, comparison of the 1919 and 1920 resolutions shows an increase in hostility: 39th Annual Convention, *Proceedings of AF of L* (June 9–23, 1919), pp. 332–333; 40th Annual Convention, *ibid.* (June 7–19, 1920), pp. 367–369.

46. *Justice*, II (April 16, 1920), 4.

47. *Ibid.*, II (October 8, 1920), 4–5.

48. 15th Convention, *Reports and Proceedings of the Convention of the International Ladies' Garment Workers' Union* [hereafter cited as *Proceedings of ILGWU*] (May 3–15, 1920), p. 106; 16th Convention, *ibid.* (May 1–12, 1922), p. 129.

49. *Justice*, II (November 19, 1920), 5.

50. The material of the next two paragraphs, except where indicated, is taken primarily from Theodore Draper, *American Communism and Soviet Russia* (New York, 1960), pp. 5, 25–51, 64–76, 215–216; Saposs, *Left Wing Unionism*, pp. 48–65; J. B. S. Hardman, ed., *American Labor Dynamics, in the Light of Post-War Developments: An Inquiry by Thirty-Two Labor Men, Teachers, Editors, and Technicians* (New York, 1928), chap. 1; David M. Schneider, *The Workers' (Communist) Party and American Trade Unions* (Baltimore, 1928), passim; Irving Howe and Lewis Coser, *The American Communist Party: A Critical History (1919–1957)* (Boston, 1957), pp. 236–272.

51. For Lewis' views, see *United Mine Workers Journal*, XXXV (February 15, 1924), 7. For the attitudes of the conventions and the *Journal*, see *ibid.*, XXXIV (November 15, 1923), 6; XXXV (February 1, 1924), 7, 19; XXXVIII (February 15, 1927), 9–10. For details on the union's struggle with the Communists, see United Mine Workers of

America, *Attempt by Communists to Seize the American Labor Movement* (Washington, D.C., 1923), and Schneider, *Workers' (Communist) Party*, chap. 3.

52. Epstein, *Jewish Labor in U.S.A.*, pp. 124–125.

53. Max D. Danish, *The World of David Dubinsky* (Cleveland, 1957), p. 48; Epstein, *Jewish Labor in U.S.A.*, pp. 366–375; Madison, *American Labor Leaders*, pp. 214–216. The latter regards Schlesinger as overbenevolent rather than capricious.

54. *Justice*, VII (June 19, 1925), 6.

55. *Ibid.*, VI (July 4, 1924), 7–8; VI (July 25, 1924), 6; VII (June 19, 1925), 6; Epstein, *Jewish Labor in U.S.A.*, pp. 138–141; Danish, *World of Dubinsky*, pp. 49–53.

56. *Justice*, VIII (November 26, 1926), 6; VIII (December 3, 1926), 1; IX (January 7, 1927), 4; IX (January 14, 1927), 4; Danish, *World of Dubinsky*, pp. 53–55; Epstein, *Jewish Labor in U.S.A.*, pp. 144–148.

57. *Justice*, VII (November 27, 1925), 4. For comments on socialists, see *ibid.*, IV (August 4, 1922), 4.

58. 17th Convention, *Proceedings of ILGWU* (May 5–17, 1924), p. 245.

59. 18th Convention, *ibid.* (November 30 — December 17, 1925), p. 225; 19th Convention, *ibid.* (May 7–17, 1928), p. 91; 21st Convention, *ibid.* (May 2–14, 1932), pp. 195–196.

60. Epstein, *Jewish Labor in U.S.A.*, pp. 163–165; Josephson, *Hillman*, pp. 274–281; Schneider, *Workers' (Communist) Party*, chap. 4; Draper, *American Communism*, pp. 221–233; 7th Biennial Convention, Report of the General Executive Board, *Documentary History* (May 10–15, 1926), pp. 66–72.

61. *Advance*, XI (November 26, 1926), 6–7.

62. 6th Biennial Convention, *Documentary History* (May 12–17, 1924), p. 279; 7th Biennial Convention, *ibid.* (May 10–15, 1926), p. 337; 8th Biennial Convention, *ibid.* (May 14–19, 1928), p. 237. The only convention not passing a resolution on Russia was that of 1932.

63. On RAIC, see Josephson, *Hillman*, p. 265. For Hillman's comments on Russia, see *Advance*, IX (November 27, 1925), 6, 8.

64. *Ibid.*, IX (March 12, 1926), 11; XIII (October 28, 1927), 6.

65. *Ibid.*, XV (January 25, 1929), 3. For information on Hardman, see Epstein, *Jewish Labor in U.S.A.*, pp. 6, 110–113, 298.

66. *Advance*, XV (January 25, 1929), 1.

67. *Ibid.*, XVI (November 14, 1930), 1, 7.

68. A group of radical labor leaders, for example, calling themselves the American Trade Union Delegation, although bitterly disowned by both the AF of L and the United Mine Workers, visited the USSR in 1927. After loud praise for the social privileges and economic freedom of the Soviet working class, they defended the absence of political freedom by arguing that the workers "do not particularly resent the refusal of the government to allow them the privilege of voting for a capitalist party which would take most of this economic freedom which has been given them by the revolution." *Russia after Ten Years: Report of the American Trade Union Delegation to the Soviet Union*

357

(New York, 1927), p. 77 and passim, esp. pp. 12–16, 32, 34–37, 43–46. For the views of the AF of L and the UMW, see *New York Times*, July 10, 1926, 28:5, and May 28, 1927, 7:2; *United Mine Workers Journal*, XXXVIII (September 15, 1927), 6.

69. *Advance*, XVIII (November 1932), 5.

70. *Ibid.*, XVI (February 7, 1930), 8; XVI (July 4, 1930), 8.

71. *Justice*, XII (December 5, 1930), 4; XIII (January 2, 1931), 5.

72. "6,000 Artisans Going to Russia Glad to Take Wages in Roubles," *Business Week* (September 2, 1931), 36–37. Of these numbers, about 85 per cent were American citizens but 60 per cent were born abroad, primarily in Eastern Europe.

73. See Chapter Seven.

74. Howe and Coser, *American Communist Party*, pp. 253–272.

75. *Justice*, XIII (September 1931), 5–6.

76. For example, *Advance*, XVI (January 31, 1930), 2, and XVII (November 13, 1931), 5; *Justice*, XIII (January 16, 1931), 4.

77. 51st Annual Convention, *Proceedings of AF of L* (October 5–15, 1931), pp. 163–164.

78. I disagree here with Lewis S. Feuer, "Travelers to the Soviet Union, 1917–1932: The Formation of a Component of New Deal Ideology," *American Quarterly*, XIV (Summer 1962), 119–149. Feuer asserts that the Soviet experiment had an enormous effect on American labor because of the Depression (p. 136).

79. *Advance*, XVI (May 2, 1930), 7.

80. Hillman, "Labor Leads toward Planning," *Survey*, LXVII (March 1, 1932), 586–588; *Establishment of a National Economic Council: Hearings before a Subcommittee of the Committee on Manufactures*, United States Senate, 72nd Cong., 1st Sess., on S. 6215 (71st Cong.), A Bill to Establish a National Economic Council, October 22–December 19, 1931 [hereafter cited as *National Economic Council*] (Washington, D.C., 1932), pp. 434–438; Josephson, *Hillman*, pp. 242–255.

81. *Justice*, XIII (January 16, 1931), 4.

82. *Advance*, XIX (August 1933), 23, 42.

83. *Ibid.*, XIX (September 1933), 2–3, 16–17, 27; *Justice*, XV (August 1, 1933), 1–5.

84. The first quotation comes from an unsigned editorial probably written by Hardman, *Advance*, XIX (October 1933), 4; the second comes from a signed editorial, XIX (October 1933), 5.

85. This phrase is from Charles W. Ervin, "Two Months of Mr. Roosevelt," *ibid.*, XIX (May 1933), 12, 23.

VII. DISSIDENT RESPONSES DURING THE FIVE-YEAR PLAN

1. Steffens to Ella Winter, August 16, 1930, in *Letters*, II, 880.

2. Matthew Josephson, "The Road of Indignation," *New Republic*, LXVI (February 18, 1931), 15.

3. Quoted by Robert H. Elias, *Theodore Dreiser: Apostle of Nature* (New York, 1949), p. 217.

4. Dreiser to Gold, September 19, 1928, in *Letters of Theodore*

Dreiser: A Selection, ed. Robert H. Elias (3 vols., Philadelphia, 1959), II, 474.

5. Dreiser et al., *Harlan Miners Speak: Report on Terrorism in the Kentucky Coal Fields Prepared by Members of the National Committee for the Defense of Political Prisoners* (New York, 1932), pp. 12–16.

6. "The Pulse of Modernity" (editorial), *Modern Quarterly,* VI (Summer 1932), 5–6; "Whither the American Writer," *ibid.,* 11–19. Granville Hicks, Newton Arvin, and Sherwood Anderson also expressed no inhibitions about joining the party. I have ignored one anonymous respondent to the survey.

7. Aaron, *Writers on the Left,* p. 160.

8. "How I Came to Communism: Symposium," *New Masses,* VIII (September 1932), 7–10.

9. Dreiser, *Dreiser Looks at Russia,* pp. 97–98, 115, 121, 123, 195–197, 245, 249, 250, 261.

10. Dreiser, *Tragic America* (New York, 1931), pp. 296, 417.

11. Elias, *Theodore Dreiser,* pp. 253–257; Dreiser, *Harlan Miners Speak,* pp. 3–16.

12. Aaron, *Writers on the Left,* p. 335.

13. Frank, *Re-Discovery of America,* p. 19. On Frank's background, see Aaron, *Writers on the Left,* pp. 192–193.

14. Frank, *Dawn in Russia: The Record of a Journey* (New York, 1932), pp. 232–233.

15. *Ibid.,* pp. 88, 13–14, 35–36, 135.

16. *Ibid.,* pp. 117–118.

17. *Ibid.,* pp. 158–160, 164.

18. *Ibid.,* pp. 230, 272.

19. Dell, "The Russian Idea," *Liberator,* V (January 1922), 26.

20. "How I Came to Communism," p. 7.

21. E. E. Cummings, *EIMI* (New York, 1933), p. 16.

22. *Ibid.,* p. 413.

23. Aaron, *Writers on the Left,* pp. 269–399.

24. Villard to Sedgwick, March 14, 1930, Villard Papers.

25. For example, see the comments of John Dewey, *Individualism Old and New* (New York, 1930), pp. 52, 60.

26. Louis Fischer, "Russia's New Revolution," *Nation,* CXXX (March 19, 1930), 322–323.

27. Bruce Bliven, "Russia in Hope," *New Republic,* LXIX (December 2, 1931), 60; Bliven, "Religion and Love in Russia," *ibid.,* LXIX (December 23, 1931), 151.

28. Robins to Samuel Levinson, Moscow, June 8, 1933, cited in Meiburger, *Efforts of Raymond Robins,* p. 172.

29. Harry F. Ward, *In Place of Profit: Social Incentives in the Soviet Union* (New York, 1933), pp. 96–97. See also, for example, Louis Fischer, *Machines and Men in Russia* (New York, 1932), pp. 65, 140–142; E. C. Lindeman, "Is Human Nature Changing in Russia?" *New Republic,* LXXIV (March 8, 1933), 95–98; Joshua Kunitz, "Food in Russia," *ibid.,* LXXIV (April 12, 1933), 232–234.

30. Ella Winter, *Red Virtue: Human Relationships in the New Russia* (New York, 1933), p. 39.

31. Jerome Davis, "A Critique of Russian Communism," *World Tomorrow*, XIII (January 1930), 23. See also Frankwood Williams, "Russia — A Nation of Adolescents," *Survey*, LXVIII (April 1, 1932), 9–10; George S. Counts, *A Ford Crosses Soviet Russia* (Boston, 1930), p. 174; Oswald Garrison Villard, "Our Attitude toward Russia," *Nation*, CXXXI (August 13, 1930), 173.

32. Colcord to Edward M. House, October 10, 1931, House Papers, Drawer 5.

33. Edmund Wilson, "An Appeal to Progressives," *New Republic*, LXV (January 14, 1931), 234–238, reprinted with slight changes in Wilson, *The Shores of Light: A Literary Chronicle of the Twenties and Thirties* (New York, 1952), pp. 524–532. On Wilson's background, see Aaron, *Writers on the Left*, pp. 180–183. For Granville Hicks's later evaluation of the significance of Wilson's article, see his comments cited in *ibid.*, pp. 438–439, n. 2.

34. "Russia Discards from Strength" (editorial), *New Republic*, LXVII (July 22, 1931), 247–248; "Leaders — Russian and American" (editorial), *ibid.*, LXVII (August 12, 1931), 327–329; "Toward an American Fascism" (editorial), *ibid.*, LXXI (June 1, 1932), 59.

35. Villard, "If I Were Dictator," *Nation*, CXXXIV (January 20, 1932), 67–70. Also "The Five-Year Plan" (editorial), *ibid.*, CXXX (May 14, 1930), 561–562; "We Need Russia" (editorial), *ibid.*, CXXXII (June 24, 1931), 669.

36. Rexford G. Tugwell, "Experimental Control in Russian Industry," *Political Science Quarterly*, XLIII (June 1928), 183 and passim; Scott Nearing and Jack Hardy, *The Economic Organization of the Soviet Union* (New York, 1927), pp. xix, xx, 46; Stuart Chase, "Russia's 'War Industries Board,'" *New Republic*, LIII (January 4, 1928), 185; Paul H. Douglas, Lewis L. Lorwin, Z. Clark Dickinson, and Joseph M. Pavloff, "The Russian Economic Situation — Discussion," *American Economic Review*, XIX, supplement (March 1929), pp. 110–130, Papers and Proceedings of the 41st Annual Meeting of the American Economic Association, December 1928.

37. For typical hostile views, see Samuel H. Cross, "The Outlook for the Five-Year Plan," *Harvard Business Review*, IX (January 1931), 169–177; Paul Haensel, in Susan M. Kingsbury, Mildred Fairchild, Calvin B. Hoover, et al., "Russian Economic Situation," *American Economic Review*, XXI, supplement (March 1931), 52-53, Papers and Proceedings of the 43rd Annual Meeting of the American Economic Association, December 1930. For typical favorable views, see Calvin B. Hoover, "The Soviet Challenge to Capitalism," *Harper's*, CLXI (October 1930), 588–598; Fabian Franklin, book review, *Saturday Review of Literature*, VIII (July 16, 1932), 837–838; A. F. Hinrichs, "Russia's Challenge to America," *Atlantic Monthly*, CXLVIII (July 1931), 107–115; Maxwell S. Stewart, "Good News from Russia," *New Republic*, LXXVI (October 11, 1933), 230–232; Gordon S. Watkins,

"Glimpses of Russia under the Soviets: Whither Russia?" *Social Science*, VI (July 1931), 293.

38. Tugwell, "The Principle of Planning and the Institution of Laissez-Faire," *American Economic Review*, XXII, supplement (March 1932), 92, Papers and Proceedings of the 44th Annual Meeting of the American Economic Association, December 1931.

39. Tugwell, letter to the editor, *New Republic*, XLVIII (October 13, 1926), 222; Tugwell, "America's War-Time Socialism," *Nation*, CXXIV (April 6, 1927), 364–367; Tugwell, *The Industrial Discipline and the Governmental Arts* (New York, 1933), esp. chap. 8.

40. William Trufant Foster, "Planning in a Free Country: Managed Money and Unmanaged Men," p. 51, in "National and World Planning," *Annals*, CLXII (July 1932).

41. Beard's plan originally appeared in *Forum*, LXXXVI (July 1931), 1–12, and is reprinted in Charles A. Beard, ed., *America Faces the Future* (Boston, 1932), pp. 117–140. On Beard's intellectual evolution, see Beard, "Rushlights in Darkness," *Scribner's*, XC (December 1931), 577–578, and Bernard C. Borning, *The Political and Social Thought of Charles A. Beard* (Seattle, 1962), pp. 9, 64, 104–105.

42. For example, Stuart Chase, *A New Deal* (New York, 1932), pp. 153–192; Dewey, *Individualism*, pp. 95, 118–120; George Soule, *A Planned Society* (New York, 1932).

43. *Ibid.*, p. 184. This book was a collection of Soule's articles published in 1931–1932. For confirmation, see Arthur M. Schlesinger, Jr., *The Age of Roosevelt: The Coming of the New Deal* (Boston, 1958), pp. 87–88, 93; William E. Leuchtenberg, *Franklin D. Roosevelt and the New Deal, 1932–1940* (New York, 1963), p. 57.

44. Edmund Wilson, "What Do the Liberals Hope For?" *New Republic*, LXIX (February 10, 1932), 345–348.

45. "Fourteen Years" (editorial), *New Masses*, VII (November 1931), 5. For a typical radical critique of liberal planning, see Robert Briffault, "The Anatomy of Liberalism," *Modern Monthly*, VII (April 1933), 154–159.

46. Steffens, "Bankrupt Liberalism," *New Republic*, LXX (February 17, 1932), 15.

47. The convention resolutions are quoted in Shannon, *Socialist Party*, pp. 211–212; Hillquit's statement is in *New York Times*, November 24, 1930, 9:1; on party history, see Daniel Bell, "The Background and Development of Marxian Socialism in the United States," in *Socialism and American Life*, ed. Donald Drew Egbert and Stow Persons (2 vols., Princeton, N.J., 1952), I, 369–371.

48. *New Leader*, XIII (March 5, 1932), 16. For a typical criticism of the USSR by Thomas, see *ibid.*, XII (February 7, 1931), 1.

49. Anna Bercowitz, "The Milwaukee Convention," *American Socialist Quarterly*, I (Summer 1932), 50. For the text of the resolution, see Shannon, *Socialist Party*, pp. 215–216.

50. "Whither the American Writer," *Modern Quarterly*, VI (Summer 1932), 11.

51. Aaron, *Writers on the Left*, pp. 196–198. The full list of signers is given on p. 422, n. 64.

52. George S. Counts, *Dare the School Build a New Social Order?* (New York, 1932), p. 23.

53. Margaret F. Gutelius, letter to the editor, *Nation*, CXXXIV (January 13, 1932), 47.

54. Arthur M. Schlesinger, Jr., *The Age of Roosevelt: The Crisis of the Old Order, 1919–1933* (Boston, 1957), pp. 198–199; Paul H. Douglas, *The Coming of a New Party* (New York, 1932), esp. chaps. 5–8.

55. Dewey, *Individualism*, pp. 33–34; Dewey, "Who Might Make a New Party?" *New Republic*, LXVI (April 1, 1931), 178, and "Policies for a New Party," *ibid.*, LXVI (April 8, 1931), 203–205.

56. George S. Counts, *The Social Foundations of Education* (part 9 of *Report of the American Historical Association Commission on the Social Studies;* New York, 1934), pp. 527–531.

57. Counts, *Dare the School*, pp. 7–10, 17 (quotation on pp. 9–10). This is a pamphlet containing Counts's association address and two others. On the background to Counts's actions, see Lawrence A. Cremin, *The Transformation of the School: Progressivism in American Education, 1876–1957* (New York, 1961), pp. 227–228, 259–264.

58. William H. Kilpatrick, ed., *The Educational Frontier: Written in Collaboration by William H. Kilpatrick, Boyd H. Bode, John L. Childs, H. Gordon Hullfish, John Dewey, R. B. Raup, V. T. Thayer* (New York, 1933), esp. pp. 22–25, 72; Cremin, *Transformation*, p. 230.

59. Schlesinger, *Crisis of the Old Order*, p. 436.

60. "Godlessness and Humbuggery" (editorial), *Nation*, CXXX (March 5, 1930), 260; *ibid.* (editorial), CXXX (March 19, 1930), 313. Although at first critical, *The New Republic* quickly became apologetic: (editorial), LXII (February 26, 1930), 28–29; "Russia and Religion" (editorial), *ibid.*, LXII (March 5, 1930), 59–60.

61. "Class Justice" (editorial), *Nation*, CXXXVI (May 3, 1933), 490; "From Breadline to Millionaire" (editorial), *New Republic*, LXV (December 3, 1930), 57–58, and (editorial), LXXIV (May 3, 1933), 320–321.

62. *New Republic* (editorial), LXXII (October 26, 1932), 271.

63. For example, "Why Do We Boycott Russia?" (editorial), *ibid.*, LX (March 16, 1932), 112–113; Oswald Garrison Villard, "Recognize Russia," *Nation*, CXXXIV (May 18, 1932), 558.

64. For examples of advocacy of recognition, see Louis Fischer, *Why Recognize Russia? The arguments for and against the Recognition of the Soviet Government by the United States* (New York, 1931); Lincoln Colcord to Edward M. House, January 13, 1931, House Papers, Drawer 5. For evidence of obduracy in Washington, see Samuel N. Harper to Walter Duranty, October 30, 1929, Harper Papers, Cabinet 1, Drawer 3.

65. *New York Times*, July 26, 1933, 1:2; October 6, 1931, 12:7.

66. Borah to Gumberg, November 9, 1932, Gumberg Papers, Box 10A.

67. Jerome Davis to Borah, March 20 and 21, 1933, Borah Papers, Box 352; Davis to Robins, April 5, 1933, Robins Papers, Box 25; Robins

to Gumberg, July 16, 1933; Gumberg to Philip F. La Follette, July 17, 1933; La Follette to Gumberg, July 19, 1933; Robins to Gumberg, August 8, 1933; La Follette to Gumberg, August 17, 1933; Robins to Gumberg, September 1, 1933 — all in Gumberg Papers, Box 10B; Harper to Bullitt, October 28, 1933, Harper Papers, Cabinet 1, Drawer 4. Robins also made a nationwide radio address about the USSR and in favor of recognition: MS, July 26, 1933, Robins Papers, Box 25.

68. *New York Times*, January 10, 4:6; March 25, 4:6; May 15, 7:1 — all 1933; Margaret I. Lamont, letter to the editor, *New Republic*, LXXIV (March 22, 1933), 162; Margaret I. Lamont (executive secretary of the committee) to William Allen White, May 13, 1933, White Papers, Box 148.

69. *Nation* (editorial), CXXXVII (November 1, 1933), 495; Browder, *Origins of Soviet-American Diplomacy*, pp. 108–112, discusses the trade and peace reasons, stressing the second as the Administration's basic motive. Browder minimizes the role of the Nazi threat. On p. 119 he also cites favorable public opinion, which I discuss in Chapter Nine. Williams, *American-Russian Relations*, p. 237, gives more weight to the trade motive.

70. Scrapbooks, reel 7, n.d. [November 16, 1933], Borah Papers.

71. "American Recognition of Soviet Union Ends Seventeen Years' Official Duplicity," *New Leader*, XVI (November 25, 1933), 3.

72. *Nation* (editorial), CXXXVII (November 29, 1933), 607.

73. "Russia and America Strike Hands" (editorial), *New Republic*, LXXVII (November 29, 1933), 61.

VIII. BUSINESS LEADERS AND THE PLAN

1. 35th Annual Convention, *Proceedings of NAM* (October 6–9, 1930), p. 12.

2. *National Economic Council*, p. 373.

3. See the caustic and illuminating analysis by Prothro, *Dollar Decade*, pp. 213–221.

4. White to Allen, December 9, 1931, White Papers, Box 136.

5. Gilbert Seldes, *The Years of the Locust: America, 1929–1932* (Boston, 1933), p. 6; Edward Angly, "Prophets without Foresight," in *America Faces the Future*, ed. Beard, pp. 59–69.

6. "The Real Issue," *Business Week*, (October 29, 1930), 40. For the same theme, see Benjamin A. Javits, *Business and the Public Interest: Trade Associations, the Anti-Trust Laws and Industrial Planning* (New York, 1932), p. 188; Wallace Brett Donham, *Business Adrift* (New York, 1931), p. 165.

7. For example, Elisha M. Friedman, *Russia in Transition: A Business Man's Appraisal* (New York, 1932), p. 487.

8. James B. Clark, "Is This Anybody's Business?" *Journal of the American Bankers' Association*, XXIII (March 1931), 737–739.

9. William N. Loucks, "Public Works, Planning and Economic Control: Federal, State, and Municipal," *Annals*, CLXII (July 1932), 114.

10. The Maple Flooring Manufacturers' Association Case and the

10. The Maple Flooring Manufacturers' Association Case and the Cement Manufacturers' Protective Association Case. Charles C. Chapman, *The Development of American Business and Banking Thought, 1913–1936* (New York, 1936), pp. 125–126; George Soule, *Prosperity Decade: From War to Depression, 1917–1929* (vol. VIII of *The Economic History of the United States*; 9 vols., New York, 1947), pp. 140–141.

11. "What Really Matters" (editorial), *Business Week* (November 20, 1929), 52; "The Castor-Oil School of Economics" (editorial), *ibid.* (July 9, 1930), 40, italics added; "Relief Reflections" (editorial), *ibid.* (February 18, 1931), 44; "Do You Still Believe in Lazy-Fairies?" (editorial), *ibid.* (June 24, 1931), 44.

12. Beard, ed., *America Faces the Future*, pp. 56–57; *Iron Age* (editorial), CXXVIII (July 16, 1931), 204–205; Donham, *Business Adrift*, pp. 154–155, 165.

13. Beard, ed., *America Faces the Future*, pp. 160–173.

14. *Ibid.*, p. 203.

15. *National Economic Council*, p. 165.

16. Swope and Harriman emphasized this point: *ibid.*, pp. 160–173, 196–264. So did Javits, *Business and the Public Interest*, pp. 183–184, and Wallace Brett Donham, *Business Looks at the Unforeseen* (New York, 1932), pp. 165–169.

17. Beard, ed., *America Faces the Future*, pp. 36–37. For a general view, see Hugo Haan, *American Planning in the Words of Its Promoters: A Bird's-Eye Survey Expressed in Quotations Collected* (Philadelphia, March 1932), pp. vii–viii.

18. Beard, ed., *America Faces the Future*, pp. 392–393, 397.

19. Fischer, *Machines and Men*, p. 85.

20. See, for example, G. L. Lacher, "Uncle Sam Ponders as Ivan Goes Industrial," *Iron Age*, CXXXI (January 5, 1933), 16–18, 21, 38–40; Friedman, *Russia in Transition*, pp. 25, 418.

21. The one was Mary Van Kleeck, director of the department of industrial studies of the Russell Sage Foundation: *National Economic Council*, pp. 523–524. For the others' remarks, see pp. 242–243, 299, 319–320, 394.

22. Jacob Javits, preface in Javits, *Business and the Public Interest*, pp. ix–x.

23. Lewis S. Feuer, using statements by leftist George Soule as evidence, claims that American ideas of planning were modeled on the Soviet Union's. Yet Feuer mistakenly ascribes to businessmen the notions of some intellectuals. Feuer, "Travelers to the Soviet Union," *American Quarterly*, XIV (Summer 1962), 144–146.

24. James Farrell, president of United States Steel, and Ralph E. Flanders, vice-president of the American Society of Mechanical Engineers and chairman of the American Engineering Council's Committee on the Balance of Economic Forces: *National Economic Council*, pp. 242, 352.

25. Schlesinger, *Coming of the New Deal*, pp. 87–89; Leuchtenberg, *Perils of Prosperity*, pp. 41–42; Soule, *Planned Society*, p. 184. Soule

also says, on pp. 204–206, that Soviet planning exerted great influence, but he does not specify those who were influenced.

26. Schlesinger, *Coming of the New Deal*, p. 176; Leuchtenberg, *Perils of Prosperity*, pp. 41–42.

27. Estimates varied: Alzada Comstock, "The Five-Year Plan and American Capital," *Barron's*, XI (January 12, 1931), 3; "Lack of Skilled Workers Weakens Threat of Russian Competition," *Business Week* (March 4, 1931), 45; "6,000 Artisans Going to Russia," *ibid.* (September 2, 1931), 36–37; *New York Times*, December 1, 1931, 13:2.

28. William Henry Chamberlin, "Missionaries of American Techniques in Russia," *Asia*, XXXII (July–August 1932), 425.

29. See the comments by John D. Littlepage and Demaree Bess, *In Search of Soviet Gold* (New York, 1937), p. 61; and "Report of A.I.M.E. on the Russian Situation; Conditions Confronting American Engineers in U.S.S.R.," *Mining and Metallurgy*, XII (April 1931), 207.

30. Chamberlin, "Missionaries of American Techniques," *Asia*, XXXII (July–August 1932), 463.

31. H. R. Knickerbocker, *The Red Trade Menace: Progress of the Soviet Five-Year Plan* (New York, 1931), pp. 82–83; George A. Burrell, *An American Engineer Looks at Russia* (Boston, 1932), pp. 20–21, 25–27, 63–64, 87–88; John Scott, *Behind the Urals: An American Worker in Russia's City of Steel* (Cambridge, Mass., 1942), pp. 42, 86–88. Note, however, that these privileges became increasingly rare as the Depression worsened in America and increased Soviet bargaining power: J. H. Carmody, "American Engineers in Russia," *American Machinist*, LXXV (October 8, 1931), 548–549; *New York Times*, January 17, 1932, 4:1, and March 6, 1932, III, 4:3.

32. A. B. Dibner, "Russia as an Electrical Market," *Electrical World*, XCV (March 8, 1930), 485.

33. Walter Arnold Rukeyser, *Working for the Soviets: An American Engineer in Russia* (New York, 1932), p. 210.

34. "Paying Proposition" (editorial), *Business Week*, (May 25, 1932), 15–16.

35. Littlepage and Bess, *In Search of Soviet Gold*, p. 304.

36. See his speech to the Rocky Mountain Club of New York in January 1918, reprinted in *Cong. Rec.*, 65th Cong., 2nd Sess. (January 31, 1918), p. 1409.

37. Julius H. Gillis, letter to the editor, "More Costs in Russia," *Mining and Metallurgy*, XI (December 1930), 593.

38. Rukeyser, *Working for the Soviets*, pp. 73–75. For a remarkably similar experience, see Burrell, *American Engineer*, p. 208.

39. Rukeyser, *Working for the Soviets*, pp. 164–165, 210. See also, for example, Littlepage and Bess, *In Search of Soviet Gold*, pp. 41–43, 106, 164–165; Clarence T. Starr, "A Dead Hand Holds Russia Back," *Nation's Business*, XIX (August 1931), 25–27, 109.

40. For example, Walter L. Carver, "Tractor Is King in Soviet Russia, Leading Huge Automotive Plans," *Automotive Industries*, LXVI (March 5, 1932), 375–378. For racial emphasis, see Rukeyser, *Working for the Soviets*, pp. 164–165.

41. Starr, "A Dead Hand Holds Russia Back," pp. 25–27, 109; Ellery Walter, *Russia's Decisive Year* (New York, 1932), passim; Burrell, *American Engineer*, pp. 177, 268–274; "Report of A.I.M.E. on the Russian Situation," *Mining and Metallurgy*, XII (April 1931), 207–208; Alfred M. Wasbauer, "Surpass America!" *American Machinist*, LXXVII (September 27, 1933), 613–615; Homer I. Trecartin, "Industrial Russia," *Iron Age*, CXXX (October 13, 1932), 567–568.

42. Rukeyser's criticism of the technical director of Asbest caused the latter's demotion to a post in Siberia: Rukeyser, *Working for the Soviets*, pp. 194–209.

43. "Report of A.I.M.E. on the Russian Situation," pp. 207–208; *New York Times*, December 1, 1930, 7:5.

44. For example, *ibid.*, November 22, 1930, 4:1; Littlepage and Bess, *In Search of Soviet Gold*, pp. 86, 109–111; Friedman, *Russia in Transition*, p. 161.

45. Burrell, *American Engineer*, p. 134; Scott, *Behind the Urals*, p. 152; Friedman, *Russia in Transition*, pp. 214–215.

46. Burrell, *American Engineer*, pp. 308–310.

47. Rukeyser, *Working for the Soviets*, pp. 9–10, 279.

48. Even Colonel Hugh L. Cooper, supervisor of the enormous Dneiperstroy hydroelectric project and president of the American-Russian Chamber of Commerce, wanted to withhold recognition until the Soviets stopped regarding capitalism as a crime: *New York Times*, December 22, 1929, II, 2:3, and September 11, 1931, 23:8.

49. G. L. Lacher, "Uncle Sam Ponders as Ivan Goes Industrial," *Iron Age*, CXXXI (January 5, 1933), 18, explicitly notes the analogy between the slogans and the New Era.

50. For example, "Trouble Ahead for Russia" (editorial), *ibid.*, CXXV (February 13, 1930), 531; "Growing Discontent in Soviet Russia" (editorial), *Barron's*, XII (October 24, 1932), 11; Walter L. Carver, "Amo and Nizhni-Novgorod Plants Lead Soviet Vehicle Plans," *Automotive Industries*, LXVI (March 12, 1932), 418–421; *Comm. Fin. Chronicle* (editorial), CXXX (December 22, 1930), 1160.

51. Browder, *Origins of Soviet-American Diplomacy*, appendix A, table 1, pp. 223–224. This is calculated from statistics in *Foreign Commerce and Navigation of the United States (1922–1939)*. Soviet figures, which are less trustworthy, describe a 50 per cent increase: Alexander Baykov, *Soviet Foreign Trade* (Princeton, N.J., 1946), appendix, table 7.

52. *New York Times*, November 11, 1930, 40:1.

53. "More than 600 Americans Are Now Working for the Soviets," *Business Week* (July 16, 1930), 24–25. This article has a useful map. Compare the 1929 total: Saul G. Bron, *Soviet Economic Development and American Business: Results of the First Year Under the Five-Year Plan and Further Perspectives* (New York, 1930), pp. 144–146.

54. "Who Is Getting These Russian Orders?" *Business Week* (February 19, 1930), 35.

55. Bron, *Soviet Economic Development*, p. 19; Dobb, *Soviet Economic Development*, p. 238.

56. "Ivy Lee, Realist, Looks at Russia," *Business Week* (January 29, 1930), 35.

57. For more direct evidence, see some of the letters written to Senator William E. Borah by businessmen favoring trade with the USSR to ease their economic plight: Henry A. Lasker, L. M. & M. Manufacturing Co., West Chester, Pa., December 31, 1930; James D. Mooney, president of General Motors Export Company, December 29, 1930; J. D. Carr, MacKay Light and Power Company, MacKay, Idaho, March 28, 1931 — all in Borah Papers, Box 328; Barnes Drill Co., Rockford, Ill., January 9, 1932, Borah Papers, Box 339.

58. "What Big Business Thinks of Russia," *Business Week* (February 12, 1930), 39–40.

59. William M. Benney, "Industrial Russia as It Looks To-Day, an Expanding Market for American Products," *American Industries*, XXX (February 1930), 21–26.

60. "What of the US.S.R.?" (editorial), *American Machinist*, LXXII (May 8, 1930), 780. Cf. "Danger Signs" (editorial), *ibid.*, LXXIII (December 11, 1930), 938.

61. For example, "To Trade, Or Not To Trade with Russia" (editorial), *Business Week* (May 21, 1930), 44.

62. For example, "The Godless Soviet Republic," *Comm. Fin. Chronicle*, CXXX (March 1, 1930), 1339–1340, concluded with a ringing condemnation of Soviet Russia as "a people without property, without love and adoration of the Source of Love," implying that the two conditions were synonymous.

63. Alexander Gerschenkron, *Economic Relations with the U.S.S.R.* (New York, 1945), pp. 41–44; Knickerbocker, *Red Trade Menace*, pp. 166–167, 197–211; Baykov, *Soviet Foreign Trade*, pp. 47–48; *New York Times*, September 29, 1930, 8:1; Dobb, *Soviet Economic Development*, p. 238.

64. Baykov, *Development of the Soviet Economic System*, p. 266, n.; Gerschenkron, *Economic Relations*, p. 46.

65. *Comm. Fin. Chronicle* (editorial), CXXXI (August 2, 1930), 677–679; *New York Times*, July 26, 1930, 14:3.

66. *Comm. Fin. Chronicle* (editorial), CXXXI (August 2, 1930), 677–679; "An Inevitable Conflict" (editorial), *Magazine of Wall Street*, XLVI (August 9, 1930), 594; *New York Times*, July 28, 1930, 1:8, 2:1; November 25, 1930, 1:4, 2:3; January 24, 1931, 27:2; "The Russian Giant" (editorial), *Nation*, CXXXI (December 10, 1930), 639.

67. *New York Times*, August 12, 1930, 37:1; August 23, 1930, 20:1; December 18, 1930, 44:5; September 13, 1931, II, 9:3.

68. "Institute Denies Russian Manganese Ore Is Dumped," *Steel*, LXXXVII (December 11, 1930), 23–24, 89; *New York Times*, December 7, 1930, II, 12:3. Ultimately, the Secretary of the Treasury ruled that there was no Soviet dumping of manganese: *New York Times*, February 25, 1931, 37:1.

69. Stephen J. Kennedy, "The Relation of Soviet Russia to the World Cotton Market," *Textile World*, LXXIX (March 7, 1931), 1094–1095;

H. A. Robicsek and R. Leonhardt, "Russia's Fabric Dumping May Affect World Markets," *ibid.*, LXXXI (April 2, 1932), 1172–1173.

70. "Congress Hesitates to Embargo Imports of Soviet Anthracite," *Business Week* (June 25, 1930), 37; "Anthracite Industry Fights to Embargo Russian Coal," *ibid.* (June 11, 1930), 11; Knickerbocker, *Red Trade Menace*, pp. 230–235.

71. "Russia Now Second Largest Producer," *Oil and Gas Journal*, XXX (December 31, 1931), 66; A. E. Mockler, "Oil Leaders Try to Induce Russian Delegates to Limit Petroleum Exports," *ibid.*, XXX (May 12, 1932), 14–15; A. E. Mockler, "World Leaders May Drop Drive for Compact Including Russia in Price Stabilization Plan," *ibid.*, XXXI (December 29, 1932), 34; "Oil Conference Failure Shows Soviets' Bargaining Advantage," *Business Week* (June 15, 1932), 10.

72. "Form American Group to Contest Soviet Trade," *Steel*, LXXXVII (October 9, 1930), 31.

73. Baykov, *Soviet Foreign Trade*, appendix, table 4; Knickerbocker, *Red Trade Menace*, p. 218; Gerschenkron, *Economic Relations*, p. 50.

74. *New York Times*, September 20, 1:3; September 21, 26:1; September 23, 1:8, 2:1; September 28, III, 1:4; September 30, 1:2 — all 1930.

75. *Ibid.*, May 23, 1:7; May 29, 6:6; September 21, 26:2; September 23, 2:2 — all 1930.

76. "Bancroft Endorses Canadien Soviet Attitude," *Barron's*, XI (March 2, 1931), 28.

77. "Fishing in Russian Waters" (editorial), *ibid.*, X (July 28, 1930), 16.

78. "We Bait Amtorg While Europe Makes New Drives for Orders," *Business Week* (July 30, 1930), 5–6; "A Policy, Please!" (editorial), *ibid.* (August 6, 1930), 40.

79. Alzada Comstock, "Crisis in Soviet-American Trade," *Barron's*, X (September 15, 1930), 11, 13; Baykov, *Soviet Foreign Trade*, appendix, table 7.

80. *New York Times*, April 27, 1931, 1:3.

81. "Russian Difficulties Increase, But Not So Swiftly as Rumors," *Business Week* (November 18, 1931), 32–33; "Courting Germany, Soviet Cuts Its Staff Here," *ibid.* (November 25, 1931), 32–33; *New York Times*, October 8, 1931, 9:1.

82. Baykov, *Soviet Foreign Trade*, p. 55.

83. For example, *New York Times*, June 27, 1931, 6:1, and September 26, 1931, 5:3.

84. Browder, *Origins of Soviet-American Diplomacy*, appendix A, table 1, pp. 223–224; Baykov, *Soviet Foreign Trade*, appendix, table 7. Again the Soviet figures differ from the American ones.

85. "Soviets' Second Plan Promises Orders Tempting to Americans," *Business Week* (April 27, 1932), 32–33; Thomas A. Morgan, *Trade with Soviet Russia*, pamphlet (n.p., February 16, 1932); Friedman, *Russia in Transition*, pp. 577, 581–582; "Russia Offers Large Opportunity for American Business, Says Colonel Cooper," *Electrical World*, XCVIII (December 26, 1931), 1135; "Moscow Pays," *Business Week* (November 30, 1932), 24; "U.S. Business Men Join Industry

Tour of Russia," *ibid.* (May 13, 1931), 40-41; E. Dietrich, "U.S.A. and the U.S.S.R.: How to Revive Our Trade with the Soviets, and Why It Should Be Done," *Barron's,* XIII (January 13, 1933), 5.

86. "Russian Fantasy," *Business Week* (April 5, 1933), 24.

87. Theodore M. Knappen, "Soviet Russia Makes Overtures to Capitalism," *Magazine of Wall Street,* XLIV (July 13, 1929), 497-499, 541-544.

88. For example, George E. Anderson, "Russian Trade and Business Morality," *Barron's,* X (November 3, 1930), 24-25.

89. Memorandum to William R. Castle by John F. Carter, Jr., of the Division of Western European Affairs, February 13, 1931, National Archives, Record Group 59:711, 61/201.

90. Jerome Davis, "Capitalism and Communism," *Annals,* CLVI (July 1931), 72-74.

91. For example, S. A. Weart, "Our Trade with the Soviets: Some Pros and Cons in Connection with Possible Recognition of Russia," *Barron's,* XIII (July 10, 1933), 18; John C. Cresswill, "What Will Russia Use for Money?" *Magazine of Wall Street,* LIII (December 9, 1933), 183, 206-207.

92. "At Least, Russia's Trade Is Fast Winning Recognition," *Business Week* (June 1, 1932), 23-24; "Russian Trade — Cotton Goods Men to Organize for Share in Potentially Great Market," *Textile World,* LXXXIII (December 1933), 2161; C. O. Willson, "Recognition of Soviet Expected to Involve Major Sales of Equipment for Expansion of Industry," *Oil and Gas Journal,* XXXII (November 9, 1933), 11-12.

93. A copy of the press release is in Box 352 of the Borah Papers.

94. *New York Times,* July 3, 1933, 1:8; August 21, 1933, 24:1.

95. *Ibid.,* November 5, 1933, II, 17:8; November 19, 1933, 31:1.

96. Baykov, *Soviet Foreign Trade,* p. 89, table 1, and p. 91; also Gerschenkron, *Economic Relations.* pp. 59-60.

IX. POPULAR RESPONSES DURING THE FIVE-YEAR PLAN

1. Estimates varied considerably. The official Soviet publication in the United States claimed that 2,000 Americans went to the USSR in 1929: *Soviet Union Review,* VII (December 1929), 196. Joseph Barnes, "Cultural Recognition of Russia," *Nation,* CXXXIV (May 18, 1932), 565, said that the totals were 2,800 in 1929, 5,000 in 1930, and 9,000 in 1931. But Bruce Bliven, "A Postcard from Moscow," *New Republic,* LXIX (December 9, 1931), 88, says that the total in 1931 was only 5,000, while "Russia, Russia, Russia," *Fortune,* V (March 1932), 57, cites a figure of 10,000 for 1931.

2. Evelyn C. Brooks and Lee M. Brooks, "A Decade of 'Planning' Literature," *Social Forces,* XII (March 1934), 429, table 2.

3. Hornell Hart, "Changing Opinions about Business Prosperity: A Consensus of Magazine Opinion in the United States, 1929-32," *American Journal of Sociology,* XXXVIII (March 1933), 666, table 1.

4. Harper to William Henry Chamberlin, October 28, 1929, Harper Papers, Cabinet 1, Drawer 3.

5. Kaltenborn to Harper, November 2, 1929, Harper Papers, Cabinet 1, Drawer 3.

6. Villard to Freda Kirchwey, January 22, 1930, and to Francis W. Hirst, February 28, 1930 — Villard Papers.

7. On increasing interest, see Harper to Junius B. Wood, December 15, 1930, Harper Papers, Cabinet 1, Drawer 3; *New York Times*, (editorial) November 25, 1930, 28:2; "From Breadline to Millionaire" (editorial) *New Republic*, LXV (December 3, 1930), 57; Edmund Wilson, "An Appeal to Progressives," *ibid.*, LXV (January 14, 1931), 234–238.

8. Nicholas Murray Butler, "Address before the American Club of Paris," June 11, 1931, reprinted in Beard, ed., *America Faces the Future*, pp. 13, 16.

9. Ray Long, *An Editor Looks at Russia: One Unprejudiced View of the Land of the Soviets* (New York, 1931), pp. viii–ix.

10. W. H. Fetridge to Harper, October 10, 1930, Harper Papers, Cabinet 1, Drawer 3.

11. Edwin James, "Russia, The Enigma," *New York Times*, November 29, 1930, 16:8. Also *ibid.* (editorial), December 20, 1931, III, 1:3; Gordon S. Watkins, "Glimpses of Russia Under the Soviets: The Land and Its People," *Social Science*, V (February-April 1930), 141.

12. Barnes, "Cultural Recognition of Russia," *Nation*, CXXXIV (May 18, 1932), 565; Corliss and Margaret Lamont, *Russia Day by Day: A Travel Diary* (New York, 1933), pp. 24–25.

13. *New York Times*, July 18, 1929, 9:1.

14. Spencer Williams to Alexander Gumberg, Moscow, May 22, 1931, Gumberg Papers, Box 9A.

15. For complaints, see Harry Stekoll, *Through the Communist Looking-Glass* (New York, 1932), pp. 6–8; Fannie Hurst, "The Russian Goose Hangs High," *Saturday Evening Post*, CCIV (November 7, 1931), 90. For favorable views, see Jay N. Darling, *Ding Goes to Russia* (New York, 1932), p. 171; Lamont, *Russia Day by Day*, p. 252; American-Russian Chamber of Commerce tour, *New York Times*, August 15, 1929, III, 1:2.

16. Harper to his mother, Berlin, August 5, 1930; Harper to his mother, Moscow, August 9, 1932; Sonya Chamberlin to Harper, July 27, 1932; Harper to his mother, October 7, 1932 — all in Harper Papers, Cabinet 1, Drawer 2; Harper, *Making Bolsheviks* (Chicago, 1931), pp. 157–160.

17. William C. White, "American in Soviet Russia," *Scribner's*, LXXXIX (February 1931), 171–182; Eugene Lyons, *Assignment in Utopia* (New York, 1937), p. 329.

18. *New York Times*, August 17, 1929, 11:8.

19. Marjorie Shuler, in William C. White, Maurice Hindus, and Marjorie Shuler, *Social Conditions in Soviet Russia: New York Luncheon Discussion, January 31, 1931, of the Foreign Policy Association* (Pamphlet 72, March, 1931; New York, 1931), pp. 18–21.

20. Adelaide Hooker, "A High Time in Red Russia," *Good Housekeeping*, XCI (July 1930), 52–53, 174–184; "How Red Is Red Russia?"

ibid., XCI (August 1930), 54–55, 194–201; "Prisoners of the Cheka in Red Russia," *ibid.*, XCI (September 1930), 42–43, 228–238.
21. William C. White, "Moscow Morals," *Scribner's*, LXXXVIII (September 1930), 277, 286.
22. For typical defenses, see Long, *An Editor Looks at Russia*, p. 80; Maurice Hindus, *Humanity Uprooted* (New York, 1929), pp. 117–118, 128, 139; Margaret Bourke-White, *Eyes on Russia* (New York, 1931), p. 43; Winter, *Red Virtue*, pp. 116, 124. For criticism, see George Sylvester Viereck, "Pyatiletka — Russia's New Economic Nostrum," *Saturday Evening Post*, CCII (January 18, 1930), 84; Eve Garrette Grady, *Seeing Red: Behind the Scenes in Russia Today* (New York, 1931), pp. 122–126, 154–155; Will Durant, *The Tragedy of Russia: Impressions from a Brief Visit* (New York, 1933), pp. 73, 77.
23. Curtiss, *Russian Church and the Soviet State*, pp. 191–237.
24. *New York Times*, February 9, 1930, 1:7.
25. *Cong. Rec.*, 71st Cong., 2nd Sess. (February 28, 1930), pp. 4522, 4525.
26. *New York Times*, February 19, 1:3; February 24, 6:3; March 24, 3:2 — all 1930; *American Jewish Year Book*, XXXII (September 1930–September 1931), 64–65.
27. Edmund A. Walsh, *Why Pope Pius XI Asked Prayers for Russia on March 19, 1930: A Review of the Facts in the Case Together with Proofs of the International Program of the Soviet Government* (New York, 1930).
28. Gumberg to Raymond Robins, February 21, 1930, Robins Papers, Box 22.
29. *New York Times*, March 16, 1930, 7:1; Villard to Hirst, February 28, 1930, Villard Papers; n. 60, Chapter Seven, above.
30. "Religion in Russia," *Outlook and Independent*, CLIV (February 26, 1930), 334; "The Blasphemous Soviet Easter," *Literary Digest*, CIV (March 29, 1930), 22–23; "Petrus v. Satanus," *Time*, XV (March 31, 1930), 21.
31. *New York Times*, March 7, 1930, 6:4, and March 17, 1930, 2:6; "The Blasphemous Soviet Easter," pp. 22–23; "The Soviet Retreat," *ibid.*, CV (April 12, 1930), 22–23; "Christendom and Sovietdom" (editorial), *Christian Century*, XLVII (March 5, 1930), 294–296; "Sowing and Reaping in Russia" (editorial), *Zion's Herald*, CVIII (March 5, 1930), 291–292; Philip S. Bernstein, "Religion in Russia," *Harper's*, CLX (May 1930), 733–739.
32. "Christendom on its Knees" (editorial), *Commonweal*, XI (March 19, 1930), 547–548.
33. MS of lecture, entitled "Russia after Ten Years," given at Sinai Temple, Chicago, November 2, 1931, in Harper Papers, Cabinet 2, Drawer 4; *New York Times*, August 13, 1931, 16:1.
34. Sherwood Eddy, *The Challenge of Russia* (New York, 1931), esp. pp. 3, 153–154, 186–211, 261–265, 269–270, 273–278. For background on the seminars, see Eddy, *Eighty Adventurous Years: An Autobiography* (New York, 1955), pp. 128, 134–135.
35. Ward, *In Place of Profit*, esp. pp. 20–85, 151, 224–225, 270–273,

324–341 (quotation on p. 75). For his earlier views, see Ward, *The New Social Order: Principles and Programs* (New York, 1919), esp. pp. 31, 377.

36. Reinhold Niebuhr, "Russia Makes the Machine Its God," *Christian Century*, XLVII (September 10, 1930), 1080–1081; "The Church in Russia," *ibid.*, XLVII (September 24, 1930), 1144–1146; "Russian Efficiency," *ibid.*, XLVII (October 1, 1930), 1178–1180; "The Land of Extremes," *ibid.*, XLVII (October 15, 1930), 1241–1243 (quotation on p. 1242).

37. Quoted in Miller, *American Protestantism*, pp. 64–65. For typical Protestant views, see L. L. Dunnington, "Some Moral Values in Soviet Russia," *World Tomorrow*, XI (April 1928), 169–171; John R. Hahn, "Will the Pendulum Swing in Russia?" *Congregationalist*, CXV (September 18, 1930), 378–379; Dunnington, "The Russia of 1923," *Zion's Herald*, CXI (October 11, 1933), 969–970; Vincent G. Burns, "The Dogs of War Are Baying," *Christian Century*, XLVII (August 27, 1930), 1034–1035; and quotations from *The Baptist* in Carter, *Decline and Revival of the Social Gospel*, p. 158.

38. Lucian Johnston, "If Francis of Assisi Came to Moscow!" *Catholic World*, CXXXIII (June 1931), 284–291 (quotation on p. 284).

39. John La Farge, "Human Obstacles to Communism," *America*, XLVII (June 11, 1932), 226–227; La Farge, "The Appeal of Bolshevism," *ibid.*, XLVIII (December 3, 1932), 201–203.

40. Walsh, *Last Stand*, p. 253.

41. *Cong. Rec.*, 71st Cong., 2nd Sess. (February 24, 1930), p. 4186. For other comments, see *ibid.* (February 27, 1930), pp. 4347–4350, 4378; (March 18, 1930), p. 5548.

42. Woll and Easley are quoted in *New York Times*, March 1, 1:8; March 2, 16:3; August 31, 15:1 — all 1930; for press opinion, see "The 'Menace' of Cheap Russian Labor," *Literary Digest*, CVI (August 9, 1930), 6–7.

43. "When the Russian Bear Is a Wheat Bear," *Literary Digest*, CVII (October 4, 1930), 5–6; "Russia's 'Dumping' War Challenge," *ibid.*, CVII (October 11, 1930), 11–12.

44. *Cong. Rec.*, 71st Cong., 3rd Sess. (January 15, 1931), p. 2199.

45. *Investigation of Communist Propaganda*: Report no. 2290 (pursuant to H. Res. 220) from the Special Committee to Investigate Communist Activities in the United States, House of Rep., 71st Cong., 3rd Sess., January 17, 1931 (n.p., n.d.), pp. 4–6, 53, 36, 45, 41, and passim.

46. *Cong. Rec.*, 71st Cong., 3rd Sess. (February 27, 1931), p. 6231.

47. For the hearings, see *Prohibition of Importation of Goods Produced by Convict, Forced or Indentured Labor*: Hearings before the Committee on Ways and Means, House of Rep., 71st Cong., 3rd Sess. on H.R. 15597, H.R. 15927, and H.R. 16517, January 27 and 28, 1931 (Washington, D.C., 1931); *Embargo on Soviet Products*: Hearings before the Committee on Ways and Means, House of Rep., 71st Cong., 3rd Sess., on H.R. 16035, February 19, 20, and 21, 1931 (Washington, D.C., 1931). For the House vote, see *Cong. Rec.*, 71st Cong., 3rd Sess. (February 21, 1931), p. 5677. For the Senate Finance Committee's

action, see Fischer, *Why Recognize Russia?*, pp. 157–158, and *New York Times*, January 3, 1932, II, 3:3.

48. *Cong. Rec.*, 72nd Cong., 1st Sess. (March 15, 1932), pp. 6089–6092.

49. Cf. "Fruits of Communism" (editorial), *World's Work*, LX (May 1931), 18, and "Our Trade With Russia" (editorial), LXI (May 1932), 17–18. For Scripps-Howard, see *Advance*, XVII (May 1, 1931), 9. For typical opposition, see "Our Trade with Russia," *Outlook and Independent*, CLVII (April 15, 1931), 520–521.

50. Gumberg to Duranty, March 27, 1931, Gumberg Papers, Box 9A.

51. "Too Much Russia" (editorial), *Saturday Evening Post*, CCIV (August 8, 1931), 20. Also, for example, Philip Wylie, "The Russians Have Beards," *ibid.*, CCIV (December 19, 1931), 21, 72–73; "Overdoing Russia" (editorial), *World's Work*, LX (August 1931), 18.

52. See Appendix A. Although the number of books on Russia declined in 1932–33, writings in other forms did not. When Norman Thomas asked *Harper's Magazine*, early in 1933, to subsidize him for articles about an intended visit to the USSR, one of the editors refused the offer because "the market is glutted at present with material concerning Russia." G. Hartman to Thomas, March 1, 1933, Thomas Papers, New York Public Library.

53. Information about the Book-of-the-Month Club distribution comes from a letter to me by Herbert M. Laskey (assistant to the president of the club), September 23, 1963. Harper's comment is in a letter to Robert J. Kerner, June 13, 1931, Harper Papers, Cabinet 1, Drawer 3. For bestseller information, see Irving Harlow Hart, "Best Sellers in Non-Fiction Since 1921," *Publishers' Weekly*, CXXIII (February 4, 1933), 528. Also a bestseller in 1931 was Grand Duchess Marie's *Education of a Princess*, but it did not equal Hindus' and Ilin's success: *ibid.*, CXXI (January 23, 1932), 366–367. Only one other American book on Russia was a bestseller during 1917–1933: John Spargo's *Bolshevism* in 1919; see *Publishers' Weekly*, XCVII (January 31, 1920), 287.

54. "Thomas Edison Talks on Invention in the Life of Today," *Review of Reviews*, LXXXIII (January 1931), 40.

55. For example, Isaac Don Levine, "The Five-Year Plan — A Menace to Whom?" *Scribner's*, XC (December 1931), 627–634; "Russia Is the Place for Communists!" (editorial), *Review of Reviews*, LXXXIV (November 1931), 31; *New York Times* (editorial), May 17, 1931, III, 1:3.

56. Quoted in "The Hoover 'Twenty-Year Plan' for Prosperity," *Literary Digest*, CIX (June 27, 1931), 6.

57. "The American Five-Year Plan" (editorial), *Saturday Evening Post*, CCIII (March 7, 1931), 24.

58. Bourke-White, *Eyes on Russia*, p. 22.

59. *Ibid.*, pp. 80, 133–135.

60. For example, Maurice Hindus, *Red Bread* (New York, 1931), pp. 69–103; Elias Tobenkin, *Stalin's Ladder: War and Peace in the Soviet Union* (New York, 1933), p. 14 (Tobenkin spent ten months

in the USSR during 1932–1933); Darling, *Ding Goes to Russia*, pp. 4, 6, 15, 60, 64–71; Durant, *Tragedy of Russia*, pp. 15–18 (Durant visited the USSR in the summer of 1932 and compiled this book from his articles published in the *Saturday Evening Post* during December 1932–February 1933); Thelma Nurenberg, *This New Red Freedom* (New York, 1932), pp. 21, 67–70, 175–176.

61. For example, Knickerbocker, *Red Trade Menace*, pp. 267–270; Lindsay Hoben, "Through Russia without a Guide," *Collier's*, LXXXVII (April 18, 1931), 52; William Armstrong Fairburn, *Russia the Utopia in Chains* (New York, 1931), pp. 47, 98, 233; Darling, *Ding Goes to Russia*, pp. 126–133.

62. Vincent Vocovich, "The Workingman in Soviet Russia: The Grim Story of His Misery," *Current History*, XXXIV (August 1931), 691–695; William J. Robinson, *Soviet Russia as I Saw It: Its Accomplishments, Its Crimes and Stupidities* (New York, 1932), p. 52; Durant, *Tragedy of Russia*, pp. 7–28, 57, 156–157, 161; Gene Tunney and Walter Davenport, "So This is Russia!" *Collier's*, LXXXVIII (October 3, 1931), 7–9, 48–51.

63. *New York Times*, April 8, 1932, 11:2; Russell Wright, *One-Sixth of the World's Surface* (Hammond, Ind., 1932), p. 101.

64. For example, Lamont, *Russia Day by Day*, pp. 257, 259; Maurice Hindus, *The Great Offensive* (New York, 1933), pp. 320, 322, 326–327; Rose Brisken, "A Case Worker in Russia," *The Family*, XIII (April 1932), 59–62; Harper's phrase appears in a letter to Will Rogers, April 29, 1931, Harper Papers, Cabinet 1, Drawer 3; Bruce Hopper, *Pan-Sovietism: The Issue before America and the World* (New York, 1931), pp. 205–213, 242–245; Frazier Hunt, "America Must Dream Again!" *Good Housekeeping*, XCI (February 1933), 206; Curtis Bok to William E. Borah, January 25, 1933, copy in Gumberg Papers, Box 10B; William Allen White to Harold Ickes, November 14, 1933, White Papers, Box 152 (White visited Russia in 1933).

65. Long, *An Editor Looks at Russia*, pp. 86–87.

66. *New York Times* (editorials), December 29, 1931, 22:3; October 27, 1932, 18:3; January 15, 1933, IV, 4:6. For other typical critiques, see "Stomach Crisis," *Time*, XX (September 12, 1932), 16–17; "Danger Signs on the Soviet Five-Year Plan," *Literary Digest*, CXIV (September 24, 1932), 17.

67. Joseph J. Spengler, "Babbitt Looks at the Depression," *New Republic*, LXXI (June 1, 1932), 66; William Henry Chamberlin, *The Confessions of an Individualist* (New York, 1940), p. 144. The over 100,000 applications to Amtorg in 1931, in response to its request for American workers to take jobs in Russia, are another indication of American views of the Soviet economic situation. See Chapter Six.

68. Secretary of State Frank B. Kellogg to Chairman of the Republican National Committee, February 23, 1928, *Foreign Relations, 1928*, III, 822–825; Under Secretary of State W. R. Castle, Jr., for the Secretary of State, to Fred L. Eberhardt, March 3, 1933, *ibid., 1933*, II, 780–782; Browder, *Origins of Soviet-American Diplomacy*, pp. 40–41.

69. "Britain's 'Truce with the Bear,'" *Literary Digest*, CII (July

13, 1929), 8; "The American Dollar Talks with Russia," *ibid.*, CII (August 17, 1929), 8–9.

70. "Russia as Customer" (editorial), *Outlook and Independent*, CLVI (October 15, 1930), 249.

71. For Cravath, see *New York Times*, August 3, 1930, 2:2; for Ottinger, see *ibid.*, August 7, 1930, 21:1; for Moore, see *ibid.*, December 5, 1930, 1:6; for Wheeler, see his three articles of September-October 1931, reprinted from *Washington Herald* in *Cong. Rec.*, 71st Cong., 3rd Sess. (February 12, 1931), pp. 4671–4674; for the Menken-Easley controversy, see *New York Times*, September 7, 1930, II, 2:6, and November 1, 1930, 19:5, as well as S. Stanwood Menken, "The Russian Dilemma," *North American Review*, CCXXX (December 1930), 660–664.

72. For exemplary opposition views, see John Spargo, "The Soviet Union: The Question of Recognition," *Current History*, XXXII (September 1930), 1072–1078; "Blunders of the Soviet" (editorial), *World's Work*, LIX (April 1930), 39–40; "Russia in Business and Diplomacy" (editorial), *Review of Reviews*, LXXXIII (April 1931), 33. For dissent, see *New York Times*, August 22, 28:8; September 6, 5:3; November 13, 38:8 — all 1931.

73. The editorial is reprinted in *Cong. Rec.*, 72nd Cong., 1st Sess. (April 4, 1932), pp. 7364–7365.

74. Browder, *Origins of Soviet-American Diplomacy*, p. 72.

75. *New York Times*, April 23, 1932, 1:5.

76. "Should the United States Recognize Soviet Russia?" *Commonwealth*, VIII (May 3, 1932), 99–100.

77. National Archives, Record Group 46. Many petitions from organizations in places as widely separated as Detroit and California were identically worded, indicating centralized coordination.

78. *New York Times*, October 6, 1932, 12:2.

79. *Ibid.*, January 10, 1933, 2:4.

80. *Nation* (editorial), CXXXVII (November 1, 1933), 495.

81. "Al Smith on Russia," *Literary Digest*, CXV (March 18, 1933), 8 (quotations come from this source). For Smith's testimony, see *New York Times*, March 1, 1933, 1:8.

82. "A Dent in the Brown Derby" (editorial), *America*, XLVIII (March 11, 1933), 543; "Recognizing Russia" (editorial), *ibid.*, XLIX (April 22, 1933), 51; "Recognizing Russia" (editorial), *Commonweal*, XVIII (August 4, 1933), 337; "Shall We Recognize Russia?" (editorial), *ibid.*, XVII (April 12, 1933), 645–647. For petitions of Knights of Columbus chapters in Long Island, Brooklyn, and Central Islip, N.Y., see National Archives, Record Group 46.

83. The quotation is cited in *New York Times*, October 26, 1933, 11:2; for the Evangelical Synod's stand, see letter from Samuel McCrae Cavert (general secretary of the Federal Council of Churches of Christ in America) to the President, November 8, 1933, National Archives, Record Group 59:711.61/346; for the Tract Society leaders, see *New York Times*, November 11, 1933, 16:6; for prorecognition evidence, see *ibid.*, February 13, 1933, 2:3; Miller, *American Protestantism*, pp.

74–75, 79, 84, 110, n. 15; "The Two Russias" (editorial), *Congregationalist*, CXVIII (April 13, 1933), 467–468; "Toward Recognition of Russia" (editorial), *Zion's Herald*, CXI (October 25, 1933), 1012.

84. 44th Annual Convention, *Yearbook of the Central Conference of American Rabbis*, XLIII (June 22–25, 1933), 113.

85. *New York Times*, April 9, 1933, II, 6:1.

86. Report of the National Americanism Commission, *Reports to the 15th Annual National Convention of the American Legion* (October 2–5, 1933), pp. 61–62. For petitions, see National Archives, Record Groups 46 and 233.

87. Eric C. H. Olson to Norris, July 2, 1933, Norris Papers, Tray 8, Box 8. For a similar anti-Semitic interpretation, see letter from Charles R. Crane to Edward M. House, October 21, 1933, House Papers, Drawer 5.

88. Paul D. Cravath, "What Recognition of Russia Really Means," *American Magazine*, CXV (April 1933), 18–19, 80–82; William E. Borah, "167,000,000 New Customers," *Hearst's International and Cosmopolitan Magazine*, XCV (July 1933), 18–19, 127–128.

89. For RFC-Amtorg arrangements, see *New York Times*, July 3, 1933, 1:8, and July 9, 1933, IV, 1:7; for patriots' silence, see Oswald Garrison Villard, "Litvinov and Recognition," *Nation*, CXXXVII (November 15, 1933), 558.

90. "Will Recognition Follow the R.F.C. Loan to Russia?" *Literary Digest*, CXVI (July 15, 1933), 8.

91. The *Sun* and other papers are cited in "What Leading Editors and Statesmen Have to Say about Russian Recognition," *National Republic*, XXI (November 1933), 23–24, 29–30, and *New York Times*, October 22, 1933, 25:4–7; for the *Times*'s comment, see editorial, October 22, 1933, IV, 4:3. Also *Seattle Times* (editorial), November 7, 1933. Even the previously intransigent *Cincinnati Enquirer* relented editorially on October 21, 1933, as did *Hartford Courant* on November 18, 1933.

92. *New York Times*, October 30, 1933, 6:2. Meno Lovenstein, *American Opinion of Soviet Russia* (Washington, D.C., 1941), pp. 139–143, extensively analyzes the data of this poll, furnishing its geographical generalizations. I present his analysis in Appendix C.

93. Under Secretary of State William Phillips to President Roosevelt, October 19, 1933, with enclosures, in Roosevelt Papers, Franklin Delano Roosevelt Library, Hyde Park. This survey dealt with only 65 editorials from 300 newspapers.

94. I have devised these totals from the raw data presented in nine pages of information entitled "Stimson Study of Russia: Analysis of Editorial Comments," March 13–April 1, 1931, located in the Herbert Hoover Archives, The Hoover Institution on War, Revolution and Peace, Stanford University. A fuller presentation is included in Appendix C. Stimson's announcement is in *New York Times*, March 9, 1931, 1:3.

95. "Russian Recognition" (editorial), *World Tomorrow*, XVI (November 9, 1933), 603.

96. *Cincinnati Enquirer* (editorial), October 21, 1933; the *Oregonian*

and *News* are cited in *New York Times,* November 18, 1933, 2:2–5, and Paul F. Boller, Jr., "The 'Great Conspiracy' of 1933: A Study in Short Memories," *Southwest Review,* XXXIX (Spring 1954), 109. Browder, *Origins of Soviet-American Diplomacy,* pp. 108–112, and Williams, *American-Russian Relations,* p. 237, discuss the motives for recognition.

97. For example, *Des Moines Register* (editorial), November 19, 1933.

98. "The Recognition of Russia" (editorial), *Commonweal,* XIX (December 1, 1933), 114–116; "Normal Relations with Russia" (editorial), *America,* L (December 2, 1933), 193–194; "The Legion Guides Right" (editorial), *Saturday Evening Post,* CCVI (November 25, 1933), 22; *Chicago Tribune* (editorial), November 20, 1933; comments cited in *New York Times,* November 18, 1933, 2:2–5.

99. *St. Louis Post-Dispatch* (editorial), November 19, 1933.

X. IN RETROSPECT

1. This biographical information comes from Anna Louise Strong, *I Change Worlds: The Remaking of an American* (New York, 1935), chaps. 1–3 (quotation on p. 34).

2. *Ibid.,* pp. 40–41, 56–60, 67–70, 88–96.

3. Strong, *The First Time in History: Two Years of Russia's New Life (August, 1921, to December, 1923)* (New York, 1924), pp. 17–18.

4. Chamberlin, *The Confessions of an Individualist* (New York, 1940), pp. 31, 36–37, 41–42, 61, 85–86.

5. *Ibid.,* pp. 68–69. For typical enthusiasm, see A. C. Freeman [Chamberlin's pseudonym], "A Revolutionary Factory," *Freeman,* VIII (October 10, 1923), 106–107 (quotation on p. 107).

6. Chamberlin, *Confessions of an Individualist,* p. 88.

7. For example, Louis Fischer, *Men and Politics: An Autobiography* (New York, 1941), p. 62; Lyons, *Assignment in Utopia* (New York, 1937), p. 96.

8. For biographical information, see Fischer, *Men and Politics,* pp. 46–47, 69–70; for evidence of Chicherin's friendship, see *ibid.,* pp. 140–141; for a good sample of Fischer's general viewpoint, see his "What Is Soviet Russia?" *Nation,* CXXXV (July 6, 1932), 6–8.

9. Lyons, *Assignment in Utopia,* pp. 3–49.

10. *Ibid.,* esp. pp. 291–292, 418–419, 455, 624–648. See also Lyons, *The Red Decade: The Stalinist Penetration of America* (New York, 1941)

11. Fischer, *Men and Politics,* p. 159.

12. Chamberlin, *Confessions of an Individualist,* pp. 102–103, 142–143, 158–159; Chamberlin, *Russia's Iron Age* (Boston, 1934), pp. 88–89, 372–377. A vivid example of Chamberlin's conversion is the differing treatment of the same anecdote concerning culture under the Soviets. In 1930 he balanced description of the propagandist character of a Kiev newspaper, once outstanding in intellectual caliber, with the growth of popular literacy since the Revolution. In 1940 he omitted the

second item: *Soviet Russia: A Living Record and a History* (Boston, 1930), p. 305; *Confessions of an Individualist*, p. 92.

13. Fischer, *Men and Politics*, esp. chaps. 30 and 37 (quotation on p. 655).

14. A 1956 study of American businessmen who visited Europe reports that they tended to change their political attitudes in the direction of the views held by most American businessmen; that is, they tended to acquire a national rather than a personal perspective. I have discovered no such uniform responses among businessmen or any other group, with the exception of the engineers (Chapters Four and Eight). Ithiel de Sola Pool, Suzanne Keller, and Raymond A. Bauer, "The Influence of Foreign Travel on Political Attitudes of American Businessmen," *Public Opinion Quarterly*, XX (Spring 1956), 161–175.

15. Berelson, Lazarsfeld, and McPhee, *Voting*, pp. 93–115; Carl I. Hovland, Irving L. Janis, and Harold H. Kelley, *Communication and Persuasion: Psychological Studies of Opinion Change* (New Haven, 1953), chap. 5; Katz and Lazarsfeld, *Personal Influence*, chap. 4 and pp. 44–45.

16. Berelson, Lazarsfeld, and McPhee, "Political Perception," in *Readings in Social Psychology*, pp. 72–85.

17. Henry F. May, "Shifting Perspectives on the 1920's," *Mississippi Valley Historical Review*, XLIII (December 1956), 425.

18. Root to Lee, March 2, 1926, Root Papers, Box 141. This letter was published in *New York Times* on March 28.

Index

Abbott, Lawrence F., 60
Abbott, Lyman, 11–12
Addams, Jane, 207, 336n, 350n
Adkerson, J. Carson, 231, 232, 233
Advance, The: on Gompers, 164;
on Communists, 177; on National Industrial Recovery Act,
184
Allied American Corporation, 116
All-Russian Congress of Soviets,
36–37
All-Russian Jewish Public Committee, 336n
All-Russian Textile Syndicate,
115
Amalgamated Bank of New
York, 140–141
Amalgamated Clothing Workers:
early history, 163–164; on recognition of USSR, 169; and
Communists, 176–177; rejoins
AF of L, 184
American Central Committee for
Russian Relief, 336n
American Chemical Society, 225
American Committee on Religious
Rights and Minorities, 247
American Express Company, 236
American Federation of Labor:
on recognition of USSR, 89;
growth, 157; decline, 160; and
Communists, 160, 173; on trade
with Russia, 161
American Foundation, Committee
on Russian-American Relations,
265

American Friends Service Committee, 77, 137, 138
American Investigation Committee on Russian Women, 141
American Iron and Steel Institute, 232
American Jewish Joint Agricultural Corporation, 87
American League to Aid and Cooperate with Russia, 23
American Legion, 89, 263
American Magazine, The, 69, 264
American Manganese Producers'
Association, 231, 232
American Manufacturers' Export
Association, 112, 238
American National Committee for
the Encouragement of the
Democratic Government of Russia, 10
American Relief Administration,
76–82, 137, 138
American Relief for Russian
Women and Children, 336n
American-Russian Chamber of
Commerce, 23, 113, 115; tour
of Russia, 236, 244, 245; on
trade with and recognition of
USSR, 237, 238
American Women's Committee for
Recognition of Soviet Russia,
207
Amtorg Trading Corporation,
114, 115, 233; advertises jobs
in Russia, 181
Anderson, Sherwood, 189

379

INDEX

381